FROM MARCOS
TO AQUINO

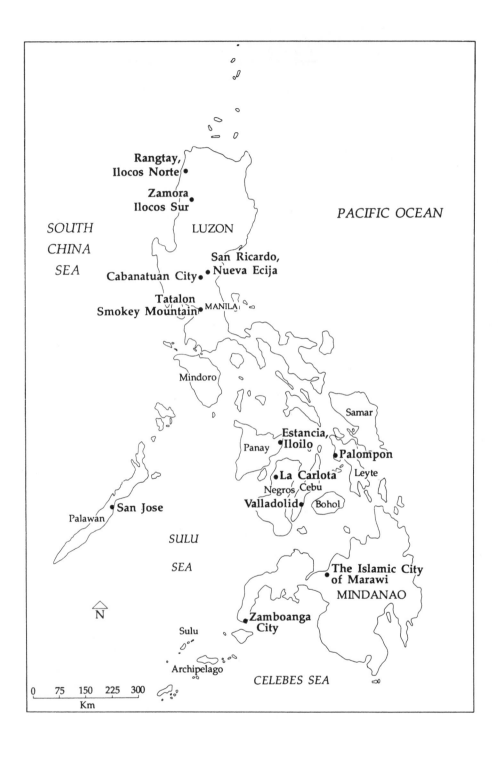

FROM MARCOS TO AQUINO

Local Perspectives on Political Transition in the Philippines

Edited by Benedict J. Kerkvliet
and Resil B. Mojares

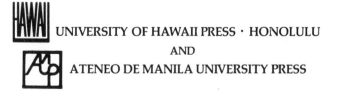

UNIVERSITY OF HAWAII PRESS · HONOLULU
AND
ATENEO DE MANILA UNIVERSITY PRESS

University of Hawaii Press edition printed in 1992

Published in North America by
University of Hawaii Press
2840 Kolowalu Street
Honolulu, Hawaii 96822

Published in the Philippines by
Ateneo de Manila University Press
Bellarmine Hall, Loyola Heights, Q.C.
P.O. Box 154, 1099 Manila

Printed in the United States

Library of Congress Cataloging-in-Publication Data

From Marcos to Aquino: local perspectives on political transition
    in the Philippines / Benedict J. Kerkvliet and Resil B. Mojares.
        p.   cm.
    Includes index.
    ISBN: 0-8248-1458-4
    1. Philippines—Politics and government—1973-1986.
2. Philippines—Politics and government—1986-   3. Philippines—History,
Local. I. Kerkvliet, Benedict J.   II. Mojares, Resil B.
DS686.5.F76   1991
959.9—dc20   91-39413
                                              CIP

University of Hawaii Press books are printed
on acid-free paper and meet the guidelines
for permanence and durability of the Council
on Library Resources

Acknowledgments

The Ford Foundation provided a generous grant that permitted us to bring together fifteen scholars for a conference at the University of Hawaii in May 1988 on the subject of this book and helped to underwrite some of the publication costs. We are extremely grateful and would like to thank especially John Humphreys and Solita del Castillo at the foundation's Metro Manila office. At the University of Hawaii we thank the University Relations Fund for additional financial support, the Center for Philippine Studies for logistical help, the Center for Korean Studies for providing us a venue for our three day meeting, and Dedania Maon for excellent administrative assistance.

We also thank Connie Alaras, Brian Fegan, and Steven Rood for participating in the conference even though they were not able to revise their papers for this volume. Stimulating commentaries and constructive criticisms by Lydia Casambre, Farideh Farhi, Vince Rafael, and Bob Stauffer helped all the authors in this volume.

We are also grateful to the Cartography Laboratory at the University of Hawaii for preparing the well-made map for us.

Ben Kerkvliet would like to acknowledge the influence of John R. W. Smail, whose emphasis on the importance of perspective in understanding Southeast Asia certainly played a role in the gestation of this project.

Contributors

G. Carter Bentley has taught at Washington University in St. Louis and the University of Washington in Seattle.

Alex Brillantes is a professor at the College of Public Administration, University of the Philippines (Diliman).

James Eder is a professor of anthropology at Arizona State University, Tempe.

Benedict Kerkvliet is chair of the Department of Political Science, University of Hawaii.

Alfred McCoy is a professor of history at the University of Wisconsin (Madison).

Resil Mojares is the Director of the Cebuano Studies Center, University of San Carlos, Cebu City.

Raul Pertierra teaches in the School of Sociology, University of New South Wales.

Michael Pinches is on the faculty of the Department of Anthropology, University of Western Australia.

Cristina Blanc Szanton is affiliated with the Southern Asian Institute, Columbia University, in New York.

Mark Turner is affiliated with the Department of Political and Social Change, Australian National University.

Willem Wolters is a professor at the Institute of Cultural Anthropology, Nijmegan University in The Netherlands.

Fernando Zialcita is a professor in the Sociology and Anthropology Department, Ateneo de Manila University.

Contents

BENEDICT J. TRIA KERKVLIET

RESIL B. MOJARES

Themes in the Transition from Marcos to Aquino: An Introduction

This book focuses on that complex of events referred to in popular shorthand as "EDSA." It is widely agreed that "EDSA" and People Power—which saw the fall of Ferdinand Marcos from power and the ascension of Corazon Aquino to the presidency—represent a significant break in Philippine history. There is little consensus, though, on what EDSA actually was and what it means. In a sense, this is to be expected. EDSA was a concatenation of events: the accelerating deterioration of Marcos's authoritarian government, widening and increasingly vociferous opposition to the government, the snap presidential election campaign of December 1985-February 1986, a military mutiny, a People Power uprising on Epifanio de los Santos Avenue (EDSA) in Metro Manila, the flight of Marcos and company, and Aquino's assumption of the presidency, followed by a prolonged struggle to stabilize and legitimate this government through such exercises as the constitutional plebiscite in February 1987 and congressional elections in May 1987 and local government elections in January 1988.

Despite the burgeoning literature on EDSA, People Power, and events prior to and since Aquino became president, there are large gaps in our understanding of the transition from Marcos to Aquino. The focus in both scholarship and reportage has been on what happened in certain areas of Metro Manila, the participation of the middle and upper strata of society, "key personalities," and the perspectives of political partisans. What was happening elsewhere in the country? How did other sectors of society view the events or "participate" in them? What was "said" in the 1986 election? There is consensus that with EDSA "something new had come to pass" and that what transpired, in textbook terms, was a "transition from authoritarianism to democracy." Has such a change, though, actually occurred? What does this transition period tell us about the Philippine polity?

This volume approaches such questions by placing national events in the context of the daily concerns of people in particular places. As previous scholarship on the Philippines and other countries has shown, a "local perspectives" approach like this is vital for a more comprehensive understanding of society.[1] Otherwise, events and their meaning are defined by a narrow, usually elite-dominated slice of society; their significance or insignificance for other locales and peoples is discounted; and the country's history is impoverished.

The essays in this volume also put these events into the flow of longer-term processes, assessing how broad economic and social changes at the local level and beyond affect people's political practices and orientations. Broadly speaking, the transition from Marcos to Aquino begins with the storm of protest in late 1983 following Benigno "Ninoy" Aquino's assassination and ends with the relative stabilization of widow Corazon Aquino's government in 1988. At the center of this period is late 1985 and the first months of 1986 when the crisis in governance climaxed. While the authors here concentrate on this time span, they view events with an eye for situating them within a larger context of changes and continuities in Philippine society.

The authors approach the subject from different disciplinary backgrounds. Most draw from an extensive knowledge about specific localities accumulated during a decade or more of frequent field work and related research. Consequently, this book offers a rich image of politics in a diverse archipelago: the commercial city of Zamboanga in Mindanao, the Islamic lakeside city of Marawi, an old coastal village in Cebu province, a medium-sized fishing municipality in Iloilo, a sugar cane district in Negros Occidental, an upland farming community in Palawan island, two poor neighborhoods in Metro Manila, a village in Nueva Ecija, that province's major city of Cabanatuan, an inland municipality of Ilocos Sur, and a village in Ilocos Norte.

Inevitably, this range is insufficient to represent adequately all of the country. For instance, no localities are included from the Bicol region, southern and northern Luzon, Leyte-Samar, or southern Mindanao. Nor, as it turns out, do we have studies in areas where the New People's Army has been strong. And we have no analyses of an upland tribal community, a religious sect village, or any number of other interesting parts of the country. To an extent, this limitation is not due to lack of trying; we invited researchers working in some of these areas but they were not able to join us. We also needed to keep the project to manageable proportions.

One value of this book is that it records, in as much significant detail as possible within the limitations of research resources and publication length, what happened during the transition from Marcos to Aquino in the various localities we have studied. We trust this will make for informative reading now and in the years to come as journalists, academicians, students, politicians, and other interested people look back on this crucial period when trying to understand the history of Philippine politics. The rich, textured analyses of these particular places should also help to preserve something of the poignancy and sense of this particular juncture of Philippine history.

Another contribution is what these essays say collectively about key aspects of Philippine political and social life. Taking a broad view of all twelve local studies, we see six themes that should be elaborated here. They concern what was happening beyond the particular places emphasized thus far in the media and published accounts, what are the immediate effects and long-term prospects of the change in government, what was the significance of the Martial-Law period, and what the events discussed in the essays tell us about the meaning of elections, the adequacy of the faction model in explaining political behavior, and the articulations between the "local" and the "national" in politics.

Beyond Metro Manila

The People Power revolt in Manila was neither completely confined to that metropolis nor was it without precedent during Marcos's rule. Resil Mojares notes that outbursts of anti-Marcos sentiment erupted in Cebu and elsewhere in the Central Visayas during elections for the Interim National Assembly in 1978 when an opposition slate of virtual unknowns completely swept the thirteen assembly seats in the region and then again in demonstrations against Marcos in Cebu City in 1980 and 1984. And in several areas of Mindanao during the early 1980s, harsh critics of the Marcos government won public office against tremendous odds. Among them, as Mark Turner says, was Cesar Climaco, who was elected mayor of Zamboanga City in 1980 and to the National Assembly in 1984, shortly before he was murdered, on an explicitly anti-Marcos platform. Scattered acts of resistance in arenas like the 1978 and 1980 elections came to be more effectively mobilized and more sharply focused after 1983 as the crisis deepened and the Martial-Law regime began to unravel. The crisis was especially acute in Negros Occidental, as Alfred McCoy demonstrates, where, particularly after 1980, developments in the world sugar market combined with the confiscatory policies of the Marcos government created a highly volatile situation of intra-elite conflict and working class militancy. Meanwhile, as is well known, popular resistance to the government was a major reason for the expansion to many areas of the New People's Army and the Communist Party of the Philippines.

During the massive EDSA demonstrations in Metro Manila on 24-27 February 1986, some parallel action occurred elsewhere. In Cebu City, citizens massed before a Philippine Constabulary camp that was friendly to the mutinous soldiers in Manila to protect it from attack by Marcos forces; in Marawi, Carter Bentley reports, people held prayer rallies and protested against local politicians who continued to defend Marcos and the crooked ballot counting that had occurred there; and in Iloilo City, Cristina Blanc-Szanton says, people celebrated Aquino's election with bonfires and dancing in the streets.

Most communities, however, particularly those outside the large urban centers, were quiet and life went on normally. Up and down the archipelago, however, people in small communities were hooked into events in Manila by an excellent nationwide radio coverage. People were especially anxious about the prospect of violence and frequently prayed among themselves that the raging dispute over who won the election be resolved peacefully before bloody fighting erupted and cause the civil war, which was already prominent in many areas, to spread further. One gathers that "EDSA" had considerable silent support in much of the country. In some areas, though, such as the Ilocos and parts of Central Luzon, people either remained firm Marcos supporters or were skeptical of the way in which Aquino forces took over the government.

After Marcos

The mood in the immediate post-Marcos period was a mix of hope and uncertainty. There was confusion as the new government in Manila purged officials in the provinces, cities, and municipalities, a controversial move that created opportunities in many places for vendettas, opportunism, and intense infighting within the anti-Marcos opposition. Coup d'etat attempts in 1986 and 1987 by factions within the military and the breakdown in the truce between the government and the New People's Army in 1987 heightened the climate of instability. In places, authority broke down, as in Lanao del Sur where the lack of a "center of power" unleashed anarchy and violence.

Many Filipinos saw "EDSA" as an "opening" in politics wherein they could act on beliefs that normally they had to hide. Willem Wolters cites the idealism of some bourgeois leaders of the pro-Aquino camp in Cabanatuan City who were anxious to pursue "new politics" based on a principled and democratic approach to governance. In a Nueva Ecija village, Benedict Kerkvliet found that poor landless families took advantage of the situation to unilaterally farm the land of a large owner. Elections in Estancia, Iloilo, Cristina Blanc-Szanton contends, became more competitive and issue-oriented during the 1986-88 period. In a Palawan community, James Eder points to a sharp decrease in cynicism about elections and a corresponding increase in the belief that government can be beneficial to average people. Michael Pinches shows that to the poor in Tatalon, Quezon City, "EDSA" was a period of communitas when the rich and poor met and participated as equals.

On the other hand, the overwhelming evidence in the essays shows that what was achieved by Aquino replacing Marcos is much more modest than what is suggested by the notion of "a transition from authoritarianism to democracy." In Negros Occidental, McCoy shows, the big sugar planters have regained their domination and have been repressing dissent more efficiently. In Ilocos Sur, Raul Pertierra concludes, the main structure of provincial and local politics has not changed significantly. Turner says that People Power has left no legacy of increased participation in governance for most people in Zamboanga City. The idealistic politicians in Cabanatuan were virtually gone by 1988. Government threats forced the poor Nueva Ecija villagers to stop farming the land they had taken over. And for the poor in Tatalon, "shaming" continues as the structures of social inequality govern day-to-day existence once more.

This is not to conclude that nothing has changed. A more accurate conclusion from the essays here is that "EDSA"—as an event to inspire people for generations to come and a momentary opening into new possibilities of political action—suggests not stagnancy but dynamism among Filipinos in various localities and classes. Hence, while no decisive reform of iniquitous social structures has taken place, EDSA has demonstrated that the social and moral resources needed for such reform are there.

Martial Law and the State

EDSA and other evidence in several of the essays indicate that Filipinos are not captives of the dominant elite's discourse and practices. While the essays, collectively considered, do not try to reconstruct the life-history of the Martial Law regime in the Philippines, a striking picture emerges: the state under Marcos was weaker than its usual "authoritarian" characterization suggests. Although Marcos accelerated the progressive shift in the locus of power from towns and provinces to the central government, the state's machinery remained insufficiently systematic to routinize people's lives throughout the archipelago. Popular consciousness remained largely uncaptured despite the Marcos government's efforts to control thought through various "New Society" organizations and such institutions as the media and schools. People were frequently cynical of the government, and the young generation even in Ilocos became a prime source for opposition to the government. Apparently by the early 1980s, fewer and fewer people believed what emanated from the ruling elite, whether it was the official version of Ninoy Aquino's death or the Marcoses' effort to cast themselves as super patrons. This is shown, for instance, in Pinches's account of poor men and women in Metro Manila privately ridiculing Ferdinand and Imelda.

The significance of Martial Law differed considerably across the country. In the frontier community of San Jose, Palawan, for example, Martial Law had little substantive impact on people's lives. But in Marawi and elsewhere in Lanao del Sur, Martial Law helped provoke a prolonged Muslim rebellion against intensified encroachments and demands by the central government. It brought for a time noticeable benefits to some localities, particularly in the Ilocos which the government favored with many public works and other improvements but also in rural areas such as central Nueva Ecija where a revitalized land reform secured tenants' rights to their fields. In several areas, such as Negros and parts of Mindanao, the adverse effects—especially from military rampages and greedy business people well connected to the powers that be—contributed directly to opposition to the government even among some of the local elites.

As the Philippine economy deteriorated in the 1980s and the government became increasingly immobilized by internal contradictions, Marcos's patronage system, which had been a key instrument for mustering support, became ineffective. Too little was distributed or done so very unevenly; too many people remained disenfranchised; the arrogance and deceit of Marcos and others became widely transparent; and the main conduit for patronage and mobilization, the Kilusang Bagong Lipunan (KBL), which never became well-institutionalized, began to fall apart.

Marcos's strong following in the Ilocos is, in a way, also indicative of the state's weakness. Accounts by Pertierra and Fernando Zialcita suggest that to Ilokanos Marcos was useful in their instrumental approach to dealing with the national government and as a protector of their preferred distance from the central government. In a way, especially in Zialcita's Ilocos Norte village, people there are semiautonomous from the national political economy because of a "remittance economy" founded on strong ties to Ilokano settlements elsewhere in the world, especially Hawaii, making them significantly less vulnerable to the worsening economic conditions in the Philippines during the 1980s.

In any case, despite differences in the impact of Martial Law across the country, the image that emerges from the essays in this volume is a population that was, in ideological terms, relatively untied. On one hand, this was expressed through avoidance, tolerance, and cynicism, factors that helped to sustain the Marcos regime. On the other, it harbored the potential for the oppositional sentiments expressed in the EDSA phenomenon.

Elections and Legitimacy

The essays here focus on elections, particularly on voting behavior, who voted for whom and why. Nearly all the studies indicate that elections remain a key institution in the patterning of political life. While its power and appeal may have suffered some erosion, the electoral process remains widely regarded in the Philippines as the way through which leaders and holders of public office gain legitimacy and the charter to govern. One notes, for instance, that EDSA was less a denial of the electoral process and more a popular undertaking to affirm it.

At the same time, cynicism about elections and politicians is common. Poor people, as Alex Brillantes's study of a Metro Manila neighborhood indicates, are often too preoccupied with making ends meet to pay much attention to elections which, in any case, they believe are frequently riddled with cheating. Similarly, a pronounced sentiment is that elections are essentially contests among candidates with little genuine interest in the problems of the poor majority, hence who wins is not terribly important to most people. Finally, they see office holders more often than not using public office for their own purposes rather than for public service.

This negative appraisal helps to explain why people may treat elections in instrumental ways—selling their votes, participating in a nominal way to please a relative or friend who is campaigning, or in other ways "working the system," as Mojares summarizes this behavior. It also helps to explain the widespread indifference when Marcos declared Martial Law in 1972, suspending most elections and disbanding Congress and other elected bodies. People were willing, partly because of the cynicism and partly in expectation of better results from government, to forego elections. As several essays here indicate, Filipinos can tolerate, perhaps even welcome, rulers not legitimated by elections so long as they deliver economic and other material improvements and maintain peace and order.

Marcos promised such a rule—a "new society" that would bring prosperity to the masses through urban and rural land reforms and economic development and that would take political power away from the oligarchy. For a while he succeeded. But by the early 1980s, if not before, a large proportion of people had concluded that he had not only failed but had made conditions much worse.

Marcos contributed further to his downfall by persistently twisting to suit his preferences those few elections that he did allow. By 1986, voters, impelled in part by a disintegrating economy and widening civil war (especially between the NPA and government troops), were determined to make the election a fair one in order to re-establish the role of elections for legitimating and meaningfully reconstituting government. Popular participation in the National Movement for Free Elections (NAMFREL), which watch-dogged the balloting and counting in much of the nation, was the most obvious manifestation of a sentiment that ran deep.

Questioning the Factional Model

Both popular and scholarly analyses typically say that factions are the basic building blocks of Philippine politics. This "factional" interpretation identifies local factions and alliances as the central components of party organization and the primary instrument for voter mobilization. According to the argument, factions and alliances cut across and entwine society's classes and are held together by kinship, friendship, patron-client relationships, and exchanges of goods and services. They pyramid into provincial and national networks but, because competing alliances are bound together by short-term ends rather than by significant ideological positions, these groupings are highly unstable. Issues and other such concerns, the argument continues, are usually unimportant to voters. Instead, the crucial question voters ponder is who is supporting or opposing whom. People support whomever their personal allies favor because ultimately such connections are what one must use in order to get any service or goods from the successful candidate.[2]

Taken together, the essays in this volume call this view of Philippine politics into question. It cannot, for instance, account for the coercion and other violence by candidates and their local advocates that McCoy finds in Negros Occidental and Bentley in Marawi. Moreover, several essays in this book reveal that factionalism is a rather blunt tool for analyzing voting behavior and accounting for the range of politics in the Philippines.

One generalization that can be drawn from several of the essays is that, during elections in 1986 and in other years, personal relationships and loyalties were not necessarily the most important considerations. In Zamboanga City, for instance, people elected Cesar Climaco largely on the basis of his stance against policies and practices of the Marcos government. Climaco defeated candidates who were better financed and had the support of the supposedly powerful national political alliances. Moreover, had the 1986 election in Zamboanga been a test of local leaders' ability to disburse patronage, then Marcos would have won by a large margin. Instead, Aquino won, primarily, Turner concludes, because of voters' assessments of the "moral standing and integrity" of the two candidates. Similarly, Eder concludes, after looking at various possible explanations for why the majority of people in San Jose, Palawan, supported Aquino, that people voted largely according to their judgments as to who would make "the better president." Szanton shows that the close election contest in Estancia, Iloilo, revolved very much around economic issues and voters' assessments of the two candidates. In Tatalon, Metro Manila, Pinches finds that underlying class tensions together with the Marcoses' arrogance greatly influenced voters to vote for Aquino. In San Ricardo, Nueva Ecija, Kerkvliet finds that land reform and corruption were the two major issues that villagers weighed when deciding their votes. An important reason why Marcos won there is that most tenants had benefited from the land reform implemented during Marcos's rule. In Valladolid, Cebu, Mojares argues that a majority voted for Aquino largely on the basis of people's weariness with the Marcos government because their lives had been getting much worse and they hoped that Aquino could reverse the trend.

The conclusion here is not that factionalism is of no importance in electoral politics. Several studies in this volume show that factional considerations are indeed factors. And in some places, such as Marawi where the 1986 presidential election had little to do with Marcos and Aquino but was principally a test of a warlord's control of the territory, alliances are extremely important (though, it should be noted, the nature of these alliances may not be what the factional model profiles).

What we conclude is that factionalism—and its corollary, personalism—is but one factor among many as people weigh their options.

Issues—such as perceived benefits from Marcos-style land reform, peace and stability, or the qualities most important for holding public office—do figure significantly in people's calculations. Even in Marawi, issues and assessments by voters of their economic situation and matters of political principles played a role in the aftermath of the February 1986 balloting when ultimately the local warlord was ousted. The image that emerges from the essays is of a diverse society of ill-joined political actors rather than pyramids of patrons and clients; and in some areas, of political monopolies built on command and coercion rather than benign alliances glued together by negotiation or reciprocity.

Possibly the factional model was more useful decades ago than it is now and then more so in some places than in others. Patron-client relations on which factions in the past leaned have been breaking down in many parts of the country as a consequence of population growth, urbanization, changing patterns of labor utilization, and growing integration of communities into the capitalist world-system.[3] The Marcos rule also contributed to this process by withdrawing or withholding resources from local elites who, consequently, could not sustain their patronage. Widening poverty during the Marcos years may also have depleted many factions of local leaders.

Even apart from these changes, we think the factional interpretation has major limitations for at least a couple additional reasons. One is that it emphasizes elections and related activity virtually to the exclusion of other forms of politics. In many parts of the country and for a long time now peasants, workers, students, and others have formed and joined petition campaigns, demonstrations, issue-oriented organizations, rebellions, revolutionary movements, and other political efforts that are not part of the election process. Some of these activities appear in essays of this volume. They suggest, contrary to the image conveyed by the factional interpretation, that politics can be grounded in economic and social concerns and that class tensions are significant in many parts of the country and have been for some time.

A second problem concerns perspective. Several essays in this volume suggest to us that if one's local perspective when analyzing elections is that of municipal and provincial politicians and their campaigners, one is likely to see considerable confirmation for the factional interpretation. Accounts from this vantage point of the presidential and congressional races in Nueva Ecija, Marawi, Zamboanga City, Negros Occidental, and Ilocos provide details of how local elites formed alliances, jockeyed for favorable relationships with more powerful politicians, and developed linkages for the sake of electoral advantages with little or no regard for social issues beyond the preservation of personal or sectoral power. If, however, one listens to the people who voted, the picture is considerably more complicated. Those alliances and linkages that dominate the discourse among the elites are only part of what common urban workers, agricultural laborers, peasants, petty traders, and others are weighing. It is from their perspective that we see the cynical and instrumental approach to participation and the assessments of candidates in terms of issues and problems crucial to people that we summarized earlier. Had previous studies of local electoral politics been more attentive to understanding the non-politicians, perhaps the factional interpretation would have required revisions much earlier.

"Local" and "National"

All the essays assess "national" developments from the standpoint of "local" communities, mainly villages, towns, cities, and provinces. While distinctions are made in the calculations people make vis-à-vis local and national elections, the essays show how closely intermeshed local and extralocal realities are such that to speak of "levels" of decision-making is misleading since the term itself suggests separate or separable realities.

The local and extralocal are related in terms more dynamic than what is suggested by such descriptions as "reflection" or "impingement." The local and extralocal are mutually constitutive: the "inside" is part of the "outside" and vice versa. Local communities are not only "affected" by broad national and world developments, they are continually being reconstituted by them such that the boundaries of village, town, and region are continually being redrawn. Simultaneously, extralocal systems, such as the nation-state, are unavoidably defined through the overall configuration of local realities.

An argument can be developed, based on the data in this book, that both the maintenance and collapse of the Martial Law regime were determined by local realities, which were, of course, influenced by forces beyond the confines of the locality itself. There is evidence throughout this volume that Marcos's rule sustained itself for so long in large measure through a skillful balancing of force and attraction, avoidance and intervention. The efficacy of such instruments rested on local experiences, predispositions, and values. These values—which, as Pertierra points out in his study of an Ilocos community, were not effectively routinized to serve the state—formed the unstable foundation of the Martial Law government. The precariousness of that governmental structure is demonstrated by how quickly it collapsed once the internal supports weakened.

These realities remain today and draw attention to how the Aquino government itself rests on a tenuous foundation. Its passage to power owes more to the favorable convergence of populist sentiments than the force of a single, organized political will anchored to a clear program of popular empowerment. Until that occurs, instability will continue to shake the government. Nevertheless, although a new era has not dawned, neither have we simply returned to the status quo ante. Experiences in recent Philippine history—whether of the sort that has raised hope or bred disillusion—have enlarged the moral and symbolic capital for the struggle to create a better society. The gain, no matter what turn history takes now, is not inconsequential.

MARK M. TURNER

Politics During the Transition in Zamboanga City, 1984–1988

Zamboanga's reputation as a peaceful, charming, and exotic city has come under fire since the advent of the Muslim revolt in the early 1970s. "Zamboanga hermosa" (beautiful) has been replaced by Zamboanga the highly militarized city, where violence and illicit activities abound. Given this environment, one might assume that electoral politics in Zamboanga is characterized by that familiar combination of "guns, goons, and gold." But this is not the case. This study traces the recent electoral history of Zamboanga and attempts to identify the dynamics of formal political competition there.[1]

Zamboanga City is located at the southwest tip of the island of Mindanao. Although officially classified as a "highly urbanized city," much of Zamboanga's large area (1,415 sq. kms.) is rural in character. The population is mainly found on the coastal plain, especially in the vicinity of the urban center which lies in the south of the city area facing out across the Basilan Strait. The hilly interior is sparsely populated, and only 20 percent of the city's area is classified as "moderately good" or above in terms of land capability.[2] Nevertheless, agriculture, including fishing, is probably the leading economic activity in terms of employment, although considerable nonagricultural employment is provided in the urban economy.

Zamboanga's strategic site makes it the focus of sea-borne trade for southwest Mindanao and the islands of Basilan, Sulu, and Tawi-Tawi. Zamboanga is the region's link to national and international trading networks. The large port and land transport industries have benefited from improved road infrastructure which has given Zamboanga greater access to its Mindanao hinterland. Commerce is the city's life-blood, and a host of wholesale and retail establishments operate in the bustling downtown area where the crowded pavements and shops complement the congested streets. In addition, there are the "barter traders" who sell goods which they are allowed to import tax-free into

Zamboanga. Strategic location has drawn a variety of other functions to Zamboanga. The city is the headquarters for the political and administrative organizations of Autonomous Region IX (Western Mindanao). Educational, media, and religious institutions congregate in the city while the Southern Command (Southcom) of the Armed Forces of the Philippines (AFP) is based there. Service industries abound, ranging from motor vehicle repairs to insurance and entertainment. There is some manufacturing, notably tuna canning, wood processing, shipbuilding and repair, shellcraft, and coconut processing.

Since the end of World War II, the city has experienced rapid population growth. In 1948, the population stood at 103,317 while in 1980, there were 343,722 persons.[3] The estimate for 1987 is 412,847.[4] Much of Zamboanga's population growth can be attributed to migration. The stream of migrants has resulted from the functional growth of the city, the exhaustion of Mindanao's agricultural land frontier, and the perception of poor economic opportunities in rural areas. Also, many have sought refuge from the fighting associated with the communist insurgency and Muslim rebellion. The result of migration is ethnic diversity. Indigenous Zamboangueños still comprise the majority of the population, but by 1980, only 53 percent of the population were first-language speakers of Chavacano, Zamboanga's own distinctive Spanish Creole.[5] Visayan and Muslim groups are well-represented in the city while there are even migrants from ethnolinguistic groups of northern Luzon. Zamboanga is still predominantly a Catholic city with 75 percent of its population professing adherence to the Catholic faith.[6] Approximately 25 percent of the population are Muslims.

The Legacy of Cesar Climaco

Any discussion of the recent political history of Zamboanga City must start in 1980 with the local elections called by President Marcos. In most parts of the Philippines, a combination of money, good organization, popular acquiescence, and electoral manipulation saw a profusion of Marcos's Kilusang Bagong Lipunan (KBL) candidates returned to office. But a few places did not succumb to KBL might. In Zamboanga City, the KBL was routed. The major reason for this opposition triumph was the newly elected mayor, Cesar Cortez Climaco.

Climaco was a professional politician who commenced his political apprenticeship in 1941 as secretary to the Mayor of Davao. He later occupied the same position in Zamboanga where he entered electoral politics, first becoming a councilor and then, at the age of thirty-seven, mayor. Various presidential appointments followed in the 1960s. He was, among other things, Commissioner of Customs, Presidential Assistant on Community Development and Chairman of the Anti-Graft Committee. With the declaration of Martial Law in 1972, he returned to Zamboanga City to farm and to become an implacable foe of Martial Law and President Marcos. Climaco formed a Zamboanga political party known as the Concerned Citizens Aggrupation (CCA). He fought in the 1978 elections for the interim Batasang Pambansa (National Assembly) under the CCA banner. Although he failed to secure the regional seat, he obtained the majority of the votes in Zamboanga. Thus, in the 1980 local elections, Climaco's CCA team captured the positions of city mayor, vice-mayor, and seven of the eight councilors.

Climaco proceeded to dominate the political life of Zamboanga until his murder in November 1984. He had been voted into office on an explicitly anti-Marcos, anti-Martial Law platform. This orientation was fiercely maintained throughout his incumbency. Climaco was a crusader for "freedom, justice, and integrity" and practiced "serving the people without any regard to fanfare and material reward."[7] He regularly fired off complaints to Malacañang and the AFP Southcom about military abuses and the appalling unchecked violence which characterized Zamboanga City. Vociferous and vitriolic criticism of other aspects of Marcos's rule was frequent. Marcos may have tolerated Climaco because of ties of personal "friendship," as a demonstration of the "health" of Philippine democracy, and because Climaco adopted a resolutely nonviolent path. Climaco's communications to Malacañang and other centers of power were often mimeographed and circulated widely. He also attended personally to his constituents. Even the poorest would approach Climaco for help. He was highly visible in the supervision of his local administration and government employees would not be asked to undertake tasks which Climaco himself would not do. In large part, his political success was due to his style rather than his philosophy. Climaco was "wacky, irreverent and wild . . . the consummate performer, the practical joker [who] poked fun at everyone, himself including [sic]."[8] He could be seen in the city astride his motorcycle with his big boots, faded denims, and long hair straggling, "over sixty but still sexy" as the children sang of him.

Climaco was a charismatic leader but not in the sense of a representative of transcendental authority. He inspired what Burns calls "heroic leadership":

faith in the leaders' capacity to overcome obstacles and crises; readiness to grant to leaders the powers to handle crises; mass support for such leaders expressed directly—through votes, applause, letters, shaking hands—rather than through intermediaries or institutions.[9]

The situation in Zamboanga City did not degenerate into the "idolatrous form of heroic leadership" which Burns sees occurring in some developing societies.[10] Climaco did, however, adopt a somewhat autocratic pattern of decision-making, taking unilateral actions with minimal consultation. Nevertheless, his brand of charisma was not antidemocratic, nor does it support Weber's view that effective electoral politics required the "soullessness" of the masses. Climaco enjoyed an "inspirational" relationship with his followers who were willing to accept his initiative because they shared the same communal identity and social philosophy.

This relationship between leader and followers was graphically demonstrated in the 1984 Batasang Pambansa elections. With a turnout that surpassed any before or since, Climaco won an overwhelming victory over pro-KBL candidate Maria Clara Lobregat and former mayor and KBL choice, Joaquin Enriquez: 85,103 to 46,750 and 14,115 votes. And this was achieved despite large KBL expenditure—Climaco typically told people to "take the money, it's yours anyway, and vote for me." The people of Zamboanga reaffirmed their support for the crusader and for the dangerous but communally prescribed path along which he led. As people now recall, it was an era of People Power predating EDSA. But there were no mass protests on the streets, just Cesar Climaco, representing a movement with some egalitarian ideals and a firm belief in the sincerity of his charismatic leadership. The presence of such a leader was essential, for after Climaco was murdered in November 1984, his brand of popular politics disappeared.

From Hero to Pragmatist

Climaco's replacement was his vice-mayor Manuel Dalipe. To many, Dalipe had been a strange choice as Climaco's running-mate in 1980. Then, at thirty-four years of age, he had no experience of running for elected office. He was a former Air Force major and bemedalled helicopter pilot who had even seen service in Marcos's Presidential Guards. In terms of formal education, he was well-qualified with four years at the Philippine Military Academy (PMA) and two years at the Asian Institute of Management (AIM).

In 1980, Dalipe had polled more votes than Climaco. But members of the CCA regarded him with suspicion because of his military background and political inexperience. A rift developed between Climaco and Dalipe, the latter being critical of Climaco's administrative style and of his relations with the military and central government. In May 1984, Dalipe demonstrated his alienation from Climaco by supporting the pro-KBL candidate, Maria Clara Lobregat, in the Batasang Pambansa elections. For this, he was ousted from the CCA. But as vice-mayor, he succeeded to the position of mayor after Climaco's murder. Dalipe immediately began to change the style and orientation of the administration.

First, the politics of conflict with the military ceased. Dalipe believed that cooperation with the AFP was the way to reduce violence and military abuses. Dalipe's military background prompted this approach and also made the new mayor more acceptable to the AFP. Second, Dalipe adopted a style of administration in keeping with the lessons on bureaucratic rationality that he had been taught at the PMA and AIM. Out went Climaco's highly personalized, charismatic, and eccentric style of leadership which focused on crisis management and crusades. Instead, Dalipe tried to improve relations with Malacañang and demonstrate his administrative worthiness through infrastructure projects. After one hundred days in office, he was judged by a leading local journalist to have "introduced positive managerial changes at city hall and done nothing that would not give him the admiration of the voters and the grudging respect of his critics."[11]

With the death of Climaco, the CCA became characterized by factional struggle as hopefuls in the party hierarchy jockeyed for support as mayoral candidates in the local elections scheduled for 1986. It became increasingly apparent that the party had been a personal creation and a vehicle for popular mobilization under Climaco. The CCA lacked formal structure and solidarity. It was focused on the person of its founder and it was his "magnetism" which both attracted people to it and which held it together. With the magnet gone, two of the councilors elected under the CCA banner in 1980 moved away from the party. Dalipe had already been ousted in 1984. Others wavered, while the elevation of the leading councilor, Susan de los Reyes, to vice-mayor meant that the CCA had lost its majority on the city council. The political mood was one of cooperation with Marcos. Dalipe maintained that Zamboanga's opposition to Marcos was "obstructionist" and hampered future development. All officials did not, however, rush to join the KBL. Although many in the political elite now saw their best interests with the ascendant Marcos camp, Climaco had left a legacy of opposition to Marcos and a belief in popular democracy.

The test of this legacy came with the presidential election of February 1986. Dalipe headed the pro-Marcos campaign and found support from three of the seven elected councilors and four out of the five appointed councilors. Sali Wali, the Regional Executive Council Chairman, and leading Muslim politician, came out strongly for Marcos as did Hasan Alam, the Barter Trade Cooperative president. Climaco's former electoral foe, the extremely wealthy Maria Clara Lobregat, also offered her support for Marcos and was identified by *The Morning Times* (18 January 1986) as the KBL leader in Zamboanga. Other lesser leaders, such as barangay captains, followed. Lawyer Ramon Lim, the younger brother of the late Zamboanga senator, Roseller Lim, led the Marcos-Tolentino Movement (MTM) in Zamboanga City. However, Mayor Dalipe was more prominent. He praised the president for his "all-out support" for the city's development and for his "generosity" and personal interest in Zamboanga. Wali repeatedly raised the specter of the communist menace and associated it with Cory Aquino. Wali also assured his Muslim constituents of Marcos's deep concern for Muslim Filipinos. Aquino visited Zamboanga and attracted a large crowd which, according to Dalipe, was "greatly disappointed by the dismal failure for an alternative program."[12]

The Aquino campaign was a low key affair. Lacking the KBL finances, which had been pouring into Zamboanga, the Aquino camp secured very little media publicity. The local arm of the national Cory Aquino for President Movement (CAPM) was led by a local lawyer and it relied, in large part, on unpaid student workers. The CAPM campaign was not coordinated with the pro-Aquino canvassing of the CCA politicians. Although local media believed that the Philippine clergy had "tactfully endorsed" the candidacy of Mrs. Aquino, the Catholic Church in Zamboanga generally kept a low and neutral profile under instruction from the archbishop. One outspoken Jesuit did achieve wide publicity for his independent line that it was a "national disgrace" that Marcos was running and that the only thing worse would be if he were to win.[13]

Violence was not a problem for the pro-Aquino camp in Zamboanga City. Zealous pro-Marcos supporters did privately warn some CAPM workers to stop their activities. There was alleged harassment of tricycle drivers displaying opposition stickers, and both sides reported vandalism to their posters. But guns, goons, and military intervention were not elements of the election campaign.

The voting was peaceful and counting proceeded without incident. Aquino secured 59 percent (69,958) of the votes to Marcos's 41 percent (49,113). The turnout was down 21 percent from the 1984 Batasang Pambansa election, despite the numerical growth of the electorate.

This is indicative of Climaco's ability to secure mass participation in the electoral process and of widespread cynicism after his death. Approximately 31 percent of eligible voters failed to go to the polls. For the 69 percent who did vote, the legacy of Cesar Climaco and opposition to Marcos was clearly demonstrated. Despite the Marcos camp's massive resources and support for Marcos from many of the city's leading political figures, the Zamboanga electorate chose not to endorse him. This election was more than a test of local leaders' popularity and their ability to disburse patronage. The presidential election involved an assessment of moral standing and integrity. On both scores, Aquino led Marcos by a considerable distance.

Following the presidential election in Zamboanga, the population's attention was riveted on events in Manila. People Power arrived on Manila's EDSA but in Zamboanga, equivalent mass action was not evident. After the premature announcement of Marcos's departure, there were a couple of peaceful marches comprised mainly of students. The vast majority of the citizenry stayed at home and followed media reports of happenings in the capital. The military at Southcom did likewise.

A Second Climaco

With Marcos gone, Aquilino Pimentel, a staunch anti-Marcos politician, assumed responsibility for local government in Aquino's new cabinet. His major task was to remove pro-Marcos officials and replace them with appointees, officers-in-charge (OIC), who were known supporters of Aquino. This OIC system would ensure local government's cooperation with the center and destroy the local KBL organizations.

In Zamboanga, the obvious targets were the pro-Marcos mayor, Dalipe, and the three elected councilors who had sided with him. The CCA was the logical place to look for possible OIC, and Susan de los Reyes, the vice-mayor and party chairperson, seemed to be the front-runner for the mayoral position. However, the CCA was not united and one group of party influentials persuaded Julio Cesar "Rini" Climaco, the late mayor's son, to compete for the mayoral position. The pro-Rini faction interpreted some of de los Reyes's actions as being pro-Marcos and suspected irregularities in the disbursement of project funds. What the faction really desired was the restoration of the Climaco name to the leadership of local politics. De los Reyes supporters in the CCA resented the candidacy of a political novice simply because he was the son of the legendary Cesar Climaco.

After intensive lobbying by the two parties, Pimentel appointed Rini Climaco as OIC mayor leaving de los Reyes as disgruntled vice-mayor. Three new councilors were appointed on local recommendation: all were hardcore CCA supporters from the Rini Climaco wing of the party. The CCA triumph did not, however, produce unity in the party. The factions merely agreed to "live together," a condition of OIC appointment decreed by Pimentel. There had been no consultation with the people over these appointments and no popular clamour for Dalipe's removal. He had, after all, been a reasonably popular mayor whose pragmatic managerial style of leadership had led him into the pro-Marcos camp where he could gain access to the resources of the central government. He was judged to be a hardworking and competent administrator who produced results. Nevertheless, when he handed over the mayorship on 25 May 1986, there were no barricades, stormy protests, or obvious displays of rancour, as in other parts of the city.

Within six months of assuming office, the appointed mayor was forced to hit the campaign trail to secure the ratification of the constitution in the plebiscite of 2 February 1987. Aquino approved the new constitution, and her ministers encouraged and even threatened local officials to ensure that the plebiscite result would be to her satisfaction. Thus, the OIC had a strong incentive to campaign for a "Yes" vote in the plebiscite. Their positions were on the line. The mayor led the ratification drive in Zamboanga and called upon all barangay captains and village officials for active support.[14] The chairman of the regional assembly, the Lupong Tagapagpaganap ng Pook (LTP), was also prominent in the "Yes" campaign. Other politicians, even former Marcos supporters, joined the "Yes" bandwagon. On instruction from the archbishop, the Church in Zamboanga adopted a neutral stance, although a pastoral letter from the Catholic Bishops Conference of the Philippines (CBCP) urged Catholics to vote for charter ratification. The Church did not even participate officially in constitution education programmes although an outspoken Jesuit did deliver a cathedral sermon in which he classified any "No" voter as a follower of Satan.[15]

There was little campaigning for the "No" cause. For those out of office, ratification of the new constitution meant elections both for national and local positions. A rejected constitution meant no elections, no chance of gaining office. Opposition to the constitution was therefore against the interests of persons anxious to test their popularity in the ballot boxes. Local political hopefuls were reluctant to pay for a campaign which, if successful, would keep them out of office. Even the proratification drive was a relatively subdued affair. In terms of local political competition, there was little at stake. What was really taking place was a vote of confidence in the president, a confirmation of her legitimacy. The Aquino camp also portrayed a vote for "Yes" as a vote for stability. The content of the constitution was of secondary importance. Education drives covered relatively few in the electorate and even then there was a lot to digest—24,000 words spread over sixty-two pages. The people of Zamboanga were participating in a presidential election in which there was only one candidate.

The poll was described as "quiet and orderly," even "dull."[16] Many polling stations were "guarded" by unarmed students while NAMFREL, the independent electoral watchdog, reported no irregularities or violence. In common with the national trend, Zamboanga gave overwhelming approval to the constitution. Eighty-one percent voted "Yes." What people gave "overwhelming approval" to was Aquino's legitimacy as president. The "Yes" victory was also an expression of the belief that Aquino was the best hope for political stability and a reduction of violence, bloodshed, and the threat of civil war. Many who had voted for Marcos in the presidential election of 1986 now cast their lot with Aquino. They no longer felt obliged to vote according to the wishes of Zamboanga's previously pro-Marcos leaders, as those leaders were inactive in the plebiscite campaign. The subdued campaigning contrasted with a relatively high turnout—79 percent of the registered voters, 20 percent more than in the 1986 election—the reverse of the previous year's presidential election. It clearly demonstrated people's concern about national politics and its potentially profound effect on the future of themselves, their families, and their community.

Even before the "Yes" victory was announced, Zamboanga's political leaders were busy making preparations for the congressional elections scheduled for May. The greatest dramas were taking place within the CCA. On 2 February, the day of the plebiscite, Susan de los Reyes, the CCA chairman, announced that she would run for Congress under the CCA banner. She claimed, it was later reported, that Rini Climaco had made a pledge to support her during Aquino's preplebiscite visit to Zamboanga.[17] The Rini Climaco wing of the CCA, however, was busy trying to decide who it would select as a congressional candidate. Four were fighting for this nomination, which would see the CCA team up with the pro-Aquino Lakas ng Bansa (LABAN). At the CCA selection meeting, city councilor Vitaliano Agan, the local coordinator of the LABAN and member of the Rini Climaco wing, won the nomination on a 30–29 vote. De los Reyes would not accept this decision. She alleged two pro-Agan voters were ineligible. More meetings followed to sort out the dispute but agreement could not be reached. De los Reyes even suggested that Aquino should be the one to choose. Then in March, Rini Climaco made statements indicating that he might be willing to run. De los Reyes countered by claiming backing from the full range of proadministration parties: UNIDO, Liberal Party (LP)-Salonga wing, Pilipino Democratic Party-Lakas ng Bayan (PDP-Laban), and the CCA. Meanwhile, one of the CCA councilors proclaimed himself the LABAN choice and demanded the total support of all in the CCA. No compromises were made within the CCA and both Rini Climaco and Susan de los Reyes filed candidacies to contest the Zamboanga City congressional seat, the former reportedly under the CCA-LABAN banner, the latter under CCA-UNIDO. Climaco was later described as "independent."

What this episode clearly demonstrates is that the CCA was no longer a coherent political party. Previously, the party and Cesar Climaco had a common identity and a common anti-Marcos purpose. The removal of Cesar Climaco revealed the lack of a strong formal structure and the party's dependence on Cesar Climaco and his particular political objectives and informal style. The departure of Marcos also removed the CCA's principal reason for existence. Although politicians continued to use the CCA label, the CCA ceased to be a political organization with a common identity, strategy, and philosophy.

In addition to the two CCA candidates there were nine others. A few sported the labels of national political parties. On the Aquino side were PDP-Laban and LP-Salonga candidates and a person claiming to be the LABAN choice. An opposition candidate adopted the Grand Alliance for Democracy (GAD)-KBL tag. He had previously been identified as a candidate of the Union for Peace and Progress (UPP)-KBL and Fuerza de Zamboanga, the latter seemingly a political creation of his own. One potential GAD candidate was so "disgusted" with exclusion from the GAD senatorial slate that he decided to run for Congress as an independent. But these party labels were of little consequence to the electorate and, as it turned out, of minimal use to the candidates. The electorate were engaged in selecting a local representative for Congress and not a political party, while the candidates quickly discovered that the new political parties had negligible resources to dispense to their provincial candidates.

Among the eleven candidates, there were no representatives of the left. None of the constituent organizations of the left's electoral vehicle, the Alliance for New Politics (ANP) contested the Zamboanga seat. This highlighted the lack of left-wing politics in Zamboanga and contrasted with other large cities in the Philippines and Mindanao. At first sight, this seems odd given the crusading anti-Marcos politics of Cesar Climaco. However, Climaco worked on behalf of traditional constitutional values, such as freedom, justice, and integrity, which were often abstract and individualistic. He was not a radical with a coherent left-wing political philosophy and program of structural reform. He was, in fact, a strong supporter of capital. Climaco was the leader of a popular movement whose principal objective was opposition to Marcos. His "heroic" leadership role may have forestalled the formation of cause-oriented groups and other political organizations of the left simply because he acted as a single focus of mass opposition. A further disincentive to left-wing political activity in Zamboanga was the massive military presence in the city. As the headquarters of Southcom, Zamboanga has large numbers of soldiers and is probably the most militarized city in the Philippines. Such an environment is not conducive to the formation of small formal organizations with radical political objectives. This is especially the case when violence is common, as in Zamboanga.

At present, there is a small umbrella-organization for cause-oriented groups called LAKAS. The national umbrella group for such organizations, Bagong Alyansang Makabayan (BAYAN), does not appear to have a Zamboanga chapter. Neither apparently does the recently formed umbrella group the National Movement for Civil Liberties (NMCL), although it identified "representatives" for all other regions of the Philippines.[18] LAKAS is run by a lawyer and a professor at a local university but it excites little interest and plays a very minor role in the city's political life. Its leader ran for councilor on one of the party slates in January 1988 but failed to get elected. Labor is generally unorganized. Efforts to organize labor meet with strong opposition from business in Zamboanga City. Unions do exist, however, with eight bargaining units covering some of the largest public and private organizations in the city. The National Federation of Labor (NFL) is the dominant force in Zamboanga's organized labor but even it is not a major actor in the city's political life. The NFL counts four large manufacturing operations as its domain but admits to considerable difficulty in establishing more unions. The opposition of business, worker ignorance of unionism, a shortage of "leaders," and the small scale and poor funding of NFL operations indicate that capital and its legal representatives currently have the upperhand. The NFL is affiliated with the radical Kilusang Mayo Uno (KMU) but receives no funding or assistance from it. Likewise no orders are taken from it. Thus, when the KMU announced a national strike in October 1987, nobody heeded the call in Zamboanga City. A further KMU "political strikes offensive" met with the same response. Strikes do occur and can be bitter and long. However, organized labor does not have a left-wing political program and appears to be fragmented. Unions do not appear to cooperate either among themselves or with the cause-oriented groups.

The radical Partido ng Bayan (PnB) has no visible presence in Zamboanga and, as with BAYAN, questions about these organizations generally reveal that people have never heard of them. They do know of the New People's Army (NPA). But the NPA, while active in neighboring Zamboanga del Sur, does not appear to operate within the boundaries of Zamboanga City. There are reports that NPA "legal teams" have conducted "social investigations" and that NPA "hitmen" have been seen in the city but the AFP regard the city as an NPA-free zone.[19] Local explanations of the NPA's absence tend to concentrate on cultural factors such as the "religious nature of the people" and the "good relationship between government and people." The current lack of a serious agrarian problem may be more important. Obvious rumblings of rural discontent are not evident. The prevailing local view of politicians and administrators is that the Comprehensive Agrarian Reform Program (CARP) is of minor relevance to Zamboanga City. The landowning Congresswoman Lobregat is a supporter of the heavily diluted version of the CARP bill. While I am unaware of the "happiness level" of rural Zamboangueños, poverty is widespread and there appear to be more tenants than is generally admitted by leaders. A survey of a district in Zamboanga City found that of 1,550 agricultural households, 23 percent fell into the "tenanted/leased" category.[20] Large areas of underutilized government land in Zamboanga City could, however, be transferred to farmers and landless laborers to forestall rural troubles. This home-grown land reform has been suggested at City Hall.

Finally, of great significance in explaining the absence of NPA is the large and easily mobilized military presence in Zamboanga City and the possibility that there is a tacit agreement with the Moro National Liberation Front (MNLF) that Zamboanga City is MNLF territory. The MNLF allegedly utilizes Zamboanga City as a center for "rest and recreation" and at present has no interest in fomenting trouble there and requires the NPA to do likewise. The NPA may respect the MNLF's wishes as they do not seek a conflict with the MNLF and also because they possibly use Zamboanga City for "rest and recreation" and logistical purposes.

The Catholic Church in Zamboanga City is no supporter of radicalism. A reported rift that existed between liberal religious orders and a conservative diocesan authority has been healed. The archbishop maintains a neutral stance in politics. This entails avoiding involvement, and hence exercising influence, in formal politics. There are no church-labor union relations and likewise none with LAKAS. The church does, however, maintain an official stance of "cooperation" with the military and a diocesan spokesman claimed to have had "no problems" with it. The church runs a Social Action Center, which initiates and implements developmental and welfare projects. These include a community-based health program, nonformal education for school leavers, a producer's cooperative, a soft loan facility, and a maternal-child health care program. Perhaps the most interesting projects are the Basic Ecclesial Communities (BECs). Elsewhere, they have challenged the status quo and so raised the ire of local elites and the AFP. Zamboanga's BECs do not appear to have acquired the "communist" tag because they presently focus on spiritual matters and their involvement in community organization has not conflicted seriously with the status quo; and, of course, there is no NPA activity in Zamboanga. Fundamentalist Christian groups are growing in the city and they are vehemently opposed to the "godless" NPA.

Returning to the election, the campaigns proceeded peacefully. Candidates attempted to demonstrate their fitness for office while exposing their opponents' unsuitability for such positions. "Black propaganda" was much in evidence, but violence or even the threat of it was absent. This lack of violence is a longstanding feature of Zamboanga's electoral politics and is quite remarkable given the general level of violence that has prevailed in Zamboanga over at least the past decade. For example, Cesar Climaco's crime scoreboard listed 889 residents of Zamboanga killed between 1981 and October 1983. *The Manila Times* (9 February 1987) announced that "Zamboanga sleeps early" because of violence. It reported that in December 1986, sixteen people were killed and twenty-three injured. Police statistics for January 1988 recorded twenty-two persons dead and fourteen injured from violent incidents. But these killings are not perpetrated by opposing groups engaged in the formal politics of Zamboanga City. Criminality and the easy access to firearms account for the majority of violence. The large AFP presence encourages crimes of violence and the casual use of firearms while it is admitted by the Southcom chief "that military and policemen are involved in syndicated crimes in this city."[21] One of the mayoral aspirants blamed the high rate of unsolved crimes on the military connection.[22] The negligible rate of detection does nothing to discourage violence while occasional excesses by the Civilian Home Defense Force (CHDF) and its urban counterpart the Active Counter Terrorist Section (ACTS) have added further to Zamboanga's reputation as a city of violence. The only murder of a political leader in more than fifty years as a chartered city was that of Cesar Climaco, and it is generally acknowledged that local political opposition had nothing to do with this assassination.

Why has electoral competition in Zamboanga been peaceful and how are cordial relations between opposing mud-slinging candidates easily re-established once the poll has been completed? One possibility is that formal politics does not assume the degree of importance in Zamboanga society that is found elsewhere in the Philippines. While the occupancy of political office in Zamboanga can bring financial rewards above and beyond official entitlements, the competition for political positions has not focused on the exploitation and monopolization of business opportunities as has happened elsewhere.[23] Representatives of the armed forces, both present and former, have allegedly assumed control of much of this action. Politicians have not assembled armed "goons" to protect and further their interests. Thus, the "warlord" has never appeared on the Zamboanga City scene. Reports of electoral irregularities are few and far between. A common Zamboangueño explanation is simply that "politics is not seen as a whole way of life, it just isn't as important as in other places." As elected politicians are simply not given the same opportunities to run logging, gambling, markets, and other "businesses" as has happened elsewhere, they have less to fight over.

A final point on the lack of political violence in Zamboanga is that the city has no vigilante force. These controversial, armed anticommunist organizations such as Alsa Masa, Tadtad and Nakasaka have sprung up in many other parts of Mindanao but have not in Zamboanga. The OIC mayor, Agan, proposed that five councilors should be sent to Digos, Davao del Sur, to study the Nakasaka operation there with a view to replicating it in Zamboanga City.[24] Mayor Agan believed that this would be an effective way of dealing with the city's endemic crime problems. Many, however, thought that the police should be responsible for law and order and efforts should be directed to improving that official enforcement agency. People did not want any more guns in Zamboanga. There were also questions about how such a group would be controlled. When the notion of an unarmed vigilante group was suggested most treated it with scorn. How could you expect unarmed vigilantes to tackle heavily armed criminals? Some queried the mayor's understanding of vigilante organizations, claiming that they had been established to fight the NPA and that there were no NPA in Zamboanga. Other people feared the possibility that a vigilante group could fall under the control of a politician who could use it for his own ends. The consensus was "no vigilantes," and so Agan's proposal was put into cold storage.

The congressional polls were uneventful. The voter turnout was 13 percent down from the constitutional plebiscite despite an 11 percent increase in the number of registered voters. Over 36 percent of the electorate did not vote. Suggested explanations for this relatively low turnout include payments made by candidates to voters for them not to vote, the coincidence of the election with the Muslim Ramadan, and the posting elsewhere of soldiers eligible to vote. Also, there were fewer material inducements to vote than in the presidential election. Finally, some did not bother to vote in a competition whose outcome they perceived to be of little direct significance to their lives. The new regime had done little to improve the lot of most people and the aspiring representatives for Congress were not seen as offering any great hope for the future.

The congressional seat was won by Maria Clara Lobregat, a result that had been predicted three months earlier in a radio station's poll. She received 46,722 votes, Rini Climaco 36,373 and Susan de los Reyes 21,784. The remaining eight candidates collectively won less votes than de los Reyes. At first sight Lobregat's easy victory seems odd. She had been soundly beaten by Climaco and the CCA in the 1984 Batasang Pambansa election, had supported Marcos in the presidential election and had been a close associate of Marcos cronies in the coconut industry, and had pitched in with the "No" campaign in the constitutional plebiscite. She had, in short, been identified with Marcos in an opposition city and had been on the losing side in Zamboanga City in the three previous electoral exercises. The reasons she won in the congressional election illustrate a number of important aspects of contemporary Zamboanga politics.

Lobregat did not have to contend with Cesar Climaco or Corazon Aquino. While the people of Zamboanga gave Aquino an easy win over Marcos in the presidential election and an overwhelming vote of confidence in the constitutional plebiscite they paid little attention to "Cory's choice" in the congressional election. In many parts of the Philippines, candidates had fought hard to be "Cory's choice" believing that the president's blessing would automatically lead to victory. There was some competition to be "the administration candidate" in Zamboanga, Susan de los Reyes eventually claiming that honor although proadministration PDP-Laban and LP Salonga candidates were also in the line-up. Rini Climaco, the administration's choice as OIC mayor, did not receive Aquino's endorsement as congressional candidate although his wing of the CCA associated itself with LABAN. In the event, party labels and Cory's endorsement counted for nothing. The electorate was not concerned with national party labels or national political figures in the selection of a congressional representative.

The consensus in Zamboanga was that the election was about "personalities." Coherent political philosophies were not part of any candidate's electoral baggage especially given the absence of left-wing candidates. Lobregat can be seen as a kindly, almost archetypal, patron who pays people's hospital bills, builds schools and clinics, is generous to the church, and, in general, helps those in need. She is very wealthy and has been seen over many years to devote some of that wealth to worthy causes. For these reasons she has built up a loyal following. Her wealth also means that there are no serious problems funding an election campaign and ensuring that the "loyal" stay in that frame of mind. But, money alone does not guarantee electoral victory, as Lobregat found to her cost in the 1984 Batasang Pambansa elections and again in the 1986 presidential contest. This may explain her much reduced, but possibly better-targeted, expenditures in the congressional elections.

Lobregat's greatest electoral aid was the split in the CCA, which saw both Rini Climaco and Susan de los Reyes as congressional candidates. If the votes of both CCA candidates are added, the sum exceeds Lobregat's winning total by 11,435 votes. A unified CCA could have beaten Lobregat whose vote was almost identical with the one she achieved in the 1984 Batasang Pambansa election. Zamboanga's betting money (always evident at election times) had assumed a Lobregat win and had been wagered on the outcome of the Rini versus Susan contest.

For Rini Climaco, his greatest advantage was simultaneously his shortcoming. He derived considerable support from being the son of the "legendary Cesar Climaco" but all of his actions as mayor were subject to comparison with what his father would have done in such a situation. He was regarded as being honest, hardworking, and possessing "integrity" but did not have the charismatic appeal of his father. Also, while he inherited a political support system left by his father he did not utilize his position as OIC to build a personal political machine in preparation for an election.[25] But an error of judgment while in office may have cost him many votes. This was his invitation to MNLF leader, Nur Misuari, to come to Zamboanga. Misuari had returned from exile to negotiate with the Aquino regime over MNLF demands for the future of the Southern Philippines. He travelled to various MNLF strongholds with a large group of armed supporters. Christian-dominated Zamboanga was very much against a visit by Misuari to the city. Eventually the meeting was held outside of the city. An indication of the level of feeling against Misuari and his demands was manifested in a petition bearing 120,000 signatures against the inclusion of Zamboanga City into constitutionally prescribed Muslim Mindanao. Christian fears about Muslim domination are undoubtedly strong, although many are quite supportive of the notion of autonomy which would enable the people of Mindanao to experience the full benefits of the wealth of the island. But when autonomy is prefixed with "Muslim" the Christian population of Zamboanga react with fear and hostility. These feelings are enhanced by the lack of central government consultation with Zamboangueños over the issue. In this climate, a preelection television commercial picturing Rini Climaco embracing Nur Misuari damaged Climaco's chances of success at the polls.

This issue—proof that issues as well as personalities do have a role in local politics—also affected voting for the Senate. The Senate competition did, however, have more in common with the constitutional plebiscite than with the congressional election. People were again asked to place a vote of confidence in President Aquino by backing her LABAN slate of candidates. The questions of national stability and moral integrity were brought to center-stage once more. In common with other areas of the country, the LABAN slate won a resounding victory, with Zamboanga's voters placing twenty-one LABAN candidates in the top twenty-four. The president's brother-in-law, Agapito Aquino, and the former minister for local government, Aquilino Pimentel, were placed lower in Zamboanga than nationally. Many Christian Zamboangueños held these two men responsible for revitalizing the Muslim secession movement. Some voters obviously withdrew their pro-Aquino support from these two leading LABAN candidates. However, their strong endorsement by the president ensured that they attained relatively high ranking in the overall field.

The all-conquering LABAN candidates were followed by the Grand Alliance for Democracy (GAD) slate, comprised mainly of powerholders from the Marcos time. Three GAD candidates made it into the top twenty-four in Zamboanga—Joseph Estrada (fifth), Romeo Jalosjos (eighth), and Juan Ponce Enrile (seventeenth). Estrada proved popular throughout the nation. Enrile performed better in Zamboanga than nationally, because of strong support from the AFP and possibly from Lobregat, the two being closely associated in the Marcos-era coconut industry. Jalosjos was well down the national list but in Zamboanga City he managed to capitalize on his local origins from Zamboanga del Norte. The electorate considered this more important than the fact that he had been a pro-Marcos member of the Batasang Pambansa and had campaigned for Marcos in Zamboanga City in the 1986 presidential elections. Other candidates from Mindanao do not seem to have garnered any support simply for being from that island. Pan-Mindanao sentiment, if such a thing exists, was not expressed in the polls.

Trailing badly behind the GAD slate came a group of the UPP-KBL team a lackluster slate dominated by Marcos associates. But if the UPP-KBL line-up received short shrift from the voters the left-wing politicians of the ANP found even less favor. Their top-polling candidate came in fifty-seventh with a mere 2,420 votes (cf. twenty-fourth with 52,859 votes). Their lowest-polling hopeful, placed eighty-first with a scant 311 votes, was Jaime Tadeo, leader of the radical Kilusang Magbubukid ng Pilipinas (KMP).

It should be stressed that the population of Zamboanga is fairly well-informed. There are nine radio stations, five television channels, one newspaper six days per week, another twice weekly, while Manila newspapers arrive daily. The mass media, especially the radio, are certainly accessible throughout the city's barangays. However, the amount of air time and column inches given to the left is negligible. When this factor is added to reasons cited earlier it is clear that the left had no chance of success in Zamboanga. Their lack of campaign funds was another severe handicap shared with the independents who jostled with the ANP and UPP-KBL for the bottom places.

The Restoration of Personality Politics

Following the congressional elections, Zamboanga's political aspirants and commentators turned their attention to the local elections for the positions of mayor, vice-mayor and twelve councilors. The president was anxious to complete the "redemocratization" of the Philippines and so allocated a high priority to early local elections. Originally scheduled for 24 August 1987, they were postponed to November and then finally set for 18 January 1988.

Speculation and announcements about who would run in Zamboanga began in May 1987. Clear from the start was that this election was exclusively local and would focus on personality politics. The contenders could not be differentiated on ideological grounds or in terms of programs of government. Money, electoral organization, personal appeal and exposure would determine the winners. A lack of money and organization militated against success for the eighteen independent candidates—one mayoral aspirant and seventeen councilor hopefuls. For all positions, the constituency was the whole of Zamboanga City, comprising some 197,267 registered voters. For an individual to cover adequately such an area and so many people required large sums of money and a well-staffed organization. None of the independents possessed such resources and none had any broad appeal of a charismatic type. Also, class-based voting blocks are virtually non-existent. Thus, the two independent labor sector candidates fared badly in the election as did all the other independent candidates. They monopolized the bottom positions in the voting tables.

Parties still dominate local electoral politics in Zamboanga City, although this is not a function of the people's ideological commitment to them. Rather it is parties who have the money to pay for the effective electoral organization which ensures widespread publicity for their candidates. Economies of scale give far better exposure to party candidates than any independent candidate could hope for. Also, the leading political personalities are associated with parties. Parties in post-Marcos Zamboanga City appear to be electoral vehicles falling into dormancy or, at best, extremely low levels of activity when there are no elections. Whether there is solidarity among elected members of the same party remains to be seen but is open to doubt.

Four major parties fielded full slates and one newly created minor party boasted three candidates. Locally, this development was heralded as the "multiparty system" in contrast to the old two-party system of pre-Martial Law days. The minor party, the United Peoples Independent Aggrupation (UPIA), resembled the independent candidates—low funding and small organization—and fared as poorly. The CCA remained split and two slates were fielded under its banner. The OIC mayor, Agan, headed one team and was backed by his predecessor, Rini Climaco. In common with the other OIC in Western Mindanao, Agan championed President Aquino and the national administration by adopting the LABAN/PDP-Laban label. However, all parties declared their pro-Aquino affiliation. The vice-mayor, Abelardo Climaco (no relation to Cesar Climaco), led the other CCA faction and was endorsed by Susan de los Reyes. No national party tag was attached to this branch of the CCA. The Liberal Party ran a slate under a former mayor, Jose Vicente Atilano, with Jose Climaco, the younger brother of Cesar Climaco, filling the vice-mayoral slot. The final slate was another indigenous Zamboanga City party, the Partido Avante Zamboanga (PAZ). Manuel Dalipe led this collection of political hopefuls. Originally Dalipe was reported as heading a new political organization of Congresswoman Lobregat. This was the Corazon Aquino Coalition Movement (CACM) which, according to Lobregat, was "a grouping of all independent political parties in the city."[26] At the last minute Dalipe ditched Lobregat's selections for councilor, inserted his own and announced the formation of PAZ. Jose Climaco, his vice-mayoral running mate until that time, bolted to the Liberal Party. The CACM ceased to exist.

The limited forty-five-day campaign, interrupted by Christmas and New Year festivities, did not permit the parties to undertake the amount of face-to-face coverage that they would have liked. Using the finances of their candidates plus contributions drawn from friends, relatives and businesses in Zamboanga City, the four slates set out to achieve maximum exposure. Once more, national parties failed to provide substantial funding. In addition to campaigning as members of a slate some candidates engaged in personal vote-drives. Peace and order and socioeconomic development were the major issues, with each party promising to solve the problems. Black propaganda was mobilized to demonstrate the unfitness of opponents for electoral office. But it was essentially the same people drawn from the same class backgrounds repeating the same messages. The candidates were almost entirely businessmen, professionals (especially lawyers) and other white-collar employees. They shared the same implicit ideology—support for capital, no structural change, maintenance of the status quo—and generally had no wish to alter prevailing class relations. There were status differences deriving from the amount of wealth or the bureau-cratic heights scaled but this seemed to have little effect on an individual's worldview.

The voting, like the campaigns, was conducted peacefully. NAMFREL adopted a "low profile." The turnout was also low with only 115,167 (58 percent) of 197,267 registered voters bothering to select their choice for mayor. Returns for the vice-mayoral poll were even lower. Over 40 percent of the registered electorate simply did not bother to vote at all. Many were indifferent as to who won, and candidates offered nothing innovative. Large numbers of the urban and rural poor may well have been cynical about the existence of any relationship be-tween voting in a local election and improvement in their personal situations. Such negative voting behavior might even be construed as a manifestation of class awareness. Material incentives to individuals, such as vote-buying, seem to have been in shorter supply than in earlier elections. The multiplication of parties and the increased size of the electorate meant that no party, let alone an individual, could provide material inducements to a large segment of voters. It was all the parties could do to pay for the food, drink, transport, radio-time, sample ballots and lider.

Agan won. Locally this was interpreted as a Visayan victory and had nothing to do with the pro-Aquino proadministration label which Agan's slate carried. Agan has Visayan ancestry. It was noted that too many Zamboangueño candidates had split the indigenous Zam-boangueño vote. What is interesting about this widespread perception is that the frame of reference makes no pretence of dealing with the results in terms of political philosophy or even party. Thus, Agan's victory is interpreted not as approval for a particular philosophy or program of government but as evidence of an ability to mobilize the large Visayan vote in Zamboanga. As Rini Climaco noted, "In this city people don't care too much about the party. They go for personalities."[27] The elected vice-mayor was Jose Climaco of the Liberal Party while the council slots were shared among PAZ (6), CCA (4) and Liberal Party (2). None of the mayor's slate were returned while only two of the vice-mayor's party colleagues won. The electorate were not voting for party slates but for personalities. Lobregat would seem to have added impetus to this trend. Originally she had declared neutrality although it was believed that she had always backed Jose Climaco. In the final days before the election it was alleged that she had given her approval and material help to a group of sympathetic candidates drawn from all parties. Political observers maintain that eight councilors fall into that category and can be expected to cooperate with Lobregat.

The winning councilors, some of whom have two occupations, are comprised of lawyers (5), businessmen (3), former public employees of senior rank (4) and mediamen (4). The last category emphasizes the importance of "exposure" in securing the support of the electorate. The elected mediamen were familiar to television and radio audiences and capitalized on this fact. Among the former public servants the exposure theme is repeated. One successful candidate had been for many years, the principal of a major secondary school while another had been a legal officer and city fiscal over a long period. Previous experience as a councilor was not in itself a great electoral asset as eight members of the new council have never held that office before. Maintaining a high profile as a councilor, however, was obviously a distinct advantage for reelection. The situation was different for mayoral and vice-mayoral aspirants. Their ranks were full of former elected officials. For example, the top three mayoral candidates, in terms of votes, had previously occupied the position of mayor. In order to have a chance of becoming mayor or vice-mayor one needs a known political name, an electoral machine, and an established following. These assets are derived from participation and success in previous electoral competitions.

A final note on the local elections concerns the obvious difficulty of mobilizing voters on the basis of class, gender and religion. The two independent labor candidates gathered very few votes and did not even gain the support of Zamboanga's major labor federation, the NFL. The new council has no representative of the rural sector, yet Zamboanga City's rural population is far larger than its urban one. No small-scale farmer, Zamboanga's typical farmer, ran for office. Indeed, none could afford to do so. One candidate, a member of a party slate, heads the farmer's association for Zamboanga City. This is a cooperative style organization which has remained an exclusively Zamboanga association. That it could not secure enough votes from

Zamboanga's thousands of agricultural families seems to indicate a current inability to mobilize fairly large numbers of farmers for solidary electoral action.

Only one Muslim candidate succeeded in gaining a council slot although sixteen Muslim candidates stood and each party slate had at least one Muslim. Muslims comprise approximately 25 percent of Zamboanga's population but do not demonstrate political solidarity in the selection of local officials. There is no strong political organization encompassing the various Muslim ethnolinguistic groups. The lone Muslim mayoral candidate polled fourth, well behind the winner though he was judged locally to have raised some Muslim political consciousness. He had received the endorsement of local religious leaders and gained an exclusively Muslim vote. But, as with the Christian population, the Muslims are politically fragmented. The Christian population is much larger and mainly votes for Christian candidates thus ensuring Christian dominance of electoral office. The one successful Muslim council candidate is in fact married to a Christian from a family reckoned to have "good political connections."

There were no women elected. Only five women stood, all for the position of councilor. Women have achieved political prominence in Zamboanga City. The current congressional representative is a woman as is the former vice-mayor. But it would appear that women require exceptional attributes to secure election and that it is difficult to mobilize a "women's vote" for women candidates.

Conclusion

The transition from Marcos to Aquino has proceeded smoothly and generated little conflict in the formal politics of Zamboanga City. Mayors have come and gone, a plebiscite has been held and congressional and local elections have taken place. All of these exercises in political legitimation mounted by the central government have passed without violence or disruption. "Guns and goons" have not been important in formal political competition. "Gold" has certainly exercised an influence, such as in the election of Congresswoman Lobregat and some of the current politicians in City Hall. But other factors can intervene. Charisma (Cesar Climaco), factional splits (the CCA), issues (Rini Climaco's perceived association with Nur Misuari), and a popular desire for moral regeneration and peace (the presidential election and the constitutional plebiscite) have all made themselves felt in electoral outcomes.

With the 1988 local government elections, personality politics has reasserted itself and anything resembling a coherent political ideology, especially of the left, is absent. A massive military presence has further discouraged the development of leftist politics. The formal political arena is not an ideological conflict zone. Elected positions have been filled by persons from privileged class positions who are defenders of capital and who are generally supportive of the status quo. They possess a form of class consciousness which does not support political initiatives to reform basic socioeconomic structures. This does not mean that action will not be taken on behalf of the underprivileged. An ambitious squatter rehousing proposal of City Hall is evidence of that. But where class interests might be threatened, then the politicians will defend them. The proposed Zamboanga City land reform scheme which focuses on distributing government land might be interpreted as a locally inspired effort to prevent land being taken from those unwilling to part with it, a defence of class interests. The council may be the scene of lively debates and disagreement but the participants possess similar perceptions of how the world should be ordered. For this reason, it is unlikely that there will be decision-making paralysis caused by a mayor from a party without any councilors and three parties having council representation. After all, they have agreed to work together with Congresswoman Lobregat.[28] She noted that through such cooperation, more project money could be obtained from central government, and in large part, this is what formal politics is all about.

Meanwhile, People Power has not provided any legacy of increased participation in decision-making for the majority of Zamboanga's population. Declining electoral turnouts may indicate a widespread awareness that participation in formal politics via voting does not have much impact on improving the socioeconomic situation of ordinary citizens. Many people see themselves as far away from power as ever. In Zamboanga, the current weakness of cause-oriented groups, labor, and the leftists means little organizational pressure to alter things. The structures of pronounced inequality which characterize Zamboanga need not anticipate any serious organized challenge in the near future.

G. CARTER BENTLEY

People Power and After
in the Islamic City of Marawi

Arrivals are instructive. [1] I first saw Marawi City, capital
of Lanao del Sur in north central Mindanao, in November 1977. I came
to study Maranao disputing for a Ph.D. dissertation in cultural anthropology. Because of unsettled peace and order conditions related to the
ongoing Bangsamoro rebellion, reactions to my plans to conduct field
research in and around Marawi had been generally negative. An earlier
application for funding was rejected, at least in part due to concerns
about my personal safety and the feasibility of my proposed research.
U.S. consular personnel in Manila advised me to stay away from
Mindanao and warned that if I got into trouble, the U.S. government
would take no responsibility and could do little to help. Filipino friends
expressed wonder at my courage or, more probably, lunacy in undertaking such a venture. Because I was aware of prevailing stereotypes
of the "Moros" who lived in Lanao del Sur, I was neither surprised
nor particularly chagrined at these responses. I thought I knew better.
I had corresponded for several years with Dr. Peter Gowing, director
of the Dansalan Research Center in Marawi City. Gowing had encouraged me regarding the feasibility and importance of conducting such
research as I planned. However, when I wrote from Manila saying I
would soon arrive in Marawi, he wrote back that for the first time in
the years he had lived in Marawi he advised that I stay away. A battle
had erupted near the city, with battalion-size AFP units trying to
dislodge Moro National Liberation Front (MNLF) guerrillas dug into
caves on Nusa Island, about 12 kilometers from Marawi near the
western shore of Lake Lanao. The whole area was extremely tense and
Gowing feared that I might get caught in the spreading political and
military crossfire.

In the end, my determination to get on with my work overrode
what was doubtless good advice. I flew to Cagayan de Oro (the Iligan
Airport was closed) and spent a couple of days traveling by road to

Marawi. I arrived in time to join spectators gathered on a hillside in Marawi and watch artillery barrages, airstrikes, and attempted amphibious landings on the rebel-held island.[2] In the aftermath of the battle, soldiers stationed around Marawi were angry and nervous, as were rebels in the area. Roads were often closed as soldiers chased rebels who had attacked one of the ubiquitous AFP or PC-INP checkpoints that dotted every road in the area. Nights and days for many weeks afterwards were punctuated by gunfire both distant and sometimes uncomfortably nearby. Because of the military situation, I was compelled to live on the campus of the Mindanao State University (MSU), a far cry from the remote village I would have preferred. Although I could move freely in and around Marawi, travel elsewhere in Lanao del Sur was difficult. It was less a matter of physical risk than of crossing unmarked boundaries between AFP and MNLF territory and becoming an unwilling, perhaps unwitting part of their war. By working within the confines of the provincial capital, this risk was reduced if not eliminated.[3] So my initial research in Marawi was carried out in a setting dominated by a political-military opposition between the Philippine government, represented by OIC Governor Mohamad Ali Dimaporo and an AFP army of occupation on one side, and the MNLF and its Bangsa Moro Army (BMA) on the other. Also on the scene were other long-established political families whose dominance in Lanao del Sur had ended with the declaration of Martial Law and Dimaporo's rise to power but who still retained substantial resources in money and manpower. I often found this complex situation a bit harrowing, but I also had a sense that it was manageable. I could choose to be politically active, in which case I would put myself at risk, or I could remain more or less neutral and be left in peace. So long as I did not present a tangible threat to any particular faction, I felt I had little to fear.

My second arrival in Marawi (now called "The Islamic City of Marawi") was in early June 1987. Before arriving, I already knew some things had changed. Local and provincial power orders have been transformed with President Marcos's flight from Manila. In addition, no Americans or Europeans lived in the city. Dr. Gowing had died, the leadership of the Protestant mission school had passed from American to Filipino hands (as it was bound to under Philippine law), the Irish missionary priests who had staffed the diocese of Marawi had left the area, and the Catholic chaplain and evangelical Protestant missionaries who had lived at the Mindanao State University had left after a series of attempted and completed kidnappings. The last two Americans had left the city in February 1987 after narrowly escaping a kidnap attempt. Most of the Americans I had known in Marawi a decade earlier told me I was foolish to return. Since I had lost touch with my Maranao acquaintances, I got no encouragement from that direction. I had little concrete information to go on, but all the signs looked bad. Still, I wanted to see old friends and at least find out if research was possible in Marawi.

As in 1977, my arrival in 1987 coincided with a notable event. The first newspaper I saw after arriving in Manila on 7 June reported that,

> Government troopers in Central Mindanao Friday pounded with 105 mm artillery fire an MNLF stronghold in Luba, Talayan, Maguindanao hours after Muslim terrorists burned Iligan City's commercial center. . . . The attack was launched following orders from military authorities to ferret out a number of Muslim terrorists believed coming from MNLF and MILF lost commands who were reportedly responsible for the series of bombings in Iligan City which burned down a sizeable portion of the City's commercial center.[4]

Newspapers also reported that the government had rejected MNLF proposals for Muslim autonomy, that factions within the Bangsamoro movement had begun fighting each other, and other equally cheering developments. Nevertheless, after a short adjustment period in Manila, I traveled to Iligan and took a couple of exploratory day trips to Marawi. Friends there warned that I would likely become a kidnap target. Many thought I should stay away. Others took a more positive view. They pointed out that so far, all the kidnap victims had been released unharmed and that a few weeks spent in the hills would certainly provide a unique opportunity to gather data. In the end, I decided to stay and do the best I could.

Some features of my stay were familiar and comforting. I was able to live with close friends from my earlier stay. The physical setting of the Mindanao State University was familiar, though several academic buildings, numerous residences, and a commercial center had been added during the intervening decade. The stunning view from the campus across rice fields to Lake Lanao, Marawi City, and the mountains beyond remained exactly as I remembered. All this contributed to a sense of being at home. Other things had changed. Where in 1977 my appearance invariably elicited cries of "Hey, Joe," this time I was greeted with "Assalamo Alaikum." Where Arab missionaries in 1977 had to endure being called "Melikano" by local children, by 1987 there were no more Americans around and children usually assumed I was an Arab visitor.

Changes in the political climate were more disconcerting. During my earlier stay, I was often assured by those opposed to the regime that once President Marcos and Gov. Dimaporo were removed from power, peace and order conditions in the province would improve. At the time, I thought they were probably right. When I arrived in 1987, I already knew Dimaporo had been forced from office shortly after Marcos had left the Philippines. In addition, overtures made by the Aquino government to the MNLF in the fall of 1986 had raised hopes that a resolution might be found to the long, desperate struggle by Bangsamoro nationalists to liberate their homeland from Filipino domination. While I found reports of kidnappings ominous, I had interpreted these as a sign that the new political order was still sorting itself out. I assumed that the political structure would soon revert to the relatively stable pattern of bipolar factions I had encountered a decade earlier. The reality I found was more complex and less hopeful. Unlike the situation in 1977, there was no clear locus of political control in Lanao del Sur. The resulting instability and uncertainty were felt as threatening in some degree by nearly everyone. Several people told me, with shaking heads, about respected political figures who had recently been stopped on the road by men "suggesting" that they might want to support their brothers in one or another armed band. It seemed no one was immune from extortion. Instead of settling down with the end of the Marcos regime, peace and order conditions had deteriorated even further. Political infighting was being waged with a savagery even Maranao found shocking. The Philippine Army had enforced an official curfew during much of my stay in 1977–79; in 1987 nearly as effective an unofficial curfew was enforced by uncertainty and fear.

Difficult peace and order conditions in Marawi limited my ability to obtain detailed information about what had happened during the Marcos-Aquino transition and what people thought and felt about it.[5] However, these conditions also comprise a large portion of what I have to tell. They indicate what has happened to the political climate since the Aquino administration came into power.

The Snap Elections in Marawi

The Islamic City of Marawi was, until recently, the smallest and probably the poorest chartered city in the Philippines.[6] It is located at the north end of Lake Lanao, where the Agus River begins its 32 km. cascade to Iligan Bay. Situated at a break in the ridge of mountains surrounding Lake Lanao, Marawi had long been a key location marked by important *cotas* (mud and stone forts). Anyone who wanted access from the north to the rich land, lake, and forest resources of the Lanao basin had to pass by Marawi. Conversely, Maranao trading, tribute-gathering, and raiding expeditions to the north coast of Mindanao, the Visayas, Luzon, and beyond also had to pass by Marawi. A Spanish invasion force tried to take control of the location in 1639–40 but had to retreat after a single season. After their more successful 1895 invasion, the Spanish built a fort on the site. Beginning in 1899, American forces expanded the military camp and began building a city to serve as a military-administrative center. For this reason, the city's layout follows an American rectilinear rather than a Spanish plaza-centered pattern. During the American colonial period, its idyllic scenery and temperate upland climate provided relief for overheated Americans and earned Dansalan, as it was then called, the sobriquet "The Baguio of the South." Since Philippine independence, it has grown in population (to its present size of around 65,000) even while suffering a series of economic reverses.[7] It serves as the capital of Lanao del Sur, the predominantly (92%) Muslim province formed by partition (from Lanao del Norte, 70+% Christian) in 1959. Marawi stands at the economic, political, and social center of the basin surrounding Lake Lanao. It has become the primate city for Maranao society. As such, it has been the focus of many government development projects, including the Mindanao State University and portions of the Agus River Hydroelectric Power Project. Nearly all public resources in Lanao del Sur are dispensed through offices located in Marawi. As other sources of income have become less secure, more and more residents of the province have come to depend on public monies for their livelihood. For these reasons, political events in Marawi reverberate throughout Lanao del Sur, often affect conditions in adjacent provinces, and occasionally draw national notice. [8]

The political landscape in Marawi had changed significantly in the months preceding the February 1986 snap elections. Since 1976, Lanao del Sur and Marawi City had been dominated by a political alliance between appointive Lanao del Sur Governor Mohamad Ali Dimaporo and Marawi City Mayor Omar Dianalan. Dimaporo had risen from his roots in Binidayan (south of Lake Lanao) to make his political career as governor and later congressman in predominantly Christian Lanao del Norte.[9] A key figure in the communal violence in 1970–71 which preceded the Bangsamoro revolt, he was appointed governor of Lanao del Sur by President Marcos in March 1976. In addition to controlling the provincial coffers, after June 1976, Dimaporo took control (as Acting President and Officer-in-Charge) of the Mindanao State University, by far the largest employer and disburser of government funds in Lanao del Sur.[10] Largely because of his close association with President Marcos, Dimaporo was remarkably successful in procuring government funds for MSU and, through MSU, for himself.[11] Campus infrastructure had done well since 1977. Buildings housing schools of Law, Business Administration, Education, Agriculture, Fisheries, and Forestry had all been added since my earlier stay, along with a new Administration Building, Student Center, Gymnasium and athletics center, and a commercial center. A few of the academic buildings lay unused as funds for furnishings, office equipment, and office materials were harder to come by. However, the campus had obviously benefited from the spate of construction, as had many of its residents.[12] Lack of classroom and library materials continued to frustrate students and faculty alike, but most persevered. The importance of the university to Marawi and Lanao del Sur is evident in Dimaporo's expressed preference for his position there to his position as provincial governor.[13]

To secure his position, Gov. Dimaporo had put together an impressive military force. When necessary he could call on several hundred armed supporters (from groups carrying such names as Special Action Forces and, unofficially, "Barracudas") in addition to the several-hundred man security force at MSU, the Lanao del Sur Provincial Guards (LSPG), well over one thousand Civilian Home Defense Force (CHDF) men dispersed throughout the province, and PC units led by officers disposed to, and sometimes ordered to cooperate with him. No less than President Marcos is said to have remarked that Dimaporo had more men and guns than the Armed Forces of the Philippines.[14]

Gov. Dimaporo's control over patronage, the military forces at his disposal, and his intimate association with President Marcos (which assured him AFP backing) all made his position in Lanao del Sur virtually unassailable. Without the positions to which he had been appointed by President Marcos, however, Dimaporo was only one among several competitors at the highest echelons of Lanao politics. For this reason, Dimaporo's power was often perceived as largely derivative. While his enemies admitted that he was untouchable so long as Marcos remained in power, they thought that the situation might change rapidly should he lose his powerful patron. In 1978, for instance, I was told, "There are ten thousand knives poised to cut Dimaporo's throat the minute Marcos falls."

Despite his domination of politics in the province, Dimaporo struggled to get the respect in Marawi he felt he deserved. Because his family's roots lay in the provincial periphery and he had made his political career on the fringes of Maranao society, Dimaporo was generally regarded as an interloper in Marawi.[15] While he had married the daughter of former Lanao Governor Mohammad Alawi Mandangan Dimakuta, a power in Marawi politics, Dimaporo was still regarded as a parvenu by the old Maranao elite.

As his wealth and power increased, Gov. Dimaporo tried to legitimate his achieved position using the traditional Maranao vocabulary
of noble titles. In 1982, he arranged to have himself proclaimed "Sultan
sa Masiu," Masiu being one of the four Maranao *pongampong a ranao*
("encampments of the lake"), the largest constituent units in Maranao
society.[16] His genealogical claim to the title was weak; in fact, several
of the other Lanao sultans refused to accept it. Despite the customary
requirement that Lanao sultans unanimously agree to any assumption
of a royal title, no one dared challenge him and his investiture took
place without incident. Shortly afterwards, Dimaporo began flying the
flag of Masiu next to the Philippine national flag at the center of the
MSU campus. This action drew private ridicule because of what was
described to me as "his preposterous presumption" that Masiu was
equal in stature to the entire Republic of the Philippines.[17] Moreover,
the MSU campus lay on land belonging to Bayabao, a different
pongampong entirely and many local residents found the flag an
offensive assertion of Masiu sovereignty. Still, no one objected openly.
"He was, after all, on Marcos's council of advisors for a time, so his
pretensions were tolerated."[18]

A second key figure in Marawi politics at this time was Omar
Dianalan, Batasang Pambansa (National Assembly) member and former
Marawi City mayor. Dianalan's descent placed him firmly among the
Marawi establishment and it was in Marawi that he had made his
political career. Like Dimaporo, Dianalan had married one of
Dimakuta's daughters, which made them brothers-in-law by Maranao
reckoning.[19] For the most part, Dimaporo had left the Marawi politi-
cal arena to Dianalan. This arrangement had worked well. Dimaporo
and Dianalan both held office under the banner of President Marcos's
KBL party; they jointly supported the party headquarters in Marawi
City; between them they administered the affairs of the capital and
province.

Once Dianalan lifted his gaze beyond Marawi City, however, the
two kingpins came into conflict. Dianalan ran for and was elected to
the Batasang Pambansa in 1984, as were Dimaporo's brother Macacuna
and son Abdullah. The two politicians clashed in early 1985 over
whether Dianalan or Macacuna Dimaporo would be appointed Speaker
Pro Tempore of the National Assembly. When Marcos announced
Macacuna as his choice, Dianalan protested that both Dimaporo and
Marcos had promised to support him for the post. Marcos's choice
was seconded by a large majority in a KBL caucus called to resolve
the appointment issue. In the aftermath of this incident, Dianalan broke
with Dimaporo and later left the KBL because, as he told the Catholic
newspaper *Veritas,*

he could no longer stand being treated shabbily by Dimaporo and the ruling party. He contested the post of Batasan speaker protempore with Macacuna Dimaporo, brother of Ali, but President Marcos picked Macacuna. "Since then, all my men, including those whose appointments I had a hand in, have been fired. Not even those with qualifications and civil-service eligibilities were spared. What they merely lacked was Ali-gibilities and Ali-fications," Dianalan charged.[21]

After this falling out, Dianalan, his father-in-law Dimakuta, and his younger brother Jiamil joined with forces long opposed to Dimaporo (in particular the Lucman and Alonto families) and switched their support to the national opposition.[22] Dianalan remarked of the new arrangement, "Politics make strange bedfellows. This is our first time to work together with the Alontos."[23] One reason Dianalan gave for his change in party affiliation was that Corazon Aquino had said she would give Muslims meaningful autonomy under the Tripoli Agreement.[24] Prior to his break with Dimaporo, Dianalan had never, to my knowledge, expressed support for Muslim autonomy. For his part, Dimaporo remained opposed to Muslim autonomy in any form.

This falling out of old allies gave particular point to the February 1986 election in Marawi. Just prior to the election, Dianalan charged that Dimaporo was "forcing government employees to swear before the Koran that they'll vote for President Marcos and that each of them will deliver 10 more votes to the ruling party."[25] Gov. Dimaporo possessed plenty of leverage. Aside from his grip on public resources in Lanao del Sur, Dianalan said,

> The Mindanao State University, of which Ali is the president, has a 450-man security guard, which Ali has converted into his own private army. Can you imagine, a campus which used to have only a handful of security guards, now guarded by 450?"
>
> He added that Ali also has 300 special action men, 200 provincial guards, 250 security guards in his different business interests, and 1,500 CHDF's distributed in 37 towns. "All these men are armed with high-powered guns," he said, in stressing why it is very urgent that the Comelec [Commission on Elections] place the province under its control.[26]

Further adding to Dianalan's worries, Lanao military commanders received orders from Manila just before the election to give Dimaporo a large number of weapons, which he then distributed to relatives, employees, and other supporters.[27]

Against Dimaporo were arrayed the Dianalans, Lucmans, Alontos, and other prominent families whose own influence had waned as Dimaporo's increased. Each could call on armed supporters of its own, though none on a scale to rival Dimaporo's. Further complicating the situation were a variety of Moro nationalist and other rebel groups in and around the city. Significantly, the MNLF, at least the Misuari faction, supported Aquino. Prior to his assassination in 1983, Benigno Aquino, Jr. (Ninoy) had talked with Nur Misuari in Europe and afterwards publicly stated his support for Moro self-determination. His statements had drawn favorable notice in Marawi, as elsewhere in the Islamic Philippines. In response, the MNLF had declared, in a March 1985 meeting, its "readiness to establish channels of communication and/or cooperation with [opposition groups] so as to hasten the downfall of the Marcos regime and the liquidation of colonialism in the Bangsamoro homeland."[28] After a meeting in Spain with Agapito ("Butz") Aquino in January 1986, Misuari sent a letter to Lanao MNLF commanders in which he endorsed Aquino's request that the MNLF do its best to ensure fair elections in the localities it controlled. Misuari went further, directing his commanders to do everything possible to assure an opposition victory. In the letter, he quoted Aquino's promise that, if victorious, the new government would respect the legitimate demands of the MNLF. KBL advertising prior to the election highlighted the meeting between Butz Aquino and Misuari and suggested Butz had agreed to the MNLF's secession demands despite Cory Aquino's denial that she had made any specific agreement with Misuari.[29] In addition to soliciting Bangsamoro support in the election campaign, opposition forces had managed to develop a nascent party organization in Marawi, a Lanao del Sur branch of PDP-Laban headed by Saidamen Pangarungan. Although he was not as well-known as some other Marawi political figures, Pangarungan was president of the Muslim Association of the Philippines (MAP), in the past an important stepping stone for aspiring Muslim politicians.

In the weeks prior to the snap elections, opposition figures in Marawi expressed grave concern about the likely conduct of the election.[30] Omar Dianalan urged the COMELEC to purge voters' lists of ghost voters in Lanao del Sur and Lanao del Norte (estimated at 40,000 and 30,000 respectively). Eventually, voter registers were purged but of eligible rather than ineligible voters. Voters and vote tabulators were subjected to intense pressure, though in some cases they are reported to have resisted.[31] As usually happens in Lanao elections, the vote totals were challenged, but the Batasan canvass gave Marcos 191,755 votes to Aquino's 28,070 for Lanao del Sur as a whole. The totals for Marawi City were somewhat closer, 16,203 for Marcos and 10,829 for

Aquino. Results in the vice-presidential race between Tolentino and Laurel were similar, though not quite so lopsided. These totals, whether they reflect how people actually voted or not, gave evidence of Gov. Dimaporo's continuing control over the Lanao del Sur political scene. Neither the national, local, or rebel opposition forces had slowed the Dimaporo vote-gathering machine.

As in the Philippines as a whole, the election itself only signaled the beginning of the drama in Marawi. Dimaporo reacted strongly when NAMFREL and Catholic officials in Manila criticized the conduct of the election. In a 15 February television interview, he warned of "bitter and bloody strifes [sic] should the combined efforts of the opposition, NAMFREL, and the church leaders succeed in dividing the Filipino people." As President Marcos struggled to hold power in Manila, Dimaporo stood firm against a rising tide of protest in the Muslim south. Students and faculty at the Mindanao State University intensified their own campus reform movement, holding prayer meetings and protest rallies.[34] Gov. Dimaporo responded by bringing units of his Special Action Force onto the campus. Most Christian and some Muslim students evacuated the area. As events moved toward a climax in Manila, the situation in Marawi became more volatile as well. On 24 February troops loyal to Dimaporo surrounded an Islamic school in Marawi where a prayer rally had been scheduled. To avoid bloodshed the rally was cancelled. Shortly after President Marcos's midnight flight from Manila, Gov. Dimaporo retreated to the MSU campus with his supporters, swearing before God that, "I will fight and protect the 'MSU-ans' to the last drop of my blood. We are going to protect this republic. We are going to protect this university from any forces that will attack."[35] Under pressure from military units, however, Dimaporo and his forces left the campus on 1 March 1986. On 3 March, he called on Defense Minister Juan Ponce Enrile declaring that while he was "still loyal to President Marcos, I am neutral to Cory Aquino and I pledge my support to you."[36] He also agreed to surrender the arms which had been issued to him prior to the election, though few guns were actually turned in and these were mostly old, some unserviceable. Dimaporo explained that his employees needed most of the guns to protect his fishpond holdings and that he no longer knew where many others were.[37] He denied having seized the MSU campus, saying instead his forces sought to quell a panic begun by the uncertain conditions in Manila. While he did not disclose his future political plans, he continued to claim to be provincial governor and president of MSU. Shortly afterwards, Dimaporo joined in a call by defeated presidential candidate (and former Cagayan de Oro City mayor) Reuben Canoy to declare Mindanao an independent republic.[38] The governmental transition was finally accomplished when, on 25 April, OIC Governor-designate Saidamen Pangarungan, with the support of his uncle PC Col. Omar Manabilang, forcibly removed Dimaporo's forces from the provincial capitol.[39] Some reports indicated substantial loss of life in the fighting.[40]

After the Revolution

Within days after President Aquino took power in Manila, those opposed to the Dimaporos began positioning themselves to take advantage of the new arrangements. Prominent Maranao politicians called for full implementation of the 1976 Tripoli Agreement on Muslim autonomy and for Muslim representation at the highest levels in the new government.[41] At the same time, these politicians began to maneuver for official appointments under the new regime. Competition was particularly intense between Saidamen Pangarungan, leader of Lanao del Sur PDP-Laban, and Princess Tarhata Alonto Lucman, the last elected governor in Lanao del Sur and a member of UNIDO. Each staked a different claim on the provincial governorship. Pangarungan had the earliest affiliation with Laban and Cory Aquino (he established the PDP-Laban office in Marawi in 1984). He also claimed to represent a new politics in Marawi, since he was not closely connected with any of the families which had dominated Lanao politics for generations. The Alontos claimed rights to elective positions taken from them under Martial Law by Marcos and Dimaporo. Also in the picture was former Marawi Mayor and MP Omar Dianalan who had campaigned for Cory during the snap elections and became her closest advisor on Muslim affairs in the period immediately following it.

Early on, the Aquino government appointed Pangarungan provincial governor, made Abbas Basran (Dianalan's cousin and former city fiscal) Marawi City mayor, named former Senator Ahmad Domocao Alonto to the Constitutional Convention (where he became assistant floorleader), made former Governor Madki Alonto Ambassador to Libya, and after an intense and divisive search, appointed Ahmad (Jun) Alonto, Jr. President of the Mindanao State University. Those appointed rejoiced while those left out became angry. The tenuously unified opposition disintegrated under competition for jobs and power. Public order suffered as a consequence.

A number of highly publicized kidnappings highlighted problems in the province. Many were attributed to Dimaporo's attempts to disrupt the government of his successor. Adding fuel to the volatile situation were a variety of "lost commands," renegade bands formerly connected with AFP and Bangsamoro nationalist units. As Noble notes,

Certainly Dimaporo's relatives and followers were responsible for the kidnaping of Father Michel de Gigord on June 4 from the campus of Mindanao State University, and probably also for that of Brian Lawrence on July 12. Probably they were not involved in the kidnaping of ten nuns in Marawi on July 11, though the actors seemed to have identical motives: revenge against the government, which had taken away power and positions, and extortion. In Father Michel's case there was an additional, personal motivation: he had been outspoken in his criticisms of the Dimaporo era at MSU.[42]

In addition to the kidnappings, several Pangarungan-owned properties in Marawi were damaged in grenade and rifle attacks.

Pangarungan's inability to control the forces of disorder became a key element in Princess Tarhata Lucman's attempt to supplant him. By August 1986, her conflict with Pangarungan had become front-page news in Manila. Pangarungan supporters warned that appointing Lucman would reestablish the Alonto dynasty in Lanao while Lucman supporters accused Pangarungan of corruption and inept governance. President Aquino first ordered the Ministry of Local Governments to resolve the conflict and then called both principals to a Malacañang conference.[43]

In the end, Princess Tarhata was appointed governor and Pangarungan became Deputy Minister of Local Governments. This did not end the competition between them, however. Most of the municipal mayors appointed by Pangarungan remained in place, protected by him in his new national position, and they complained vociferously about their new superior, Gov. Lucman. Others joined in, including Omar Dianalan's brother Jiamil from his position in the Office of Muslim Affairs and Cultural Communities. Throughout early 1987, both sides continued their offensives, in part through reports by sympathetic newspapermen and letters to Manila papers, in part through efforts to undermine their opponents' local support, impede delivery of government services, and otherwise disrupt life in Marawi City and Lanao del Sur. Former Gov. Dimaporo watched gleefully as his successors tried to destroy each other and used his still considerable resources to assist them in the process.

External events also had considerable impact in Marawi during the year after Aquino's accession to power. An opening toward resolution of the Bangsamoro revolt appeared to have been made when President Aquino met Nur Misuari in Jolo on 5 September 1986. Afterwards Misuari undertook a series of "consultations" with the Muslim populace of Mindanao and Sulu. In Marawi, a crowd of several thousand greeted Misuari's appearance, many fully armed and wearing

MNLF uniforms.[44] AFP personnel were reportedly shocked at the hero's welcome accorded Misuari and appalled at the quality and quantity of arms carried by his supporters.

After a somewhat hopeful beginning, negotiations between the government and the MNLF stalled, then sputtered toward an indefinite conclusion.[45] Throughout early 1987, government negotiators and leaders representing various Moro nationalist factions postured and protested, with the MNLF finally setting the May congressional elections as a deadline for completing the negotiations.[46] Settlement hopes receded as government positions gradually reverted to those established under the Marcos regime.[47] The collapse of negotiations on 9 May generated disappointment and a sense of betrayal among Muslim residents of Marawi.[48] Concern rose that warfare might break out once again between AFP and rebel forces.

In Marawi itself, the contribution of rebel forces to the political situation was complex. Bangsamoro nationalists were as fragmented as were the "legitimate" politicians. All three major Bangsamoro factions were represented in the town, as nearly as I could tell in more or less equal numbers: the MNLF Misuari group (forces loyal to Nur Misuari), the MILF (Moro Islamic Liberation Front, led by Salamat Hashim), and the MNLF Reform Group (directed by Dimasangkai Pundato, aka "Jack Dimas").[49] Who was affiliated with each faction was sometimes unclear and what position each faction might take if war broke out remained uncertain. What the events of early 1987 did make clear was that there remained in Marawi a great reservoir of ill will toward the national government and the potential for mass civil-military disorder.

A flurry of incidents in late June and early July 1987 further mobilized public sentiment against the government. On the night of 29 June, a vehicle carrying five men, two Malaysian *tableeqhs* (religious workers) and three Maranao, was ambushed by soldiers stationed near the bridge linking Lanao del Sur and Lanao del Norte. All five were beaten, stabbed, and shot. Far more than the death of their kinsmen, the killing of foreign missionaries outraged Marawi Muslims.[50] The following Saturday morning (4 July), a demonstration was held in Marawi to protest the killings. An estimated three thousand participants marched past AFP checkpoints. Many taunted the soldiers, who responded by shouting, sarcastically, "Allahu Akbar" ("God is great"), "moklo'" (Visayan, roughly "dirty scum"), and by miming masturbation. Only a few days earlier, on 1 July (about 4 pm), two Maranao girls had been stabbed to death at a spring where both Maranao and soldiers often went to fetch water. Most residents believed the killer must be a Christian soldier. The failure of the police to find the killer lent credence to the suspicion since the AFP was assumed to protect criminals in its midst.[51] The Army moved expeditiously to identify and try the killers of the Malaysian missionaries—something no one believed would have happened had all the victims been Maranao—thereby forestalling a diplomatic crisis.[52] Nevertheless Marawi remained polarized, the Army representing the Republic of the Philippines and the Aquino government on one side, the Maranao populace on the other. Maranao politicians maneuvered uncomfortably between the two.

Meanwhile, in the domain of "legitimate politics," the approach of congressional elections scheduled for 11 May, the first competitive elections under the Aquino regime, prompted realignments among the various Lanao political factions.[53] In April, following a plea by Omar Dianalan's father, who was seriously ill at the time, the Dianalan and Dimaporo families resolved their differences during an emotion-filled meeting held midway between Marawi and Binidayan. Once again, they were allies. Thus, despite the fact that Dimaporo remained a Marcos (or perhaps more an Enrile) loyalist and ran as the KBL congressional candidate in Lanao del Sur District 2 while Omar Dianalan stood as Cory Aquino's PDP-Laban candidate in Lanao del Sur District 1, the two stood together in opposition to UNIDO (Liberal Party) Gov. Lucman and her nephew Jun Alonto at MSU.[54]

The congressional campaign in 1987 was conducted with typical Maranao fervor. Spending was lavish; vote-buying and pressure tactics were ubiquitous.[55] Both Dianalan and Dimaporo led the initial canvassing in their respective districts but with relatively small pluralities. Dimaporo reportedly received only 37 percent and Dianalan 30 percent of votes cast in their respective districts (see table 1).[56] Jamel Lucman, a rebel returnee and member of the Region XII Autonomous Region Assembly, nearly beat Dimaporo in his home area, receiving 32 percent of the vote. In the District 1 contest, the Alontos backed Mamintal Adiong, who ran second and who might have won had not Normallah Pacasum, Gov. Lucman's daughter, run against Adiong (reportedly against her mother's wishes) and split the votes of the Alonto-Lucman bloc. Dimaporo backed Manguntawar Guro, who ran sixth, but was not displeased to see Dianalan, once again his ally, win over the candidate supported by his long-time enemies. Probably the most interesting development was the emergence of the Ompia ("Reform") Party led by Dr. Mahid Mutilan, the director of a local Islamic school. With little preparation, less money (and reportedly no vote-buying), and communicating its message through the network of *madaris* (Arabic-medium schools) staffed by its *ulama* (learned) members, Dr. Mutilan still managed to collect 12 percent of the vote, finishing ahead of several better-known candidates. While not all Marawi residents were comfortable with the entry of religious leaders into electoral politics, most of those with whom I spoke indicated that the Ompia Party had made a substantial impact on the election and probably would do even better in the future.

The dispersal of votes in this election was a far cry from the near unanimity in the presidential elections fifteen months earlier. While the provincial board of canvassers declared Dianalan and Dimaporo winners, none of their opponents was willing to concede defeat. All candidates alleged misconduct in the elections, usually against each and every competitor, resulting in such a tangle of challenges that COMELEC personnel in Manila saw little prospect of ever deciding the issues on legal or evidentiary grounds.[57] By early September 1987, the Congress had been in session for over two months, but no winner had yet been confirmed in either Lanao congressional race.

After the congressional campaign had run its course, the frequency of kidnappings and other acts of violence increased in Marawi.[58] On 8 July, two female employees of the Department of Social Services were kidnapped but were released unharmed five days later. On 9 July, a female (Visayan Christian) student helper in the MSU College of Community Development and Public Administration was shot to death in a campus building. While the university's chief of security accused the MNLF of having committed the murder, others implicated a recently discharged security guard. This incident led to student demands for better protection, demands which President Alonto irritably dismissed as unreasonable. Morale on the campus plummeted. On 22 July, two teachers in the MSU High School were kidnapped by heavily armed men during a flag-raising ceremony at the center of the campus. This daring daylight raid represented a blatant challenge to the authority of MSU President Jun Alonto, whose office stood only a stone's throw from the plaza.[59] On 7 August, sixteen people riding in a Fiera utility vehicle from MSU toward Iligan were kidnapped just after leaving the campus. Those taken included thirteen students, two faculty members, and one member of the university staff. After several days, the kidnappers and their victims were located on Balt Island, not far from the home of former Gov. Dimaporo. The kidnappers initially demanded 500,000 pesos for release of the captives, later raising the demand to 62.5 million pesos, calculated to be one-quarter of the MSU annual budget.[60] This time the challenge to President Alonto was explicit as, in addition to the ransom, the kidnappers demanded that Alonto be removed from his position.[61] Ex-Governor (and newly elected if undeclared Congressman) Dimaporo was approached about trying to free the captives, since they were being held near his home and one of the kidnappers was reputedly a leader of his "Barracuda" gang, but he reportedly refused to help unless Gov. Lucman personally appealed to him. This she categorically refused to do. The military issued shoot-to-kill orders, blockaded the island, and prepared for an airborne and amphibious assault. On 17 August, following negotiations conducted by Gov. Lucman's son, the captives were released. Almost incidental to this massive drama, on the same day as the MSU kidnapping, a sixth-grade student at Dansalan Junior College, the Protestant missionary high school in Marawi, was also kidnapped for ransom. He was released a few days later after Muslim religious leaders interceded on his family's behalf. Just after the MSU victims were released, the wife of the National Power Corporation manager for northern Mindanao was kidnapped from her home in Iligan, reportedly by three Maranao men posing as car repairmen. At the time I left Marawi, she had not yet been released.[63]

Clearly financial gain motivated many of these kidnappings but political capital was also a goal. Payment of ransom is never publicly acknowledged in Lanao kidnappings, though the amount paid in each case is usually known, or at least is thought to be known. That amount can be viewed as a rough measure of the effective political power of the officials forced to pay (as well as of the value of the hostages), for in the case of kidnapped students, professors, social service workers, and so forth, it is usually responsible office holders who pay the price of maintaining peace and order. The greater the official's power, the lower the ransom paid. The Alonto family was generally believed to have paid between 150,000 and 300,000 pesos to gain the MSU captives' release and this relatively large amount indicated that the public perceived the Alonto-Lucman regime as a weak one. Moreover, the fact that MSU had become such a target of disruption indicated that those who stood to gain power at the Alontos' expense felt they had found the family's weakest point.

Since my departure from Marawi in August 1987, I have been able to gather only a few bits of reliable information. In local elections initially scheduled for November 1987 but finally held in February 1988 (after several weeks of delay), Dr. Mahid Mutilan, head of the Ompia Party, was elected mayor of the Islamic City of Marawi. To outsiders, his election was alternately hailed as a breath of fresh air and dreaded as the long-awaited arrival of Islamic fundamentalism in Maranao politics.[64] Dr. Mutilan did mobilize the large network of Islamic schools (madaris) in his campaign, but the tone of his campaign was thoroughly secular, emphasizing the dismal service-delivery record of past mayors. After his election, he began efforts to clean up the huge piles of garbage that littered Marawi streets, to create a workable telephone system, and so forth. How much he has been able to accomplish I have been unable to ascertain, though local residents to whom I talked in November 1989 said conditions in Marawi were not much improved.

MSU has remained a center of political strife and of peace and order difficulties. In February 1988, the university administration declined to allow an American librarian and a Dutch Foundation representative to visit the campus, even though their agencies had provided substantial funds for buildings and library improvements. The MSU leadership complained that, under the prevailing conditions, it could not assure the safety of its visitors.

Gov. Dimaporo is still an important political figure in Manila and in Lanao as well. His name was associated with the August 1987 coup attempt and, after the December 1989 coup attempt in Manila, his name was linked with reports of a secret plan to proclaim an independent republic in the southern Philippines.[65] He never explicitly denied involvement in either coup attempt, instead daring his accusers to confront him publicly.

In the November 1989 referendum on the creation of a Muslim Autonomous Region, the Islamic City of Marawi was one of the few parts of Mindanao where voting favored the Aquino government's autonomy proposal. More notable, however, was the very small turnout, likely resulting from an MNLF call to boycott the election.[66] Thus, popular dissatisfaction with the government, political fragmentation, and civil disorder—trends which emerged in Marawi immediately after the Marcos-Aquino transition—appear to have remained strong in the several years since.

Signs and Portents

In Lanao del Sur, the February 1986 elections served less as a test of President Marcos's popularity than of Gov. Dimaporo's control over the regional electoral process. Despite the efforts of powerful opponents—including his former allies, the Dianalans—Dimaporo passed the test with flying colors. According to the official count, his candidate received 87 percent of the vote in Lanao del Sur and over 60 percent in Marawi, the center of opposition to him. The vote totals reflected Dimaporo's primacy in Lanao politics, whether they were achieved through his personal popularity, manipulation of registration and voter eligibility, vote-buying, ballot-box stuffing, voter intimidation, or control over the tabulation process. They did not appear to reflect sentiments regarding national issues. Even Aquino's support for Muslim autonomy had little impact, despite the unquestionable popularity of her position on this issue. Dimaporo publicly framed the election in terms of whether the largesse he had been able to distribute throughout the province would continue should President Marcos lose. Privately he threatened those who opposed him with reprisals. This strategy had served him well for over a decade. With Marcos gone, however, Dimaporo's control over the apparatus of government in Marawi eroded rapidly.

While Marcos's departure shook the foundations of Dimaporo's empire, however, it did not crumble completely. Rather than deal directly with President Aquino, Dimaporo declared his loyalty to Defense Minister Juan Ponce Enrile, a move which deflected the threat of military action against him.[67] This enabled him to stay in the game and, if he could no longer hold the unquestioned center in Lanao politics, he remained strong enough to prevent anyone else from doing so.

Given the widespread dissatisfaction with Gov. Dimaporo's autocratic rule I found during my earlier visit, I expected that Marawi residents would respond positively to democratization under the Aquino regime. Even if early hopes for Muslim autonomy were not realized, still the political process was considerably more open than it had been under Marcos and Dimaporo. The pattern of voting in the congressional election seemed to signal that political participation was alive and well in Lanao del Sur. However, instead of excitement or relief, the prevailing mood I found in 1987 was one of despair. My notes are replete with comments such as, "The situation now is so bad. It has gotten out of hand," "Everyone is afraid of those private armies. They are nothing but bandits," "People say all our leaders are crazy. They are all politicians. They are only interested in themselves and they have forgotten the people. But what can we do? Only maybe we can go to the hills."[68] Despite the loosening of military control, reinstitution of the writ of habeas corpus, removal of an oppressive overlord, and a new ability to speak and act freely, I found most Marawi residents more tense and less hopeful than they had been under military occupation a decade earlier.

From the perspective of an outsider, the lives of Marawi residents (at least Muslim ones) appeared at least as secure in 1987 as they were in 1977–79. Murder and mayhem occurred no more frequently than in 1977–79. The number of kidnappings had increased, but the victims were almost always outsiders. Government funds continued to pour into the city, and Maranao generally perceived themselves as better off materially than most other Philippine Muslims.[69] Yet they also seemed to feel less secure.

This apparent paradox dissolves when Maranao concepts of power and social order are taken into consideration.[70] Like many other Malay-Indonesian peoples, Maranao consider the normative social condition to be one of being ruled, to stand in tributary relation to a center of power.[71] Where other Southeast Asian peoples conceive of power as deriving from the favor of ancestors to whom one sacrifices or the accumulated *sakti* of ascetic practice, Maranao locate the ultimate source of power in the blessing (*barakat*) of a remote and all powerful god.[72] It is this power that animates the world and that makes human actions effective.[73] The power of a true leader, someone worthy of being supported, will radiate over those supporters and enhance the effectiveness of their actions as well.[74] Consequently, Maranao seek out persons who display signs of leadership and whose actions have proven effective. These are the ones who possess the *barakat* and it is through them that order is brought into the world. So long as power is focused at a single point, in a single person (or descent line), the surrounding people and places may bask in the prosperity, fertility, and security which are produced by proximity to a leader's radiant power. As power ebbs in a center, control erodes and disorder follows as people struggle for an effectiveness that no longer comes so easily.

During his tenure, Gov. Dimaporo was recognized as a supremely effective leader. With his removal and the failure of anyone of comparable stature and effectiveness to replace him at the center of things, the world became less secure, at least in the view of most Maranao with whom I spoke. They told me that Lake Lanao is receding, threatening the rice crop and making it hard for worshipers to perform the necessary ablutions before prayers.[75] Cattle rustling is on the rise. Farmers are afraid to till their fields lest their work animals be stolen. Bandits are everywhere. The roads are not safe. Gov. Lucman is a good person but a weak leader. Some candidates ran in the congressional election just to sow disorder, to prevent any of the good candidates from winning. Now that Dimaporo is gone, Maguindanao congressmen will get a university for Cotabato, the external units of MSU will become independent and the Marawi campus will wither away. Marawi will become even poorer. Most people join the MNLF because they seek real leaders, people they can look up to. Marawi has gotten so dirty that the smell of garbage would drive Allah away. Community extension workers can't do their jobs because travel isn't safe even for Maranao. The whole *basak* (the rice-growing area east of Lake Lanao) has been without electricity for so long, frustrated residents cut the power lines and sold them for scrap.

Some of these complaints are accurate; others are exaggerated. Cu-

mulatively, they serve as a barometer of the public mood. It seems that
Gov. Dimaporo's absolutist rule created a sense of order and security,
even for many of those who opposed him. Many of the same people
who attacked him vociferously a decade earlier now complain of the
eroding infrastructure and lowered efficiency in the delivery of public
service since he left.   In fact, the intense factional struggle which
pervaded Lanao politics since early 1986 did impede service delivery.
Marawi was dirtier than I remember it, though on one trip into town
I saw front loaders clearing the streets of head-high piles of garbage.[76]
Apparently banditry was on the rise. The roads certainly were not
well-traveled at night. The political scene lacked any clear locus of
control, a condition which well-publicized kidnapings served to
highlight. Dimaporo touched a sensitive nerve when he declared that,
"No one is in control in Marawi."[77]

If Gov. Dimaporo was so effective, and his governance is so sorely
missed, why should there have been so much resistance to him in the
first place? Most outside observers pointed to his abuses of power, his
Draconian methods for dealing with those who dared defy him, and
his appropriation of state resources for his personal and family benefit.
Yet Maranao have historically shown relatively little concern for
nepotism, legality, or even morality in the exercise of power.[78] I believe
instead that he failed to display features of character and deportment
which Maranao associate with leadership, with exalted descent, and
with possession of *barakat*. The ability to create around oneself a sense
of order and emotional balance is such a sign. This Dimaporo often
did not do. His histrionic oratory, his brusqueness, his grandiose
professions of faith in God, and his transgressions of Maranao etiquette ran counter to Maranao images of leadership as contained and
controlled energy.[79] In contrast to Maranao images of aristocracy,
Dimaporo was considered by many to be pushy and crude. In contrast,
Gov. Lucman displayed the polished demeanor traditionally associated with leadership. She claimed to have established order where her
predecessor Pangarungan could not, to have liberated kidnap victims,
and, in general, to have kept the forces of chaos under control. For
instance, in a letter to a Manila newspaper she declared, "Strong and
powerful though Ali Dimaporo may be, I have kept him on his good
behavior."[80] She worked hard to cultivate the appearance of a leader,
but she lacked the economic and military resources to command respect,
and her claims to be in control in Lanao del Sur rang hollow.

The Maranao have experienced periods of rapid change in the past,
during which their institutions proved remarkably resilient.[81] Yet it
seems to me that in the decade during which I have followed Maranao

affairs, new and disconcerting changes have begun taking place. As the Maranao have been drawn, unevenly but ever more firmly, into the orbit of the Philippine state and, through it, into the remote periphery of the capitalist world system, the material bases for traditional Maranao social relations have eroded. Where in the past the products of labor circulated (if unequally) through bilateral kin networks to the general benefit, members of the Maranao elite have begun to exploit state power to escape the political and economic claims of their kinsmen.[82] Productive property has been privatized at an accelerating rate and kinsmen and supporters have come increasingly to resemble employees and tenants. In large part, this change is a product of state policies aimed at integrating the Maranao by coopting the nobility and turning the mass of the population into a dependent peasantry.[83] In past times, relations of inequality (and economic exploitation) were masked by a "symbolic economy" of rank honor (maratabat) which tied kinsmen together in a community of sentiment and (presumed) shared interest. The economic and military support given to one's datu (which consisted primarily of a share of harvests and military support when called upon) was returned in the enhanced maratabat which devolved to all that datu's supporters. Under this ideology, Maranao were enjoined to strive for wealth and power, as the very existence of each descent line (bangsa), the basic building block for social order itself, depended on the willingness of each and all to contribute his or her energy to the struggle.[84] This symbolic economy of honor allowed substantial economic inequality to coexist with an ideology of egalitarianism.[85] As events during the Martial Law period indicated, however, where resources are dispensed from above, through authoritarian patrons in Manila, the scramble for resources comes increasingly to resemble a disenchanted "economy of naked self-interest" where brute force rules and political legitimacy becomes a distant dream.[86]

Out of the social stresses and contradictions created by this process of political-economic incorporation arose the Bangsamoro rebellion. The movement toward Moro independence initially promised liberation from external domination and the fragmentation of experience that accompanied it.[87] However, while the rebellion has continued sporadically, hope has faded that it might succeed in releasing the populace from its malaise.

To some degree, this disillusion reflects the passage of time. Many of the young revolutionaries with whom I spoke a decade ago have assumed positions within the system they once sought to destroy or transform. Their places are being taken by younger people who, in their turn, seek to prove their valor, courage, and honor by military exploits. For many, though, the vision of social transformation that fueled Bangsamoro nationalism has been lost. The struggle has become routine, something the young do simply because they are young. Some informants, including MNLF cadres, say that the movement's leaders have lost contact with how people feel, that their image of the future is no longer compelling, and that the revolution has been absorbed by the constant struggle for power, prestige, and position that is everyday Maranao politics.[88] Still, the stresses and contradictions that generated the Bangsamoro movement remain along with a widespread sense that radical change is required within Philippine Muslim societies if they are to survive.

To the opposed ideological poles of tradition and modernity (as defined by the colonial and postcolonial state), the Bangsamoro movement added a third ideological and political force. But other voices are now being heard as well. The Ompia Party heralds the emergence of an overtly religious force in Lanao politics, though what its impact will be remains unclear. In the late 1980s, I found more young Maranao receptive to revolutionary Marxism than a decade earlier. Maranao now face a dissonant welter of vocabularies for political action: tradition, modernity, Islam, nationalism (both Philippine and Bangsamoro), and Marxism. These are being combined in multifarious ways, especially by such adept politicians as Ali Dimaporo, who manages to combine Maranao tradition, Western modernity, and Islam in an improbable yet politically effective manner.[89]

How all this will affect Maranao society in the long run is not clear. Perhaps increasing numbers of Maranao will seek alternative forms of political action. Perhaps the Maranao, who have thus far proven resistant to prophetic religious movements (unlike many of their Christian and highland neighbors), will prove more susceptible in the future. Perhaps more revolutionary forms of political consciousness, such as that promoted by the NPA, will take hold. Perhaps Maranao traditions will be reinvigorated. I have seen some evidence of all of these in Lanao (and elsewhere in the Muslim Philippines). At this point, it is hard to tell which trend will prove most significant in the long run. From the Maranao perspective, however, the recent past is clearer. With the Marcos-Aquino transition, things began to fall apart in Marawi more profoundly than ever before. There now exists a struggle to reestablish political control and order in the Islamic City of Marawi. It is a struggle in which there have so far been no clear winners but in which the residents of the city have been the losers.

Results of 1987 Congressional Elections, Lanao del Sur

District 1

Candidate	Votes	Percentage
Omar Dianalan	27,057	30%
Mamintal Adiong	20,082	22%
Lininding Pangandaman	12,157	13%
Mahid Mutilan	10,631	12%
Normallah Pacasum	9085	10%
Manguntawar Guro	9044	10%
Others	3525	4%
	91,581	101%*

[3,481 votes from the Municipality of Kapai were recorded but remained untabulated due to challenges.]

District 2

	Votes	Percentage
Ali Dimaporo	27,964	37%
Jamel Lucman	24,490	32%
Pangalian Balindong	21,016	28%
Others	2595	3%
	76,065	100%

SOURCE: Legal Department, COMELEC, Lanao del Sur

*Error due to rounding.

RESIL B. MOJARES

Political Change in a Rural District in Cebu Province

News of the "EDSA Revolution" came to the rural district of Valladolid (municipality of Carcar, Cebu province) as the events themselves unfolded in Manila. Radio was the main source: ownership of radio sets in Carcar is around 70 percent; and five or six of the leading AM stations in Cebu City carried an excellent 24-hour coverage of events in the national capital through hookups with Manila stations and monitors from American, British, and Australian news broadcasts. News also came by word of mouth from residents who had seen the daily Manila or Cebu newspaper or had just come in from the Carcar *poblacion* (municipal center) or Cebu City, an hour away by bus.

In Cebu City (1980 population: 490,281), with its mass media facilities (fourteen radio stations, four TV stations, two daily newspapers) and organized political groups, public support for Corazon Aquino was made evident: when it was reported on radio on 24 February that the "Aquino-sympathizing" Camp Sergio Osmeña of the Philippine Constabulary near downtown Cebu would be attacked by the "loyalist" forces of the Army's Camp Lapulapu in the city's outskirts, a large crowd massed to protect the "rebel camp" with "people power"; when a local radio station started a fund drive for the "heroes of EDSA" in the afternoon of 25 February, 60,000 pesos was raised in two hours (two boys, escorted by their father, turned in their piggy banks; someone appeared at the station with a dozen of native sleeping mats to be sent to the people holding vigil at EDSA); and some Cebuanos actually flew to Manila to be on the scene. On the night of 25 February, when word came in that Ferdinand Marcos had fled the country, Cebu City residents trooped to the city's central park (Fuente Osmeña) for a spontaneous, festive celebration of what was perceived by many as a "popular" triumph.

In Valladolid itself, those who stayed by their radios learned about the fall of Marcos as it happened. Most, however, were to learn about it only the day after. The mood in Valladolid was somber: the most common sentiment was one of prayerful relief (*nahuwasan,* as in the passing of a fever) that events did not take a bloody turn. There were those saddened by the fall of Marcos not simply out of charity but the conviction that Marcos, after all, "had done a lot as President." There were many who were not quite sure what to think: "Manila is too far away" (*Layo ra kaayo ang Manila*), and the dull compulsion of economic survival afforded little space for reflection. After all, for the elderly rural resident who has witnessed four or six changes in the national administration—although the events of 1986 were indeed exceptional—experience tended to compel a realism, if not cynicism, about the prospects for substantive social or political change. Yet, there were many too who felt that the end of Marcos was long overdue and that perhaps people can now look toward the future for some meaningful changes.

Aquino, after all, won in Valladolid—as she did in Carcar and the province of Cebu—in the February snap presidential elections. And subsequent events confirmed support for the Aquino presidency (at least by the conventional indicator of the electoral vote). In the 2 February 1987 plebiscite for the Constitution—billed as a confirmation of the Aquino presidency—Carcar and Valladolid turned in an 88 percent "Yes" vote (19,840 against 2,597 in Carcar; 2,496 against 305 in Valladolid). In the May 1987 and January 1988 elections, pro-Aquino parties and candidates overwhelmed the opposition (where it still existed) in Carcar and Cebu province.

What does it all mean? The larger picture of the past decade-and-a-half includes what, on the surface, have been drastic political changes: martial rule (1972–86), the unprecedented expansion of the Communist Party of the Philippines, and the somewhat uncertain return to the structures of a liberal-democratic government. We need to inquire not only into how these large events have affected people in a particular locality but how local realities themselves are expressed in or have determined the large events. Such an inquiry is not only essential for the understanding of these events and the phenomenon of regime-change but valuable as well for current theoretical debates in anthropology and political science on the relationships between "local" and "extralocal" systems.

My point of entry into this problem is the rural district of Valladolid in the municipality of Carcar in southern Cebu, central Philippines.[1] It lies 45 kilometers south of Cebu City, axis of Metropolitan Cebu which is the country's second largest urban concentration.

Constituted of two barangays, Valladolid and Tuyom, with a combined area of eight square kilometers and an estimated population of
8,000 (7,274 in 1980), Valladolid is an old community with a known
history that stretches back to the sixteenth century. Though still
primarily agricultural, it is today—like other mainstream villages in
the country—a complex district with a marked degree of internal
economic differentiation and patterns of inside-outside relations.

I shall take a long-term view of the district to understand what
social transformations have taken place in the area over the long
duration and, thus, better appreciate changes in the local polity. Such
an approach necessarily includes a view of the larger worlds into
which a locality opens out. Historical change has created communities
"open" to the world (region, nation-state, world-system) and has, at
the same time, redrawn their boundaries in complex ways. That locality
is an artifact of history has important theoretical, methodological, and
stylistic consequence. At the simple level of procedure, this demands
that one should see it as something that is provisional, the meaning-
fulness of which is something that must be continually tested. Since
the determinants, mediations, and consequence of events and perspectives are not strictly local, nor do they lie solely in the present, the
analysis must necessarily involve an accordionlike movement in time
and space, between past and present, and between local and extralocal
systems of significance.[2]

I shall focus on elections as index to broader changes in local and
wider polities. Elections are a key institution in Philippine politics:
exercised in limited form in the late Spanish colonial period (with the
election of municipal officials by selected members of the propertied
class) and then widened considerably with universal suffrage under
American auspices in the twentieth century. Elections have been held
with marked frequency throughout the present century (Even under
Marcos rule, twelve elections, referendums, and plebiscites were held.).
They involve such large numbers of the population (26.4 million voters
today, with 1.2 million in Cebu province) that Filipinos often think of
politics in terms of elections.[3]

There is also something in the nature of the election itself which
makes it an instructive focus. Elections are a mechanism for the renewal
of political leadership and a legitimation-ritual, part of the process
by which a political system reproduces itself. In this sense, they are
not unbounded, open and free. Restrictions are placed on the production and circulation of meanings. Yet, as a source of discourse on
politics, elections are also an area in which other voices can be heard
and, to the extent that such voices gather strength, a medium that
alters the way in which persons and worlds are constituted. Elections

render visible divisions within society whether through the positive function of bringing these to the open realm of public debate or the negative one of masking or excluding them from this realm.

What changes in the practice of elections have taken place in Valladolid? In responses to random interviews conducted with adult residents of Valladolid in April-May 1987 on what changes in popular electoral practice have taken place over the past half-century, the stress has been on the continuities of political practice. While, indeed, "times have not changed" (drawn from the fundamental sense that "we are still poor," *pobre lang gihapon*), people are at the same time sensitive to the fact that the times are, in fact, not quite the same. In the matter of elections, certain themes express this change: (1) the disappearance of the old village-wide "patrons"; (2) the difficulties in predicting voter behavior (*Dili na nimo maseguro ang tawo*, "You can no longer be sure about people"); and (3) the "symbolic slippage" of elections, or the decline in their power to compel participation and belief.

Disappearance of the Patron

A contrast villagers themselves draw between past and present is that the past were the days when certain key individuals or families controlled, or had effective influence over, the electorate of Valladolid and could deliver the vote of the barrio in municipal, provincial, or national elections. This is no longer the case. Today, there is a multiplicity of lower-order *lider* in place of the old village-wide patrons. *Pulitika* (politics) is less orderly and smooth (*husay*) and more unpredictable. While *before* and *after* comparisons tend to bias perceptions in favor of "difference," a historic shift undoubtedly exists and requires explanation.

Underlying this shift are economic changes that have taken place over a whole century. At the start of the present century, Valladolid was a farming community with a population of 3,000 (2,689 in 1903), in seven *sitio*, subsisting on the cultivation of sugarcane (around 50% of village farmland), corn and coconuts (40%), and maguey and other crops (10%). Despite the clear economic inequalities, Valladolid was a fairly coherent community: well-settled (with families having two-to-six generations of residence in the area), with people bound in a common farming economy and interlinked by crosscutting horizontal and vertical kinship ties (i.e. consanguineal, affinal, ritual). The three richest families in the barrio (i,e. Regis, Gantuangco, and Enriquez) owned close to one-half of the village land (in addition to landholdings in neighboring barrios and towns); were residents linked downwards to other families by affinal and ritual ties; and performed the functions of traditional patrons (e.g. sponsoring formal education, religious projects, and cultural activities). They did not, either separately or together, manage haciendas but maintained scattered holdings cultivated by relatives and tenants. There was a measure of village egalitarianism as there was a large number of independent landowners and big tenants. Around 100 households (in a total of 500 households in the village) owned no land but many of these had access to tenancy arrangements and secondary sources of subsistence (e.g. fishing, trading, handicraft production).

At the turn of the century, the Regises, Gantuangcos, and Enriquezes were already well-entrenched as the *dakung tawo* ("big men") of the area: donors of church and school sites, principal organizers and financiers of fiesta celebrations—including a lavish annual theatrical spectacle called *linambay*—and brokers of the village in its relations with municipal and provincial authorities. When national elections grew in importance after 1916 (with the enfranchisement of a larger population and the expansion of State bureaucracy), these three families—with their economic resources, social status, and corps of tenants and dependents—became not just village patrons but local political leaders. They could deliver large blocs of vote and themselves served as elective town officials (with two Gantuangcos, Constancio and Leoncio, serving as Carcar mayor). There was lively competition among members of these families—they rarely voted as one—both for benefits that were inward-oriented (status and authority in the village) and outward-oriented (prestige and influence in the town or city).

The situation today is not quite the same. After a long period when the village was demographically static (due to factors like outmigration)—the population increased at an annual rate of only 1 percent from 1900 to 1960 (from 2,500 to 4,000)—there was a marked expansion of the population in the 1970s, from 4,793 in 1970 to 7,274 in 1980. The municipality of Carcar showed the same trend, increasing from 45,806 in 1970 to 60,824 in 1980. Valladolid (which became two barangays, Valladolid and Tuyom, in 1982) is now larger, more complex, with a current population of 8,000 in fourteen sitio, around 1,300 households, and a more mixed economy. The crop distribution pattern has changed: corn and coconut (70%), vegetables (12%), rice (8%), fruit trees (6%), and maguey and others (4%). Sugar has disappeared.

It is difficult to detail the shifts in occupational patterns due to limitations in the census data and the problem of comparability of available statistics for the early twentieth century and the present period. Government census data for the period 1903 to 1980 indicate that in Cebu province, the proportion of workers in agricultural to non-agricultural sectors has remained relatively steady over much of the present century, dropping only slightly from 51 to 48 percent over the period from 1903 to 1980. The municipality of Carcar shows a drop from 50 to 47 percent.[4] Viewed in the context of such factors as increased population, higher man-land ratio, and little change in technology, the slow expansion of the nonagricultural sector suggests increased pressures on limited land, high rural underemployment, and a greater mix of farm and off-farm work. For Valladolid, the rise in population, increasing parcellization of land, and higher landlessness indicate that significant numbers of the local population have been either removed from agriculture or occupy marginal positions in it. This is suggested in part by the increase in the number of farm families who obtain income from nonagricultural pursuits.[5]

The history of Valladolid over the present century has seen the drainage of resources out of the village—in terms of goods, capital (directly or indirectly, through taxes, rents, and terms of trade), manpower, and, most important, power. A clear illustration is the alienation of local resources to nonresidents. Today, 43 of the 63.6 hectares of fishponds in Valladolid-Tuyom under long-term lease from the government are controlled by a Cebu City businessman. Over the past seventy years, village land owned by nonresidents (those who do not reside either in Valladolid or Carcar, including members of old Valladolid families who have moved out of Carcar) has more than doubled.[6] Other changes in the landholding structure indicate the increased marginalization of local families: small farms have become even smaller and more people have been pushed out of farm employment.

Landholding Patterns, 1914 and 1987

	1914	1987
Number of lots	772	1,252
Number of owners	406	686
Average lot size	.9594 ha	.6049 ha
Nonresident owners	18	65
Landholdings	60 has	132.7 has

An analysis of landownership by family names, with 1914 as a base, shows that 39 families have gained, 109 have lost (with 51 disappearing from the rolls of owners), and 7 have maintained the same holdings. The rate of landlessness has doubled: of the estimated 1,300 households in Valladolid today, between 500 and 600 do not own any land. Many of the 1914 families who either gained or maintained landholdings actually suffered a reduction because of the increase of households per family. The change has affected the three dominant early twentieth-century families themselves: their landholdings reduced, they have either relocated to the town or city or have ceased to perform the role of village patrons.

Status of the Three Leading Families, 1914 and 1987

	1914			1987		
	Land/Owners/Average			Land/Owners/Average		
Regis	118.2	13	9.1 ha	98.3	16	6.1 ha
Gantuangco	91.5	6	15.2	30.5	20	1.5
Enriquez	90.6	3	30.2	71.5	17	4.2

All these have affected political practice in Valladolid. Interview respondents are one in asserting that there are no longer village-wide leaders in the mold of the old patrons. By the 1950s, we have the last of the traditional patrons of Valladolid—Constancio Gantuangco and Leoncio Gantuangco, who served as Carcar mayor in 1941–42, 1946–50 and 1952-55, respectively. The incorporation of Valladolid into wider economic and political systems drained resources and power away from the local community. This occasioned the economic decline of the old village elite as well as a changing ethos (a redirection of interest from intravillage prestige-building to outward-oriented entrepreneurial activities) that left the field open for small political entrepreneurs.

Instead of the traditional patron, there is now a large number of *lider* and political specialists. An early twentieth-century borrowing from English, "lider" (unlike the Cebuano *agalon*, "master" or "lord") connotes a more particularistic, instrumental type of leadership. It is commonly used to refer to leadership exercised for specific ends, such as mobilizing people for undertaking a project or supporting a candidate.[7] The shift in time has not only been from agalon to lider but from big to small lider. In Valladolid today, in a population of 8,000 (with a voting population of around 3,300), there are from twenty to thirty lider who can influence from 50 to 100 voters as against the three or four patrons in a village population of 4,000 (with around 1,000 voters) in the prewar period. The lider's following revolves around sitio or neighborhoods, kin groups, and economic or social alliance groups. In addition to the lider are specialists and workers who make up a more elaborate campaign machinery: *movers*, a larger group of lower-order lider whose influence and responsibilities in a campaign are more specific (e.g., to campaign among even smaller groups of voters or families); *cabos,* those who are responsible for shepherding a group of voters, of from five to twenty, to the polling centers on election day; and others who are hired for election-day services at from 50 to 100 pesos such as *ushers* (those stationed at polling centers to guide voters to their precincts), *runners* (messengers, errand boys), and precinct *watcher.*

All these suggest a turn toward specialization, specificity, and differentiation in electoral practice. With the loose articulation of local and national systems, however, these values index not so much "political modernization" as a fragmented and fluid polity. The fragmentation of the population has, for one, freed residents from the old loyalties. Populist attitudes are prominent: mistrust of traditional politicians, cynicism about the status quo, and the framing of contradictions in terms of the "people" (*katawhan*) and the power bloc of the rich (*datu*) and mighty (*dagku*). It is common to hear remarks like "Landlords can no longer tell the tenants how to vote" or "All politicians are the same." While such disengagement from familiar loyalties makes mobilization difficult, it also makes for a more democratic situation. Yet, the absence of compelling principles around which significant masses of people can be organized also makes for the phenomena of seeming depoliticization and demobilization in the contemporary village.

Withdrawal of the Voter

Voter withdrawal from the political process does not seem to be borne out by high voter turnouts in elections (of around 80 percent in recent elections). Turnout statistics, however, are partial indicators, particularly if viewed in the light of three factors: (1) the compulsions of the law (President Marcos decreed penalties for nonvoting), (2) the compulsions of tradition (formal education and immersion in the rhetoric and experience of close to a century of popular elections), and (3) the unintended or informal benefits to be derived from participating in an exercise which primes the circulation of material and symbolic goods.

The need is to attend to the motives and quality of voter participation. Queried on their reasons for voting, Valladolid residents are usually initially stumped, thinking an answer is superfluous. When pressed for an answer, they usually raise a textbook explanation which, however, places the stress on *katungdanan* (duty) rather than *katungod* (right). In practice, the ethic of "working the system" appears to be dominant. On one hand, this takes the form of opportunistic "raiding" and appropriation of the goods in circulation, as in vote-selling, called *mangopras* (selling copra for emergency cash) or *mangahoy* (gathering and selling wood). On the other, this may take the form of "playing the game," evading the claims of the state on one's beliefs through nominal participation.

A study of electoral practice indicates not only keenness of competition but the degree to which candidates and campaigners have to go further afield to get to the voters. This is shown in the increasingly intensive exploitation of mass media. A survey of the six leading AM radio stations in Metro Cebu during the May 1987 campaign period shows that around 50 percent of the combined daily airtime of these stations was devoted to partisan political propaganda (broadcasts of party meetings, commentaries or talk shows, and jingles). In the prewar period, public rallies (*miting*) in town centers and major barrios made up the campaign itinerary. Today, in addition to the mass rallies (now held on a daily basis in Cebu City and aired on radio), neighborhood and district *pulung-pulong* (forums) and intensive house-to-house campaigning characterize electoral campaigns. It would seem that, in a reversal of the customary practice called "the moving contrast," it is now the superiors who must do the "moving" instead of subordinates "moving forward" to approach superiors. Cebuano terms like *kamang* ("crawl toward an object") and *kuot* ("extract with difficulty"), applied to what is required to get to voters, indicate a situation where much more labor is expended to get voters to participate. It is in this context that one has an explanation for the resort to hardsell techniques, fraud, physical coercion, and the use of money for buying lider and voters. (In recent elections in Valladolid, votes were bought for 20 to 50 pesos, equivalent on the average to a farm worker's wage for three days. Even in the Marcos era, when there was a mock quality to elections, money was still expended to get people to vote.) A common observation on postwar politics is that vote-buying has become more open and rampant. The popular statement *Kuwarta na lay palihokon* ("It is money that does the moving") points to a situation where elections are nourished by money (which can move "faster" and talk "louder") rather than persons or ideas.

In prewar elections—such as the elections of 1922 and 1924 in Carcar—such practices as *hakot* (ferrying voters in hired trucks or rigs to public rallies and polling centers), *pakaon* (feeding the voters), and *panghulga* (intimidation) were already common. Yet, it can be said that, at a point in time, these were practised or perceived as extensions of traditional patronage and control functions. Feeding clients and dependents, in particular, as is customarily done in fiestas, has a certain legitimacy and the requisite diffuseness that marks traditional patronage. In many ways, this is no longer the case where patrons have disappeared or lost legitimacy: lider are not autonomous lords but political middlemen who must, in the main, rely on more naked forms of coercion or more contractual, particularistic exchanges with their clients. Moreover, there may be a shift here as well from forms of collective voter-herding (in which "big men" compete either for power and prestige as deliverers of votes, or for pork barrel, communal benefits for localities) to free-form, open-field competition for individual or particularistic benefits.

It is admittedly difficult to calibrate these shifts or document the basic assumption that the intensification and overelaboration of campaign practices speak not only of a step-up of the candidates' competition for a *share* of the market but the contraction or enervation of the market itself. Like "quality," "withdrawal" is a problematic concept and may be misleading: the recoil or retreat from electoral participation may at the same time suggest that people are being politicized and organized in other forms and directions. Still, as we shall discuss later on, there are no significant power blocs organized along nontraditional lines, although the beginnings of such groupings are to be found in Valladolid. There is instead a shifting field of relations: alliances and linkages which can be active or recessive and which may overlap and supersede each other, depending on contexts, situations, and combinations. There are the claims of past, present, and future (favors given, contracts in force, promises made) and culturally formed notions of what is proper or right in given situations. And there is, finally, the sense of provisionality about political commitments declared or given. Hence, predictions about political behavior require an accounting of a wide range of factors and sensitivity to temporal shifts in the value of such factors.

Decline of Ritual Power

There is a built-in tendency in a ritual system, such as elections, to weaken or suffer from "symbolic slippage." Hence, the need to periodically repeat its performance. Repetition, however, is not enough; contextual factors are important. Despite common observations concerning the passion of Filipinos for elections, there is something of a surface quality in the intensity of competition and, beneath the surface, a real enervation in the power of elections to compel participation and belief.

In local communities, an important reason for the decline in the quality of participation is that less and less power is available in the localities at the same time that local residents are disengaged from the centers or levels where real power is accumulated. We have adverted earlier to the "drainage" of wealth and power from the village. On the basis of its municipal income, Carcar has declined from a first-class to a third-class municipality. At the beginning of the century, Carcar was known as the *segunda ciudad* of Cebu province, a center of trade in southern Cebu and with its own rich agricultural hinterland. The decline of agriculture (especially sugar cultivation) and the failure of local industries to develop has relegated Carcar to the provincial backwaters. At the same time, government policies biased in favor of centralization have sapped local units of power and initiative.

An examination of Carcar Municipal Council records from 1952 to 1987 (the only such records available in Carcar) shows the limited fiscal resources available to the municipal government and its dependence on external aid and patronage for such development projects as roads, irrigation, farm credit, and schoolhouses. The bulk of the municipal income (ranging from 55,000 in 1952 to 1.4 million pesos in 1986), mainly raised from real property taxes and municipal licenses, goes to maintaining the local bureaucracy (salaries and operational expenses). In 1953, only 10 percent of the municipal revenues of 54,588 pesos that year went for development purposes such as infrastructure. National government assistance is sought for even small improvements like a barrio artesian well, the asphalting of a few kilometers of road, or the building of foot bridges.[8]

Today, Carcar, with an estimated population of 70,000 (60,824 in 1980), has become an "exurb" of Metro Cebu, part of the structurally undeveloped semiurban zone that covers a large part of east-central Cebu (from Carcar to Liloan). Carcar residents commute regularly to Cebu City, where they transact business, attend school, or have employment. Unemployment in Carcar is high, unofficially estimated by municipal authorities in 1986 at 15 percent underemployed and 25 percent unemployed.

Like many Philippine towns, Carcar is still largely agricultural (60.62% of the land is devoted to corn, coconuts, and other crops), with a predominance of small farms (4,027 out of 4,068 farms in the municipality are less than five hectares in size), and a high rate of tenancy (around 67% of rice and corn lands). The few modern agribusiness and aquaculture concerns in the town are owned either by *poblacion* or Cebu City residents. In the poblacion itself, there are around 500 registered commercial establishments concentrated in small business (i.e., eateries, retail stores, services). There are no industries outside of furniture and blacksmithing shops and (the most important) the largely unorganized small-scale rural shoe factories in the barrios close to the town center.

The same situation is to be found in Valladolid where the barangay government is even more ineffectual as a pivot for local development. The two barangay councils of the area have virtually no funds outside of occasional small-change revenues from permits (e.g., for public dances) and the token share they get from certain taxes and, particularly during the Marcos era, doleouts (disguised as "special development assistance") from the Manila government. Largely a postwar creation, the barangay council was formally strengthened during the Marcos era. In Valladolid, however, it commanded few economic and political resources compared to the more informal government of wealthy traditional patrons in the early years of the century who worked through such instruments as the local chapel association, various project committees, or their personal linkages to village households or to state officials outside the village.

The general phenomenon has been the shift of the locus of power away from local communities (i.e., the barrio, the town). Local government posts have become more important as instruments for extracting benefits from the outside, for brokering between the locality and the national government, and for filtering back to the countryside what resources have been drained out of it by a central state and capitalism. Local officials have considerably fewer resources to dispense. In an environment of scarcity, however, what powers they do have remain important: as gatekeepers in a vertically structured bureaucracy, they can control the flow of benefits from the outside, and, as local officials, they have petty powers to harass and petty spoils to distribute to clients. Yet, in the main, their powers are neither autonomous nor decisive.

Something of this phenomenon can be seen in the character of political leadership in local communities. In both barrio and town, government officials do not have the elite status of their counterparts in the early years of the century. This is dramatically illustrated in the case of Valladolid. Turn-of-the-century *cabeza* (village heads) included members of the Regis, Gantuangco, and Enriquez families who, among themselves, controlled almost half of the village land. Cabeza Miguel Enriquez and Salvador Gantuangco, for instance, owned 77.5 and 29.8 hectares, respectively. Today, the barangay captains of Valladolid and Tuyom are, an owner of a small backyard shoe factory and houselot of 250 square meters and a landless retired policeman respectively.

Valladolid Under Martial Law

This was the general situation in the Valladolid area when Marcos declared Martial Law in 1972. There was no overt or organized opposition in both barrio and town to the new order. In a series of resolutions, the municipal government dutifully hailed the imposition of Martial Law and the subsequent initiatives of the Marcos government.[9] Carcar and Valladolid turned in "Yes" votes in the various Martial Law-period referendums and plebiscites.

The only political disturbance took place in the morning of 17 November 1973, when soldiers of the 344th Co. of the Philippine Constabulary (PC) came in an army truck and raided a seminar of the Federation of Free Farmers (FFF) held in one of the houses of the barrio.[10] The seminar was attended by around fifty farmer-participants not only from Valladolid but other places in the Visayas and Mindanao. The soldiers arrested twenty-five farmers (including two women), herded them to the Constabulary camp in the southern town of Sibonga and, later, to detention quarters in Cebu City where they were booked for violation of a Martial Law order prohibiting mass assemblies without a PC permit. They were released three weeks later, after it was determined that they were engaged in nothing more subversive than instruction in farmers' cooperatives and land reform (and also after FFF national president Jeremias Montemayor came to Cebu to intercede on their behalf).

Like other barangays in the country, Valladolid organized a Samahang Nayon in 1973, with an initial membership of around sixty, and various arms of the revitalized barangay government (i.e., Kabataang Barangay, Tanod, and Lupong Tagapayapa). The barrio received benefits from the national government: a barangay high school was opened, though it is only partly operational; the village was energized in 1980 under the Cebu Electric Cooperative (CEBECO), although only 30 percent of Valladolid households are today served by electricity; and several artesian wells were installed. (All projects were properly marked as "Projects of the President and the First Lady" and of their man in Cebu, Governor Eduardo Gullas.)

More important was the inclusion in 1973 of the 500-hectare Hacienda Osmeña—which had become Carcar Development Corporation (CARDECO) in 1968—in the land reform program decreed by Marcos in 1972. Owned by the Osmeña family, political enemies of Marcos, the hacienda was the major land-reform site in Cebu province. Of the 500 hectares of the estate, 362.7 hectares (717 parcels) were transferred to 586 tenants. Of these, 29.8 hectares (51 parcels) were in

Valladolid, with forty-nine tenants involved. A portion of the estate
(83 hectares) remained with CARDECO and has been developed as a
housing project. (State compensation for CARDECO was 1.09 million
pesos in cash and government bonds.) A choice portion of 54 hectares
was acquired in 1983 by the Valladolid Integrated Farm Co. (VIFCO),
a Filipino-Chinese firm based in Cebu City and engaged in livestock
and permanent-crop agriculture. In sum, land reform beneficiaries in
Carcar received an average of slightly more than half-a-hectare each
and, as of 1988, only a small number have actually received titles to
the land.

No radical change took place during the Martial Law period. Despite
the pretensions of Marcos for building a popular democracy, old
patterns of dependence and containment were fostered and centralizing trends in the state strengthened. The Marcos era was not radi-
cally different from previous administrations in the experience of
villagers. The restrictions on political competition may have deprived
villagers of opportunities to establish or activate linkages with patrons
or play off one leader against another; yet, villagers knew that the
short-term gains to be gained from electoral contests were not that
crucial. Besides, the Marcos government continued to dispense state
patronage and, in certain respects, more benefits were received by the
village from Marcos than from other presidents. Villagers knew enough
of democratic government to know that Marcos's continued stay in
power was an anomaly. They were willing to tolerate it for so long
as there was a perceptible improvement in their condition (seen chiefly
in terms of more jobs, better wages and tenancy contracts, and favorable prices). The lack of such improvement created the potential for
the anti-Marcos sentiment that existed in Cebu virtually throughout
the entire Martial Law period.

The reservoir of anti-Marcos sentiment in Cebu was fed from other
sources. In the last elections before martial rule—the 1969 presidential
election (when many felt that Marcos cheated opponent Sergio
Osmeña Jr., Cebu's political kingpin, of the presidency) and the 1971
senatorial and local elections—Marcos was badly beaten in Cebu.
Though there was no overt resistance in Cebu when Martial Law was
announced in 1972 (and virtually no New People's Army activity),
Marcos knew that Cebu was not friendly territory.

The first clear expression of opposition to the Marcos government
did not come in 1986 but in the elections for the Interim National
Assembly on 9 April 1978. Thirteen assembly seats were contested in
the Central Visayas or Region VII (with 1,826,316 voters in 1977). A
ragtag opposition group that called itself Pusyon Bisaya (Visayan
Fusion) fielded a complete slate against Marcos's party, the Kilusang

Bagong Lipunan (New Society Movement). The contrast was very stark: the KBL had a stellar slate that included the most prominent names in the region (including Osmeña, Durano, Cuenco, and Gullas) against a ticket of virtual or relative unknowns.[11] The election provided an opening for a populist expression of resistance. In panic, the KBL in Cebu attempted to manipulate the election results, yet it was done so crudely that there was no way they could ensure a credible outcome. After a long delay (and with Malacañang willing to settle for what was a "merely local" opposition victory and to turn it into a testament of "free elections"), the Commission on Elections proclaimed all thirteen opposition candidates winners on 17 May 1978. Such was the euphoria of victory after the election that a common boast was that "even if the opposition had fielded a dog against the Marcos candidates, the dog would have won."

This was a populist reaction to the Martial Law government that foreshadowed the events of 1986. It was organized less around clear political leaders or counterprograms as it was a coming-to-focus of a popular disenchantment with government. It was not sustained: the Pusyon Bisaya, which was not much of an organization to begin with, splintered with the cooptation of some of its leaders. Still, Marcos rule remained far from hegemonic. On three occasions in 1980, the Martial Law government was denounced in freedom marches, noise barrage demonstrations, and sitdown strikes involving thousands of participants led by anti-Marcos Cebuano politicians. On 4 July 1980, a "Freedom March" organized by the National Union for Liberation (NUL)—a coalition of the ideologically moderate opposition to Marcos—was aborted when demonstrators were dispersed with water hoses. Thirty persons (including two members of the National Assembly, a former congressman, and two former Cebu City mayors) were arrested for illegal assembly. On 21 September 1980, on the eighth anniversary of Martial Law, some 5,000 Cebuanos gathered at Fuente Osmeña, the city's central park, and then marched to the provincial capitol bearing a coffin, signifying "the death of democracy." A violent confrontation with the military was narrowly averted and twelve persons were arrested (led by a National Assembly member, a former congressman, and the manager of a local radio station which functioned as the demonstrators' communications center).[12] The most violent manifestation came on 19 May 1984, when a large crowd gathered at the provincial capitol to protest the results of the May 14 National Assembly elections. In a long pitched battle between an armed military-police force and stone-throwing demonstrators, one demonstrator was killed and many were injured. Though the odds were stacked in favor of the administration and the opposition was splintered, the main opposition party in this election—Coalition Panaghiusa (Unity Coalition)—swept Cebu City (winning two seats) and had one candidate (out of six) elected in the province. In Carcar itself (voting as part of the province), the vote was divided between three opposition candidates and three proadministration bets.[13]

Structure of Loyalties

In the 1986 snap presidential election and its aftermath, various factors converged to give fuller and wider expression to popular disenchantment with the Marcos government. Corazon Aquino won over Ferdinand Marcos in Cebu Province, Carcar, and Valladolid. Around 80 percent of the voting population turned out to vote. At provincial, municipal, and submunicipal levels, Aquino won convincingly though she won with less than 50 percent of the total voting population.

Presidential Election Results, 1986

	Registered Voters	Votes Cast	% of Votes Cast	Voter Turnout
CEBU PROVINCE	1,161,211			80.4%
Aquino		502,709	53.7%	
Marcos		431,786	46.2%	
CARCAR	27,199			78.9%
Aquino		13,057	60.7%	
Marcos		8,420	39.2%	
VALLADOLID	3,286			80.6%
Aquino		1,677	63.3%	
Marcos		972	36.6%	

What local realities are expressed in these results? In Valladolid, an analysis of the nature and distribution of the vote shows that such explanatory concepts as class and clientilism do not neatly sum up political behavior. In Valladolid, support for Marcos came from barangay officials (whose support, in most cases, drew less from ideological conviction as the sense that it was proper they being in government) and people who felt that Marcos had done something for the village in the way of agrarian reform and local improvements. Local members of the FFF, including those detained in the 1973 incident, voted for Marcos. The local machinery of the Kilusang Bagong Lipunan did not work as well as in previous elections. After twenty years of Marcos, faced with the most organized national electoral opposition since Martial Law was declared, even avid Marcos supporters had the sense that the administration's material and symbolic capital was overdrawn and a change of government was imminent. The local KBL machinery broke down as local leaders defected or skimmed off the "Marcos money" for the campaign (a practice called *kopras,* if done by those who receive the money, or *kapon,* if done by those who are supposed to distribute it).

On the other hand, support for Aquino came from local oppositionists, most notably the "San Miguel group" (*taga*-San Miguel), a core of around seven politically active families whose heads work in the San Miguel Corporation plant in Metro Cebu and who look up to Bernardo Noel, a Carcar political figure who is SMC personnel manager in Cebu, as their *lider.* The central management of San Miguel Corporation in Manila supported Marcos (in fact, San Miguel products were included in the postelection boycott movement announced by Aquino), but the rank-and-file was for Aquino. In the case of Valladolid's "San Miguel group," the factors at work were a combination of factional (the Noel group was oppositionist in Carcar during this period) and categorical factors (the group, due to its steady city employment, is the more urban-oriented of the village factions).[12] In addition, there was the perception that Aquino was supported by the Catholic Church which—combined with the public image of Aquino as a strongly moral person—was a factor in a community which, aside from being a parish with a resident priest, has a network of thirty-four *kapilya* (*sitio* or neighborhood chapels).

In postelection interviews, the most common explanation offered by villagers for voting against Marcos was that they were "tired" (*puol*) of his continued stay in power and that it was time for a change (*kausaban, bag-o*). The word *puol* means "being sated" or "feeling worn": in the specific context of its use, it signifies less an active negation as social weariness, political fatigue, or the feeling that an existing order has outlived its justification—that it no longer makes much sense.

Villagers were aware of talk of corruption in government, and by Marcos himself; yet, they either did not know what to make of it precisely ("we just hear about it") or tended to be dismissive ("it is nothing new"). They, however, *knew* that their lives were not getting any better and had, in fact, deteriorated (*nagtikuskos*) due to poor yields, high prices, low wages, and joblessness.

The inchoate, ad-hoc populism which fueled Aquino's triumph at the polls also characterizes the support for her presidency today. It is a support founded less on a sense of what the Aquino government promises for the long future than on a tenacious yet provisional faith that people will "survive" (*buhi gihapon*), a basic optimism which grants a new government charter for rule, so long as it does not make the chances for survival even more restricted or difficult. Such a meager, minimalist faith is an ideological artifact of hegemonic processes, a product of a history that has kept people largely powerless, yet one which, given the fact that hegemony is never completely total and that even the most restricted rural worlds are never completely closed, can expand into larger, maximizing demands.

Valladolid is what may be called a conservative community. It is, residents claim, peaceful: the local Katarungang Pambarangay (the dispute-processing forum organized under the Marcos administration) processed 565 recorded cases (and around 500 unrecorded ones) from 1982 to 1987, an average of around 170 cases per year. Of these, less than ten were referred to the courts and only two cases were actually filed. All the cases (except one attempted homicide) are petty in nature: complaints about stray animals damaging crops, slander, and drunken behavior. (However, in this connection, a case may also be made for the reality of low-level violence: alcoholism, neighbors' quarrels, and tensions over property rights—partly indicated by the warning and off-limits signs one sees marking plots and houseyards in the village today.)

The communist insurgency is generally viewed as something taking place outside the village. Mobile elements of the New People's Army operate in some of the mountain barangays of Central Cebu (including Carcar) but the economy and terrain of Cebu island are such that CPP-NPA activity in Cebu has taken a largely urban orientation, with party organizing and selective armed action gravitating around Metro Cebu (its peripheral mountain barangays and the depressed, heavily populated barangays in the metropolitan area itself). Official and unofficial sources estimate NPA armed guerrillas in the whole Cebu province at less than 200.

The 11 May 1987 congressional elections—billed as the first real free election after Marcos—present something of a map of the political loyalties in the Carcar-Valladolid area. The five main candidates for congressman of Cebu's First District (to which Carcar belongs together with Talisay, Minglanilla, Naga, and San Fernando) were Antonio Bacaltos (lawyer, Partido Panaghiusa, the official administration candidate), Jose Aznar (lawyer, PDP-Laban, of a family that owns a university in Cebu City), Miguel Enriquez, Jr. (lawyer and popular radio commentator prominent in the anticommunist movement in Cebu, of UNIDO), Felipe Regis-Abellaneda (a retired military officer, Nacionalista Party), and Miguel Rentillosa (small Carcar shoe factory owner, Partido ng Bayan). Two others filed their candidacy and got a few votes.

The Aquino presidency (with Aquino still at the crest of her popularity) was not at stake: all candidates declared support for the President; criticized, or distanced themselves from the Marcos regime; and competed over who best served the democratic aims of the Aquino government. Candidates sought to establish some association with the Aquino family (no matter how tenuous) through messages of endorsement, photographs, recall of personal links, and others. Much of the contest, therefore, was waged over local concerns or the "local meaning" of national issues.

Enriquez and Regis-Abellaneda had claims to being "of Valladolid." Both did not reside in the barrio but Enriquez had landholdings, tenants, and relatives in the barrio, while Abellaneda was connected to the still wealthy Regises of Valladolid. Yet, both lost in Valladolid. Enriquez raised the issue of "fighting communism" as the main theme of his campaign. It did not prove too effective: he lost not only in Valladolid but in Carcar and the whole district. On the other hand, Rentillosa, the candidate of the left-wing Partido ng Bayan, plagued by various problems (logistics, organization, failure to articulate a clear message), also lost in Valladolid, Carcar, and the district.

The ideological factor did not prove effective although the vote showed fairly well-defined ideological blocs of vote. Rentillosa and the PnB senatorial candidates received practically the same number of votes: around 500 in the municipality and around 20 in Valladolid. The "Marcos vote" was also well-defined: the senatorial candidates of the KBL (which had no candidate for First District congressman) each received around 1,000 votes in the municipality and around fifty in Valladolid. Carcar and Valladolid elected twenty-three Aquino candidates out of 24.

Congressional Election Results, 1987

Candidates	District	Carcar	Valladolid
Bacaltos	50,223	6,288	1,003
Aznar	31,734	5,259	422
Enriquez	22,928	5,626	812
Abellaneda	5,639	2,128	332
Rentillosa	1,228	501	21

Interview data indicate a wide range of motives underlying voter behavior: particularistic estimates of past or prospective benefits (as a resident remarks, *Asa gani ta mabuhi, tua ta gyud:* "Where we can make a living, there we will be"); the influence of superiors and peers;

factionalism; and categorical imperatives (support for the government, anticommunism, and others). These variables crosscut and overlap such that prediction is extremely difficult. A single voter or household is characteristically enmeshed in a network of debts and relations such that he will have some reason for voting for any of three or four candidates (e.g., a link of kinship or coresidence, a past favor to a family member, a promise of some benefit, a debt to a landlord-lider, the attraction of ideas). Hence, it is difficult to determine, unless one is privy to all the facts, how a household or person will finally vote.

On election day, 11 May 1987, I was standing in the schoolgrounds of the Tuyom Elementary School, conversing with a local public schoolteacher, Rosvias Alesna, who is also an active political lider of the barrio (in fact, there is a pending administrative complaint with school-division authorities against him for electioneering). He has been an active lider for many years; he knew the people coming into the grounds and could estimate (for my benefit) how this or that person would most likely vote. As we were conversing, somebody arrived with the news that "Kumander Mike," the leader of the NPA in the Carcar area, was gunned down, his throat slashed with a bladed weapon, near the Carcar-San Fernando boundary.[15] It was the big story of the day but from the reactions of those present, it was something that had happened—was happening—somewhere else. Rosvias and I went back to observing the election proceedings, with Rosvias once more sizing up for me the political loyalties of those who were coming in to cast their votes. In the end, however, turning reflective, he said: *Dili na nimo maseguro kon unsa ang naa sa hunahuna sa tawo* ("You can no longer be certain about what is in a person's mind").

Prospects of a New Order

The people at EDSA clearly gave voice to the sentiment of a large sector of the population. In the 7 February election, the barrio was a microcosmic EDSA, with support for Aquino coming from the traditional opposition, the Church and urban-oriented "middle elements." The case of Valladolid, however, also shows the inchoate character of the base of support for the Aquino presidency. We must not slight the fact that Aquino received the votes of less than 50 percent of the voting population (i.e., provincial, municipal, and barangay levels) in the 7 February election; that 20 percent of the voters perhaps did not feel too strongly about the issues for them to cast their votes; and that, despite the claims of a more politicized citizenry in the wake of EDSA, only 76 percent of the voters of Valladolid cast their vote in the three recent political exercises (the 2 February 1987 plebiscite and the 17 May 1987 and 18 January 1988 elections).

In the final analysis, economic realities make for much of what is both real and vulnerable in the Aquino government's base of support. The factors we have discussed—the disappearance or decline of patrons, the "withdrawal" of the voter from the electoral process, the problematization of elections, the absorption of the district into a wider economy—suggest a halfway polity, one that is not effectively formed or organized around national leaders, parties, or programs of government. Marcos, in his time, did not rest on a stable base. Neither does Aquino.

The Valladolid polity is fragmented and volatile, turned not only toward the local lider and concerns but turned outwards to the city and nation. Within the locality itself, the population pressure on available resources has led to more diverse and complex economic arrangements: the combining of multiple employments, of farm and off-farm work, occasional jobs in town and city, and multiple or overlapping linkages to brokers and middlemen.[16] One is tempted to apply the concept of "involution" to Valladolid except that involution—with its stress on internal elaboration rather than the processes of fragmentation and destitution—makes strategies of economic survival seem "aesthetic." Moreover, the dry agriculture of Valladolid (irrigated rice occupies less than 10% of the agricultural area of both Carcar and Valladolid) presents a less absorptive environment compared to Java.[17] Hence, it is less the image of stability of the overall social system which is dominant as that of disaggregation.

Moreover, the residents of Valladolid no longer circulate within the old village boundaries. The Carcar poblacion is only fifteen minutes away by pedicab or tricycle and Cebu City, an hour away by jeepney or bus—vehicular movement between these points is regular throughout the day. Interviews with Valladolid residents of the 18–30 age group indicate a highly mobile population of commuters and short-term migrants, ranging through a geography that includes not just Carcar but Metro Cebu, Manila, and other places in the country. Since the wider economy is itself structurally undeveloped, there are limits to the fields that villagers can occupy outside the village. Characteristically, young Valladolid residents have (or have had) urban employment in marginal sectors: as salesgirls, clerks, small-factory workers, construction laborers, domestic servants, or helpers in the service sector.

The classic image of the structure of Philippine politics is of a multitiered system of factions and patron-client networks extending from local to national levels and organized around local, particularistic, and noncategorical ends.[18] The political disruptions of the past decade-and-a-half (martial rule, the phenomenal rise to power of Aquino, and a communist challenge that is at its strongest in Philippine history) highlight the limited explanatory power of the "classic" model.

The polity of contemporary Valladolid is not so elegantly structured. Loyalties are not so neatly orchestrated, clients are more active than passive, and dissensus is more real than consensus. The old occupational categories (landlord/farmer/tenant) are no longer adequate or tenable: persons and households are engaged in a wide variety and mix of occupations; they are linked vertically to multiple patrons or brokers and horizontally to partners, friends, and allies. With such factors as the shift to leasehold arrangements (a 75:25 norm in Valladolid in favor of the tenant based on income from the traditional crop of corn), many of those who continue to till other people's land are no longer traditional dependents: spreading-out risks (i.e., cultivating parcels belonging to different landowners, mixing incomes from farm and off-farm work), raising crops and livestock beyond what the landowner can legally claim, or using the law to protect their livelihood rights. Furthermore, even the lowliest Valladolid resident is not village-bound: he has a store of urban experience and is aware of a world of power in which there are actors other than his landlord, employer, patron, or boss.

As history stands in Valladolid, one has a disaggregated and protean social formation in which people are not constituted as classes or traditional economic, social, or territorial blocs. In such a setting, resistance (as in EDSA) has primarily taken a popular-democratic form rather than one based either on class or traditional alignments. It is largely unorganized and can be articulated in the discourse of the ruling elite or disarticulated from such a discourse and articulated instead into the discourse of the dominated class.[19]

What light does this cast on the transition of government from Marcos to Aquino? The Valladolid experience shows that despite the lack of organized resistance to martial rule in many parts of the country, Marcos rule was far from hegemonic. Despite the proliferation of the instrumentalities of the state at the local level, the population could not be effectively mobilized and a large part of it remained hidden, beyond the effective reach of the state. This hidden population came into momentary view in the opposition victory in Cebu and the Central Visayas in 1978, and in the Cebu elections of 1984, and then in the February 1986 election and its aftermath. All these manifestations, however, do not constitute an organized counterhegemonic project.

These facts suggest that we must reject any totalizing interpretation of recent changes in Philippine political history (whether it is the advent of authoritarianism in 1972 or the reinstallation of democracy in 1986). At the same time, the same facts are arguments against "closure" (in reductive interpretations that say "Nothing has changed"). Instead, they speak of dynamism and openness: there is an accumulation of power, of the symbolic capital for struggle, at the level of localities and, more important, the expanding communities which villagers now inhabit. Such capital is still largely unaggregated: it may be dissipated or appropriated by the ruling elite (or sections of it), but it may also be conserved, built up, transformed, and put to more effective use on behalf of popular or class interests.

In Valladolid today, clientilism and factionalism coexist with categorical imperatives. The district has nontraditional groups: occupational organizations—such as the FFF chapter and the local Fishermen's Association of the government-funded Cebu Resource Management Project (CRMP)—cooperatives, neighborhood chapel associations, and other formal and informal groups held together, albeit in different degrees, by shared economic and cultural interests. At the same time, there is a great deal of individual and class initiative as shown by rural entrepreneurs in Valladolid and Liburon (another Carcar barangay) who have established backyard shoe factories without state assistance and tenants who have shifted to commercial vegetable production even in the face of landlord resistance. While there is, as yet, no mobilization of such acts at higher levels of economic and political action, they suggest new possibilities in political development.

Valladolid is just one small rural district but, unexceptional as it is, it provides us with an insight into the larger picture of contemporary rural society in the Philippines. It is a district where a relatively cohesive agrarian community under the sway of traditional landlord-patrons has given way to a fluid social field of disaggregated households, economic sets, and alliance groups with multiple links to persons, groups, and institutions not only within but without the village. It is, in this sense, a "free field" which can be organized around a number of alternative centers: a sea marked by contrary currents but one in which the communist guerrilla (in Mao's familiar image) can swim, yet one too that can be organized around other models of empowerment, including that of a renewed national government sensitive to the age-old needs of its citizens and the dynamic social configuration of its constituent communities. The village is not an artifact of custom: it is—like the nation itself—contested ground, a field of challenge and opportunities.

CRISTINA BLANC-SZANTON

Change and Politics
in a Western Visayan Municipality

Against the background of longer-term socioeconomic
trends and specific changes in patron-client and class relationships in
Iloilo province since World War II, particularly in the northeastern
municipality of Estancia since 1967, this essay analyzes the transition
from Ferdinand Marcos to Corazon Aquino in the 1986/1988 period
and the phenomenon of "People Power." It tries to capture political
changes and continuities, from a Visayan municipal, as well as
provincial perspective. It is grounded in the assumption that one
important aspect of the national political process is the daily practice
of politics and what this means to both the wealthy and powerful
people as well as the ordinary citizens in the municipality.

The 1986 presidential, 1987 congressional, and 1988 municipal
elections have been viewed as potential turning points in the Marcos/
Aquino transition. In this essay, these elections are analyzed: (1) against
the backdrop of pre-Martial Law municipal, provincial and national
elections and the understandings on which they operated; (2) in terms
of the effects of Martial Law since 1972 on local politics; and (3) in
the context of longer-term economic, social and political changes and
their effects on the political process. Elections are seen as special
times of intensified interpersonal exchanges and heightened feelings,
potentially crystallizing at one moment in time longer-term changes
in interpersonal relationships and perspectives. The particular circumstance of People Power in the transition from Marcos to Aquino generated a great wave of emotional commitment as well as many
conflicting loyalties that translated into actual voting practices and
local perceptions of political change. In dealing with these practices
and perceptions I shall consider: (1) the local understandings of
democracy, (2) the extent to which municipal politics in Western

Visayas are tied to personalistic patron-client models of social relationships rather than issues, such as land reform, and (3) the role played by family politics before, during and after Marcos's reign.

In the background are long-term changes brought about by the country's socioeconomic transformations and processes of administrative centralization which are manifested in the changing style of family politics, the rise and demise of particular town/barrio projects (such as municipal cooperatives and the National Food Administration centralized rice-marketing system during Martial Law) and the new social awareness of drugs, prostitution, tourism, illegal gambling and law-and-order problems in the municipality.

The historical dimension is important to answer two questions that Filipinos today frequently pose themselves: (1) To what extent have the 1987 congressional and 1988 municipal elections shown a return to the pre-Martial Law style of politics? (2) Is there evidence of a return to "business as usual" in politics, or are there manifestations of deep-seated change?

Data for this essay were collected during eighteen months of fieldwork in 1967 and 1968 in Estancia and other towns in Iloilo province, as well as during visits lasting from approximately two weeks to two months, every two years from 1970 to 1989. The visits became the basis for an earlier book and subsequent articles on aspects of contemporary life and post-World War II changes in Estancia.[1]

Data on the same municipality also generated monographs by David Szanton on the town's entrepreneurs and on ongoing changes in the local fishing industry.[2]

While David Szanton and I initially focused on social relationships related to economic entrepreneurship rather than on the political process per se, we also realized at that time that factional politics played a very significant role in the life of the town. My own interest since then in Thai municipal politics before and after World War II in relation to national politics and local class formation (1982) as well as in the role of Filipino women in politics (1981, 1982) made me collect further systematic information about elections and people's perceptions of politics.[3] This culminated in about a hundred two-to-three-hour random open-ended interviews in the town and surrounding barrios in June 1986, partially repeated in June 1988 and again briefly in 1989. These allowed me to follow current economic, social and political changes in the municipality and highlighted again how politics and social relationships based on entrepreneurial enterprises (land, fishing, food processing) are intricately intertwined.[4]

Estancia in the 1986 Campaign

When I reached Iloilo City almost three months after the 1986 elections, I was told that Aquino had won in the city by 25,000 votes. Feelings had been running high. There had been demonstrations by unions, workers, and farmers prior to the elections, in which they asked for government support in lowering fertilizer and pesticide costs or increasing palay subsidies, among other things. Catholic nuns had been lying down on the pavement in a show of passive resistance to block the actions of local police against the demonstrators. Large crowds were brought from the barangays to the Sport Stadium at 15 to 50 pesos a head to support a Marcos visit. And people flocked to see Corazon Aquino, the newcomer.

After Aquino's win was announced, people had danced in the streets for three nights and lit bonfires. Even those who were not sure about how she would perform in office regarded these events with great emotion. People generally felt that something unusual and exciting had occurred.[5]

In the five districts of Iloilo province (San Enrique, San Dionisio, Passi, Sara and Carles), Cory Aquino had apparently obtained an overall victory by 20,000 votes. She had won in the first three and lost slightly to Marcos and the Kilusang Bagong Lipunan (KBL) party in the last two. However, in most municipalities the voting had been close. In Estancia (district of Sara), Marcos managed to obtain a slight advantage of 358 votes, according to the official count.[6]

The election in Estancia brought few formal speeches and none of the mass celebrations witnessed in Iloilo City (nuns demonstrating, bonfires, dancing in the streets), but only a big party held by a pro-Aquino opposition leader after the election.[7] People, however, spoke about the personalities and issues of the election with great emotional intensity. There was a sense of expectation. Many hoped that the election would bring effective solutions to their country's and town's problems.

The citizens of Estancia also experienced some surprisingly different election activities than those they were accustomed to. There was evidence of the beginnings of a local party machine by UNIDO, house-to-house campaigning in the town and barrio by Iloilo students and nuns, local priests delivering campaign speeches after mass, members of the town's middle class distributing anti-Marcos newspapers, and NAMFREL officials closely supervising the elections. Old elite allegiances were competing with new concerns in a deteriorating economic situation, and there were national-level conflicts between political parties

(UNIDO, PDP-Laban), played out among their newly appointed officers-in-charge (mayor and vice-mayor).

What was also clear was that the traditional patterns of voting determined by previously dependable factional two-party politics and vote-buying were breaking down. This was occurring in an economy which was seriously stagnating after almost two decades of expansive growth.

Changes in Estancia

The Economy

The municipality of Estancia, at the eastern tip of the island of Panay, Western Visayas, is economically based on middle-level fishing, farming, and marketing. The content of its social relationships changed significantly, however, through the entire twentieth century, interacting with social and economic changes in the country as a whole. These changes are reflected in the differences between the 1967 and 1986–1988 elections.

What I found on my first visit to Estancia in 1967 was a coastal, medium-sized rural municipality of some 14,000 people, quite prosperous compared with communities in its sugar-growing hinterlands. Located on the outskirts of the rich, rice-growing Iloilo plain, it was heavily dependent on fishing production and on wholesale and retail marketing activities that peaked during its two- to three-day weekly town market.[8] The town was known then as the "Alaska of the Philippines" because, thanks to its pier facilities, it had become a collection center for dried and fresh fish from the Western Visayan Sea for weekly shipments to Manila's Chinese wholesalers.[9] There were large fishing outfit owners in town, usually also landowners, with 100-plus-man crews fishing throughout the Visayan Sea and as far as Palawan. Besides fishing, the surrounding coastal and interior barrios and neighboring islands grew rice, sugar, coconuts, and vegetables. When people came to Estancia to sell their dried or fresh fish, they also shopped for their weekly needs. Thus, the town had become a commercial center for more than a 100-km radius with flourishing shops, retail and wholesale business establishments, doctors, pharmacies, and restaurants. The municipality, and especially the town proper, appeared economically prosperous at the end of the expansive 1960s, compared to the more depressed sugar-growing Eastern Iloilo municipalities such as Anilao where farmers, smallholders and sugar workers were engaged in bitter feuds with landlords and were experiencing serious economic constraints.

By 1986, Estancia had changed surprisingly little in some respects. The surrounding countryside had remained very rural, with little evidence of industrialization or significant local growth. And there were signs of economic deterioration rather than growth. There were abandoned sugar wagons sitting in uncut sugar fields in Estancia's outskirts, and the town proper had, through local mishap and ineffective leadership, lost its deep sea pier, the key to fish shipments to Manila. Despite improved facilities and newly cemented and reclaimed areas, the weekly market had not shown marked growth since 1967. It served the same surrounding region, but the number of stores and services had decreased with the decline of the Manila fish trade. There was less confidence in Estancia's potential for growth than there had been in 1967.

In the two years after Aquino came to power, Estancia began to show signs of economic rejuvenation, although it did not look markedly different.[10] By July 1988, there were new government-funded plans to further enlarge the market area, complete repairs on the pier and improve water and electrical power supplies. The fishing business had also improved. There were a number of individual economic success stories in fishing and marketing. But these success stories were purportedly those of outsiders rather then locals.[11] Bureaucrats complained ever more bitterly about low salaries, and businessmen appeared cautious about the impact of Aquino's economic policies. Landlords appeared generally disgruntled by the accelerated implementation of land reform. Farmers were unhappy about rising fertilizer and pesticide prices and low government-controlled rice prices. And food costs had not been sufficiently lowered to match stagnating salaries.

Informal conversations with townspeople from all walks of life as well as barrio folk left impressions of other changes, progressively evident since the early 1970s. From the early 1980s on, a number of houses became noticeably "modern," with cement walls and/or corrugated iron roofs. They were described as "houses built with dollars," the result of remittances from family members working in the U.S. or Saudi Arabia. The same was true in the countryside so that recent local wealth became identified with external sources of income.[12] The main pattern of social mobility in 1986, and still in 1988, was to have at least one family member working overseas rather than to engage in local entrepreneurial enterprise. With more than 50 percent of the families in town now having at least one family member abroad according to our estimates, which were confirmed by a recent survey (D. Szanton, pers. comm.), the entire town became changed by the new transnational remittance economy. Those who remained in Estancia dreamed of a similar economic boom for themselves, perhaps facilitated by the higher education of their brighter children, and by a stroke of good luck.

In 1988, there were also increased problems relating to law and order. Illegal gambling dens, some sponsored by local elite families, were flourishing, although denounced in provincial newspapers as "mafias" involving local officials.[13]

The town had been "invaded" by outsiders, transients, and "people one did not know," with informal estimates pointing to "the new faces around" representing up to 40 percent of the people one met in the streets. Streets were now considered unsafe in the evenings. There had been cases of holdups, robberies, rape and beatings, and "bad drug trips." The local police, still under the Philippine Constabulary, was understaffed, underequipped, underpaid, and thus, generally discouraged. There had also been accusations of police corruption.[14] There were some positive signs but also general concern and uneasiness in this latest stage of the town's post-World War II history.

The Electoral Scene

The main feature of politics in Estancia from 1947 to 1971 was a reasonably stable and not overly exploitative regime by a powerful local family. The "beloved Mayor," member of a fishing and landowning dynasty that had migrated from the Tagalog area a generation earlier, was raised in the town, served five terms, and was reelected three times without opposition. He was a nonpracticing medical doctor who provided free services to the needy in the barrios, and was generally seen as a benign patronal figure. His unmarried brother, who directed the fishing outfits owned by an older sister, was a violent, hard drinking brawler. The sister, a shrewd businesswoman, had married into an old landed family, the Aclaros. With her fishing business, the landed interests of her in-laws, but primarily her inherited, large island of Bayas (mostly a coconut plantation) opposite the town, she controlled a large block of votes, and could pretty much swing an election. Her brother-in-law was a businessman, who was politically and economically well-connected in the capital, Manila. So the Reyes-Aclaro family, building alliances with some of the town's sixty-six businessmen and small landowners, reigned in the town from 1947 to 1971, despite opposition by other elite town families, also in fishing and landowning.

Electoral support was one strand of the complex web of exchanges and reciprocal obligations that tied together landowners/fishing outfit operators and their workers. Townspeople carried a very conscious and vividly prevalent image of where everyone else, particularly men, were located in the system of interlocked factions (i.e., pyramidal support systems) in the community and its extensions regionally and nationally.[15] While the system of electoral factions was still going strong, other forms of association also existed, based on professional, religious and/or socioeconomic grounds (e.g., Cursillo, Lions Club, Rotary). This factional system, however, was beginning to break down in Estancia in the 1960s. Patrons were increasingly less "patronal" and were more interested in their young obtaining higher education and moving into a professional, middle class urban life. They were replaced on the farm by more anonymous, less committed, salaried overseers. The middle-aged sugar or rice landowners felt less welcome, even potentially threatened, when visiting their fields. Many in the town and the province carried firearms, "just in case."[16] Clients, on the other hand, still tried to activate their patronal support systems through personal requests or by establishing *compadrazgo* relationships but, often, they ended up by asking, in this less reciprocally responsive system, for special favors based on a broader, "right to survive" appeal, rather than the specific, preexisting, reciprocal patron-client expectations.[17]

At the same time, with eight out of ten men in the barrios of Estancia having run for election at one time or another, the electoral system functioned on both multiple and increasingly single-stranded reciprocities, with a heavy reliance on the use of "pork-barrel" funding and vote-buying. Politics was definitely a pragmatic rather than issue-based practice.

The 1967 election in Estancia was a traditional carrot-and-stick, family-dominated, factional, vote-buying affair with minor, shortlived postelection retaliations by the victorious Reyes-Aclaro family (landowners and outfit operators) against opposition families, mostly outfit operators and businessman (Appendix, A). These included the transferring of schoolhouses, a rule-book crackdown on illegal fishing, and the implementation of unpopular ordinances. Control of the electorate by the reigning faction, closely allied to Marcos, continued to be tight and without a major challenge. In the four years after the 1967 election, however, the aged mayor died of cancer, part of the pier was destroyed, and lives were lost in a docking accident. Neither repairs to the broken-down water system nor the long-promised electric system had materialized.

The 1971 election marked a rupture in local politics as a major opposition challenge was mounted against the Reyeses whose power was showing signs of slippage. There were outsiders as mayoral candidates and goons hired all around to intimidate opposing party members.

This election drained the Reyes family resources, forcing them to sell much property. Postelection retaliations ran deeper and longer than before, and the weak and inexperienced new mayor, who had been raised in Manila, had none of the patronal influence of his uncle, hated his new position and preferred to rely on his aged vice-mayor to run things. He frequently reported drunk to his office and progressively lost the respect of his electorate.[18]

By 1972, the young mayor, abetted by a family scheme to recoup the costs of a too-expensive election and to pay business loans to Chinese moneylenders, was under investigation in Manila for misadministration of the Estancia Cooperative Society, which was organized to sell lower-priced goods to its capitalizing members (i.e., 22 Estancia barrios and 205 stockholders). In fact, goods were sold at higher prices, no accounts were kept or reported to shareholders, nor were dividends returned in the face of a claimed profit of 10,000 pesos in the first year.

Impact of Martial Law on the Local Economy and the Reyes Faction

The declaration of Martial Law set in motion a whole series of intended and unintended consequences at the local level. It completely transformed for a time the town's mode of livelihood and socioeconomic relationships. And it happened at a time when the Reyeses' power was particularly weak. Thus, they were not as able, as established political families in other towns, to shelter themselves—and the town—from the political/economic effects of Martial Law and the Marcos regime through the 1970s and 1980s.

The strict implementation under Martial Law of the prohibition to use dynamite (and firearms for that matter), together with the worldwide hike in gasoline prices, revolutionized the fishing industry of the town. In less than a year's time, fishing outfits, such as the *basnig* or *largarete*, had to cope with a 400-percent increase in the cost of fuel, and a 10 to 40 percent reduction in catches. A new fishing method, the *kurantay*, was developed and became the mainstay of the town. It is done during the day rather than at night, and it uses a small pumpboat with a single-stroke engine and two to three crewmen.

Although in 1967, some twenty people in town owned the large and expensive fishing outfits (over 100 crewmen, 100,000 pesos) responsible for a large proportion of the town's fish production, and influencing its political life, there were by mid-1974 some 1,000 fishing outfit operators in the town of Estancia proper, mostly teachers, shopkeepers or smaller fishermen, rather than the large landowners of the past. This disrupted existing patron-client systems in fish production, and the whole rhythm of fishing and resting, fish drying and marketing, etc., was transformed. By the midseventies, the landowning and fishing "capitalists" in town were thinking of shifting to larger, more modern outfits, in a bid to reestablish the patterns of capital-intensive fishing boats with large crews.

It should be added that complete shifts in the fishing technology are not uncommon and already occurred before and after World War II in Estancia (1925: beginnings of *lawag* and of *basnig*, 1946: beginnings of *palopok*, 1951: beginnings of *largarete*).[19]

Martial Law also very purposefully aimed at sapping the power bases of provincial oligarchs and patrons, by centralizing power and increasing the presence of the state at the local level. The mayors lost control over the municipal police, which was placed under Philippine Constabulary commanders, often Ilokanos, now assigned to each province. The power of PC commanders—in enforcing laws, regulations and licensing, as well as the midnight curfew, in controlling people's travel and confiscating all unregistered firearms—grew over time. This was compounded in Estancia by the fact that the pre-Martial Law Chief of Police was accused of running a gambling operation and forced to resign. Though ultimately acquitted, because somebody was hired to take the blame, he could not enter the force again. So the Reyeses lost a long-standing personal connection to the police.

When Congress was dissolved by Marcos, Congressman Aldeguer's role as go-between and useful provider for the northern Iloilo provinces was abolished. The government became more anonymous and distant. Manila was now a place of bureaucracy, from the point of view of the municipal councilmen, requiring much loss of time and with fewer available personal contacts, a far cry from the often efficient responses to previous requests of help channeled before Martial Law through Congressman Aldeguer. The Municipal Council of Estancia continued to send pleas to Manila bureaucrats for help in improving the water system and the pier, for example, but to little avail until many years later. Although electricity was extended to the town as part of a nationwide program in the late seventies, further inequality resulted since only houses along the main streets and next to the electric lines (usually homes of well-to-do people) could obtain electricity at little expense, while the internal sitios of the poor had to pay much more to be reached by electrical power.

Another example of these government attempts at centralization, and their problems, was the Rice Marketing Scheme. In the late 1970s, the Marcos government, after completing the establishment of the barangay system, attempted to centralize the marketing of key commodities. The newly created National Food Authority established a Rice Marketing Scheme which aimed to offer good rice at a low price and avoid the price hikes imposed by greedy rice merchants—or at least that was the pitch. In fact, the government-subsidized Rice Marketing Scheme as adopted by the Reyeses, and placed in the hands of a Reyes cousin with a store near the marketplace, provided very poor quality rice at medium-high prices and, combined with political pressures, threatened the businesses of local rice-wholesalers. There was much fear in Estancia in the midseventies that the same system might be applied to local meat or fish marketing. Again, a potentially useful scheme was diverted and misutilized because of insufficient knowledge of local conditions and lack of appropriate monitoring from the center.

Government programs were often diverted locally for lack of personalized supervision. And centralization contributed to disrupt, purposefully or unintentionally, the systems of patron-client recipro-cal exchanges that were still operative, even though these exchanges were already manifesting significant evidence of stress in 1967 espe-cially in the case of landowners/outfit operators and their tenants, leaseholders or crews. It also deprived the patrons of the unregistered firearms they were increasingly using for protection. It was not surprising then, that in 1974 members of the town's middle class would in our informal conversations refer to Marcos as a "communist." The local middle class felt under attack and deprived of their customary tools for power, and defined the term "communism" in pragmatic rather than ideological terms.

By the early 1980s, fishing techniques in the municipality had undergone new transformations. There were reinvestments by wealth-ier landowners/fishing entrepreneurs, and a few successful shopkeep-ers and teachers, of large capital (200,000 pesos capital each for at least 25 crewmen) into baby purseines, catching mackerel at night as before. Smaller *bulbotan* (30,000 pesos, ten crewmen) and *arong* (2,000 pesos, three to four divers) became also quite popular among former fishing entrepreneurs as well as merchants and teachers.[20]

Fish production had preserved its somewhat broader base while allowing more capital-intensive productive activities. Some patron-client versions of employer-employee relationships had been rees-tablished in the fishing business by the early 1980s. They were, however, much less effectively activated during the 1986 election (and again in 1987 and 1988, as we will see) compared to the election in 1967.

By February 1986, municipal elections appeared to be much more based on policy issues than primarily on personalized patron-client relationships, relatively narrow stranded reciprocities, and ad hoc vote-buying. Landowners and outfit operators who tried to influence workers and/or clients often triggered *balimbing* or split voting in families. People bragged of not being bought. Those who allowed themselves to be bought were roundly condemned by popular opinion. Aquino seemed to inspire a very personal sense of trust in the people. The poor saw her as well-meaning; the middle class felt she was personally incorruptible, compared to Marcos. At the same time, however, some people utilized a class model in their evaluation of Aquino, with leaseholders and tenants seeing her as a wealthy landlord, and therefore unreliable on land reform matters, and landowners feeling divided allegiance toward her. All in all, there was a much more complex voting picture than twenty years earlier.

Difference in the 1986 Election

In 1986, the newly appointed officers-in-charge, Mayor Jose Mosqueda and Vice Mayor Jose de los Santos, were members of two prestigious political families that had alternately been allied and opposed to the long-time "reigning," Marcos-supporting Reyes.

The 1986 presidential vote was in keeping in some ways with the old pattern of allegiances, i.e., with the barrios and the portion of town usually opposed to the Reyes family (Paon AB, Bulaquena, Logingot, Estancia IIB to IIIA) voting more heavily for Aquino, and the part of town and barrios always completely controlled by the Reyes family (Bayas A, B, C in particular and Estancia Zones I to IIA) voting more heavily for Marcos. But the voting was close (see note 6), suggesting that people had also expressed their own wishes. Moreover, the handling of the election was noticeably different than in the past.

Townspeople expressed to me some of these differences as follows.

1. Landowners (like the appointed officer-in-charge owning land in Canoan, who had openly shown a preference for Aquino) or fish outfit operators (like one operator to whom the KBL had promised an iceplant in Paon) had not forced their tenants or fishing crew employees to vote their way. They had not picked them up to accompany them to the polls and watch them vote. Little pressure, if any, was also brought by each party either by recalling old favors

or conditioning new ones, a system of enforcement well known to voters.

The Reyes family, on the other hand, did apply strong pressure on coconut tenants, wage workers, and house renters in Bayas and Estancia, to vote for Marcos. This resulted in a split vote in some families where a wife voted the expected way, while the husband, expressing the new sense of hope generated by the opposition, voted for Aquino.

2. Monetary incentives given by the Reyes family in the marketplace failed to work as effectively as they had in the past. People spoke smilingly about the small amount given (20 pesos), which they felt showed the family's diminished economic power and was certainly not enough to influence this important vote. Many took the money and voted as they wished, completely disregarding any obligation that their acceptance of the money presupposed.

Market vendors, for example, voted predominately for Aquino, despite the Reyes family's improvements to the marketplace because they believed she represented change and an improved economy. They had also decided that the Reyes clan, no longer in full control of the police force and law enforcement, would not be able to retaliate against them for their disloyalty under a new regime.

3. Fish crewmen and farming leaseholders focused on their economic situation and overall concerns about reliance and trust. Fish crewmen in the coastal barrios expressed economic reasons for voting for Corazon Aquino, but they also openly spoke of love for Cory. They acknowledged her lack of experience, but seemed to trust her in spite of this lack:

> "What is the reason for the change? Because he (Marcos) has been in for a long time and the prices of commodities are very high. That is the reason why we should change him. Salaries are very low, while prices of commodities are very high."
>
> "Cory won—but Cory does not know the work of the politician, has no experience at all. What is the real reason? They were for Cory? They voted for love of Cory—they liked her. Families, entire families."

Agricultural workers in the interior barrios also expressed this new sense of hope and love (gugma) for Mrs. Aquino—even those who had not voted at all, too absorbed in the desperate daily effort of making a living (pangabudlay ka lang todo para makakaon): "The

day will come when she will send some people to see how the
poor live and also the farmers and what help she can give."

Farmers (leaseholders) were most concerned about the issue of
land reform and attended both KBL (Marcos) and UNIDO (Aquino)
meetings. The Aquino speakers, however, did not stress land reform, speaking more about the general concept of democracy, while
the KBL regularly emphasized Marcos's commitment to land reform.
So farmers voted predominantly for Marcos. They were now
anxiously waiting to hear Aquino air her views on the land reform
issue. They were clearly not satisfied with her position, or lack
thereof, during the election, as our conversations indicated.[21]

4. The interruption imposed by Martial Law was followed in the 1986
   election by the creation of new factional politics and the beginnings
   of a UNIDO party machine in Estancia. National level conflicts
   between UNIDO and PDP-Laban were echoed locally. It has been
   argued elsewhere in this volume that UNIDO/Laban/KBL combinations in part reproduced the pre-Martial Law Liberal/Nacionalista
   dual party system and practices.[22] Prior to Martial Law, party
   affiliations were certainly more important and more evident in presidential and congressional elections than in municipal elections. And
   there seemed a greater concern and adamancy in 1986 about the
   issues the parties stood for (democracy vs. economic cronyism) than
   in elections of the past, certainly a novel feature in Philippine
   elections.

5. There were other organizational changes in town. A NAMFREL
   (National Movement for Free Elections) group of volunteers had
   been set up to monitor the election in conjunction with the local
   Knights of Columbus. The priest of Estancia was honorary chairman of the group. It provided for an inspector and substitute as
   poll-watchers, and an inspector and substitute for the "quick-count"
   of votes. This group also prepared a checklist of voters and set up
   a Voter's Assistance Center in the elementary school.

6. The Catholic Church became quite active in this election, with the
   Estancia parish priest campaigning vigorously for Aquino. He said
   special masses for the election and urged congregants to vote for
   her. The Church saw in Aquino new hope for the resolution of the
   country's problems. The parish priest's successor, a militantly
   nationalistic young man, who exemplified the young priesthood's
   outlook, obviously planned to connect Estancia organizationally,
   and philosophically, with broader Catholic movements in the rest
   of the country.

Another group that wielded some influence on the 1986 election were the Charismatics.[23] The small (15 members at first) Pentecostal movement, had been growing, despite conflict with the old parish priest. By June 1986, it had 400 members, mostly Catholic. The new priest was preparing to offer mass for them, and many of the town's prominent people had become members. It was seen by the priest as a potential basis for structuring and organizing the Christians into communities that would mobilize town and country toward the development of Christian issues.

While there was no effective official intimidation and little vote-buying of common citizens, there had been some large-scale buying of some prominent citizens. But despite the continuation of many of the old election practices, there was plenty of evidence that new concerns and practices, both organizational and issue-based, had become part of Estancia's election behavior.

Was the 1986 Presidential Election a Fluke?

The congressional elections of May 1987 further demonstrated that old political practices in Estancia would have to meet continuing challenges from a less predictably malleable electorate. The town saw more active elite politics in the town than in the presidential elections of 1986. At stake was the recreation of personal networks and linkages to parties and national politicians by the local political families. The newly elected congressman for the Northern District of Iloilo was Tupaz, from Barotac Viejo, who, thanks to his wife's family connections, controlled many northern Iloilo municipalities (Ajuy, Enrique, Anilao, San Rafael, Barotac Nuevo), though he apparently lost in his own hometown. Sara, the base of former Congressman Aldeguer, was largely controlled by Tupaz's opponent, Salcedo, who ultimately lost after a close election. Tupaz, despite the help of the Reyeses, and especially the Ravenas, old acquaintances of his, lost in OIC-controlled Estancia by 120 votes, in a contest that generated some very heavy betting. He, however, fulfilled his preelection promises by strongly recommending Rainier Ravena as vice-mayor on the Reyeses' ticket in January 1988. It was hoped that he would also build the road from Barotac to Estancia, as promised.

The February 1988 gubernatorial election in Iloilo saw the defeat of Olive Lopez, member of an old Iloilo family, despite her PDP-Laban affiliation and strong support from four out of the five congressmen of Iloilo, and their allied mayors. According to Estancia councilmen, she had not spent enough on votes, only 28,000 pesos in Estancia, for example, while her opponent, Gringo, was much more generous, winning heavily despite the support of only one Iloilo congressman. Again betting was extensive.

Both elections appear to indicate (1) the diminished effectiveness of local patrons, mayors and congressmen, in delivering votes through patronal connections, and (2) the new importance of open-ended vote-buying in those more elite-based congressional and gubernatorial elections, only occasionally neutralized by a focus on issues.

The municipal elections, postponed from May to August to November 1987, finally took place in January 1988. In Estancia, it saw an unusual proliferation of candidates with different party affiliations: (1) a Liberal Party ticket, very comparable to pre- and Martial Law times, with Reno Aclaro as mayor, Rainier Ravena as vice-mayor, and both new and former councilmen, with Reyes backing; (2) a PDP-Laban Party with the incumbent Jose Mosqueda as mayor and a newcomer, Melina Requinto, a very successful young businesswoman, as vice-mayor, and some new councilmen; (3) a weak UNIDO Party with a businesswoman as mayor and the son of a former vice-mayor as vice-mayor; (4) an Independent Party with many old-timers, including Rolando Alpasan, the popular fishing outfit operator, as vice-mayor; (5) the incumbent Vice-Mayor Nonong de los Santos running under the PDSP-Bandila Party as lone vice-mayor (he could not convince others to run with him); (6) a skeleton Nacionalista Party; and (7) many more independent or lone party candidates (see appendix).

The fierce competition encouraged attempts to "buy" or sway candidates or voters; these were not always successful. There was, however, no use of goons and violence as in 1971, and the candidates were predominantly local residents. The votes were spread out among many. There was a reasonable showing for Reno Aclaro who, with the help of Bayas, came out second; Rainier Ravena made it as vice-mayor, though there were also strong showings for Melina Requinto, who could have won if she had received the Bayas vote. Rolando Alpasan preserved the strong support of his crewmen and fishermen but did not do so well elsewhere. Six councilmen on the Reyes ticket and two popular councilmen on the Independent Party ticket also won.

There were both new and old features to this election. The elites and politicians played games with each other even more so than usual. Party tickets attempted to steal each other's candidates, or at least to pay for their presence on a ticket (but not all of these candidates received the money promised). Candidates also proposed favors or funds to have their names carried in other party tickets but did not always succeed at the last minute.

There was extensive vote-buying, at 50 pesos a head, but often it did not bring the desired result. We were told by one retired mailman in town that he felt people were too wise now to sell their votes, they would rather vote on issues. Payments were made in a nonpersonal way, with money often left on people's tables but with no face-to-face attempts to persuade them. Consequently, many took money from one candidate and felt no compunction in voting for another.

Landlords as a rule did not pressure their tenants too hard about voting choices. They did at times ask them to vote for a certain ticket, or for certain candidates within a ticket. They did not always succeed, however, in influencing their votes. Only a few raised threats of eviction, as in the old times.

Another unusual feature of the 1988 municipal elections was a popular meeting of all council candidates who presented themselves, and in some cases their programs, to the voters about a week before the elections. The meeting, a complete innovation for Estancia, was sponsored by the Knights of Columbus on a stage in the marketplace. It glaringly revealed the inadequacies of certain candidates and the abilities and good intentions of others. Again, it suggested concern for issues and reliable personalities, rather than for factional politics and purely pragmatic exchanges of goods for votes.

The proliferation of party affiliations, six in all, did not transform itself into a dual party opposition as in the past, at least for the period covered by this study. The Liberal ticket, made up of former KBL men, won, but both Independent and PDP-Laban made substantial showings, with UNIDO and Nacionalista tickets trailing behind. Municipal elections had changed from the mechanical Liberal/Nacionalista duality of 1967 to a more complicated multiparty system potentially indicative of the future (see appendix).

Nongovernmental organizations participated, but not quite as intensely as in the 1986 presidential elections. There had been youths from Babol and Ravena campaigning in the barrios, but the new priest had not campaigned from the pulpit as in 1986. The Charismatics greatly decreased in number and had failed so far to fulfill the great promises of two years earlier. They apparently felt discouraged by the complexity of the task. The new parish priest, however, was actively promoting among his flock the Catechumenic Training recently sponsored by Rome. Grassroots organizations, such as credit unions with Swedish or US foundation funding and self-help pressure groups (KAMI, Small Fishermen Association) fighting the large fishing outfits' disruption of shallow-water fishing, were appearing in the barrios, responding to immediate needs and local concerns.

The Land Reform Office in Balasan became a real presence in the Estancia barrios, where it was promoting since mid-1987, following Corazon Aquino's wishes, a rapid completion of the Land Reform program. Farmers were quite pleased in June 1988 with Aquino's performance with regard to land reform.[24] They could now show markers on their land and Certificates of Land Transfer, although there were other sources of concern. In some areas, because of strong resistance from the landlords, there was concern about the smooth completion of the land reform process. Farmers worried about their lack of receipts from landlords for past and present payments and about the mode of payment. Farmers were also concerned about the rapid rise of prices of fertilizers and pesticides since the year before. They saw themselves squeezed between controlled rice prices and rising costs.[25]

They were often already forced to resort to borrowing advances (*alili*) from the town's moneylenders at high interest at planting season or taking secondary jobs (agricultural or fishing outfit labor, dry fish business, tricycle driving) during slack time to generate cash. As a farmer in Lonoy put it:

Formerly we like Marcos, now we like Cory. Cory looks after poor people.

But he also added:

I think formerly is a little better because we rent only; during harvest time up to planting time, we still have in store one or two sacks of palay left for us. But now life is so hard because the price of commodities has gone up . . . Also the price of chemicals has gone up.

Land reform has thus had two interesting effects on rural Estancia voters, both of which were reflected in our conversations. On the one hand, it made them feel that Aquino cared for them, that she was willing to cross the landlords who had voted for her in 1986, that her government was not allowing landlords to set the price for the land but rather establishing it for them. "She protected the poor." On the other hand, as a particularly conservative former tenant put it,

Now the land is under land reform and tenants won't have to feel ashamed or pressured to vote for their landlord.

And he also added that

the tenants' children even now cannot be pressured by their parents to vote for their landlords. They do not feel they "owe gratitude to them" and want "to exercise their own free will."

Land reform is obviously going to further affect the deteriorating rural patron-client relationships, already challenged by the changing economic conditions of the post-World War II period. It will continue to disrupt the control over voters' choices, formerly exercised by landlords and fishing outfit operators. People may still appeal to a right to survive to force their former patrons or the "rich and powerful" to help them. Candidates, in order to attract them, will be faced with indiscriminately buying votes with cash or favors (a strategy that has already proven only partially successful), forcing voters to the polls, or attempting to sway voters with ideas and policy issues (something they were attempting in 1986, 1987 and 1988).

The Significance of the 1986 Election

Many processes of change have been affecting the Visayan countryside over the last forty years, some very short-range, others with longer-term implications. Martial Law and its multiple local consequences accelerated the slow deterioration of patron-client ties already initiated by the growth of a more urban-based middle class geared to provide manpower for an incipiently industrializing country. The economic deterioration, isolation, and processes of centralization experienced by the municipality through the late Marcos period prepared it quite effectively for more class- and issue-oriented political concerns.

The liberating message of Aquino in 1986, full of hope at a time of very serious economic constraints (laborers earned 25 pesos a day and had to work three days to be able to afford a pound of chicken), was welcomed by many. But for those who had rejoiced and done well under Marcos or considered themselves still tied to the Marcos political framework, Aquino was seen as a potentially dangerous, blundering threat.

There were also problems of interpretation of her message at the rural level in 1986. In February 1986, she had strongly appealed for democracy. She and her followers, however, assumed at the time that the ideological implications of a democratic stance would be understood by the Filipino population, much as they would be by an American population, that they would know how to translate it into applied meanings, i.e., more effective people's participation in policy formulation and increased government concern for people's rights. They did not bother to give specifics about what they planned to do in such important domains as land reform or support to local entrepreneurial activity. The message tended to be general: "Democracy will make it all happen for you! Just give it a chance!" It was poured into ears that had not had the opportunity to absorb the philosophical underpinnings of democracy in their school and home lives, had not grown up with it, had not studied it in history books as part of their own histories, were not as deeply concerned as Americans with the interaction between individual achievement and the common good. What Visayan rural dwellers needed, what they could best understand, were well-focused reassurances and specific confirmations, to translate those generalities into policy issues relevant to their everyday lives. Faced with a continued lack of specifics, tenants and leaseholders still preferred in 1986 the clearly laid out promises by Marcos. The locally educated middle class also considered Aquino's "American-style politics" as not quite Filipino, while the foreign-educated middle-class could much more easily understand her message.

This problem of communication was being faced again in 1987. The constitutional emphasis on democracy translating into human rights and redistribution (late 1986 to February 1987) has been accompanied by delayed economic and political planning in key areas such as land reform. Democracy has been blamed for slowing down legislative action. But, as we have seen, there was by mid-1988 still much trust in Aquino as a well-meaning leader. Aspects of her moral legitimacy were still intact. She alienated some of the landlords but seemed to have gained for the moment the trust of the Estancia farmers, who attributed the problems of the economy and land reform to those surrounding her rather than to Aquino herself. Again in 1988, rural or poor voters saw themselves as a "we" category, jointly facing the often opposing interests of landlords and the wealthy. Cory Aquino had shifted, however, in their perception, from being a "they" to becoming an ally. She was, however, to face still greater challenges ahead.

The analysis of a series of elections as special events in an historical continuum gives us the following conclusion.

1. There are considerable differences in the way elections were practiced in Estancia from 1967 to 1988. Organizationally, recent elections showed increased numbers of parties, more central government presence, greater role of grassroots organizations, shift from goons to NAMFREL inspectors, and others. Substantively, they showed a shift from more or less multistranded and pragmatic exchanges of goods for votes to changed expectations by both patrons and clients. They have shown ultimately an increased independence of the electorate, a situation in which candidates have to sway

voters more often on the basis of policy issues, personality or performance rather than by sheer force, exchange of goods, or purchase.

2. More importantly, these contrasts have stressed an important relationship between modifications in the patron-client relationships and the political process. Processes of change in the countryside were modifying people's utilization of the old style of patron-clientship. The obligations felt by patrons toward clients had already greatly diminished by the late 1960s and clients were appealing to a more elemental right to survive to activate some of them. The obligations of clients to their patrons were further challenged by Martial Law, land reform and other economic constraints. Local candidates, especially at the municipal level, have thus generally lost control over their clients' votes and must now attract the electorate in other ways.

Policy issues are likely to continue to be an increasing part of people's assessments of their politicians or elected officials' performances. The proliferation of new parties may be here to stay. Perceptions of "we-they" will go through further modifications. But all these will take place "Filipino style"—in other words, we are likely to see, with the continued development of a transnational set of political understandings, the crystallization of modified Filipino versions of politics—democracy and communism—both more cosmopolitan and uniquely historically Filipino. I do not believe that we have gone back to the Estancia of 1967 with the election of Reno Aclaro in 1988, but we are rather graduating progressively to the political understandings of the 1990s, that will have differentially absorbed all these previous Filipino/Visayan experiences.

APPENDIX

Changes in Municipal Election Patterns in Estancia, Iloilo (1967–1988)

A. 1967 Election (1968–71) One Single Reyes Ticket/No Mayoral opposition

Name	Position	Occupation	Other Councilors for 1968–71		
			Name	Position	Occupation
Eusebio Reyes*	Mayor	Professional M.D. (deceased)	Sergio Bañes*	Councilors	Fishing outfits
Serafin Dema-isip**	Vice-Mayor	Fishing outfits/land	Antonio Alpasan*		Landowner/coconut
Pedro Morales	Councilors	Businessman/market	Marcial Aclaro*		Commerce
Julio Sitchon*		Accountant	Antonio Regalado		
Romeo de los Santos*		Landowner/fishing outfits			
Reno Aclaro*		Landowner/nephew mayor			
Cristeto Sinense		Landowner			
Pastor Cordero		Landowner/coconut			
Antonio Babol		Bank			
Democrito Bacos		Commerce/fishing outfits			

B. 1971 Election (1971–1975) — Two tickets: Reyes/Aclaro and Betita/Ravena

1971 Election — Reyes/Aclaro Ticket			1971 Election — Opposition Ticket		
Name	Position	Occupation	Name	Position	Occupation
Reno Aclaro*	Mayor	Landowner/nephew mayor	Mio Betita (Iloilo)	Mayor	Business/land/fishing
Julio Sitchon*	Vice-Mayor	Accountant/agent (deceased)	Romeo Ravena	Vice-Mayor	Fishing outfits/land
Venancio Cudilla*	Councilors	Land/transportation	Acedre Acebuque	Councilors	Fishing outfits (deceased)
Jose Matta*		Business agent	Rolando Alpasan*		Fishing outfits/land
Reynaldo Baylon*		Commerce	Sergio Bañes*		Veterinarian
Antonio Tiples*		Commerce/fishing	Alex Barba		Fishing outfits/land
Marcial Aclaro*		Landowner/coconut	Pedro Morales		Commerce/meat
Virginia Reyes*		Wife of former mayor/restaurant	Aning Corteza		Pharmacist/landowner

*Winners of election.
***Was also a winner of election; became mayor after Eusebio Reyes's death from cancer in 1968. First councilor Rene Aclaro was subsequently selected as vice-mayor.

C. Appointed Officials

1975–80

		1986–88 Appointed Officers-in-Charge		_Occupation_
Reno Aclaro	Mayor	Jose Mosqueda	Mayor	Landowner
Julio Sitchon	Vice-Mayor	Jose de los Santos	Vice-Mayor	Land/business
	16 Councilors	Jose T. Barba	Councilors	Fishing outfits
		Ruben Rivera		Commerce
		Herman Alpagan		Fishing outfits
		Rainier Ravena		Landowner
		Romeo Astronomia		Teacher
		Melina Requinto		Fishing/landowner
		Nicanor Magnifico		Teacher
		Alex Barba		Fishing outfits
		Oscar Gomes		Business
		Daniel Babol		Business

1980–85

Reno Aclaro	Mayor
Romeo Ravena	Vice-Mayor
	10 Councilors

D. 1988 Election (1988–90) — A multiparty system

PDP LABAN-LAKAS NG BANSA

Jose C. Mosqueda	Mayor
Melina C. Requinto	Vice-Mayor
Angelo Abagatnan	Councilors
Angel Alpasan, Jr.	
Jesus Andreo	
Jose Barba	
Salustiano Germentil	
Manuel Inventor	
Procopio Matta	
Porferio Castill (Withdrew)	

NACIONALISTA PARTY

Sergio A. Bañes, Sr.	Mayor
Florencio Aguilar	Councilors
Nelson Banico	
Rachel Placencia	
Manuel Tan	

PDSP-BANDILA PARTY

Jose Ma. L. de los Santos	Vice-Mayor

Continued

Appendix continued

LIBERAL PARTY

Reno R. Aclaro	Mayor	3,876 votes
Rainier B. Ravena	Vice-Mayor	2,797 votes
Donaldo Babas	Councilors	3,397 votes
Ruperto Bacos		
Alexander Barba		2,643 votes
Rene Cordero		4,160 votes
Benedicto Demapendan		2,290 votes
Cesar Leonidas, Jr.		2,307 votes
Alberto Rogador		3,354 votes
Eduardo Sulayao, Sr.		

INDEPENDENT PARTY

Venancio R. Cudilla, Jr.	Mayor	
Rolando B. Alpasan	Vice-Mayor	
Procopio Bano, Sr.	Councilors	
Reynaldo Baylon		2,792 votes
Heliodoro Buaron		
Ricardo Trance		
Adriano Crisme		
Edgardo Ventura		
Samson Divinagracia, Jr.		
Jose Ferrer		
Adriano Tiples, Jr.		3,696 votes
Vicente Ulla		

UNIDO PARTY

Mita D. Morales	Mayor
Julio V. Sitchon, Jr.	Vice-Mayor
Enrique Alunday	Councilors
Ruel Baballo	
Crisol Bellido	
Antonio Bermudez	
Pedrito Bucane	
Vanny de la Cruz (Withdrew)	
Manuel Mendia	
Carlito Roche	

ADDITIONAL CANDIDATES

Alessandro S. Babol	Mayor (Independent Party)
Danilo O. Montero	
Wilfredo Y. Tee	

PDP-LAKAS NG BANSA

Virgilio P. Paciente

NACIONALISTA PARTY

Alejandro Malata
Genaro S. Punay

UNIDO PARTY

Armando Anala
Celina Bullos

ALFRED W. McCOY

The Restoration of Planter Power in La Carlota City

The January 1988 local elections were the final step in the restoration of planter power in the Philippine province of Negros Occidental. Although the province's resilient sugar planters had survived three empires and two republics during their century-long history, they finally seemed threatened with extinction in the last years of the Marcos regime. For over a decade, the dictatorship had plundered the country's sugar industry, extracting its surplus through institutional corruption and confiscatory decrees. Compounding this crisis, the world sugar market crashed twice (1976–79 and 1983–86) to prices far below the Philippine cost of production. By 1985, planters had cut cane cultivation sharply, producing massive unemployment and near–universal infant malnutrition in this monocrop province.

As planter social controls withered, legal protest marches swelled to unprecedented proportions and the region's communist guerrilla force quickly grew into one of the archipelago's largest. Impoverished and powerless, dissident planters were forced into an uncomfortable alliance with the lower class protest movement to force concessions from the Marcos regime. Moreover, after three centuries as a profitable global commodity, cane sugar seemed to be approaching a long–term decline in product demand. During the early 1980s, the U.S. bottlers of Pepsi and Coca-Cola, the world's largest sugar consumers, began sweetening their soft drinks with a corn extract called "super-fructose," slashing demand in the Philippines's main market. Even the fall of the Marcos regime threatened the planters. When President Corazon Aquino proclaimed that "the sugar industry is finished" during her first official visit to Negros in October 1986, it seemed a death sentence for both sugar and sugar planters.[1]

Within a year, however, the Negros sugar planters had regained much of their power. Abolition of the Marcos trading monopoly, combined with successful diversification and a rise in the world sugar price, brought the province back from the brink of economic collapse. Instead of basic reform, President Aquino's political program aspired to a systematic restoration of the status quo ante martial law. Through congressional and local elections, Negros planters recaptured much of the autonomy lost during the Marcos years. Only a few months after the February Revolution, the Aquino administration doubled the combat forces on Negros and assigned competent commanders who soon seized the initiative from the New People's Army (NPA).

In studying such a commercialized society, we must be careful to avoid the model of localized social equilibrium that is often used in analyses of the Philippines. In particular, much of Western writing often describes Philippine politics in terms of patron-client ties, a pattern of reciprocal exchange between superiors and inferiors that maintains society in a state of equilibrium. Defined by Lynch, refined by Lande, and modified by Machado, this analysis excludes considerations of coercion and exploitation in favor of an imagined symbiosis between landlords and tenants or between mill owners and laborers.[2] Even Kerkvliet's study of the Huk peasant revolt explained violence as a consequence of the collapse of clientelism, not as an essential and enduring element of Philippine rural politics.[3] Indeed, Kerkvliet argues that the "patron-client relationship . . . was based not on compulsion or force but on reciprocity. . . . In order to get what the other had, landowners and villagers each had to give something that was considered fair. Hence, theirs was a symbiotic relationship."[4] This vision of Philippine villages and towns operating through such social reciprocity is not appropriate for Negros Occidental with its century-long history of sectoral conflict and systemic violence.

To understand Negros, we must consider the regional, national and international factors that have impinged upon its local politics. Since Negros Occidental generally produces over 60 percent of the Philippines' sugar crop, long the country's leading export, the province's collective fortunes are tied to the world market, bilateral relations with the United States, and national economic policy. The planters must combine local political control with national economic influence. Yet the province, as home to 2.3 million people scattered across thirty-two cities and towns, is too large and complex for a carefully nuanced study. At the same time, the boundary between the local and provincial is plastic, requiring discussion of both in order to grasp the dynamics of the transition from Marcos to Aquino in Negros Occidental.

Perhaps the best way to balance the complexities of national, provincial, and local interactions is to focus on a single municipality— while taking care to place events in their wider contexts. As the hacienda enters an agonizing transformation from community to agribusiness, Negros municipalities have acquired increased political importance. Worker ties to their plantations attenuate as they become wage laborers forced into the nearby towns in search of work and shelter. In this transition period, the hacienda is losing coherence as a community and the municipality is in the process of gaining it. Moreover, the nation-state, although influential in Negros Occidental, still remains distant in Manila, allowing many of its institutions to retain a strong provincial identity and a de facto autonomy of action. In this context, La Carlota City, a sugar town in central Negros, seems an appropriate case for a closer study of the politics of transition.

As an observable political entity, La Carlota only exists during elections. For it is only then that all the externals who hold the city's power actually exercise it. After fifteen years of periodic research and residence in La Carlota, a sense of the city's political dynamic had eluded me. While mill and plantation were constantly animated by production and industrial conflict, I found City Hall, by contrast, almost moribund. Offices were overstaffed with clerks being rewarded for support in the last elections, but there was little administrative product. I went through the files and interviewed ageing politicians but failed to define any coherence that made La Carlota City a meaningful unit of political analysis.

Then, in January 1988, I returned for the local elections to discover an intensity of political conflict that contrasted markedly with the normal administrative lethargy. The absentee politicians arrived from the capital in armed convoys; the commander of Task Force Sugarland descended in a helicopter gunship; and leaders of the militant sugar workers union came by jeepney from the head office in the capital to campaign. And as soon as the electoral trends firmed from the precincts, they left again to transmit their orders by radio and memo. During these few days of formal electoral politics, all of the broader political tensions within the City's sugar society emerged with striking clarity.

The Setting

Extending for some 16 miles from the flatlands of the Negros plain up the steep slopes of Mt. Kanlaon volcano, La Carlota City is, by history and geography, a sugar town. As peasant pioneers and planters cleared the virgin forests in the late nineteenth century, the Spanish regime established La Carlota as an inland municipality. There is no coastal fishing, little lowland rice, and no remaining forest. Even within

Negros Occidental's monocrop economy, La Carlota's dedication to sugar is extreme. In 1971, for example, 80 percent of the city's 6,364 arable hectares were planted to sugar.[5]

The landscape hints at the broad contours of La Carlota's political economy. Instead of the nestled, manicured look of peasant farms in Iloilo or Ilocos Norte, La Carlota has open, sweeping vistas sculpted by the imperatives of tropical agribusiness. Just before harvest in the boom year of 1975, I climbed the brick smokestack of an old Spanish mill to see an unbroken, silvery green carpet of cane leaves spreading from the coast across the rolling plains to sweep up the broad, denuded flanks of Mt. Kanlaon on the horizon. The landscape was surprisingly empty for a municipality with a population of 55,000.

The hacienda punctuates the landscape and defines the structure of La Carlota's society and politics. This unique plantation system imposes an inequitable social system with a marked contrast in life-styles between planter and workers. While the larger planters live in elegant mansions in Bacolod and Manila, the typical two-room worker cottages are nearly bare—a few cooking utensils, a change of clothes, and two or three pieces of furniture. Like other Negros planters, La Carlota's *hacenderos* are remarkably mobile—radioing instructions to their *encargado* managers as they shuttle between homes in Manila and Bacolod, or appearing for brief inspections in their chauffeured vehicles. By contrast, permanent workers are relatively uneducated and immobile, often living out their lives in a single hacienda where they work during the six-month season and "stand-by" during the dead time between harvests.

The town center confirms this stark social contrast. Although La Carlota has been one of the Philippines' richest municipalities for over a century, there is remarkably little material evidence of its prosperity. Unlike Silay City to the north with its blocks of imposing planter mansions, La Carlota's more modest town houses are home to the city's middle class of small planters, technicians, and local merchants. Built during the sugar boom of the 1930s, the grand city hall has the space to highlight its emptiness. Like planters on the surrounding haciendas, the mayor and his senior officers are often absentee officials, holding the office but not present to exercise power which, in any case, lies elsewhere.

Nearby on the same broad plaza, La Carlota's Catholic Church, a massive nineteenth century masonry structure, has played a variable role in the town's politics. A bastion of planter power until 1986, the Church has now become the main center of working class mobilization. Fifteen minutes drive from the plaza lies Central Azucarera de La Carlota (or Central La Carlota), the second largest sugar mill in

Negros and the city's largest employer. Although the Central has enormous influence, its management only intervenes in local politics to protect its interests—for example, to ask the City's police to break militant unions.

From the outset, La Carlota's politics were shaped by the clearing of the plantation frontier. Instead of a mythic past of village amity, social relations in La Carlota were marked, *ab initio,* by systemic violence and conflict. Although some planters may have cleared unoccupied lands, several expropriated vast tracts from peasant pioneers through a combination of fraud, corruption, and violence. During the 1870s, for example, a Spanish colonial investigation found that Teodoro Benedicto, ancestor of Marcos's sugar crony Roberto S. Benedicto, had expropriated 11,200 hectares in the La Carlota area by bribing the local mayor and employing gangs of armed men to burn out the small farmers who had cleared the land a decade or more before.[6]

By the time La Carlota's landscape had been cleared in the 1880s, its plantations had a distinctive character that would survive, in some form, for another century. Unlike the patrimonial haciendas elsewhere in Negros, La Carlota had commercial plantations run, almost from the outset, as agribusinesses. Although there were individual Spanish haciendas elsewhere in Negros, La Carlota alone had a large community of resident Spanish planters and managers, *peninsulares* not *mestizos,* whose descendants owned large farms until the 1970s. While Filipino planters settled in towns such as Silay and Bacolod, La Carlota's remained absentee investors, thereby creating a pattern of family-corporate farming and preserving the city's large plantations. While inheritance has fragmented much of north Negros into fifty-hectare blocks, La Carlota still has farms, often family corporations, with areas undiminished since the nineteenth century. In 1986, for example, Eduardo Cojuangco owned about 2,145 hectares in the La Carlota Mill District, while Roberto Benedicto had 1,214 ha.[7] Although there has been a marked decline in the average cane area per planter during the first half century of Central La Carlota's records—from 186 hectares in 1925 to 154 hectares in 1950, and 64 hectares in 1975—the survival of family-corporate farming still allows large planters to maintain their influence over City politics.[8]

In the past 100 years, La Carlota has been a cockpit of social conflict. In 1896, a local sugar worker known popularly as Papa Isio launched a peasant revolt on the slopes of Mt. Kanlaon that continued until 1907. In 1926, "Emperor" Florencio Intrencherado's mass messianic uprising seized La Carlota municipal hall for a day and killed the local police chief. Between 1931 and 1950, the region's first modern labor union, the Federacion Obrera de Filipinas, launched four strikes at

Central La Carlota. Once independent unions reemerged after the anticommunist repression of the 1950s, La Carlota again became a center of union agitation. The province's leading labor union, the National Federation of Sugarcane Workers, organized its first plantations in the La Carlota district in 1971 and launched its most militant strike at Central La Carlota a decade later.

Even in La Carlota, however, such resistance is episodic. During the long sugar booms of 1909–41 and 1948–75, many workers identified with their haciendas, which remained, until the 1970s, akin to a comprehensive life support system. On the more beneficent plantations, workers received free housing, light, water, rice loans, and medical care. During the periodic troughs in the world sugar market, planters have reduced wages, hours and benefits—often with disastrous consequences for their dependent workers. In such an extreme monocrop economy, workers have no source for survival outside the haciendas. Without plantation wages, workers often face hunger if not starvation. Thus, worker consciousness shows mercurial swings from craven submissiveness to militant, violent resistance.

From clearing the island's forests in the 1860s, Negros plantation labor remained in short supply until the sugar slump of the 1930s. Since then, through a long-term natural increase in population and a 40 percent reduction in the U.S. sugar quota in 1934, there has been a constant labor surplus. Exploiting this glutted labor market, planters have used a mix of market pressure and coercion to impose a steady reduction in wages and benefits to levels that were, by the late 1970s, below a healthy caloric minimum.

Within the Philippines, La Carlota's social system is thus doubly distinct. Negros is the only Philippine sugar region with large administered plantations. And in Negros, La Carlota has achieved the most advanced form of corporate sugar farming. In such an intensely commercialized society, we must be guarded in our use of patron-client analysis. Even in the most patriarchal of plantations, planters and workers appear to deal with each other through class-based organizations—labor union versus planter association. Although a few La Carlota planters do engage in personalized reciprocal relations, most maintain too great a physical and social distance for such direct contact. Even when planters and their workers interact through vertical ties, it appears to involve the limited exchange of specific planter patronage for short-term political support, not an ongoing patron-client bond.

Over the past century, the planters have dominated La Carlota's politics to secure the essentials of export cane sugar production—land, labor, capital, and market. At the outset in the 1870s, capital came from apolitical foreign merchant houses—British, American, and Spanish. Thus, planters, Spanish and Filipino, used their influence with the colonial state to secure low-cost land and adequate labor. Anxious for development, the Spanish regime cooperated by legitimating land expropriation and using its constabulary to control labor. Later, between 1903 and 1916, the U.S. colonial state enacted laws that extended the planters' political range beyond Bacolod to Manila and Washington, D.C. In 1916, the U.S. Congress created an autonomous Philippine legislature which the planters soon used as their base within the emerging Philippine State to lobby for new essentials—access to the U.S. market, liberal loans from the Philippine National Bank (PNB), exemption of sugar from land reform, and repressive labor legislation.

Given the planters' national and international perspective, we must ask why they would bother with municipal politics. Indeed, for most of the past century, La Carlota's planters have remained aloof from local politics, concentrating their resources instead on provincial and congressional elections. Although the municipality's role in local land titling commanded the planters' attention in the late nineteenth century, its more limited role under U.S. colonial administration had little to offer. After independence in 1946, mayors were given greater control over police and the local budget. But it was not until La Carlota won an autonomous city charter in 1965 that the planters began to play an active role in municipal politics as candidates and campaign managers.

Mass Politics Prior to Martial Law

Whether causal or coincidental, the emergence of mass politics in La Carlota followed the construction of Central Azucarera de La Carlota in 1917. As modern, well-capitalized processing mills, the centrals created an independent wage labor force in the heart of the province's sugar districts, breaking the uniform oppression of the closed plantations. Most importantly for the province's political history, the construction of the mills allowed the emergence of a populist politics. Through a subtle and almost imperceptible process, the modernization of milling gradually imposed a rationalization of work practices in related areas, notably plantation and waterfront. Increased production and profit gradually facilitated capital accumulation for mechanization of the plantations and a consequent reduction in labor demand.

A few statistics illustrate the scale of change. In the La Carlota milling district, which covered three towns at the base of Mt. Kanlaon, a 12-million-peso factory replaced 55 hacienda muscovado mills worth only 8,000 to 97,000 pesos each.[9] The new milling technology permitted a rate of capital accumulation extraordinarily high by Philippine standards. In 1925, for example, Hacienda San Jose, the largest in La Carlota, retained 1,097 metric tons of raw sugar after milling its crop at the new Central. As its 55 percent share from milling the cane of the district's 124 haciendas, the Central retained 22,777 tons of raw sugar. Eight years later, Hacienda San Jose's production had risen by 73 percent to 1,903 tons while the Central's had risen by 248 percent to 79,168 tons.[10]

As economic pressure upon workers increased, improved communications also introduced radical ideas of working class brotherhoods and unions to the once-isolated sugar districts. The Central linked every hacienda with a 147 kilometer grid of narrow-gauge railways, breaking down the isolation of the planter regime and facilitating the entry of people and ideas into the plantations. Moreover, the mills split the once homogeneous *hacendero* class into planters and millers, locking them into an intense, thirty-year conflict over the sharing ratio of milled sugar. In the interstices between elite factions, workers could now find, on occasion, the social space for quasiindependent mobilization.

The subsequent spread of the province's first trade union, the Federacion Obrera de Filipinas (FOF), directed worker resistance toward electoral and industrial goals. As the mills passed the cost of the Depression on to their workers, FOF launched a general sugar strike in 1931 against five Negros Centrals and their waterfronts. When strikers closed Central La Carlota, management appealed to the district planters for scabs to break the strike. Still battling the mills over sugar sharing ratios, the La Carlota planters, like those elsewhere in Negros, refused to support the centrals.[11] In the end, the mills won through State intervention when the Negros Governor called in Constabulary troopers to break the strike at bayonet point. In the 1931 elections, FOF campaigned for the planters' candidate, Isaac Lacson, who scored a major upset over the incumbent governor, then identified with the mills.[12] In his campaign speeches, Lacson had promised that planters would award their workers 10 percent of any increase in share of milled sugar won from the mills—clear indication of a planter-worker alliance.[13] For the first time, an independent mass organization had played a significant role in provincial politics. For the next twenty years, FOF played upon the fissures in Negros society to maintain an industrial presence and influence the outcome of elections by allying with one or another of the competing political factions in the province.

But in the early 1950s, planters combined political maneuvering and coercion to break the FOF, depriving the workers of an advocate in La Carlota. For the next twenty years, the four unions that succeeded the FOF were, to varying degrees, corrupt and company-dominated.

While the new Republic's leaders proved intolerant of leftist unions, they did allow, if only by default, a greater authority for municipalities and their mayors. The colonial state had used its arbitrary authority to restrain the excesses of local power brokers, but the weaker Republic fostered a de facto provincial and local autonomy. In Negros under Gov. Rafael Lacson's warlord regime of the early 1950s, the municipal mayors and their police became his main political base. Hostile toward any opponent, he directed his most extreme violence at opposition mayoral candidates.

In La Carlota itself, Mayor Democrito Canlas was a consistent winner. If nothing else, his string of five unbroken electoral victories from 1937 to 1957 indicates that he was, by character and background, suited to this new style of politics. A medium-sized landowner, Canlas allied with Gov. Lacson in the late 1940s and, like all Negros mayors, acquired extraordinary authority. To prevent Huk communist penetration, Gov. Lacson required that all workers leaving their towns carry a pass from their municipal mayor—an edict that gave officials direct control over local lives. Working with the Special Police, Canlas formed his own union and won an exclusive bargaining contract for the Central's work force.[14] Although aligned with Gov. Lacson and his SP, Canlas was strong enough to maintain a certain independence. When the Governor's SP wanted to parade through La Carlota with the mangled corpse of Moises Padilla, opposition mayoral candidate from nearby Magallon, Canlas refused them entry.

In 1959, Canlas finally lost office to arch-rival Jaime Marino, his predecessor as mayor in the 1930s. A small planter with 37 hectares of sugarcane and son of a former mayor from the 1920s, Marino, an aristocratic and eccentric man, won congressional and local approval to upgrade La Carlota from municipal to city status in 1964, a change that greatly increased its budget and fiscal autonomy.[15] The changed charter, combined with some militant worker strikes, finally encouraged the candidacy of a leading planter. Backed by the Canlas machine, planter Luis Jalandoni, Jr. defeated Marino for mayor in 1967. Reelected in 1971, Jalandoni, like most incumbents, had his tenure extended without election for another decade when Marcos declared Martial Law in 1972.

Jalandoni's victory involved the leading planters directly in municipal politics for the first time and, thus, represented a major change in La Carlota politics. As a member of an important planter family, Mayor Jalandoni lived in Bacolod and visited La Carlota only occasionally to supervise Hacienda Cristina, 130 hectares of prime sugar land close to the town center. During his decade as the city's Martial Law administrator, he was an absentee mayor just as he had been an absentee landlord. He conducted most City business by two-way radio from Bacolod and relied upon his nephew, Roberto "Bob" Cuenca, leader of the Asociacion de Agricultores de La Carlota y Pontevedra, the district planters association, to manage his political affairs.[16]

While Jalandoni seemed an almost diffident patron in the manner of the prewar generation, his nephew Cuenca typified the younger planters who regarded labor as a commodity and violence as a political essential. Although he never ran for local office, Cuenca would dominate the La Carlota's politics for the next twenty years— marshalling money and arms to elect surrogates as mayor, first his uncle and then his brother-in-law, and to deliver the City's votes to regional and national patrons.

Martial Law

Although Marcos styled his Martial Law dictatorship as "a revolution from the center," Negros Occidental was one of the few provinces where he actually carried out his promise of antioligarchic reforms. In the months before Martial Law, Marcos had fought a bitter, humiliating public battle against the powerful Lopez brothers, leaders of the Negros sugar bloc and his chief political patrons. In an apparent effort to break the Lopez political base, Marcos used Martial Law to restrain planter autonomy and plunder their assets. Always wary of Negros, Marcos turned the province over to his college classmate and closest crony, Roberto S. Benedicto, a native Negrense who had sided with Marcos during the Lopez split.

Under Martial Law, Mayor Jalandoni's administration distinguished itself by its loyalty to two masters—the Marcos regime and, after 1975, its regional plenipotentiary, Ambassador Roberto S. Benedicto. When Mrs. Imelda R. Marcos advocated "dendro-thermal energy" (i.e., wood-fired generators) to replace petroleum during the 1973 oil crisis, La Carlota became the "City of Ipil-ipil."[17] Responding to Madame's directive, Mayor Jalandoni organized the planting of over three million of these fast growing trees. His faction joined the ruling Kilusang Bagong Lipunan Party and remained, unlike most Negros planters, loyal to the end.

In allying with Marcos and Benedicto, Mayor Jalandoni recognized that the power equation between State and province suddenly reversed with the declaration of Martial Law. No longer dependent upon regional power holders for blocs of votes, Marcos could now impose central State authority upon all the provinces. Most importantly, Marcos abolished the de facto local autonomy that had evolved under the Republic by disarming private armies and placing town police under Constabulary control. With the closure of Congress, Negros Occidental, and its sugar bloc in particular, suddenly lost the national fulcrum that had enabled planters to force export quotas and agricultural credit from the national government. By transforming both quotas and credit from prizes of provincial power into instruments of central control, Marcos soon held a whip hand over Negros Occidental.

Marcos, however, could not afford to demolish the old structures of elite power because he lacked a military or civil bureaucracy of sufficient strength to control the provinces directly. Rather than eliminating local warlords altogether, in several regions Marcos subordinated them to regional authorities, drawn from his kin and cronies, who used a monopoly over a particular crop or product to control their assigned region. In the case of Negros Occidental, Roberto S. Benedicto, a local planter and Marcos intimate, became "sugar czar" and KBL Party chief for Region VI, the five provinces of the Western Visayas. Aside from his enormous economic power, Benedicto controlled the appointment of all government officials in Negros—municipal, judicial, and military. Now subordinated to Benedicto, the preMartial Law power men continued to control their Negros territories—Armando Gustilo in the north, the Montelibanos in the center, and, more loosely, the Gatuslaos in the south.

In La Carlota City, the structure of power was more fluid than this model of Martial Law politics might imply. In stereotypic north Negros, warlord Gustilo, also president of the National Federation of Sugarcane Planters, preserved his private army and handpicked his zone's half-dozen mayors. Only nominally allied with Benedicto, Gustilo maneuvered constantly to expand his de facto autonomy, finally replacing Benedicto as national sugar crony in 1985. Although the Montelibanos preserved their power in the area immediately surrounding the provincial capital of Bacolod, their influence over La Carlota waned with the abolition of the Second Congressional District that had joined the two cities. After 1975, moreover, Marcos's two most powerful cronies, Roberto Benedicto and Eduardo Cojuangco, Jr., purchased extensive plantations in the La Carlota district, many Spanish-owned, eclipsing the Elizaldes and reducing the authority of the city's political elite. Although both had local connections, Benedicto by birth and Cojuangco by marriage, their presence in La Carlota was clearly a product of State resources beyond the reach of even the wealthiest local planter. By 1985, Cojuangco owned 2,145 hectares and Benedicto 1,214 hectares in the La Carlota milling district—dwarfing local planters Bob Cuenca with 311 hectares, Mayor Jalandoni at 92 hectares, and ex-mayor Jaime Marino with 36 hectares.[18]

Faced with this formidable presence, Bob Cuenca, La Carlota's leading planter-politician, adjusted his alliances. Although once close to the Montelibanos when they led the sugar bloc, after Martial Law Cuenca first aligned himself with Benedicto and then shifted toward Cojuangco in 1985 as Benedicto's influence waned.[19] The Cuenca group prospered from their alliance with Benedicto. While other Negros planters suffered costly delays, Benedicto's Philsucom sugar monopoly paid the La Carlota planters promptly.[20] So favored, La Carlota's leaders opposed the Negros planter revolt against Benedicto that began in 1981.

Under Benedicto's patronage, the Cuenca machine strengthened its hold on La Carlota. Its mayoralty candidate, the incumbent Jalandoni, crushed long-time politician Jaime Marino in the 1980 local elections, getting 13,513 votes to Marino's 2,025. In May 1979, a fire had swept the City's commercial district, destroying the City's electoral rolls. On election eve seven months later, the local electoral office suddenly reconstituted the roll by asking barrio captains, all loyal to Mayor Jalandoni, to list eligible voters in their areas. Evidently, the master list excluded several thousand opposition voters and multiple-listed planter loyalists in two or three different barrios. In the words of Supreme Court Justice Claudio Teehankee, the new electoral roll caused "chaos and confusion on election day with thousands of flying voters having been allowed to vote while thousands . . . were allegedly unable to vote for having been excluded from the list."[21] In his petition to the Supreme Court, defeated candidate Marino claimed that Mayor Jalandoni's men "took advantage of this situation by hauling flying voters, trucks by trucks, into the voting centers, and thru the connivance of the Chairman and poll clerks, said flying voters in thousands of them were allowed to vote." When Marino's protest finally reached the Supreme Court five years later, Chief Justice Fernando ruled that "there was clearly a lack of regularity in preparing the list of voters" but dismissed the complaint on the grounds that time must have remedied the situation.[22]

Such political control facilitated the planter attempt to shed surplus labor from their haciendas. During the episodic sugar crises of the late 1970s, Negros planters realized that their cost of production at 5.5 cents per pound was more than twice the 2.5 cents for efficient producers like Australia.[23] Initially, Negros planters tried to cut costs and improve yield by purchasing heavy tractors for deep plowing and tilling. In 1974, the sugar planters transformed a World Bank credit scheme for medium-sized farmers into a tractor purchase scheme for large haciendas.[24] In 1974–75, the World Bank thus provided the sugar industry a subsidized tractor capital of 180.2 million pesos, a figure that compares favorably with 724 million pesos for all government crop finance in the same period.[25] Continuing until 1980, the World Bank's massive support for tractor credit helped eliminate water buffalo and plowmen from the cane fields of La Carlota's large plantations.

"Mechanization is the solution to rising labor costs," proclaimed Philippine Sugar Commission (Philsucom) Chairman Benedicto in a 1980 television interview. "I know because I have fully mechanized three of our farms and we found our cost has gone down . . . We have of course the mechanization of the Hodge System which we will demonstrate soon in the pilot farms."[26] On Benedicto's orders in 1978–79, the Philsucom experimental station in La Carlota ran trials of mechanical harvesting on his own Hacienda Carmenchica in nearby Pontevedra.[27] Once world prices revived in 1980, Negros delegations, encouraged by Benedicto, toured the Queensland cane districts and returned convinced that mechanization of field cultivation was the solution to their historic inefficiency. By October 1981, nine La Carlota haciendas, led by Elizalde, had imported Hodge implements from Australia for lands totalling 1,542 hectares.[28] Initial experiments at Elizalde's Hacienda Esperanza indicated that Hodge mechanized farming could cut costs by eliminating 90 percent of labor demand.[29] As local machine shops copied implements for a fraction of import cost, Philsucom predicted that most farms over 50 hectares would soon mechanize.[30] With 77.7 percent of its sugar area in blocks larger than 50 hectares, La Carlota had far greater potential for massive labor displacement than some other districts.[31]

In anticipation of labor displacement, leading La Carlota planters began evicting workers from their haciendas. Throughout a decade of acquisitions that amassed about 10 percent of the district's sugar land, Cojuangco required mass eviction of all workers as a condition of purchase. Similarly, Benedicto evicted all residents from the Elizalde farms he purchased in 1983–84.[32] By 1982, mechanization had already eliminated 50 percent of labor on his 370-hectare Hacienda Carmenchica and promised to displace as much as 90 percent.[33] Thus, by 1981, mechanization had begun reducing employment in a district with a serious labor surplus.[34] When the world sugar crisis struck Negros with the force of a typhoon in 1983, La Carlota's workers were already suffering from widespread unemployment and malnutrition.

The Workers' Challenge

As hacienda benefits, patronage, and work withered in the 1980s, workers turned to peer organizations for support. Behind the spectacle of banners and 100,000 strong rallies lay long-term social changes that threatened planter hegemony.

For both the clergy inspired by Vatican II and lay activists animated by the nationalist ferment of the 1970s, the province's dehumanizing poverty and declining living standards demanded social transformation. Under the leadership of the liberal Bishop Antonio Fortich, activist clergy encouraged Basic Christian Communities (BCC) dedicated to empowering the impoverished and organized the province's militant union, the National Federation of Sugar Workers (NFSW), which grew steadily during the 1980s. Moreover, the New People's Army (NPA) guerrillas, led by two former diocesan priests, expanded rapidly in the uplands of southern Negros during the early 1980s.

The first sign of this ferment came at Central La Carlota in 1982 when the NFSW launched a three-month strike that pitted the Catholic Church and union against La Carlota's mill and planters. With 5,000 members in La Carlota and 40,000 in Negros, NFSW represented a major political challenge to both planter dominion and the Marcos regime's policy of cheap-labor exports. Influenced by the self-awareness seminars the NFSW had sponsored since its founding in the City ten years earlier, the Central's workers seemed to have embraced the union as a vehicle for personal and social transformation. Launched in late January 1982 to restore real wages, the strike dragged on until early May when both union funds and worker resistance were exhausted.[35] Although beaten, gassed, and threatened at gunpoint, over 600 strikers, the great majority of Central workers, maintained a picket that blocked entry of cane trucks for almost three months. In the end, it required the combined resources of mill, planters, City, and military to break their determination.

Although not directly affected, Bob Cuenca and his planters committed their resources to breaking the strike. For three years, PAFLU union leader Jose Liansing, City vice-mayor and Cuenca ally, had resisted NFSW's claim for a bargaining agreement at the Central on grounds that his union represented a majority of workers.[36] Once NFSW won a bargaining contract and mounted pickets in January 1982, Cuenca, in the words of one Elizalde employee, "collected armed men from the planters and . . . smuggled them into the Central by the back road." Afraid that "the NFSW would spread to their haciendas," the planters also "recruited scabs from their haciendas to work the mill."[37] As the strike entered its second month, Mrs. Cuenca led a delegation of planters' wives that approached the strikers with food, pleading, without success, for the processing of "their unmilled canes in the farms."[38]

After six weeks of low-level violence, the Central finally smashed the strike with a major military operation on March 14. On the eve of the exercise, Mayor Jalandoni appeared before the pickets for the first time and demanded their dispersal. "If you go on stopping the cane trucks and scabs from entering the Central, many people are affected," he said. "Even other nations are affected. So please let them in. I understand what it means to stop the Central. I am also a haciendero."[39] At dawn the next day, 600 strikers and their families faced 500 soldiers and 300 armed goons and security guards. Confronted with such overwhelming force, the strikers withdrew, allowing cane trucks to enter the mill. Although the pickets continued for another six weeks, security forces, supported by Army troops, now kept the mill open.[40]

An emerging political struggle over mechanization and unionization suddenly disaggregated when Negros plunged into the worst economic crisis in its modern history. After two years of good sugar prices that peaked at U.S. 45 cents per pound in 1980, the world price crashed to historic lows below 7 cents in late 1983 and 3 cents in 1986. In Negros Occidental, sugar production dropped by nearly 50 percent from 1.2 million tons in 1982 to 625,000 in 1986.[41] Similarly, in the La Carlota mill district, gross tons of cane ground dropped from 1.4 million tons in 1980–81 to only 760,500 tons in 1985–86.[42]

The impact of the protracted crisis on the sugar workers was devastating. Negros planters abandoned an estimated 25 percent of their lands and paid reduced wages on those that remained in production.[43] Even before the crisis, a 1983 survey of 155,000 Negros Occidental schoolchildren found 29.8 percent seriously or moderately underweight, compared to a national average of 22.2 percent.[44] As the crisis deepened, Bacolod Provincial Hospital opened a special Mal-Ward filled with extreme and often fatal malnutrition cases. By early 1986, UNICEF calculated that there were 142,000 children with second degree malnutrition among the province's total population of 2.1 million.[45]

As an extreme monocrop zone, La Carlota suffered a similar rate of hunger. In May 1985, an *Asiaweek* correspondent surveyed plantations in Barrio La Granja, La Carlota—finding most families eating rice once every two days, an emaciated nine-month infant being fed on boiled rice water, and a worker's family surviving on field frogs.[46] After the sugar price collapsed, so many planters in the upland La Castellana zone abandoned their lands that the Central was forced to curtail rail service on several lines.[47]

While hunger spread, the Negros working class mobilized as never before. On 10 December 1984, Human Rights Day, for example, the Church and NFSW sponsored a five-day Lakbayan procession from the island's north and south that brought 80,000 people to Bacolod's plaza.[48] Since its rival union NACUSIP was compromised by its alliance with Benedicto, the personification of management, NFSW grew rapidly from 47,000 Negros members in 1984 to 70,000 three years later.[49]

La Carlota's planters responded to the crisis with efforts so limited in scope that they are best called cosmetic. In February 1985, Mayor Jalandoni and Bob Cuenca, president of the Asociacion de Agricultores, imposed a production tax on La Carlota's planters to establish the Buas Damlag Foundation with 2 million pesos for livelihood projects. Among La Carlota's population of 55,000, the Foundation funded only 3,262 recipients. Among the 22,284 hectares of sugar lands in the district, planters allocated just 639 for workers' emergency farm plots.[50] With such limited support from state and employers, the District's workers turned to mass organizations. As the NFSW's membership expanded, the NPA's Propaganda Organizing Teams spread from guerrilla zones on the slopes of Mt. Kanlaon into the lowland haciendas surrounding the City center.

Despite the gravity of the crisis, Benedicto's Philsucom continued its expropriation of the province's sugar profits, a policy that forced an alliance between radical workers and bankrupted planters. The planter revolt had begun in 1981 as the world sugar price surged 700 percent above its 1978 low. Benedicto, as Philsucom chairman, seemed inclined to retain the profits. Dissident planters organized in Bacolod and their leader, Mrs. Corazon Zayco, petitioned the Supreme Court for the abolition of Philsucom's sales monopoly.[51] Several days later, NACUSIP, the conservative union allied with Benedicto, published a full-page "Prayer and Thanksgiving" in the national press raising "our voices in thanksgiving for all the guidance [Y]ou have given to President Marcos and Ambassador Benedicto . . . to save the sugar industry from collapse."[52] For the next three years, the dissidents mounted a sustained critique of Philsucom that won support from industry influentials, notably Guillermo Y. Araneta, manager of Central Ma-ao and member of the milling family displaced by Benedicto twenty years before.[53]

Under Benedicto's patronage, Philsucom had banned private sugar sales and required all planters to sell to its trading monopoly at a fixed price—a policy that denied the industry, 60 percent located in Negros Occidental, of profits between 11.6 and 14.4 billion pesos from 1974 to 1983.[54] The policy meant a massive expropriation of resources and, combined with the global sugar crisis of 1983 to 1986, brought many planters to the brink of bankruptcy.

When the World Bank pressed Marcos to restore free-market sugar sales in late 1983, Benedicto maneuvered deftly to preserve Philsucom's monopoly. After dumping 300 tons of illegally imported sugar on the domestic market, he then announced that planters were free to sell their sugar at depressed local prices.[55] However, those who wished to contract Philsucom as their exclusive sales agent would, he announced several days later, receive crop loans and the right to export to the U.S. where the price was three times the world market.[56]

Several months later, in the May 1984 legislative elections, Negros planters inflicted a humiliating defeat on Benedicto. In the 1978 elections for the Interim Batasang Pambansa, Benedicto's KBL slate had captured all fifteen seats for Region VI under a system of one electorate per region. Under the revised 1984 rules of one electorate per province, Benedicto, still KBL chairman for Region VI, had to share the party's candidacies for Negros Occidental with provincial leaders—three for Gustilo, one for Montelibano, one for Gatuslao, and two for himself. Throughout Region VI, all Benedicto's candidates lost, including his cousin Teodoro Benedicto who ran in Negros. Capitalizing upon popular disaffection, the province's three supralocal leaders—Gustilo, Montelibano, and Gatuslao—had dumped Benedicto's men without hurting their own, thus breaking his power in Negros. At a postelection rally in Bacolod, the opposition burned Benedicto in effigy.[57] After the elections, Benedicto's enemies intensified their assault on Philsucom, ultimately stripping him of any real power.

Cojuangco—with 6,000 employees, 7,000 hectares of prime land and 16 million pesos per month in new Negros investments—soon replaced Benedicto as the province's leading crony capitalist. Unlike the local planters who remained wedded to sugar, Cojuangco had diversified aggressively. After evicting the workers and plowing under the cane rattoons in the late 1970s, Cojuangco had converted Hacienda Candelaria's 600 hectares into an integrated coconut-cacao farm that was a model of synergy and profit.[58] Until the EDSA revolt toppled Marcos, Cojuangco continued to court the Negros planters with his proposal to refinance the entire sugar industry in exchange for control of sugar marketing. If his bid had been successful, Cojuangco would have won a powerful horizontal monopoly over a key sector of the Philippine consumer economy—first, raw sugar; then sugar-based beverages (Coca-Cola and San Miguel Beer); and, finally, the foundation of Filipino consumerism, the corner variety (sari-sari) stores that market these products. Benedicto's forced fusion of provincial and national power had proved volatile. By contrast, Cojuangco's clever complementation of his national and local investments was making him the Philippines's first major monopoly capitalist.

In the dictator's final months, conflict between regime and opposition intensified across the country. In 1985, the Marcos regime supplied its loyalists with infantry weapons to expand their private armies, banned at the outset of Martial Law but reorganized a few years later as official militia. Known formally as Civilian Home Defense Forces (CHDF), these militia represented Marcos's attempt to restore control through a more violent repression. Concerned by the spread of the NPA and NFSW, leading Negros planters won new troop deployments and increased their own CHDF militia to a total of some 300 men—Gustilo 100, Benedicto 70, Cojuangco 59, and lesser numbers for a few planters.[59] In 1985, there was a parallel rise in human rights violations. Summary executions doubled from twenty-four in 1984 to fifty-four in 1985, while those massacred increased from nine to twenty-nine.[60] The NFSW's secretary-general noted that in 1984, six union organizers were murdered in Negros, a change in the previous pattern of simple harassment.[61]

Undeterred, the Negros opposition continued to challenge the power of the regime's planter allies. With the formation of the "cause-oriented" Bayan coalition in June 1985, opposition planters and workers formalized their alliance in a coalesced board—Romeo Guanzon, sugar planter and former Bacolod City mayor, as chairman; Fred Pfleider, planter and retired military officer, vice-chairman; and Edgardo Estacio, vice-president of the NFSW, secretary-general .[62] In retrospect, it was a remarkable coalition joining Romeo Guanzon—planter, life-long friend of warlord Gustilo and future president of the planters federation—with the most radical working class leaders in the province.

With the support of planters and labor, Bayan launched an ambitious Welgang Bayan, a three-day transport strike, in September 1985. Directed by six strike centers across the province, including one at La Carlota, Bayan's thousands of demonstrators immobilized Negros Occidental. On the second day at Escalante in his north Negros territory, Gustilo, now rearmed by Marcos, mobilized local police and two CHDF militia companies to confront the massed human barricades. When demonstrators refused to disperse, the local police chief, apparently acting on Gustilo's direct command, ordered his men to fire on the crowd of 5,000 with rifles and machine guns, killing 21.[63]

In the wake of the massacre, the fragile Bayan coalition collapsed, crippling the Negros opposition during the February 1986 presidential elections. Within hours of the Escalante shooting, Bayan Chairman Romeo Guanzon, Gustilo's close friend, resigned, blaming his own membership for the shooting. Without the moderating planter influence, Bayan-Negros followed the ill-advised boycott position taken by its national executive. Bayan leaders resigned their posts in the Cory Aquino for President Campaign, leaving opposition planters in control and denying themselves future presidential patronage. Bayan's boycott met with strong opposition. "We here in Bayan-Negros campaigned for boycott for five days," recalled its secretary-general Edgardo Estacio. "In our Bacolod rallies, people booed us. So we stopped the campaign and simply were inactive."[64]

Needing allies in Negros after Benedicto's eclipse, Marcos now relied directly on provincial leaders like Gustilo to mobilize votes in the 1986 presidential elections. In exchange, Gustilo demanded that his former north Negros congressional district become a separate province. Only weeks before the February election, Marcos complied, forcing the legislation through parliament and appointing Gustilo governor of Negros del Norte—with Col. Francisco Agudon, an officer known for his extralegal violence, as his provincial Constabulary commander. As Philsucom's leader, Gustilo expropriated the national government's famine relief shipments and used them as patronage for the campaign.[65] With characteristic toughness, Gov. Gustilo won a unique Comelec order banning Namfrel citizen poll watchers from his province. On election day, he mobilized his militia, "Dober Force" and "Panther Force," to drive Namfrel from the precincts.[66] With the opposition split and the right rearmed, Gustilo used fraud and violence to deliver a crushing 66 percent majority for Marcos in Negros del Norte.[67]

In Negros Occidental proper, fraud ranged from moderate in towns like La Carlota, where the KBL remained strong, to insignificant in Bacolod, where Montelibano's relations with Marcos had cooled. In La Carlota, the leading Marcos loyalists—Benedicto, Cojuangco and Elizalde—spent heavily for the President, raising KBL payments for each "family leader" to an unprecedented 50 pesos. The Cuenca group campaigned hard for Marcos, and their CHDF militia, financed by the Asociacion de Agricultores, roughed up a pro-Aquino planter and beat six Namfrel poll watchers.[68] Claiming that ballots from twenty-six of the City's eighty-three precincts were improperly tallied, Aquino supporters filed a formal and futile protest that could not block the Cuenca machinery from scoring a massive majority for Marcos.[69]

People Power in La Carlota City

After the EDSA uprising of February 1986, Negros Occidental began a year-long transition to a new political order. The KBL powers were in exile or eclipse, the left had forfeited its leadership and there were no strong political parties. President Aquino appointed as her acting governor, Daniel Lacson, a reformist planter and shipping executive who became the weak political center in a polarized province.

In this transition period, municipal politics acquired an exceptional importance. For first time since World War II, supralocal authority had collapsed and politics devolved to the municipalities. Under its program of normalization, moreover, the new regime was rebuilding the political system from the municipality upward. Acting under President Aquino's revolutionary powers, her Department of Local Governments purged the KBL provincial and municipal officials elected in 1980 and appointed supporters from her diverse coalition as officers-in-charge (OIC). It was here then at the municipal level that resurgent planters and the fading people's movement struggled for power. As both sides understood, the coincidence of regime change and sugar crisis had created a unique opportunity for a fundamental transformation of Negros society. Simply by foreclosing on the 80 percent of sugar lands with overdue crop loans, President Aquino could have fulfilled her promise of land reform—thereby destroying the planters' wealth and social power. While the cause-oriented groups still staged vigorous, albeit smaller, rallies for land reform and human rights, the planters, now deprived of State patronage, organized an armed underground.

Although planter control had muted local dissent in the months before EDSA, during the next two years La Carlota became a major political battlefield. Two appointments placed the City's main institutions on the side of social change—the populist Edgardo Canlas as OIC Mayor in May 1986 and activist Fr. Gregorio Patino as parish priest in September.

During much of 1986, La Carlota had a populist city government that seemed, in many ways, a realization of the EDSA uprising's ideals. Son of veteran City politician Democrito Canlas, Mayor Edgardo "Gado" Canlas, then 41, was a medium planter and transport operator "conscientized" by his participation in Church activities. Active in the anti-Marcos opposition as the City's Liberal Party president, Canlas won appointment as OIC Mayor through his movement contacts when the Aquino administration purged the province's KBL incumbents. Instead of resisting like others, Mayor Jalandoni, incumbent for the past twenty years, called on the new appointee's father, his former ally Democrito Canlas, then 85. "This is the only way I can repay my debt to you," said Jalandoni referring to the elder Canlas's critical support for his election in 1967. "If anyone else were appointed mayor of La Carlota my consent would not be such a simple matter." The two embraced warmly and, three days later on May 6th, Gado Canlas was sworn in without opposition, becoming one of the province's four mayors identified with the new populist politics.[70]

Despite his elite background, Mayor Canlas's administration was decidedly "propeople." Instead of applying the city's 1.8 million pesos revenue grant to the usual fiestas or beautification projects, he used the funds for over a thousand small-scale livelihood projects to sustain the city's working class during the sugar crisis—32 sows, 20 carabaos, 500 goats, 1,000 breeding ducks, cooperatives, and petty manufacturing. "If the poor had a complaint, I would speak to the planters," recalled Canlas. During the previous twenty years, Mayor Jalandoni, by contrast, had often called upon police or military to support the planters. Moreover, in a controversial move, Mayor Canlas appointed Edgardo Estacio, NFSW vice-president and Bayan secretary-general, to the City council.[71]

By the time Bishop Fortich assigned Fr. Gregorio Patino to La Carlota in September, the city's planters were active in the province's rightist underground and could mobilize to oppose his appointment. "When I arrived here, the planters planned to barricade the church," recalled Fr. Patino, "but over a thousand BCC members from my Bacolod parish accompanied me in a cavalcade of trucks and jeeps. There was no welcome but there was no barricade either." Soon after his arrival, the planters hung streamers outside the church reading "Do Not Support Priests that Adhere to Communism." As rumors spread that Fr. Patino was an armed and active member of the Communist Party, the planters began boycotting the Church.[72]

Committed to the principles of liberation theology and the practice of community organization, Fr. Patino encouraged the formation of Basic Christian Communities. His predecessor, Fr. Antinero, opposed the concept and La Carlota had remained one of the few parishes in Negros without any BCC. Working through traditional parish structures—the October rosary crusade, the Barangay Sg Virgen prayer group, and the 500 mothers receiving regular famine relief—he organized a year-long series of seminars that moved systematically from ritual to social awareness. Starting with the creed, code and cult, Fr. Patino added a social dimension which was, as his assistant Fr. Nueva explained, "new to the people here since the Church had been conservative for so long." In just nine months, La Carlota had thirty-two active BCC with 100 to 150 families each—a substantial portion of the City's 45,000 nominal Catholics.[73]

Although BCC in many Philippine parishes are modest prayer groups, Fr. Patino shaped La Carlota's into vehicles for social and political transformation. In a 1988 interview, Fr. Patino explained that the "purpose of organization is to enable people to gain power to govern themselves and to stand up against anything that tries to oppress them." Such organization requires education for "economic and political analysis so they will understand the root causes of their problems at local, national and international levels." Worship is not, in Fr. Patino's theology, an end but a means: "We aim to transform a traditional pietistic and conservative religion to allow religion to liberate us from unjust structures. Processions have issue placards; novenas have issues . . . that reflect the sectoral struggle of the people." Such a theology represented a direct challenge to La Carlota planters. "They are opposed because the people will come to understand the root causes of their problems—feudalism, paternalism and exploitation," explained Fr. Patino. "The rich will lose their control over the people during elections. If you shine a flashlight on a thief, he will become angry because he wants the dark."[74]

In late 1986, the new propeople leadership of Church and City sponsored two province-wide peace marches to support a ceasefire with the NPA. Fr. Patino's parish issued a "Pentecost Primer" decrying the "heightened state of violence" in Negros, criticizing Aquino's "total war against the insurgents" and advocating "the peace that will reign when people are no longer captives of the violent structures that destroy them."[75] In the November Peace Pilgrimage, the central Negros contingent of 5,000 assembled at the La Carlota Church for a mass and then marched down the provincial highway—land reform placards and union banners waving, Mayor Canlas and Councilor Estacio in the vanguard. On December 10th, La Carlota City and Church officials led an even larger crowd that again trooped for four days to Bacolod City, merging with columns from north and south to form a parade of 100,000 people, one of the largest in Negros history. Marching in their midst was the NPA's guerrilla leadership—Commander Nemesio Demafiles, Fr. Frank Fernandez, Fr. Vicente Pellobello—unarmed and down from the hills to participate in the local ceasefire talks. At the rally's emotional peak, Bishop Fortich, chairman of the National Ceasefire Committee, embraced NPA Commander Demafiles.[76]

The Resurgent Right

During the year after the ceasefire's collapse in January 1987, La Carlota's planters combined elections and repression to recover their waning hegemony. With its victory in the January 1988 local elections, the Cuenca group finally broke the City's populist movement, thereby regaining a degree of autonomy and authority they have not enjoyed since the declaration of Martial Law in 1972.

In 1986–87, as the global sugar market revived, the planters, now free from Philsucom's marketing monopoly, were again able to accumulate profits. By 1988, 183 planters with coastal lands, including 46 in the La Carlota Milling District, were making unprecedented profits exporting pond-fed prawns to Japan.[77] With Gustilo's political eclipse, some local planters, notably La Carlota's, gained access to some of the $14.3 million in famine relief then entering Negros and used it on a discretionary basis to rebuild their political followings.[78]

Canada's late entry into this massive humanitarian effort had a direct bearing upon politics in La Carlota City. After a meeting with President Aquino and Gov. Lacson in May 1986, External Affairs Minister Joe Clark ordered the Canadian International Development Agency (CIDA) to prepare a five-year, $100 million Philippine aid program within just ninety days, an unprecedented speed. Jettisoning its normal procedural checks, CIDA authorized $11 million for a hastily organized Negros Rehabilitation & Development Fund controlled by Gov. Lacson and a Canadian consultant named Greg Forbes, a Nova Scotia native married to a Filipina.[79] In the early 1980s, as an agronomist for the Negros plantation company Gamboa Hermanos, Forbes had advised planters, La Carlota's among them, on ways of cutting labor costs by mechanizing sugar cultivation.[80]

When Bob Cuenca's Buas Damlag Foundation, an arm of his Asociacion de Agricultores, applied for 8.7 million pesos to aid displaced sugar workers, Forbes endorsed the project and introduced Cuenca to the Canadian Embassy's Counsellor for Development. Although "a bit nervous about this project," Counsellor Jim Carruthers assessed Bob Cuenca's group as "progressive planters willing to have orderly change." Relying on Forbes to monitor the project, the Embassy approved Cuenca's 8.7 million pesos program, CIDA's largest single grant in Negros.[81] In mid 1987, a source inside the Asociacion de Agricultores reported that the Buas Damlag Foundation was purchasing gasoline for Cuenca's militia at the rate of about 10,000 pesos per week. When confronted with this allegation, Counsellor Carruthers admitted that up to 20 percent of the Buas Damlag grant, or 1.75 million pesos, could be diverted to political or paramilitary ends without detection.[82] In a city with a daily wage of twenty pesos, a million pesos could purchase a vast amount of patronage and power. Repeating this pattern throughout the province, CIDA granted $1.7 million to planter groups, denied aid to the NFSW's farm plot program, and offered only $38,000 to grassroots organizations.[83] In this competition for external aid and local support, CIDA sided resolutely with the rightist planter and played a key role in his restoration.

A review of the Buas Damlag Foundation's budget indicates the scale of CIDA's impact upon La Carlota politics. As the sugar crisis worsened, Bob Cuenca had slashed Buas Damlag's budget from 2 million pesos in 1984 to 1 million pesos in 1986. Dividing 1 million pesos among the Foundation's 9,702 beneficiaries produced an average grant of 110 pesos, about the same amount that Cuenca paid his village leaders for their votes in the 1986 elections. Although too small to finance development, such grants were sufficient for patronage payments.[84] By contrast, CIDA's grant of 8.7 million pesos to the Foundation was intended for only 4,260 projects, an average of 2,053 pesos each. The eight-fold increase in the Foundation's overall budget expanded Cuenca's electoral patronage, while a twenty-fold increase in per-project funding allowed room for extensive graft. By mid-1987, several of Cuenca's employees at the Asociacion de Agricultores were convinced that he was diverting CIDA funding to his new paramilitary forces.[85]

By late 1986, Cuenca's group had already emerged as leaders of the planter underground arming for rebellion against the State and repression of workers. Alienated from the new regime and angered by President Aquino's October declaration that "sugar is dead," the Right, led by planter Esteban "Sonny" Coscolluela, formed the Negros Independence Movement and began stockpiling arms for a threatened secessionist revolt. "Negros is a wealthy land, colonized by Manilans, exploited by them, and siphoned of its riches" declared the Movement's manifesto. "Now they tell us we are poor and would like to donate a can of milk to a dying Negros child . . . What has Negros done to deserve this from the people who grew fat on the toils of Negrenses?"[86] Aside from their attack on Manila and its threat of land reform, the rightist planters launched a sustained propaganda campaign against the thirty-five or fifty-four communist clergy who supposedly controlled Bacolod's diocese.[87] Masked and armed with costly automatic weapons, planters paraded before international television cameras to dramatize their threat.[88] In 1987, moreover, the Negros planters' improved finances and political position allowed them to arm paramilitary forces. In La Carlota alone, Cuenca built a force of 220 riflemen—the largest single private army in the province's history.

If 1986 was a year of populist politics in La Carlota, then 1987 saw the restoration of planter power through the overlapping processes of election and repression. By reviving a bicameral Congress and giving it control over land reform legislation, President Aquino's constitution became a vehicle for rapproachment with alienated local elites such as the Negros planters. In February 1987, Gov. Lacson used the constitutional plebiscite to forge an open alliance with the former KBL stalwarts, including the Cuenca machine of La Carlota. The armed independence movement active only a few months before quieted, and conservative planters joined Gov. Lacson in campaigning vigorously for ratification of the new constitution.

Similarly, the May 1987 congressional elections allowed the Negros planters to rebuild their legislative leverage within the national government. In the fourth district comprising La Carlota and five other municipalities, the campaign became a costly three-way battle among wealthy sugar men—Antonio Oppen, Eduardo Cojuangco's brother-in-law; Guillermo "Baby" Araneta, the manager of nearby Central Ma-ao and a leading critic of Benedicto's Philsucom; and Edward Matti, a wealthy molasses trader closely allied with Benedicto. Initially, the Cuenca-Jalandoni group committed to Oppen. But, as money started flowing for Matti, Cuenca switched, leaving Jalandoni to manage Oppen's campaign. According to observers, Matti's funds came from Benedicto, who was determined to punish Araneta for his attacks on Philsucom; from Cojuangco, who was equally determined that his brother-in-law would be defeated; and from Fred Elizalde, who was competing with Araneta's adjacent Ma-ao milling district for scarce cane. While Oppen and Matti both ran as candidates of the Lakas ng Bansa Party (LnB), Araneta ran under the Liberal Party, headed by his relative Judy Araneta Roxas. OIC Mayor Canlas, also a Liberal, campaigned for Baby Araneta, his ally in the anti-Marcos movement.[89]

In the end, cash became the currency of the election. Oppen's campaign manager, Bonifacio Peña, the neophyte warlord of Pulupandan, exhausted his funds in a flood of patronage at the outset, leaving little for election day. Working through the Cuenca machinery, Matti made community contributions for basketball courts or cleaning drainage ditches, paid his family leaders weekly allowances of up to 500 pesos for six weeks, and, on election day, gave each of his voters 30 pesos in cash. The number of votes correlates well with the amount of money expended: in La Carlota City alone, Araneta spent 112,000 pesos for 3,572 votes; Oppen about 800,000 pesos for 5,293 votes; and Matti 2 million pesos for 10,655 votes.[90] With ample funds and good management, Matti won the seat with nearly twice the votes of his nearest rival, Oppen.

The results were the same throughout the province. All seven congressmen-elect were planters identified with their class and industry. Gustilo's successor as president of the National Federation of Sugar Planters, former Bayan chairman Romeo Guanzon, won the Bacolod seat, and the leader of the anti-Benedicto planters, Mrs. Hortencia L. Starke, won the Sixth District.[91] Once in Congress, the Negros delegation worked to weaken land reform legislation. On September 2nd,

Congressman Guanzon filed H.B. 941 allowing a generous landlord retention limit of 24 hectares—a measure that effectively ended the chance of genuine land reform.[92] With their political isolation ended and legislative influence restored, the Negros planters could again use the State to serve their sectoral interests.

These elections also saw the eclipse of the organized left as an electoral presence in Negros. When the entire Partido ng Bayan (PnB) senatorial slate appeared at a La Carlota rally, for example, only 750 people attended. Although they won 15 percent of Negros Occidental's vote, their best result anywhere, the leftist PnB candidates still finished far behind the rightist Grand Alliance for Democracy. After the elections, the Negros chapters of Bayan and PnB dissolved.[93]

Paramilitary Repression

As their relations with the Aquino administration repaired in 1987, the planters formed a close alliance with local military commanders. After a decade of incompetent leadership and inadequate resources under Marcos, the Armed Forces now marshalled sufficient forces and fire power to confront the 700 to 1,000 NPA guerrillas on Negros island. The Constabulary provincial commander, Lt. Col. Miguel Coronel, devised a comprehensive anticommunist campaign that had thirty-eight "Bionic Teams" indoctrinating workers and students in every Negros town. In their public discussions of communist penetration in Negros, these teams identified the NFSW, the Basic Christian Communities, and Task Force Detainees as the leading communist front organizations.[94]

By mid-1987, this pattern was particularly evident in La Carlota. With military support, Cuenca and his planter allies organized the Philippine Constabulary Forward Command (PCFC), a local militia of 100 men, and an Alsa Masa vigilante unit of 70 to support the City's 50 police—forming a large private army of 220 men. By diverting funds from the Asociacion de Agricultores and Canadian aid, Cuenca supplied his PCFC with mobility and firepower—M-16 rifles, pick-up trucks, gasoline, and two-way radios. Their presence was visible and intimidating. By midyear, Miguel "Butch" de la Concepcion, a Cuenca ally and owner of 59 hectares of sugar land, was jogging daily at dawn around the plaza with his trainee vigilantes, shouting in time—ALSA!, jog jog, MASA! Whether on foot or mobile patrol, the PCFC squads conducted themselves in a surly, threatening manner. Moreover, the City police, utterly unreformed despite the dictator's downfall, harbored several killers known for their death-squad activities.

Statistics on human rights violations for 1987 show both an upward trend throughout Negros Occidental and marked concentration in La Carlota. After dropping from 443 in 1985 to just 100 in 1986, political arrests in Negros Occidental reached 487 in 1987. Similarly, after dropping from fifty-four to twenty-three, "salvagings," or death squad murders, climbed back to thirty-seven.[95] While many of the earlier murders had been random, most of those killed now were affiliated with NFSW or Bayan. This repression was particularly strong in the La Carlota district. Of the ninety-five NFSW members arrested in Negros Occidental during 1987, more than half, or forty-nine, were in the La Carlota district. Similarly, of the eleven NFSW members salvaged, four were in La Carlota.[96] Each of these numbers represents an incident of calculated terror that had a chilling effect on union activism. Each was a part of an attempt by the planter machine and local military to destroy the NFSW in La Carlota City.

The campaign started on 15 June 1987, when thirty paramilitary troopers entered Hacienda Paz and interrogated a twenty-two-year-old worker named Richard Ordona about his alleged support for the NPA. Within hearing of residents, the troops tortured him from 9:00 P.M. to 1:00 P.M., puncturing his skin and cutting open his stomach with a short knife. When he refused repeatedly to identify alleged NPA supporters in the barrio, he was finally executed with a single shot.[97] Local police did not investigate the murder. After militia shot up the village the next day, some ninety-three families fled to the City under the protection of the populist OIC Mayor, Edgardo Canlas, and were housed in the City gym. When they finally returned to their homes, a PC detachment occupied the plantation and later forced workers to "surrender" to the government formally as if they were NPA guerrillas.[98]

For the next three months, the PC and planter militia harassed strong NFSW chapters in the La Carlota area. On June 18th, for example, Butch de la Concepcion led thirty-two uniformed militia into Haciendas Consuelo, Paz, and Purisima where they fired their automatic weapons into the air as a warning against joining the NFSW.[99] In mid-July, Constabulary and militia forced several hundred NFSW members on six La Carlota District haciendas to "surrender."[100] On August 5th, the Constabulary detained Elma Alcala, president of the NFSW, at Hacienda Consuelo for ten days without warrant and tortured her, in the presence of her husband, to confess her communist affiliations. Recalling the incident five months later, Mrs. Alcala, a tiny, thin woman in her mid forties, trembled and wept as she described how an army lieutenant punctuated his questions with slaps across her face and blows to her upper body.[101]

That same month, the war came to La Carlota. Operating on the slopes of Mt. Kanlaon, Task Force Sugarland encountered an NPA base camp and called in air support. During a day-long battle visible from the City below, two helicopter gunships raked the volcano's slopes with forty rockets and their .50 calibre machine guns.[102] In September, as a part of a province-wide offensive, an NPA patrol stopped a sugar train two kilometers from Central La Carlota and burned the locomotive with gasoline.[103] After that operation, however, the NPA guerrillas withdrew from the La Carlota area and could no longer serve to check the planters' militia.

By late 1987, the NFSW's La Carlota branch, once the most militant in the province, was broken. Key chapters had "surrendered" to the military, and militants had asked central office to stay away for fear that contact would mean arrest. As the NFSW's chief organizer Roy Mahinay explained, in La Carlota "the members are afraid to go out because there are spies about who point to the members when they march."[104] When the mayoral campaign started in late 1987, La Carlota's planters had already crippled the City's main vehicle for worker mobilization.

The Election in La Carlota City

Compared to the fiesta atmosphere of pre-Martial Law elections, the January 1988 mayoralty campaign in La Carlota was a passionless exercise of power, lacking the usual feasting, parades, fraud, and violence. Although simultaneous with the election for provincial governor, La Carlota focused on the local contest since the incumbent Gov. Lacson was running unopposed, supported by all the KBL planter factions including the Cuenca group. Criticized by the rightist planter in 1986–87, Lacson had gradually won their support by his adamant opposition to land reform, ability to deliver famine-aid patronage, and access to President Aquino.

With his patronage restored and opposition silenced, La Carlota's "warlord" Bob Cuenca could afford to observe electoral proprieties. Despite the deceptive quiet, these elections were the capstone in the reassembly of planter power. While the populist ex-mayor Gado Canlas ran with the support of the Church and union, his rival Juancho Aguirre, Cuenca's brother-in-law, had the backing of the planters, the mill, and the military.

The contrast between the two campaigns was most evident at their headquarters. Built of dark hardwood in the art deco tropicale style of the 1930s, the Canlas house sits on the City's wide plaza facing the three-storey columns of the Presidencia. The house was protected by a single police bodyguard, brother-in-law of an NFSW leader, and a clutch of supporters standing by in the Canlas bus company waiting shed. The heart of the campaign was three tables in the open kitchen at the rear of the house. While Mrs. Canlas supervised the feeding of the poor and middle class supporters at one, the other was meeting place for members of the two families who have dominated La Carlota politics for the past half century, Gado Canlas and his council candidate, Jaime Marino Lim, nephew of the ex-mayor. At the third, a mahjong game of the mayor's friends and relatives continued throughout the campaign. Closed meetings retired to a *sala* with an air of fading gentility—prewar furniture, a portrait of the family patriarch "Democ" Canlas, and wide plank floors.

Although the rival candidate, planter Juancho Aguirre, had his own house just down the street from Canlas, it was empty save a few guards. Symbolic of his subordination to the town's warlord, Aguirre campaigned from Cuenca's house at Hacienda Cristina just outside the *poblacion*. As the ten-foot steel gate opened to admit autos, 14 guards, each armed with an automatic weapon, controlled access to the fortress-like compound. Parking in front of Cuenca's modern house at the compound's center two days before the election, we met the second line of defense. As I approached the front door, planter and paramilitary leader "Ange" Rodriguez came around the side of the house with a Colt .45 under his arm. Ten feet behind, Alsa Masa commander "Butch" de la Concepcion, a stocky *mestizo*, covered him, fingering the automatic pistol concealed under the hem of his bullet-proof vest.

Inside, Bob Cuenca sat at the head of one of two tables that served as the motor of his electoral machinery. Throughout the campaign's final stages, he worked there surrounded by his entourage—Atty. Dick Teruel; planter ally Antonio "Tony" Trebol, manager of Hacienda San Miguel; and more than a dozen lesser *lider*. Behind him was a row of blackboards with columns of numbers listed by precinct. Sitting at the other table with long voter lists and stacks of pesos were accountants and clerks. A delegation of his *liders* from Hacienda Malaga arrived during our visit, and approached Cuenca to report "about 406 votes" in their area. After Cuenca approved, they sat down with the clerks to go over the voter lists and take receipt of cash at the rate of 20 pesos per voter. "Imagine that," Atty. Teruel remarked as the cash was counted out, "last night we got so busy with the work that we gave some leader 50,000 pesos instead of the 10,000 pesos we owed. That's not the kind of mistake you make unless you get real busy." There was laughter from both tables.

In contrast to the emotion and idealism in the Canlas house, the atmosphere inside Hacienda Cristina was of a cool, at times cynical professionalism manifested in a wry machismo, joking about errone-ous payouts or listing the dead as living voters. While Canlas carried himself with the humility of a Catholic *cursillista*, Cuenca exuded an aura of authority, commanding, brash and, at times, arrogant. Anyone could approach Canlas in his home, but access to Cuenca, the man behind the candidate, was protected by three layers of security and a claque of *lider*. If Canlas's campaign evoked the brotherhood of the Kristianong Katilingban (BCC), then Aguirre's was an extension of the *amo/dumaan* (master/worker) relation. Canlas's campaign was a populist crusade, while Cuenca's showed the sinews of power—assault rifles, a tank, helicopter gunships, two-way radios, and pick-up trucks.

Church and Central were the other fulcrums of power in this campaign. During the months before elections, the rightist planter continued to harass Fr. Patino. In July, he had received a death threat: "Your Days Are Numbered, Christian Crusade Against Communism." When he drove into the villages on parish work, a car with tinted windows and no license plate followed.[105] "In this election," Fr. Patino stated two days before balloting, "they [the planters] are not cam-paigning against Gado Canlas but against me."[106] Undeterred, the Church circulated 2,000 copies of a leaflet titled "Ten Guidelines for Voters in the Coming Elections." Several of the injunctions seemed pointed at Cuenca. Number five, for example, advised: "Do not vote for a candidate who offers money, employment or other favors in exchange for your vote. One who tries to do this is corrupt." Number eight read: "Wolves and sheep do not eat together yet. Do not vote for one who has expelled workers from their land, who has dismissed laborers without a just cause, who has tortured and killed."[107]

For the first time in La Carlota's history, the Central's manager actually campaigned house to house in the worker compounds that surround his milling factory. With cane supply critically short, manager Jack Teves had to please the president of the Asociacion de Agricul-tores, Bob Cuenca. A taciturn technocrat without a populist touch, Teves offered his workers a blunt message: "Help someone who can help the Central. And if you don't, then maybe you can work somewhere else."[108]

Instead of the customary *miting de avance*, the final mass rally, La Carlota's plaza was empty on election eve. Instead, Cuenca's liders moved through the villages distributing stacks of envelopes with each voter's name written on the front—20 pesos for the individual voter, and 50 pesos for each family leader. Reflecting Cuenca's confidence, the payment had dropped far below the 50 pesos for voters in the 1986 presidential elections and 30 pesos in the 1987 congressional contest. With our two-way radio tuned to Cuenca's frequency, we picked up a message near midnight—forty men, who turned out to be armed militia, had arrived and needed to be housed. At the Canlas campaign kitchen, the news aroused concern. If Cuenca was cutting his costs, then he might be holding force in reserve.

On January 18th, the elections proceeded without incident and seemed, superficially at least, a model democratic exercise. At 8:00 A.M., I approached the long lines of generally youthful voters at La Carlota South Elementary School and, in a loud voice, asked "how much are we all making today?" There were shouts up and down the queue of "twenty pesos," and, laughing and smiling, a few youths waved their payment envelopes. Inside the school, Precinct No. 1 for the voters from Hacienda Cristina seemed a mirror of plantation society. A wiry man in aviator sunglasses monitoring the queue of workers had been one of the guards on Hacienda Cristina's steel gates the day before.

As an official Comelec observer, I entered the precinct and seated myself next to a Cuenca poll watcher, a woman in her early twenties who introduced herself as Miss Jamora from Hacienda Cristina. "I couldn't get a job until Juancho [Aguirre] got me a temporary post in City Hall as a clerk," she explained. "When Gado [Canlas] became OIC, I was fired out and went back to the hacienda . . . So if Juancho wins, I can get my job back."[109] As we talked, the queue of 62 voters, all workers from Hacienda Cristina, moved through the polls. Most were barefoot with gnarled hands; blackened toes splayed wide by working barefoot in the fields; their best clothes, patched and tattered; wide gaps in their teeth; and arms so thin that sinews and veins bulged beneath the skin. As they seated themselves to write out longhand the 24 names of their choices—one mayor, one vice-mayor, ten councilors and a dozen provincial officials—three teachers, the official inspectors, moved up and down the rows of child-sized desks as if supervising an exam. Many of the older workers from Hacienda Cristina were illiterate, Ms. Jamora explained, and needed the teacher's help in filling out their ballots. For such poor, I thought, 20 pesos was a lot of money.

After stopping at the church where several priests reported a universal 20/50 pesos payout, we drove out to Barrio Consuelo, polling place for the precincts surrounding Central La Carlota. Arriving just after 11:00 A.M., we found Central manager Jack Teves standing outside the main gate, sweating under the hard tropical sun. Arms folded on his chest and two armed security guards at his back, Mr. Teves was staring hard, as he had been since the polls opened, at each pedestrian who passed through the main gate to the nearby polls. At dawn, security guards at the Central's main gate had cancelled entry permits for tricycles contracted to carry Canlas supporters from villages on the other side of the mill compound. In all probability then, those arriving by tricycle were Aguirre voters and those on foot were for Canlas. As one voter put it, by just standing and staring, Mr. Teves was "making his presence felt."

That afternoon, we drove west into the foothills of Mt. Kanlaon to observe the voting at Hacienda San Miguel, a large plantation owned by the mother-in-law of Cuenca ally Antonio "Tony" Trebol. Entering Precinct No. 76, a classroom in the local primary school, just after 3:00 P.M., we noticed that the three women working as electoral clerks, all teachers at the school, had opened the ballot boxes and were sorting the ballots. Knowing that opening a ballot box outside the tally center was illegal, I asked where the candidates' inspectors were. One of the teachers pointed to Aguirre's watcher, a young man named "Boy," and said that Canlas's watcher was in the bathroom. After we complained about the anomaly, the teachers, with angry retorts, slammed shut their registry books and cleared the table of electoral materials. As tempers flared and sharp words flew, I disengaged and went to the back of the classroom where I noted a poster on the back wall, "Nutritional Status of Pupils." Among the classroom's 67 pupils, drawn mainly from nearby Hacienda San Miguel, 48.2 percent of males had suffered from mild to severe malnutrition in June 1987.

As I was taking these notes, a pick-up truck stopped in front of the school and the passenger shouted for Boy, Aguirre's inspector. The passenger was Noe Serdena, barrio captain and labor contractor at Hacienda San Miguel, who handed "Boy" a stack of white envelopes. Returning to the precinct, Boy placed envelopes marked "Teacher" on the table in front of each. When one of the teachers slipped the envelope in her bag, we asked what it might be. She answered: "Panihaponan siguro. (Probably our dinner.)" After pocketing their illegal payments, the teachers announced the closing of the polls at 3:30 P.M.—a full thirty minutes before the legal hour. When we challenged their order, they explained that the precinct's voters, almost all from Hacienda San Miguel, had voted en masse at 8:00 A.M.

After the polls closed, we drove back toward the City and entered the Hacienda Cristina compound just after 5:00 P.M., the steel gate swinging open at our approach. The guard in aviator glasses we had met in Precinct No. 1 that morning flagged us down, saying: "Mr. Cuenca has asked if you might not be able to come back tomorrow. They are having a conference now." Indeed, the compound was full of pick-up trucks and troops—seven security guards at the gate with automatic rifles and six Army soldiers guarding a light tank with a

.50 caliber machine gun parked outside Cuenca's house. As we pulled away, a helicopter gunship landed carrying Col. Rene Cardones, Task Force commander, for a meeting with Bob Cuenca, Congressmen Matti, Tony Trebol, and other La Carlota planters.

We spent most of that evening at La Carlota City High School watching the teachers from Barrio San Miguel count the votes from Precinct No. 76. As the teachers read and tallied each ballot on a master list before a small crowd, runners from both campaigns appeared periodically. By 8:15 P.M., Precinct No. 76 had given Aguirre 140 votes and his vice mayor 141, against 1 for Canlas and 0 for his vice mayor. As I stepped outside the classroom, I overheard San Miguel's barrio captain Noe Serdena muttering to himself in the dark, his stocky frame shaking with rage: "This is awful . . . Canlas got a vote . . . I'll demand a recount." When I asked the reason for his anger when his candidate Aguirre had scored such a crushing victory, he answered: "We don't have many votes so we have to keep them all together. Besides we all agreed to go for Aguirre. Last May [in the congressional elections] I was able to get zero for Araneta . . . and gave nearly all to Matti." Serdena speculated that the teachers might be cheating or may have misread a name.

Standing there in the darkness that night, I was struck by the contrast in the conduct of the elections in Precinct No. 1 downtown and No. 76 in remote San Miguel. In the poblacion precincts, the rules and rituals of balloting were rigidly observed—voter lists were posted, the Cuenca's poll machine watchers kept their distance and the ballot boxes were opened at the tally center. In San Miguel, by contrast, plantation workers marched into Precinct 76 en masse and voted with their field foremen helping them fill out the ballots. There the poll clerks opened the boxes illegally, refused access to the registry, and closed the polls thirty minutes early.

At midnight, we went to City Hall, the grand Presidencia, where the Board of Elections was meeting to approve the final precinct tallies. About fifty Liberal Party members loyal to Canlas crowded the room. Noting the complete absence of Aguirre followers, the Board Chairman asked, "Where is the winning party? Perhaps they are so far ahead with this landslide that they don't need to be here." After a well-timed pause, he won a laugh from the Liberal crowd: "And perhaps that is because there has been a lot of money flying all over town today."

The chairman's cynicism seemed to highlight a certain hollowness to the electoral procedure. Canlas supporters concentrated on protecting the integrity of the formal electoral process—copying and recopying long lists of precinct tallies. While they focused on the accuracy of the numbers, an invisible political machinery, integrated with the hacienda structure, worked to manufacture those same numbers. Under the tight controls of the plantation system, there was no need for the planters to perpetuate the usual frauds—brownouts, ballot box snatching, and flying voters. Their network of hacienda *lider* had mobilized the voters and bribed the teachers to insure that the ballots were favorably handled. Lopsided majorities in a few plantations and Central precincts overwhelmed the support for Canlas from some urban poor and plantation workers. Reinforced by repression and cash, the natural social controls of mill and plantation produced these wide margins.

A study of the city's final precinct tally sheet shows that these incidents we had witnessed were indeed representative of the electoral process in La Carlota. In the final tally, Bob Cuenca's candidate, Juancho Aguirre defeated Gado Canlas by 14,273 votes to 5,687—a margin of 2.5:1.[110] If we compare urban versus rural results, poblacion precincts show a ratio of 2.4:1, plantations 3.2:1, and Central 2:1. Assuming that the levers of social control were not applied, then these ratios ranging between 2:1 to 3.2:1 would be repeated, with minor variations, across the city.

In fact, Aguirre did not win a uniform majority but, instead, scored extraordinary margins in a few limited localities. Even adjacent precincts, clustered in the same polling place, show widely divergent results based, not on differences in social composition of the electorates, but on the capacity of the Cuenca machine to exert pressure through personal contacts. All residents of the plantations surrounding Barrio Nagasi, for example, are sugar workers. But casual field hands living in an independent resettlement barrio gave Canlas a 75 to 71 majority while workers in Hacienda Esperanza, owned by the exiled crony Roberto Benedicto, gave Aguirre a 91 to 4 margin (22.8:1). By contrast, at nearby Hacienda Najalin, owned by Elizalde y Cia., the manager did not press hard and his workers voted for Aguirre by a 125 to 38 margin, a normal 3.2:1 ratio. Other areas show a similar pattern. In Barrio Consuelo, for instance, just outside the Central gates, voters from Purok Mainabayan, a strong union area, favored Canlas by 89 votes to 87, while those inside the Central compound, where manager Jack Teves had campaigned so hard, voted for Aguirre 230 to 43 (4.3:1).

In the plantations southwest of the poblacion, NPA influence and planter repression were at their strongest. Aguirre scored a modest 88 to 54 margin (1.6:1) in one precinct and a 166 to 80 margin (2:1) at another—still far below the plantation norm of 3.2:1. Aguirre won an even narrower margin in a third: 110 to 93 (1.2:1). Clearly, planter terror had not yet broken worker resistance in this area.

Although Aguirre's overwhelming 2.5:1 majority seemed to mock the Canlas campaign, the Cuenca machine's grip on the electorate had, in fact, weakened since 1980. At the height of Martial Law, Cuenca's uncle Luis Jalandoni, Jr. defeated Jaime Marino by 13,300 to 2,025 votes, a 6.6:1 ratio. In the context of accelerated social change, the work of union, Church, and NPA had clearly loosened the planters' hold on the electorate.

After the Elections

As in La Carlota, Negros planters won office by wide margins throughout the province in the 1988 local elections. Running without a serious opponent, Gov. Lacson scored a huge majority and then lent his support to the successful planter campaign to blunt the threat of land reform. Throughout the province, only two cause-oriented mayors survived the planter restoration—Rowena Guanzon in Sagay and Roland Ponsica in Escalante, both in the north Negros area where the spirit of popular resistance to Gustilo's warlord regime was still strong.

After the elections, repression continued against Church and union. Two weeks later, just before midnight, an unknown assailant fired an automatic weapon into the windows of the NFSW's national headquarters in Bacolod City. The next morning, five bodies, shot through the head in like manner, were found at five locations where a soldier or police officer had been killed by the NPA in the past few months.[111]

The military played upon a break in the NPA's regional command to foster a parallel split in the NFSW. In early 1987, the charismatic NPA commander, Nemesio Demafiles, and a half dozen supporters, all urban cadre, had broken with the Party over broad issues of correct revolutionary strategy and tactics.[112] After the January 1988 elections, Demafiles sought protection from the Bacolod Police, bringing with him his legal sector ally Edgardo Estacio, a former NFSW vice-president who had broken with the union after his defeat in the La Carlota local elections. After denouncing communist penetration of the NFSW for several months at rallies and over radio, Estacio's group of nine NFSW dissidents founded their own union, DIWA, in January 1989.[113] Throughout this period, the ongoing repression against the NFSW— salvagings, arrests, and mass surrenders—continued throughout Negros and remained particularly strong in La Carlota.[114]

With the union in retreat and the broad left movement broken, the planter Right concentrated its campaign on the Catholic Church. After eight years of episodic efforts, the planter Right, supported by the military, launched a sustained attack on Bishop Fortich and his radical priests. As a part of a general shuffle of diocesan clergy, Bishop Fortich had ordered Fr. Antonio Atillaga to transfer from Our Lady of Fatima parish in suburban Bacolod to the main church in a north coast town. On the day of his transfer, 15 July 1988, several thousand demonstrators, escorted by Constabulary troops, barricaded the four entrances to the Bishop's compound in downtown Bacolod. For eight days, angry crowds maintained their pickets round the clock, supported by periodic visits from PC Commander Lt. Col. Miguel Coronel, Congressman Romeo Guanzon, and prominent planters.[115]

Two days after the barricades came down, the Papal Nuncio, Cardinal Bruno Torpigliani, arrived in Bacolod for a consecration and was met with a mass demonstration. Organized by the province's planters, notably the Cuenca group from La Carlota, the demonstrators charged that the diocesan clergy "has been heavily infiltrated and influenced by the Communist Party of the Philippines."[116] At a private audience with the Nuncio, the rightist planter, including the spokeswoman for their armed underground, Atty. Luz Dato Lacson, criticized Bishop Fortich. In January 1989, after the Bishop had submitted a pro-forma resignation on his 75th birthday, Pope John Paul II, acting upon recommendation of the Nuncio, announced his acceptance. Given Bishop Fortich's distinguished career, many of his priests had expected a cardinal's cap instead of forced retirement.[117]

Similarly, tensions between Church and planters worsened in La Carlota during the months following municipal elections. After more anti-Church streamers appeared on La Carlota's plaza, Fr. Patino banned two leaders of the local right, Butch de la Concepcion and Junjun Sicangco, from parading their *santos* in the 1988 Holy Week procession. Since these life-sized images are a source of elite prestige, both planters displayed theirs at the Concepcion pharmacy in La Carlota, protected by armed guards to deter amulet seekers. "I did not go with the procession since there was report that I would be killed," explained Fr. Patino. "On Good Friday, as the procession was passing South Elementary School, the entire building exploded in flames. To us it looked like arson. My reading was that the aim of the fire was to panic the people and then shoot me in the confusion."[118]

With both Church and union now on the defensive in the lowlands, the AFP marshalled five infantry battalions on Negros for a major campaign against the NPA's liberated zone in the island's southern highlands, known popularly as the "CHICKS area." When the NPA overran an Army detachment at Candoni in April, the AFP retaliated with a combined air-ground offensive that swept 35,000 villagers into refugee camps for three months.[119] That same month, the Sugar Regulatory Administration ordered all centrals to collect a five-peso contribution on each picul of milled sugar for payment to the PCFC militia, in effect providing 40 million pesos in planter funds for repression.[120] Building toward a strike force of ten regular infantry battalions and a substantial paramilitary presence, the Aquino administration seemed to be seeking a purely military solution to the Negros insurgency.

Conclusion

Viewed from the perspective of La Carlota City, the transition from Marcos to Aquino seems a restoration rather than a revolution. Through his expropriation of sugar profits, Marcos had exacerbated historic tensions within Negros society, forcing the smaller planters into opposition and their workers into rebellion. In the last months of the regime, extreme poverty, compounded by hunger and repression, fostered a deepening and broadening mass movement that seemed poised to threaten planter control over the province. Whether this movement could have continued had Marcos survived is impossible to say. It can be argued with greater certainty that Aquino's accession to the presidency stifled, at least for the time being, such a possibility.

Although the EDSA Revolution inspired an emotive rhetoric of reform in Manila, Aquino's administration has in fact brought the reality of intensified repression to La Carlota. Underpaid and unmotivated, the Marcos military proved an inefficient mechanism of repression. Marcos's attempted centralization denied power to local elites but failed to create an agency with an effective provincial reach. In specific, Marcos denied provincial officials private armies and patronage police but did not marshall his military to fill the void. By so weakening elite controls over the provinces, Marcos had inadvertently created the social space for a mass political mobilization.

Aquino's restored local elites have proven a more efficient instrument of control. Their fusion of near-perfect information with private militia has achieved an efficacy of political violence beyond the capacities of Marcos's weak authoritarian state. In seeking to restore control over the countryside, the Aquino administration has, by stages, combined the Republic's localized elite controls with Marcos's centralized military repression. During her first year in office, Aquino imposed policies that alienated these elites—central selection of local officials and the threat of land reform. Once she had restored local elections and invested Congress, an assembly of established political families, with control over land reform, antagonism subsided and an alliance with provincial elites emerged. In its second year, the Aquino administration sanctioned an alliance between these elites and her regional military commanders, thereby reinforcing repression.

This systematic violence in defense of the Negros social order highlights the inadequacy of the clientelist model for the analysis of Philippine politics. If the study of this peculiar provincial society has any utility for our broader understanding of the Philippines, it is to alert us to the prevalence of class-based violence. Even though they are useful in highlighting the element of conflict, these broad class categories cannot adequately explain how Negros planters negotiate the social divide and manipulate politics to maintain their dominance. If an inherent class conflict defines the basic structure of Negros politics, then the clientelist model, albeit modified, is the basis of the system's daily dynamic. Indeed, this study of Negros reinforces this point by showing the limitations of both models as complete and exclusive explanations for local politics.

In Negros, with an impoverished mass and a small elite, there is both a greater need for patronage and less capacity to distribute it evenly. Thus, extremes of wealth and poverty, without the social salve of widespread patronage, require a constant violence, in operation or in reserve, to maintain the existing order. Through their discretionary use of clientelism, the planters have, in the half century of mass electoral politics, employed a small group of loyalists, militia, and political leaders to deliver a mix of patronage and coercion sufficient to maintain control. Restrained and bankrupted under Marcos, the planters lost the material basis for their control over Negros politics. Now rearmed and refinanced under Aquino, the planters have recovered the instruments of power and restored their control over the province.

JAMES F. EDER

Political Transition
in a Palawan Farming Community

How community residents participated in the Marcos to Aquino transition is examined by this essay. The first part describes the general ethnographic setting and examines in turn the history of the wider region in which the community is embedded, the socioeconomic structure of the community itself, and the circumstances surrounding the February 1986 elections, an election in which Aquino defeated Marcos by a margin of 427 votes to 273 votes. The second part analyzes this election result in terms of the voting preferences of the 266 households who participated in it, households known individually by their demographic, economic, and social characteristics. This analysis aims to determine, as closely as possible and in terms of proximate variables, why each of the 266 households voted as they did. The final part of the essay uses this analysis as a point of departure to address some wider issues concerning the nature of local politics in this part of the Philippines.

The Setting

The data examined in this essay were obtained in San Jose, a Cuyonon-speaking, upland farming community of about 300 households, located eight kilometers from Puerto Princesa City, the capital of Palawan province. I first resided in San Jose during 1970–72, while conducting dissertation research on the interrelationships between agricultural development and the emergence and institutionalization of social inequality since the founding of the community, forty years earlier. During the years that followed, I turned my attention to another research project elsewhere on Palawan island, but I continued to make periodic, brief visits to San Jose and kept abreast of changes taking place there. I found these changes to be of such interest that from

January to July 1988, I undertook a detailed restudy of the community aimed at understanding such evolution as had occurred, since the time of my previous research, in patterns of agricultural production and in the nature of community agrarian structure. This restudy examines, in effect, one local community's experience with nearly two decades of Marcos-era "development," a period including the Martial Law years, the economic crises of 1984–85, and the transition from the Marcos administration to the Aquino administration in 1986. This restudy also provides the basis for most of the discussion below, although I draw upon my earlier research as well.

Palawan island, like Mindanao before it, enjoys a reputation of being one of the Philippines's last frontiers. Long, mountainous, and the fifth largest island in the Philippines, Palawan is rich in natural resources. It is still heavily forested, and in fact, contains the country's only remaining large, undisturbed stands of tropical forest. Palawan is known as well for its rich fishing and mineral resources. But beginning early in this century and accelerating greatly after World War II, the steady stream of land-seeking migrant farmers has poured into Palawan, leaving land-poor areas in Luzon and the Visayas, in search of a better life on the frontier. These migrant homesteaders have cleared the island's narrow coastal plains, creating on both sides a series of scattered, rural agricultural communities.

One such community is San Jose. Until 1930 a virtually unoccupied stretch of forested flatland, San Jose was settled in the decades that followed by migrant farmers from Cuyo Island, 300 km. distant in the Sulu Sea. Cuyo island had been Spain's only significant mission and military station in the Palawan region; Puerto Princesa, in contrast, Palawan's capital today, was not even founded until 1872. Cuyo's inhabitants, who share close linguistic affinities with the residents of Antique and Iloilo, lay first claim down to the present of being "Palaweños." Driven by population pressure at home, and traveling first by sailboat and later by motor launch, Cuyonons began emigrating to mainland Palawan in the latter part of the nineteenth century. Those who arrived in San Jose during the 1930s and 1940s were preoccupied, during their early years on Palawan, with shifting cultivation of upland rice and with clearing the virgin forest from their homesteads. With land abundant, roads and public transportation poorly developed, and no significant regional market for agricultural produce, life was subsistence-oriented and considerable social and economic equality prevailed in the community—as it did through much of rural Palawan down through World War II.

San Jose's developmental trajectory, however, began to change significantly during the 1950s. In 1950, when the community's population then totaled forty-five households, vacant land for homesteading was exhausted, but births and in-migration continued to swell the population in the years that followed. Subdivision, for sale or inheritance, of many of the original homesteads allowed many of these later arrivals to obtain at least some land, such that by the time of my initial study in 1971, San Jose remained primarily a community of smallholders.

In 1971, the population of the community was 112 households. An all-weather road had long since been constructed to connect San Jose with Puerto Princesa, where San Jose enjoyed a reputation as a "successfully developing" community (one of the reasons I chose it for study). Community residents, in fact, enjoyed generally rising incomes and standards of living, the latter comparing favorably with those of elsewhere in rural Palawan and the rural Philippines, generally. San Jose's prosperity, however, was not based on irrigated rice, a more familiar Philippine agricultural pattern, but on a commercialized upland (i.e., nonirrigated) agriculture made possible by increasing demand for fruits and vegetables in the Puerto Princesa marketplace, as the town itself grew dramatically during the post-World War II years and particularly after about 1965. By 1971, many San Jose farmers pursued vegetable gardening or tree crop farming as a way of life; many residents also received cash incomes from small stores or off-farm employment. Continuing opportunities to earn subsistence, through fishing or through short-fallow cultivation of rice, corn, or rootcrops, also contributed to the generally robust nature of community economy.

Variation between households in such factors as time of arrival, farm size and location, and farming ability and motivation ensured that, by 1971, these various economic activities were combined in different ways and proportions on different farms and underlaid a considerable degree of socioeconomic inequality.[1] But, by rural Philippine standards, generally, agrarian conditions were relatively favorable. Of the community's 112 households, 70 percent owned at least one hectare of land, and only about 15 households, entirely landless and without steady urban employment, could better be described as "tenants" or "squatters" rather than as "owner-operators." Income was broadly distributed, largely because the variety of economic activities ensured that a family's income-earning prospects were only partly determined by the amount of land it owned. Thus, even farmers with only one hectare of land could achieve satisfactory, middle-level standards of living by combining farming with marketplace trade or operation of an offshore fish corral. For 1971, in the rural Philippines as a whole, the poorest 40 percent of the population received only 13.3

percent of total income; in San Jose, the poorest 40 percent received about 23 percent of total income.[2]

One of my reasons for restudying San Jose in 1988 was to see how these relatively favorable agrarian conditions of 1971 had survived seventeen more years of in-migration, household developmental cycling, and Marcos-era "development." The nature of the development that did occur after 1971 was inevitably influenced by President Marcos's declaration of Martial Law in 1972. But the influence has been less than elsewhere, as Palawan—except for its fishing grounds, minerals, and timber—was and remains relatively peripheral to the Philippine economy as a whole; and San Jose, lacking such resources in any case, has never been coveted by powerful political or economic interests outside. In its immediate impact, Martial Law in San Jose had generally the same consequences as in the Nueva Ecija village studied by Kerkvliet. There Martial Law did not also directly affect the day-to-day economic endeavors of most residents and was hence not a significant issue for them.[3]

Nearby Puerto Princesa was significantly affected by the declaration of Martial Law and its aftermath, and in ways that continue to reverberate through San Jose economy and society. The Western Command of the Philippine Army established a major base on the outskirts of town, ostensibly to control problems with subversion and rural unrest that threatened to spill over into southern Palawan from Mindanao. Much new wealth moved into the town, and much old wealth prospered because of (1) the opening of large tracts of land in southern Palawan to corporate agricultural enterprises, (2) the discovery of oil off the northwest coast of Palawan, (3) the town's enhanced social and political importance, and (4) the road-building and construction activity that these other changes generated. All of these developments were given some additional stimulus and direction beginning in 1982 with the inauguration of the Palawan Integrated Area Development Project (PIADP) funded by the European Economic Community (EEC).

In 1972, Puerto Princesa was made a chartered city, and a modern airport and many new government offices subsequently opened there. By 1981, the greater Puerto Princesa City area included more than 55,000 persons; more than a third of this total lived in the city proper, while the remainder were distributed in San Jose and thirty-four other rural barangays. By 1988, the estimated population of the area was 84,000 persons. An additional 7,000 persons, Vietnamese refugees, inhabited a refugee camp established at the outskirts of the city some years before.

As these and other changes occurred in the wider region, San Jose grew dramatically between 1971 and 1988—from 112 to 278 households—even as it continued to maintain its reputation as a prosperous, successfuly developing community. In 1980, for example, it was found by public health officials to have the best nourished schoolchildren of any rural community in that part of Palawan. The community was electrified in 1977 and by 1988, more than 90 percent of households had electrical connections. Most families had only added electric lights, but a good number also had televisions, videocassette recorders, and refrigerators. A new high school had been opened in the community, and families in all economic circumstances appeared to be more likely in 1988 to send children to high school and college than in 1971.

These and other improvements in living standards were underwritten by a sharp increase in demand for farm produce after 1971: the city itself burgeoned due to in-migration and internal growth, and the military base and the Vietnamese Refugee Camp (VRC) added significant demands of their own. In addition, the national highway linking San Jose and Puerto Princesa City had been widened, and the network of feeder roads in San Jose itself had been expanded and improved. Increased productive investment in the community was visible in some new stores and in tracts of previously fallow land now planted to tree crops. There were some new forms of land use as well. In 1986, an agribusiness concern specializing in cotton began operations in Puerto Princesa, and by 1988, a number of San Jose farmers were attempting to grow it. More than ever, though, vegetable gardening remained the basic agricultural lifeway in the community, although here too there were changes, most notably with respect to scale and to patterns of labor use.

Most visible of all the changes that had occurred in San Jose between 1971 and 1988 were the many new houses that had been constructed. New houses appeared in part because some long-time, better-off residents had built new ones for themselves, in part because some children of residents had recently married and established independent households, and in part because there were many new arrivals in the community. Some of these new arrivals were rural folk from land-poor areas elsewhere in the Philippines, the same sort of people who had settled San Jose all along. But others were town dwellers, of all income levels, driven by overcrowding and high real estate prices in the town proper to seek living space in nearby farming communities. In consequence, real estate prices have risen dramatically in these communities as well, motivating many farmers to subdivide part of their farm land into residential lots for sale to townspeople. Many such townspeople in San Jose do not engage in farming at all; for them San Jose is simply an attractive, semirural "bedroom" community. This influx of outsiders, of diverse ethnic backgrounds, also began to change the heretofore largely Cuyonon-flavor of San Jose, and for the first time one could hear long-time San Jose residents comment that "they didn't know their neighbors."

Of the total of 278 households present in 1988, 63 households had been present during my earlier, 1970–72 research; the remainder of the 112 households then present had either died out or had moved on to other communities, testimony to the marked mobility of persons in frontier areas such as Palawan. Of the remaining 1988 households, 96 households had been created as the result of developmental cycling within households present in 1971—i.e., as the result of the marriage of a son or daughter and the subsequent establishment of an independent household. The remaining 119 households present in 1988 represented entirely new arrivals to the community after 1971—the sorts of migrants just discussed.

While San Jose had prospered visibly during 1971–1988, it remained an open question—one of the subjects of my current research—how this prosperity was being shared between the various social segments in the community and how any differentials in that "sharing" were reflected in changes in landownership, labor relations, and so forth. During a brief visit I made in 1981, for example, everyone complained of the effects of the high inflation rate, and the opinion was often expressed to me that only a few residents had really prospered during the previous decade, while most were struggling just to maintain their previous standards of living. On the other hand, even in the depths of the national economic crises of the mid-1980s, San Jose farmers did maintain their standards of living and escape the impoverishment that struck other rural communities. Further, by 1988, things looked better; a lot of money was in circulation and even poor residents commented that it had become relatively easy to earn it. But differences between households in living standards were greater than ever, and previously unknown patterns of labor utilization had appeared: contract cotton farming, monthly laborers in the larger vegetable gardens, overseas workers.

In short, while no simple polarization was evident, complex processes of differentiation were clearly at work, processes of the sort said by Koppel to constitute a "rural transformation" in the Philippine countryside.[4] Processes of differentiation were most visible in San Jose with respect to the growing variety and importance of secondary, off-farm income sources, for both men and women, in households still primarily dependent on farming. Such differentiation, and the complexities of community economy generally, frustrated any simple "class" analysis of community socioeconomic structure, an issue to which I return below.

The February 1986 Election

The foregoing was the general setting, then, in which San Jose residents found themselves in 1985, on the eve of the February 1986 presidential election. That particular election must first be placed in the context of a long and proud tradition of trouble-free elections throughout Palawan; from my first arrival there in 1965 down to the present, I have never heard of even a single incident of the sorts of poll-related violence that plagues elections elsewhere in the Philippines. The pre-election situation was said to have been tense but quiet; a kind of wait-and-see attitude prevailed. The KBL mustered a highly visible and well-funded campaign throughout the Puerto Princesa area. In San Jose, the principal Marcos *lider* (local political leader) was Pedro, a long-time NP member, the head of a large kin group, and *barangay captain* since the late 1960s. About eight other local liders, mostly of upper social standing in the community, assisted the Marcos campaign there. PDP-Laban forces mounted an analogous group of liders in San Jose, headed by Ricardo, a young and progressive farmer long said to be "waiting in the wings," as it were, to run for barangay captain himself in the event of a local election. He coordinated his efforts with Aquino's campaign manager in Puerto Princesa City; when the latter was appointed OIC City Mayor following the Aquino takeover and the subsequent replacement of local officials, he in turn appointed Ricardo as OIC barangay captain.

The two campaigns differed in scale but were otherwise similar, both to each other and to previous election campaigns in San Jose. Each set of *lider* prepared a master list of all voters and their known candidate preferences; each side then devoted the campaign to trying to keep its voters in the fold while trying to capture fence-sitters and cajole any opposition voters believed to be only weakly committed and hence vulnerable to persuasion. There were differences of opinion about the degree to which fear and uncertainty may have muted the Aquino campaign effort. Ricardo, for example, said that rumors of pro-Marcos goons caused him to limit his campaigning to daytime hours and that, during the one Aquino rally in San Jose, he was the only Aquino *lider* willing to speak publicly. In a similar vein, another Aquino *lider* claimed that during his house-to-house efforts he kept to the "bushes" and trails and avoided the more visible feeder roads. The accounts of others, in contrast, made such statements seem melodramatic. Many ordinary voters on both sides agreed that the campaign was not only peaceful but conducted in a nonintimidating atmosphere. They pointed out, for example, that when Aquino came to Puerto Princesa City for a PDP-Laban rally, numerous San Jose residents attended. (Some recalled that Aquino's motorcade from the airport was marred by KBL-inspired placards and signs bearing such messages as "Cory—Queen of the Communists," and "A Vote for Aquino is a Vote for Communism." Also, when Aquino began her speech at the rally, the local radio station, which was featuring live coverage, suddenly went off the air.)

On election day itself in San Jose, each side customarily rewards the party faithful with free transportation back and forth to the polling place and with a large communal meal. There was a substantial inequity in the amount of funds that each side had available for this purpose; Marcos's *lider* received abundant transportion money and four thousand pesos for their communal meal, which allowed them to slaughter several animals, while Aquino's liders had to get by with little transportation money and 450 pesos for food.

Despite such differences in scale (which are not unusual), Aquino won handily in San Jose. In the weeks and months that followed, San Jose residents experienced much the same sorts of uncertainties that overtook the rest of the country. There was also considerable tension within the community due to the bitterness of some pro-Marcos *lider* over the election outcome there; "they couldn't accept it," as one resident put it. There were no untoward incidents, but a number of Marcos supporters, including the president of the Catholic Association of San Jose, ceased attending Church for a spell. They were angry at the priest, it was said, for his allegedly pro-Aquino sermons during the campaign. After Marcos fled, some residents said they were saddened; others said they were overjoyed, or angry, or apprehensive. There was later some unrest (but no violence) in Puerto Princesa, when city employees barricaded themselves in the City Hall to prevent the new OIC Mayor from taking over. Again, however, none of this spilled over into San Jose.

Table 1 shows the actual outcome of this election in San Jose. Two sets of figures are displayed. The first set, the actual vote count following the election, shows that the Aquino forces were victorious over the Marcos forces by a margin of 427 votes to 273 votes. Ideally, the analysis below would revolve around these figures—i.e., around how people actually voted. The problem, of course, is that we do not know how any one person "actually" voted. What we can know, and work with, is the second set of figures in table 1, which displays how household heads *said* they voted or *were said to have voted* by others. These latter data were gathered by myself and two local research assistants in January 1988, in the early stages of the above-described restudy of San Jose. I limited our data-gathering efforts to the preferences of household heads, rather than attempting to survey all voters, for reasons of economy in data collection and because I assumed, as San Jose residents do themselves, that all members of the same household vote the same way. (Most San Jose households consist either of simple nuclear families or are extended downwards to incorporate temporarily the spouse of a married child.)

We obtained these data with little difficulty. The nature of Philippine electoral politics is such that the voting preferences of many, even most, households in rural communities are publicly known by election day. Simple recall, either by my research assistants or by other informants, proved adequate to compile much of the data in table 1. The balance of data was obtained by seeking out the household heads individually. Finally, we reviewed the raw data—how each of the 266 households were said to have voted—with the principal *lider* of both the Marcos and the Aquino campaigns, making corrections as necessary. Given these circumstances, I had considerable confidence that the data displayed in table 1 were valid.

Despite my reasons for confidence, even a cursory comparison of the two sets of figures in table 1 shows that something is amiss: they are not in the same proportions. Thus, according to my recently gathered data, and assuming that household size was not a factor and that my assumption about household voting solidarity is correct, Marcos should only have received 34 percent of the total votes, but in fact, according to the actual vote count, he received 39 percent of

Table 1. February 1986 Election Results (San Jose)

	Actual Vote Count	Household Heads (1/88 count)
AQUINO	427	175
MARCOS	273	91
Total:	700	266

the total—about thirty-five more votes than he should have. This discrepancy noted, of course, it is easy to think of many reasons why one should *not* have confidence in my recently gathered data: given the outcome of the election, it would not be surprising if some persons who actually voted for Marcos would later claim to have voted for Aquino; perhaps the assumption that households vote as a bloc is incorrect; and so on. (On the other hand, of course, it could be claimed that perhaps my own data are correct and it was the actual vote count that was fraudulent.)

In point of fact, however, I believe each set of figures to be quite accurate, in its own way. With respect to the actual vote, I have no reason to suspect that it was fraudulent. With respect to my more recent data, there is little reason to suspect post election misrepresentation of voting preferences; when the opposing *lider* reviewed our raw data, only for 15 households was there any disagreement between them about how they were alleged to have voted. (That these opposing *lider* would *agree* on how 251 out of 266 households voted in the election is compelling testimony to the public nature of voter preferences in the community.) Because of my greater confidence in the data obtained from the Aquino camp, I have included all 15 of these households with the 175 pro-Aquino-households shown in table 1. Were we to remove them, however, it would have the effect of increasing Marcos's share of the total to 36 percent.

Most of the inconsistency, between the two sets of the data in table 1, apparently derives from two sources. First, approximately fifteen persons were registered to vote in San Jose but were not resident there; some, for example, were former residents who had since moved to town. As it happened, almost all of these non resident voters voted for Marcos. Second, some pro-Aquino household heads did not in fact "carry" their entire households, because some of the pork-barrel jobs that appeared in the community prior to the election (see below) were offered to voting-age children in such households, and perhaps also because the votes of some of these latter individuals were bought by pro-Marcos *lider*. (For the present election, this is strictly the speculation of pro-Aquino *lider*, some of whom thought it was suspicious that the wife of the pro-Marcos governor, who owns a substantial farm in San Jose, was seen visiting some poorer residents in the company of her bodyguard during the days before the election. In past elections, single, adult male voters, particularly of lower socioeconomic status, were frequent targets of vote-buying efforts.)

These things said about the lack of parallelism between the two sets of data in table 1, I shall simply assume that the second, more-recently obtained set is sufficiently valid for purposes of the analysis below.

Who Voted for Whom, and Why

Our question now becomes, then, why did each of the 266 households in table 1 "vote" the way it did? There are three different
approaches one can take to this question; they overlap somewhat but
I believe they are worth pursuing separately for the light each sheds
on rural voting behavior.

The first and perhaps the most obvious approach is simply to ask
the voters themselves—in this case, the household heads, why they
voted as they did. I asked a lot of people, in private, why they voted
as they did; most or all of the other contributors to this volume did
the same. Here and there I picked up a few tidbits—a frank acknowl-
edgment of an obligation incurred by virtue of employment or a debt
of gratitude to a *lider*, an expression of concern about corruption or
communism, and so forth, issues to which I return below. Most of
the reasons proffered directly by voters were not very illuminating,
however. They tended to be *mababaw* or "shallow" statements (as my
research assistants put it) about which candidate was "the best person
for the job," and so on. This is not, of course, to deny that this last
is an important question, but to express some skepticism that this
procedure was leading us to anything useful about the causes of voting
behavior. Did a man, for example, who said he voted for Marcos
because he feared communism really fear communism, or did he vote
for Marcos for some other reason, which he didn't want to talk about
or wasn't even thinking about at the time I interviewed him—a debt
of gratitude owed to a lider, perhaps—and simply use the communism "issue" (which certainly figured in the campaign) as a rationalization for his behavior?

With this first approach, in short, one quickly gets bogged down
in a classic anthropological conundrum: the reasons people give for
their behavior may not be the "real" reasons, or at least not the reasons
that satisfy the investigator.

The second approach is to leave the people out of it, as it were, or
at least leave out their alleged reasons in favor of a more objective
focus on their demographic, economic, and social circumstances. In
the case at hand, after all, besides knowing how these 266 households
voted, I have access to a variety of *other* data about them, data which
might help us uncover patterns in voting behavior. Age, occupation,
social status, religion—these are some of the factors known to influence the outcome of American elections; could similar factors be
operating here as well? In point of fact, of course, given what is known
or assumed about Philippine elections, I have no apriori reason to
expect any simple correlations in present case, but since I already had

the data in hand I thought some negative testing would at least be useful and, after all, one never knows what one might turn up.

Tables 2 to 5 classify the 266 households according as they supported Marcos or Aquino and cross-classifies them, in turn, according to time of arrival in San Jose, primary income source, estimated socioeconomic status, and neighborhood membership. These tables suggest some possible associations that may merit closer examination. Table 2, for example, shows that Aquino did particularly well among long-time San Jose residents as opposed to newer arrivals; table 3 suggests that she did particularly well among residents whose primary source of income was nonagricultural; and table 4 suggests that those at the extremes of community socioeconomic structure, as opposed to those in the middle, were most likely to support Aquino. Unfortunately, the measures used in these tables are either too simplistic or too confounded by other variables to make any of these correlations informative or convincing. After tabulating more field data and doing a finer-grained analysis, I will pursue this inquiry. (Only table 6 in this set is statistically convincing; it demonstrates an unsurprising correlation between neighborhood coresidence and voting preference in San Jose and anticipates some of the explanatory factors to which I now turn.)

The third approach to explaining the data in table 1 turns to the more private and personalistic factors emphasized in the factional model of Philippine electoral politics.[5] According to this model, neither the issues themselves (our first approach) nor voters status and class circumstances (or second approach) are as important in determining voter behavior as are personalities and personalistic relationships. The latter are central, it is said, because electoral political alliances are in fact constructed top-to-bottom upon a network of kinship and patron-client relationships, held together by various forms of patronage (jobs, political favors, etc.) and associated *utang na loob* obligations. Voters use their votes, in effect, either in thanks for some

Table 2. Voting Preferences of 173 Households,
Classified by Time of Arrival

	Time of Arrival in San Jose		
	Before 1971	*After 1971*	
AQUINO	44	62	
MARCOS	17	50	
Total:	61	112	173

Table 3. Voting Preferences of 196 Households,
　　　　Classified by Principal Income Source

| | Principal Income Source | | |
	Agricultural	Non-Agricultural	
AQUINO	44	89	
MARCOS	30	33	
Total:	74	122	196

Table 4. Voting Preferences of 186 Households,
　　　　Classified by Estimated Socioeconomic Status

| | Estimated Socioeconomic Status | | | |
	High	Medium	Low	
AQUINO	9	80	36	
MARCOS	1	47	13	
Total:	10	127	49	186

Table 5. Voting Preferences of 265 Households,
　　　　According to Neighborhood

| | Neighborhood | | | | | |
	One	Two	Three	Four	Five	
AQUINO	37	22	34	24	62	
MARCOS	14	8	33	20	11	
Total:	51	30	67	44	73	265

Table 6. Voting Preferences of 67 Households, Classified by Voting
　　　　Preferences of Husband's or Wife's Parental Household

| | Voted same or different as parents? | | |
	Same	Different	
Co-Household Head is:			
SON of another San Jose household	30	4	
DAUGHTER of another San Jose household	24	9	
Total:	54	13	67

previous personalistic assistance or in the anticipation of some future assistance. If these are the kinds of factors that matter in Philippine elections, how constrained by them were our 266 households in their voting behavior?

Government employment figured in the election in the following way. About eight households voted for Marcos because, in each, one member had a permanent job in a city or provincial office that incurred the obligation to "support the administration" during an election. This is considered normal. On the Aquino side, about two or three households had such jobs, arranged by then-Assemblyman Mitra. In addition, and again on the Marcos side, about fifteen, short-term pork-barrel PIADP jobs became available just before the election, thereby ensuring fifteen votes (but not fifteen households—see above) for Marcos. Thus voting to protect or to give thanks for employment, while important for some people, was a relatively minor factor in the election.

More important—and harder to identify—is the web of patronage that extends into the countryside from provincial and city officials and politicians. The political favors such voters do for rural voters range from the innocent (expediting some paperwork) to the questionable (a load of gravel for someone's driveway) to the outright illegal (payroll padding), but all nominally incur an *utang na leba* (*utang na loob*) obligation that might be called up at election time. In San Jose, with its high density of kinship ties, people in need of assistance are said to go typically to their better-off kin in the community and in the city, rather than to government officials or politicians. This circumstance may make patronage (apart from kinship, and excluding the provision of employment) a less important determinant of voter behavior here than elsewhere. In terms of the number of votes it explained in the January 1986 election, patronage in the sense used here was, at most, on a par with government employment in its importance. (One Aquino supporter, ridiculing the efforts of the Marcos-era governor and city mayor to reclaim their offices during the January 1988 local elections, claimed that the web of *kurakot* or "corruption" that they had established while in office reached down to the barangay level and helped explain some of Marcos's San Jose vote total. Who she had in mind I do not know, but any substantial graft would likely have involved the same pro-Marcos political *lider* or government employees already discussed.)

Kinship is another factor known to be important in Philippine elections. It was certainly important in this and other elections in San Jose, if difficult to separate from other factors in the "factional model" (since, as just noted, one's better-off kin are a primary source of employment, loans, and political favors). One man, for example, seemingly apolitical himself and without much enthusiasm for either Marcos or Aquino, told me that he voted for Marcos because his father was a Marcos lider. He could, of course, have gone against his father, but "it would have looked bad," he said, and there was no reason to. I learned of others whose votes could be explained in this fashion, and many residents commented on the importance of kinship in voting behavior. At the same time, however, they would often point out that the very density of kin ties in the community meant that many voters had close kin on both sides in the election, rendering meaningless such simple generalizations as "people tend to vote like their relatives."

Particular cultural importance is attributed, however, to the parent-child tie as a determinant of voting behavior (e.g., as in the case above), so I decided to examine that behavior in the sixty-seven households voting in the January 1986 election for which either the husband's household of origin or the wife's household of origin was also present and voting in that election. Table 6 shows that these married offspring voted the same as their parents in 80 percent of the cases. The association applies to both married sons and married daughters; while Table 6 suggests that the association may be more marked with respect to *sons*, the difference (between sons and daughters) does not appear to be statistically significant.

Interestingly, of the 54 households which apparently followed the electoral lead of the husband's parents or wife's parents, only 15 households voted for Marcos, several less than the 18 households expected on statistical grounds (i.e., applying the proportions in table 1). While this deviation is likely not statistically significant, it suggests that Aquino benefited at least as much as Marcos did from "kinship" as a determinant of voter behavior. (Note that this particular test, in table 6, does not exhaust the possible influence of kinship on voting behavior in San Jose. Note too that the influence of kinship in this test is confounded with the influence of coresidence; individuals whose parents reside and vote elsewhere probably resemble them less in voting preference.)

Finally, somewhat beyond these immediate considerations of employment, *utang na loob*, and kinship out of which political factions and party memberships are said to be fashioned lies the issue of political partisanship itself. While clearly related to these constituent factors, party membership in the election displayed a perplexing autonomy of its own, visible in the large numbers of voters on both sides who were simply *sa partido*—"for their party." I still remember one of my first conversations about the election, with one of my best friends and informants in the community, a young (and so I thought) progressive-thinking married woman. "So, who did you vote for in the presidential election?" I asked. "Marcos kami!" she replied, grinning sheepishly. I couldn't believe it, and told her so: "You voted for that turkey?!" We laughed some, because I really couldn't believe it; she was one of the people I had kept in touch with in San Jose since the time of my first research visit, and I had known her for years as a bitter critic of Marcos-era corruption. She explained her behavior thus: true, the election was ultimately between Marcos and Aquino, but what it really was in San Jose was a replay of the NP-LP contests of old, in which the newer party labels (KBL, PDP-Laban) did not figure so much as Marcos's old identification with the Nationalista Party and the opposition's identification with the Liberal Party. What she said, in effect, was that she wasn't voting for Marcos so much as she was voting NP—which had been her alignment in the past and which, not incidentally, was the alignment of most of her husband's kin, who traditionally composed a large and influential NP voting bloc in San Jose.

I didn't pursue the issue much further in her own case, but I was intrigued. I later encountered others who also explained their voting behavior by simple reference to party affiliations of old, without any discernible social or economic "motive" of the sorts just discussed. Such statements suggested, as noted above, an emergent quality to party memberships that confounds efforts (such as the preceding) to weigh separately the importance of patronage, kinship, and the like—factors which, at the least, may not be operative during any particular election. Such statements also suggest an interesting line of inquiry: might there not in fact be some significant continuities between the NP-LP factional alignments of old and the present cleavage between Marcos supporters and Aquino supporters? Because I had been present in the community during the 1971 local election for town mayor and governor, and as I had also recorded, as in table 1, the voting preferences of households then resident in San Jose, I was able to test this proposition against a small sample of households: the 53 households that were resident in San Jose in both 1971 and 1986 and who voted in both elections.

Table 7 classifies these households according as they voted NP or LP in 1971 and crossclassifies them according as they supported Marcos or Aquino in 1986. Table 7 shows that 36 of these households voted NP in 1971; Nationalista Party candidates in fact won by a large margin in San Jose as a whole that year. Table 7 also shows a revealing phenomenon: of the 17 households who voted LP in 1971, all but 2 households supported Aquino in 1986. In contrast, by 1988, the 36 one-time NP households showed no such association with Marcos and were, in fact, evenly split between the two candidates.

Table 7. Voting Preferences of 53 Households Who Voted
in Both the 1971 and 1986 Elections

	1971		
	LP	NP	
1986:			
AQUINO	15	18	
MARCOS	2	18	
Total:	17	36	53

I showed this table to Ricardo, the principal lider of the Aquino campaign in San Jose, and asked him what he thought of my informant's claim, that the contest had basically been a sort of NP-LP affair. Well, he said, it could indeed be seen in that light, and it certainly wasn't surprising that former LP voters would choose to support Aquino. But he pointed out that many former NPs had, like himself, become disillusioned with the Marcos administration and, having "learned to think for themselves," joined the opposition. Large numbers of former NP voters, apparently, did precisely that, giving Aquino her San Jose election day victory.

Discussion

If substantial numbers of voters remained sufficiently unencumbered by the constraints of employment, kinship, *utang na loob,* and prior party membership to "think for themselves" on election day, the problem remains that we can still not be sure of what they were thinking for themselves about. Certainly, it is a little facile to assume that they all thought virtuously about which candidate was most qualified to guide the ship of state. Ricardo's idealism notwithstanding, at least some of the long-time NP voters who abandoned Marcos to join the Aquino camp did so not because they were "pro-Aquino" but because they were, for whatever reasons, *silag kay Pedro*—"angry at Pedro," the longtime, pro-Marcos barangay capitan. In short, at least some people were using their votes to signal their support or rejection of their own (community) *lider,* not the actual candidates for national office.

An extreme but revealing example of this sort involved Pedro's eldest daughter, an apolitical married woman who had long followed her father's lead in community elections. Pedro, however, now about sixty-three years old, had recently remarried, following the death of his wife (and mother of his five married offspring) some years before. Pedro's daughter was angry with her father over the remarriage, as under Philippine law it meant a significant dimunition in the estate that would be shared among the children. She chose, or so it was said, to publicly rebuke her father for his decision by rejecting his traditional family political leadership and voting for Aquino. Her behavior was not only extreme but idiosyncratic—Pedro's other four children remained in the Marcos camp—but it is a sobering reminder of how personal Philippine politics can in fact be. Indeed, others were said to have signaled their disapproval of Pedro by voting for Aquino as well. Some ordinary residents were offended by, or had grown tired of, his autocratic personal style; others, it was said, one-time political allies, had become angry over unfulfilled promises of spoils in previous elections.

Such observations, like table 7 itself, are consistent with a cynical folk view of Philippine elections: that they are basically contests between the "ins" and "outs," in which the old "outs"—the losers in the last election; in the case at hand, the former LPs—are still out, having acquired in the interim no reason to support the reelectionist candidate and hence providing the core of the opposition. Here they are joined by some of the former "ins"—in the case at hand, some one-time NP supporters—who, having failed to garner a share of the spoils or having otherwise fallen out with their one-time allies following the previous election, have become disaffected. In this folk view—which has been invoked, I believe, to explain why the Philippines had no reelectionist president until Marcos—there was nothing particularly virtuous about those who "broke with their party" to support Aquino, nor was there anything particularly remarkable about the election itself.

None of this, of course, is very flattering to the rural Philippine electorate. The analysis implies, for example, that voters who "thought for themselves" about the January 1986 presidential candidates represented a sort of residual category, a group of voters who had no other reason to vote for one candidate or the other—no government job, no *utang na loob* to a lider, no other constraining economic or social circumstances—and could therefore indulge their personal preferences. Worse, the analysis implies that even as a residual category, the voters who thought for themselves are a suspect group, because there is no assurance that they were in fact thinking about anything less selfish than where greener pastures might lie for themselves personally in the future.

There is some truth to these implications, but they do some injustice—perhaps considerable injustice—to voter motives, and hence to the nature of local-level Philippine politics. Despite the skepticism I expressed earlier, to the point of dismissal, about voters' own stated motives for supporting one candidate or the other, the fact of the matter is that numerous people did vote for Aquino precisely—indeed, only—out of a genuine belief that she would be a better president—better because she would be less corrupt and more responsive to the needs of the people. Many people voted this on belief, furthermore, without any expectation of personal reward should Aquino ultimately win. I believe Aquino won in San Jose for no more complicated reason than this.

Similarly, at least some people really did vote for Marcos in the earnest belief that communism was a serious political threat to the well-being of the country and Aquino was "soft" on communism. I talked at length with one such man in January 1988, who complained bitterly about how the CIA had engineered Marcos's downfall and about how Reagan was preventing his return to the Philippines. I had known him in 1971 as an upper-status farmer who had accomplished much on his own initiative; he feared communism then as well for the economic leveling he said it would bring. Now he cited the recurring assassinations and other incidents in Manila as evidence of an accelerating drift to the left since Aquino took office. I didn't approve of this man's politics, but I could scarcely conclude that he wasn't "politically conscious," or that he was insincere in his political beliefs.

To conclude that there is room for both "selfish" and "selfless" interpretations of voter behavior may itself seem a little facile. But I was in fact fascinated by the range of perceptions held by San Jose voters about the nature of the electoral process itself. At one extreme were those party regulars who themselves saw an electorate in much the same way that Hollnsteiner and Lande did—an electorate in which most or all votes were or would be fully determined, as it were, by the structural principles of factional politics.[6] At the other extreme were those who tended to dismiss all of this as passe or at least as only relevant to understanding the voting behavior of a few. These persons also tended to resent the claims of liders that they, as voters, were *dara*—"carried"—by this or that party. They seemed, instead, to envision an electorate largely unencumbered by factional obligations— an electorate free to shop, as it were, for the best candidate for the job. These two views of the electoral process coexist, at least in part, because both kinds of voters coexist.

With these "unencumbered" voters particularly in mind, let me turn now to a wider issue: what sort of government leaders do they desire to have? Nobody really votes "selflessly," of course, and the real issue is one of immediacy; even the most altruistic-appearing voters are presumably influenced by some sort of vision of greener pastures for themselves further down the line, should their own candidate be elected. This vision is widely believed to be influenced by a voter's class circumstances, and Kerkvliet, in fact, found that class awareness was a factor in the presidential election in the Nueva Ecija community he studied (with poor peasants tending to support Marcos and the landless tending to support Aquino).[7] The gist of my own analysis above was that differences of this sort did not figure in San Jose's election. But San Jose residents may nevertheless be class aware, in ways simply not manifested in voting patterns at election time, because (as Kerkvliet says) elections alone may provide too limited an arena in which to observe this phenomenon. To pursue this possibility, I hence return briefly to the question of San Jose's own socioeconomic structure. I indicated earlier that this structure was complex and difficult to characterize; here I would like to examine some of these complexities with an eye toward the issue at hand.

A good place to begin is to explain why I did not attempt, in my "second approach" to data analysis above, to correlate voter preferences, between Marcos and Aquino, with categories representing the amount of land each household owned or controlled. This approach, implicit (but not quantified) in Kerkvliet's analysis, would seem an obvious, even crucial, test of the possible importance of "class awareness" to voter behavior, with the number and type of land-based categories employed determined by local production arrangements and the quality and detail of the data obtained. But in San Jose, such categories likely would not illuminate voter behavior because they do not illuminate economic behavior. First, most households residing in San Jose now apparently derive the bulk of their income from off-farm sources. For some, but not all, of these latter households, agriculture is a significant secondary income source, and there are still the many households whose primary income source remains farming. But for the community as a whole, the importance of landownership to economic well-being ranges from very important to irrelevant.

Second, even those households which derive all or a significant part of their income from farming—for whom land ownership is presumably important—may not easily be disaggregated into "land-based" categories. For one thing, it is hard to capture in simple categories important gradations in land security. To "own" land in the narrowest sense is to possess titled land; but many San Jose farmers, who acquired and have long occupied their land under homestead laws, and who consider themselves "owners," do not yet possess clear titles, although they have applied for titles at the Bureau of Lands and pay real estate taxes annually. Other residents are "inheritors"—currently landless, but who expect (but cannot count on) some portion of a parental estate. Still other residents rent land for their agricultural production activities; others "squat," rent free, on the land of friends or kin. (That a number of vegetable gardens use land rent free, while others pay rent only on the order of 500 pesos per half-hectare per year, further suggests that "landownership" is a less crucial variable here than elsewhere.) For another thing, and as these observations suggest, land use is as important as land ownership. Some relatively prosperous vegetable gardeners, with little or no land of their own, employ two or three monthly laborers. They are technically "landless," and yet they are closer to "rural capitalists" in their economic behavior than are their poorer, landed-counterparts who pursue more traditional, land-extensive production activities.

To this setting, we must add complexities in labor use; the multiplicity of economic activities, even within single households, makes it difficult to operationalize even such seemingly basic concepts as "occupation" and "primary source of income." In one household, for example, not unusual, the wife attends market daily, both to sell her own produce and to engage in the buy-and-sell trade. The husband manages their three hectares of tree crops, he occasionally hires unskilled labor (to assist in the more onerous farm chores) or hires himself out as a skilled laborer (he knows some carpentry), and he engages in some petty entrepreneurship (he sprays mango trees to promote flowering, in return for a share of the harvest). Numerous other activities, involving different production activities, could be cited; the point is simply that many San Jose residents enter into different relations with the means of production at the same time, rendering impossible the demarcation and juxtaposition of clearcut collectivities of households standing in common relationships to those means.[8]

Added to this lack of class crystallization—or rather, contributing to it—is the marked geographical and (for some) socioeconomic mobility experienced by households in Palawan communities such as San Jose. One of my most striking findings when I returned to San Jose in 1988 was that out of the 112 households originally present in 1971, only 63 households remained. Some of the other 49 households had broken up or become extinct, but most had simply left the community for other locales and better economic opportunities. That such opportunities can still be found on Palawan reflects a congeries of related circumstances: low population density; a predominantly upland agricultural technology; a smallholder-dominated agrarian structure; and a relatively equitable, "middle-oriented" income distribution. (These circumstances also help explain, I believe, Palawan's earlier-noted tradition of nonviolent elections, as well as the virtual absence, throughout the province, of NPA or vigilante activities.)

It remains a question for my current research to determine the extent to which domestic cycling and geographical mobility among San Jose households between 1971 and 1988 were actually associated with upward or downward socioeconomic mobility. But as van Schendel observed among the Bangladesh peasants he studied, individual and household mobility experiences and expectations of this sort scarcely promote development of the more subjective aspects of "class consciousness."[9] More could be said about these issues, but I trust it is apparent why, like van Schendel, I will continue to eschew artificial class categories in my analyses in favor of simple groups (as in tables 3 and 4) representing different kinds of occupations or levels of socioeconomic well-being.

Returning now to the "greener pastures" question and if San Jose's voters are not apparently class conscious, what are they conscious of? The assessments they make of the Aquino administration to date are helpful in this regard. Support for Aquino grew after the February 1986 presidential election; in the May 1987 congressional election, Ramon Mitra, a close ally of Aquino known to be her personal choice for Speaker of the House, overwhelmed the Marcos-linked opposition candidate. Those who continue to oppose the Aquino administration cite the peace and order situation in Manila and the continued NPA insurgency in the countryside as evidence that she is not in control. Some residents also counted the 1987 Mendiola incident against her; one pointed out that Marcos confronted protestors all the time without killing them. Those who speak favorably of the Aquino administration, however, consistently emphasize two things: the restoration of democracy (there are regular elections again), and the improved economic climate (it's easier to make a living now).

Of these two concerns, I believe the concern with the state of the economy to be paramount and, if I may speculate a bit, in the following way. Standing back and looking at San Jose as a community of owner-operators, and excluding the small minority of persons who can in fact accurately be described as "tenants" or "agricultural wage workers," the overall ambience remains one of general prosperity. The "opportunities to be enterprising" remain broadly accessible; individual initiative, entrepreneurship, and hardwork can be rewarded by socioeconomic advancement. (I realize this sounds a little Arcadian, and so I add that many San Jose residents, of all socioeconomic levels, talk about their community in similar terms. Also, for them and for myself, such alleged community attributes are only by way of implicit comparison with other rural Philippine communities in less promising circumstances.)

In such a setting, it is not surprising that land reform or other proposed government efforts to redistribute wealth are not important political issues in the community. What people do appear to want, quite simply, are government leaders who will do their parts to keep the existing economic competition fair and open—to maintain an economic atmosphere in which rural residents succeed or fail based on their own personal effort and acumen. Sure, many San Jose residents were angered by the megacorruption of Marcos and his cronies. But what really angers them is to learn that many of the improved cattle distributed in Palawan under the Livestock Dispersal Project of PIADP went to rich farmers or to the allies of politicians. While there may be lots of opportunities to be enterprising, life is still tough, and government should make it a little easier for the ordinary folks to compete—not a little tougher still.

What elections are about, in this perspective, is the attempted replacement of corrupt officials with honest ones. People recognize that elections are a highly imperfect mechanism for this purpose, but it's the only one they have, so at least they should occur regularly (hence the need for "democracy"). In the 1988 local elections, the campaign slogan *mabuay sa sirvicio* ("a long time [government] service") was used against the Marcos-era Puerto Princesa City mayor running for reelection while allied with Mitra and Aquino. This ironical turn of phrase is heard throughout the Philippines, I suspect, each election time. One woman voted for this man's opponent for mayor; she didn't know, she said, whether he would be corrupt or not, but she knew the ex-mayor was corrupt. *OK naman si Aquino*, she added, *piro cong tula dan den lamang ang dalagan i ang gobierno digue sa Palawan . . .* —"Aquino's fine, but if thing's don't change here in Palawan. . . ."

These and other comments I heard during my 1988 visit suggest that there may indeed have been local-level counterparts, albeit more subdued, to the momentary "opening" in the Philippine national politics that appeared to accompany "EDSA" and its aftermath. In San Jose, this opening took the form of a significant decrease in cynicism about the electoral process and a corresponding increase in the belief that government can, in fact, be made to work democratically in an even-handed fashion. As the particular comment cited above suggests, however, the potential for peaceful change created by this opening is already being squandered.

MICHAEL PINCHES

The Working Class Experience of Shame, Inequality, and People Power in Tatalon, Manila

Two issues are the concern of the present essay. The first is the people power uprising of February 1986 and my continued uneasiness with the explanations that have been given for it, specifically relating to the involvement of Manila's working class. The second more general issue concerns the structure and culture of social inequality in Manila and the ways in which they manifest themselves in consciousness, interpersonal relations and political action. Thus the major question the essay addresses is: how was Manila's working class involved in the events of February 1986 and did this involvement represent an acceptance or rejection of the existing sociopolitical order? Despite the proliferation of literature following the overthrow of the Marcos regime this question has received very little attention.[1]

The material I use is drawn mainly from research in an urban worker community in the Manila squatter settlement of Tatalon.[2] It concerns social relations between the people of this community and others like them—a people commonly known in Manila as the "urban poor" or *masa* (masses)—and the people they in turn describe as the *mayaman* (rich) or the *burgis*, to use a term popularized from the late 1960s, meaning bourgeois. While the people of Tatalon sometimes distinguish other strata in Manila society, depending on the situation or issue at hand, it is this "dichotomic conception" which predominates as they reflect upon themselves and others around them.[3] This conception may lack sociological sophistication, but since I am primarily concerned here with the people's own imagery, I too employ the same model. Elsewhere I have argued that the people of Tatalon are best viewed, both in terms of livelihood and outlook, as a part of Manila's working class and hence I reject as inadequate the more common label, "urban poor."[4] Nevertheless, this label forms a part of Manila's political parlance and here I use it interchangeably with working class and *masa*.

The aspect of social relations between rich and poor that I focus on concerns what people in Tatalon commonly refer to by the Tagalog term *hiya*, normally translated as shame or embarrassment. For the most part, I am concerned here with the more intense emotion of shame. The term *hiya* is sometimes used alone, but more often arises in various derivative words.[5] These words figure prominently in daily conversation about interpersonal relations. Indeed, in one tradition of Philippine sociology, *hiya* is referred to as a key factor in understanding society and culture in the Philippines.[6] While drawing attention to the importance of the concept, the normative consensus model usually found in these studies fails to examine the structured political, economic and social contexts in which *hiya* arises, or is invoked. It generally ignores the variable and often ambiguous meanings given to the term and, in particular, it fails to consider the significance of shame in terms of class relations.

Here I argue that the behavior and feelings denoted by the term *hiya*, and its derivations, can act both as instruments of subordination to the prevailing social order, and as expressions of class resentment and action. *Hiya* is thus revealed as at once an element of both hegemonic and counterhegemonic processes. Both the feeling of shame and the act of inflicting shame are important to an understanding of working class involvement in the People Power uprising of 1986.

Tatalon, The Visayan Area

The squatter settlement of Tatalon houses over 20,000 people. Many of them are former peasants who left a life of poverty in the countryside in search of a more prosperous existence in the city. The people of Tatalon live in a number of local communities, some of which are founded on provincial-linguistic ties. Families and individuals rely heavily on networks of mutual help, and it is in the local communities that these are most fully developed. The community in which I worked comprises over one thousand people. It is known locally as the Visayan Area because it has been populated mainly by Cebuanos migrating from Leyte and other Visayan provinces since the 1930s. The largest group trace their origins to the municipality of Palompon in northwest Leyte.

While the great majority who have settled in Tatalon experience increased incomes and view life in Manila as better than life in the countryside, most live an existence of unstable employment and insecure residence. In the Visayan Area, most workers earn a living as manual laborers in construction, manufacture and service industries and, though many are self-employed, about two thirds are wage-workers.[8] The people live mainly in self-built houses, comprising one or two rooms constructed largely from reused timbers and galvanized iron. An increasing number of families have television sets and other electrical appliances, though most have only a few pieces of furniture, usually home-made or produced by local carpenters. The vast majority of families have incomes below levels officially deemed necessary for covering minimum living expenses and nutritional requirements.[9]

In the Visayan Area most people have few clothes and other personal possessions, and their income is mainly devoted to food, most of which is purchased daily. Malnutrition is a common experience among the children and many people suffer tuberculosis, influenza, gastroenteritis, skin diseases, and other poverty-related illnesses. The people also suffer the constant anxiety of insecure residence. As squatters, all have been periodically harassed by officials and the agents of powerful real estate interests, while some have been evicted and had their houses demolished. Over the last years of the Marcos administration, piped water was connected to many dwellings, and concealed drains and concrete walkways were installed through much of the neighborhood. For those with access to them, these services are looked upon as a welcome improvement over previous living conditions, though many people still have to provide their own water and drainage, while waste disposal continues to present difficulties throughout the community.

The people of the Visayan Area, like people of other squatter settlements, are not uniformly disadvantaged. There are differences in the quality of their houses, in the age and cost of their clothing, in the food they eat and in their expenditure on family religious celebrations. There are also significant differences in the levels of formal education. Since 1979 local inequalities have become more stark as many men gained relatively well-paid construction work in the Middle East and as others were laid off work in factory and construction retrenchments that came with the economic crisis of the mid 1980s. Overall, the more longstanding residents have improved their incomes, both through overseas contract work and through the collection of rents as more newcomers have come to live in the neighborhood. Nevertheless, job security is such that the relative prosperity enjoyed by some families is often only shortlived.

Though material hardship is a constant source of anguish for people in the Visayan Area, equally striking is their vibrant collective life and sense of community. Important household activities are conducted indoors but only during the sleeping hours do people close themselves away from their neighbors. The focus of day-to-day life, when people are not away working, shopping or at school, is found in the public outdoor spaces where people wash their clothes, pump and collect water, play games, drink together, engage in discussion or humorous exchange, and, in general, pursue the activities they enjoy. Regular face-to-face contact between neighbors is treated as both normal and desirable. Apart from the informal day-to-day interaction within the community, locally organized dances, Christmas and New Year celebrations, along with wakes and other such activities also draw individuals into regular group life. The people of the Visayan Area often associate their sense of community with their common identity as Visayans, or more specifically as people from Palompon, Leyte. Many also associate it with the large number of kin most of them have in the neighborhood. Many of these kin relations are traced back to the countryside but most have been given social meaning in Manila. The same is true of shared regional-linguistic ties.

In large part, the significance of these relationships is to be found in mutual help: in finding work, in acquiring food, clothing and money, in borrowing household items, in conducting courtship and disputes, and in obtaining information, advice and protection. Personal relationships differ greatly in the extent to which such help is sought and given, yet there is a general understanding that residence in the Visayan Area obliges one to help and entitles one to seek help. Moreover, such views merge with a local wisdom about the state of the world, the meaning of success and failure, and the character of rich and poor in the Philippines. Particular individuals hold contending ideas; indeed debates are common and lively, but most opinions, experiences and information are aired and evaluated publicly.

While the Visayan Area expresses communal solidarity, vis-à-vis the outside world, it is also a collective vehicle through which the people come to terms with and participate in this outside world. Thus, alongside the common sense of identity and the local esteem that comes with sharing and mutual help, internal status differences are judged according to the same criteria as prevail in Manila at large. Differences in income, occupational standing, job security, educational achievement and private consumption play a big part in the way the people evaluate each other and seek recognition. In this sense the Visayan Area is coextensive with and a microcosm of the outside world. Thus, while the local perspective on national politics offered by the Visayan Area is in certain respects unique, it also arises out of a series of conditions and circumstances that prevail among Manila squatters in general.

Tatalon, the State, and the "EDSA Revolution"

Tatalon is divided administratively into two *barangay* or wards, each with its own barangay captain. These wards are in turn subdivided into districts, each with its own barangay councilor. Before the declaration of Martial Law in 1972, these were elective positions but between 1972 and 1982, barangay captains and councilors were appointed. Government-controlled elections held in 1982 saw only minor changes in the makeup and activities of the councils. Throughout this period the barangays functioned primarily as agents of authoritarian rule and worked closely with the police and Philippine Constabulary in maintaining control over the squatters. While many people sought assistance from the barangay officials, nearly all regarded them with suspicion and fear.

The other principal arm of government in Tatalon is the National Housing Authority which, since 1979, has been implementing a major redevelopment scheme as part of its nationwide urban housing program. Under this scheme parts of Tatalon have been subdivided and lots have been sold on a mortgage basis to longstanding residents. Recently settled squatters have been evicted or forced onto other vacant sites in Tatalon. For a number of years, the National Housing Authority has operated an office in Tatalon and through its surveys, public meetings and distribution of notices, has had a significant impact on the people. For most of this time it has worked closely with the barangay councils. It has been a major source of anxiety and apprehension among the people.

The most politicized issue facing the people of Tatalon and most squatters elsewhere in Manila is land tenure. Squatters throughout Manila have strenuously resisted periodic attempts by landowners and officials to evict them, and in many cases, violent confrontations have ensued. Such encounters have occurred often in Tatalon and this settlement has a reputation as having been one of the city's most militant.[10]

Like other presidents and political leaders before him, Marcos sought to win a popular base among the poor of Manila in reference to the issue of land tenure. Indeed, from the mid 1970s, the Marcos administration tried more than any of its predecessors to control the city's squatters. In part, this involved evictions on an unprecedented scale, a policy which had the support of property developers, but which aroused much resentment and opposition among squatters and groups supporting them. Yet the Marcos program also involved "sites and services" schemes of the type being implemented in Tatalon.[11] At the time of its political demise, the Marcos government had processed or was processing the claims of thousands of families through these schemes. While the majority of squatters in Manila were not included, the program offered some hope that in the future they might escape the insecurity and stigma of squatting. The program was carefully presented as an act of generosity and patronage by the First Couple, who, on a number of occasions, visited Tatalon and other settlements to win support and to distribute certificates of "award." Schoolchildren were taught to sing songs of thanks and their parents were instructed to applaud and display pro Marcos banners during these visits. The speeches and leaflets presented on such occasions stressed the generous patronage of the First Couple couched in the populist rhetoric of the "New Society."

When the presidential elections was called in 1985, the Marcos administration appeared to wield much influence in Tatalon. Both the National Housing Authority and barangay councils campaigned for a Marcos victory, various forms of largesse were offered, and many people depended directly or indirectly on Marcos-controlled State patronage for their livelihood. Perhaps most important, the Marcos government's redevelopment program was welcomed by the majority as a relief from years of struggle over a secure place to live in, despite the continued uncertainty over mortgage repayments. If nothing else, the level of intimidation that the Marcos regime had been able to instill among the people of Tatalon seemed enough to guarantee electoral victory, especially given the apparent lack of organizational and military power available to the Aquino opposition. Indeed, once the election results were tallied, the Marcos party publicly announced victory in Tatalon, and among the urban poor generally, largely on the basis of its housing and urban land reform program. However, even official figures showed that this victory was by a slender margin and applied only to the barangay most affected by the redevelopment program. Taking the two barangays of Tatalon together, both Marcos and opposition figures showed an electoral victory for Aquino. Within the two barangays, the pattern was also uneven. In the Visayan Area, where the government's redevelopment program had been most fully implemented, 57 percent of voters were recorded to have supported Aquino. Given the regime's institutional powers and its record during previous elections and referendums, these results were quite remarkable.

More interesting than the official results however, was the mood of opposition that built up in Tatalon during the campaign period, and particularly after the election, when many, who said they had voted for Marcos, changed sides and joined the protest rallies that culminated in the overthrow of the government. All through this period,

Aquino's supporters in Tatalon had been the most vocal. It was their talk and camaraderie that dominated the public arena, along the roads, alleyways, and clearings. It was they who displayed the most enthusiasm, good humor, and confidence. Most of those who attended the Marcos rallies went for the money and other gifts available, while those participating in the antigovernment demonstrations generally paid their own fares and brought their own meals. In the election aftermath, they comprised the great majority.

Not all people in the Visayan Area had taken an equal interest in the election: some remained skeptical and showed limited interest even as the mutiny by some sections of the armed forces was being staged. But increasingly, throughout the election period and during the civil disobedience campaign and protest rallies that followed, more and more people were drawn into the political arena. Keeping up with the latest news broadcasts over the Catholic radio station, on television, through the newspapers, and by word of mouth, as relatives and neighbors returned from the streets, became a major preoccupation.

I do not have any figures on the proportion of people in the Visayan Area who were present outside the military barracks and television stations where the final drama of Marcos's defeat was played out. Certainly most stayed at home, many of them fearful of the outcome. Nevertheless, I estimate that the majority of the youth in the community and a high proportion of the men joined the crowds that flocked to EDSA. Some said they responded directly to the call of Cardinal Sin, head of the Catholic Church, and a great many said they would not have gone had it not been for this directive and the large presence of nuns and priests. This was not, however, the sole reason for participating. Many said they went out of curiosity, or because their friends and relatives were going, or simply because "everyone was there." Some went with their families, some with their friends or peers (barkada) from the community, and others with their work mates from outside the community. Most only stayed during the day, to come home late in the evening and, in some cases, to return early the following morning. Some, notably young men, stayed overnight, sometimes taking their own sleeping mats and blankets, sometimes availing themselves of those brought by others in the crowd. Food was also taken and shared—often with complete strangers.

In the final days, students stayed away from school and many workers took time off from work to go to EDSA. Though participants from the Visayan Area always went in groups, they did not congregate in any particular locations, but say they moved around and merged easily with the rest of the crowd. As different pockets in the crowd chanted political messages, or prayed the rosary, people from the

Visayan Area joined in. Continuing their discussion from Tatalon, some talked with their companions, or others around them, about the problems they associated with Marcos rule—high prices, unemployment, corruption, the large foreign debt, and so forth. But in recalling these experiences, the people of Tatalon lay most stress on the camaraderie, the vitality and the enjoyment of the occasion. Many describe a fiesta atmosphere. Even those remaining at home, but keeping up with events through their neighbors and radio broadcasts, describe similar feelings in Tatalon. Once it was known that the Marcos family had left the country, similar scenes to those that occurred elsewhere in Manila broke out in the Visayan Area and in Tatalon generally. People banged tins, laughed, danced, greeted each other, and generally celebrated in a manner that they describe as being like New Year's Eve.

The Politics of Shame

The involvement of people from Tatalon in the presidential elections and popular uprising of February 1986 cannot be understood simply, or even primarily, in terms of electoral politics or support for either Marcos or Aquino. Certainly the desire by many people to remove Marcos was strong; conversely, many saw much appeal in the apparent sincerity and honesty of Aquino. Indeed much debate and discussion among people in the Visayan Area referred to the respective strengths and weaknesses of the two candidates. However, more fundamental than these issues are matters concerning social relations between the people of Tatalon and those they describe as the rich or burgis, and the extraordinary character that these relations assumed during the events of February 1986. An important dimension of these relations concerns the politics of shame.

Much of the literature touching on social and political relations between different classes in Philippine society either stresses normative consensus and reciprocity or economic exploitation, political repression and conflicting material interests.[12] What one approach lacks in sensitivity to political-economy and social conflict, the other lacks in careful cultural analysis. Both generally suffer in their failure to adequately explore the differences and tensions that are to be found in the attitudes and social practices of dominant and subordinate groups.[13]

As I have indicated, material deprivation and economic hardship are fundamental to daily experience in the Visayan Area. They are a constant source of anxiety and discontent. Yet material deprivation is always mediated and given meaning through social relations. What matters most to people in Tatalon is the way others attribute or deny value to them as human beings. It is primarily in this context that wealth differences are to be understood. Indeed, it is the common burgis tendency to portray the lives of the poor purely in terms of material deprivation that people in the Visayan Area find so degrading and shaming. Seen as eking out a bare hand-to-mouth existence, they are effectively denied their own humanity and culture. Hence, the common satirical rhyme spoken in Tatalon:

Isang kahig, isang tuka
Ganyan kaming mga dukha.

One scratch, one peck
that is the life for us, the poor.

For people of the Visayan Area, the feelings of shame and the act of shaming are common to the daily experience of interpersonal and interclass relations. As has been observed widely in the Philippine literature, shame is frequently used or invoked as a principal sanction in reciprocal relations, most notably in those involving a debt of gratitude (*utang na loob*).[14] The pairing of shame and debt of gratitude arises generally in interpersonal relations, but it is of particular importance in relations of patronage, including political patronage.[15]

In many ways, the Martial Law years saw the Marcos family establish themselves as supreme patrons. Thus in Tatalon, Christmas gifts would be dispersed through the National Housing Authority or through barangay local officials as presents from the First Couple. Relief aid and State employment were distributed in a similar fashion. But most significant in Tatalon and the Visayan Area was the Marcoses' use of the urban redevelopment scheme to cultivate a sense of moral indebtedness. The people of Tatalon had fought vigorously for decades to avoid demolition and eviction and this scheme, which allowed most residents to remain in the settlement, thus appeared to offer a valuable source of political support. That there was to be no state subsidy, that the people would have to pay commercial rates, and that many had already paid in money and in kind to government officials and real estate operators, were downplayed as the whole exercise was elaborately conducted as an act of presidential generosity and compassion (*awa*).

This cultivation of moral indebtedness was the focal point of Marcos's presidential campaign in Tatalon. National Housing Authority and barangay officials regularly reminded people of their debt of gratitude over the "gift" of land, and promised those who had not so far gained secure tenure that this would come if Marcos was reelected. The theme of patronal benevolence was invoked by Marcos campaigners in different ways throughout the country, and in Tatalon this was not limited to the issue of land tenure. Government employees and local officials were also reminded of their loyalties and debts of gratitude to the First Couple. For those not bound by these sorts of obligations, there was the cruder source of debt, established through monetary gifts distributed in the weeks and days before the election. Implicit in all of these moves was that gratitude and the fear of shame would ensure electoral support for Marcos as the appropriate act of reciprocity.

Patronage politics undoubtedly brought the Marcos regime significant electoral support. A number of people in the Visayan Area cited a feeling of personal debt over the house lots they had been awarded or the jobs they had been given, and said explicitly that they would have felt ashamed had they not voted for Marcos. Indeed, when it was discovered that Aquino had received most of the votes, a number of local officials, visibly shaken by this result, accused others in the community of being ungrateful, of having no shame.

Conspicuous generosity, debts of gratitude, and the sanction of shame are clearly not the only elements to political patronage in the Philippines. Ultimately, the principal element is institutional power and the reality or threat of State violence. This element was most pronounced during the Marcos years and with nearly every reference to presidential generosity and moral indebtedness, was the veiled threat of retribution or suffering, should particular individuals or communities not support the regime. Some people in Tatalon looked upon Marcos's strength and preparedness to use force as a positive attribute, especially given the perceived threat of civil war which the government had played up during the campaign. Believing the opposition party to be lacking in political and military might, many people supported Marcos for primarily pragmatic reasons—they did not want to be on the losing side and risk the consequences. Yet this pragmatism also extended to taking a public stance of support for Marcos, but voting for Aquino.

While the power of the Marcos party was seen by some as a positive attribute, nearly everyone in the Visayan Area expressed ambivalence over this. For the most part, the repressive side of the regime's character worked against its reelection, once it became clear over the final weeks and days that the President's might had waned in the face of concerted opposition. For years, people in Tatalon had lived in fear of the government; some had lost their lives at the hands of the military, many had been injured, arrested and detained and virtually all had

suffered harassment or intimidation of some kind. While these circumstances had increased the authority of local people appointed to
barangay office, there was deep-seated resentment among the majority of ordinary people who felt they had no choice but to endure their
hardship in silence.

A common feeling in the Visayan Area was that a good government needed to be strong to prevent social disorder, but that Marcos's
rule had been excessively harsh. Likewise it was generally accepted
that private enrichment came with high public office, but again that
the Marcos family had taken corruption and extravagance to unac-
ceptable extremes, robbing the country of its wealth and leaving it
exhausted and defenseless. Hence, a common saying among Visayans
in Tatalon was, "*Marcos Tikuskus,*" *tikuskus* referring to the figure of
a person pitifully hunched in foetal position unable to move for the
pangs of hunger.

Perhaps the most deeply felt grievance against the Marcos regime
was the contempt with which the people felt they were being treated.
In the newspapers, on television and radio, and occasionally at public
meetings in Tatalon, they would hear passionate speeches from the
Marcoses about how the regime intended to uplift the lot of the poor,
about how it would give or had given the people the land they had
longed for, and so forth. But people in the Visayan Area knew from
painful experience that none of these had come to pass, indeed, that
no serious attempt had been made to help the poor. The cost of the
Christmas gifts they received were often outweighed by the bribes
they had to pay government officials, and while they welcomed the
opportunity to win legal status in Tatalon, most had no illusions about
the fact that it was they who had to pay for the land and the cost of
providing water, drainage, and pathways. Some sarcastically said they
thanked President Marcos for his signature, that being all that he had
contributed. At one Tatalon public meeting, Imelda Marcos had
addressed a crowd pronouncing in dramatic tones her compassion
for the poor and her pledge to give the people their land. Amidst
polite clapping, one man held aloft a small pot of soil calling out
simply "one pot of land (*isang pasong lupa*)." Normally people in Tatalon
would not take the risk of airing their disbelief with such sarcastic
defiance, but this man's actions were echoed later by others as they
returned home.

When Martial Law was declared in 1972, the government responded
harshly to any forms of dissent in Tatalon, particularly in the light of
the settlement's former militancy. Even mild criticism was denied a
legitimate place in the life of squatters. In 1979 when the Housing
Authority commenced work in the settlement, it began a series of

meetings which were announced as opportunities for the people to, at last, air their views and participate in the planning process. However, these meetings were nearly always attended by highly visible armed military personnel and were conducted in such a manner as to stifle serious debate. It was common after such occasions to hear someone remark: "They are just making fools of us (*Niloloko lang nila tayo*)." Sometimes after such statements the people would add that they could do nothing to change this because they were "held by the throat (*hawak sa leeg*)."

These experiences and feelings add a second dimension to the significance of shame in patron-client relations, one that is touched on only rarely in Philippine sociological literature, namely the act of shaming. Here the issue is not the embarrassment and humility that are felt, because of failure to fulfill a debt of gratitude. Rather, in the instances cited, people say that the Marcoses, and government officials generally, treat them without respect and insult their dignity, that is that they make them feel ashamed ("hiniya kami"—"we are made to feel ashamed"). These acts of shaming do not so much bring inner feelings of embarrassment or loss of face; rather, they arouse resentment and hostility. Thus, the failure of many people to vote for Marcos had as much to do with the issue of shame as did the fact that some felt obliged to vote for him. Before pursuing further the political significance of shaming behavior, I wish to return to the first dimension of shame as it concerns the inner feelings of social inadequacy.

Structure, Symbols, and Subordination of Shame

In Tatalon, the feeling of shame is used to describe the painful experience of everyday life. For the people with whom I worked, the experience of poverty, hardship and subordination is not just the experience of having to go without in a material sense; more fundamentally, it is the experience of not being valued as human beings, of having to endure humiliation, disapproval and rejection, of constantly having one's dignity challenged.[16] These feelings of shame are not so much brought about by one's failure to fulfill a debt of gratitude, or by some misdeed or negligence, rather they are inflicted from above by virtue of one's life's circumstances; they are embedded in the structure of class society.

For those denied access to status, wealth and opportunity, the institutions of inequality bring with them a sense of inferiority. Thus, in Manila's social division of labor, Tatalon people learn through bitter experience that, while others may live comfortably without having to work, they themselves must work to survive. Yet they also learn through their work experience that they are expendable and can easily be reduced to destitution. Moreover, in the structure of labor relations they learn that their time is less valued than that of their bosses. They receive less money for it, and while they often have to wait for hours, even weeks to be paid or to arrange a short meeting over a problem they might have, their superiors control their activities at a moment's notice.

People in the Visayan Area also contrast their own relatively low levels of formal education to those found among the people they describe as the burgis, and they know, when they go for a job, or have dealings with officialdom, or need medical attention or legal assistance, that they will be disadvantaged. They feel humiliated by the fact that they cannot provide for and protect their families in the same way those among the *burgis* can. They are painfully aware at Sunday mass, for example, that their children often do not look as strong and healthy as the children of the burgis sitting along the central aisle. And they know in all kinds of public ceremony that it is the rich, not they, who occupy pride of place. They know that in death too, there is inequality. Should they oppose the government, they could easily be liquidated and the media would pay them little attention, but should someone like Benigno Aquino be murdered, and this is far less likely, it would bring wide publicity. Their wakes, funerals, cemeteries, and headstones too, are less prominent than those commanded by the *burgis*. In short, the people of Tatalon know only too well that, in the social hierarchy of Philippine society, they occupy a position near the bottom.

From these conditions and experiences spring an endless variety of situations and actions that can bring shame. The labels of poverty, propertylessness, and uncertain employment are inescapable—they are embedded in one's speech and language skills, in one's command of etiquette and bureaucratic procedure; they are evident in the texture and usually the color of one's skin, or in the condition of one's teeth, dentures and hair; they can often be seen in one's posture and gait, or in the quality of one's attire, jewelry and makeup, in the type of food one buys, in the location of one's home, workplace and school, or in the company one keeps. In Manila, both rich and poor have an acute sensitivity to these signs and symbols of human value. They represent an intrinsic part of the dominant hegemonic order and find expression in popular cinema, magazines, newspapers and books, in television programs and billboard advertising, as well as in interpersonal relations. In Tatalon, the sensitivity to these labels carries with it much pain and self-doubt, so that when people find themselves in the company of others more privileged than themselves, or are faced with this prospect, they commonly say "we feel ashamed" ("*nahiya kami*" or simply "*nakakahiya*").

The nature of the subordinate consciousness being suggested here cannot be understood simply in terms of signs, symbols, and ideology. To a large extent it is born out of pragmatism as is particularly evident in employment. For example, a number of workers in the Visayan Area have openly rejected the industrial structure and regimented work practices established by their employers, only to find themselves unemployed and unable to support their families. Thus, most workers accept the regimentation and authoritarianism that come with working for a boss, because they know of no viable alternative way of making a living. Some workers describe the feelings of shame that arise here not merely as an outcome of the lowly position they are placed in, but rather as a consequence of withholding or concealing their discontent. It is also in this context that workers speak of having to "sacrifice" themselves for the good of their families. Not only do they have to endure the hardship of the working life itself; they also have to learn to live with the practice of repressing their own anger.

Furthermore, when people in the Visayan Area agree that the Philippines has to be ruled by people who are wealthy and who have high levels of formal education, they are not simply internalizing a dominant value system, but are reflecting upon their own experiences. In politics, they are well aware of the fact that the candidates who win need to spend a lot of money on elections, and that they themselves simply do not have that amount of money. They also recognize that many established bureaucratic and administrative procedures used in government require learned specialist skills which they have been unable to acquire. Moreover, the legitimacy attributed to credentials gained through formal education owes much to the fact that people in Tatalon themselves experience limited success on the basis of school certificates. In a similar way, many people in Tatalon gain local status and self-esteem on the basis of conspicuous consumption, a practice that the burgis also engage in. However, the outcome of participation in such systems of achievement is that most people find themselves bound to accept the logic of their collective subordination since, as a group, they are never able to acquire the same educational or consume status as the burgis.

The structures and symbols of inequality experienced by people in the Visayan Area foster feelings of inferiority and shame, but they also promote discontent and the desire for a better life. This inspires many to work hard and to tolerate hardship so that they, or their children, may escape their predicament through schooling or private consumer status. A second way in which the people deal with their devaluation in the wider society is through avoidance and social closure, that is by minimizing the number of shaming or degrading situations in which they find themselves, and by withdrawing behind social boundaries that distance them from the rich and give prominence to principles of solidarity and mutual help. This, in large part, explains the vitality and enjoyment associated with community life in Tatalon. Though the world of the burgis—of employer, landowners, officials and teachers—is ever present, it is not as intrusive within Tatalon as it is outside. Inside the settlement and within its constituent communities, like the Visayan Area, there reigns a limited autonomy which allows people to assert and express themselves in ways that are not possible at work, at school, at church, in government offices, or in busy shopping centers. At home, in the Visayan Area, the contemptuous eye of the burgis can be kept at bay and commonality enjoyed. In part, the practices of sharing and mutual help found within the community are adaptive strategies aimed at dealing with material hardship and uncertainty. But they also provide an alternative moral setting within which the people are able to assert, in common, the dignity and humanity otherwise denied them. Thus, within the Visayan Area, one finds the contending themes of status hierarchy and egalitarianism constantly being played off against each other.

Social Encounters and Class Conflict in Shaming

The structures and symbols of social inequality in Manila engender feelings of inferiority and shame among the people of Tatalon, and though they also engender feelings of discontent, these feelings are largely absorbed in the quest for upward social mobility or through practices of avoidance and withdrawal. Moreover, in attempting to explain their disadvantaged position, most people in the Visayan Area are more inclined to attribute this to the bad luck of having poor ancestors than they are to blaming the rich or the social system. However, this is not the full picture.

It is useful, for analytical purposes, to treat the structural and symbolic dimensions of social inequality separately from the social encounters through which they are acted out. But it is also necessary to examine these encounters: it is here that we can appreciate more fully the ambiguous qualities of shame. So far I have treated the burgis as if they were simply passive beneficiaries of an unequal social order. This is not the case, for in general, they practice similar shaming behavior toward the people of Tatalon as did the Marcoses. Thus, when members of the Visayan Area carry with them the various labels of poverty described earlier, it is not only their behavior that is affected. Indeed, it is largely the response that these symbols elicit among the burgis that is important.

The general experience of people in the Visayan Area is that the burgis response is one of contempt, ridicule or patronizing sympathy. This is often communicated in body language—for example, through the look that fails to even recognize a person's presence, a feature of burgis behavior that people in Tatalon often simply refer to as *"no pansin"* ("no recognition"). Alternatively, the behavior of the rich is often described by the term *matapobre*, meaning in general that they are snobbish, but more particularly, as the term suggests (*mata* - eye, *pobre* - poor), that they greet the poor with a mannered gaze of condescending scrutiny. People also speak of other more subtle forms of body language which they interpret in a similar way.

In verbal communication with employers, officials, teachers or priests, people in Tatalon often feel that they are being spoken down to. Students frequently complain that they have trouble learning at school because they are "too ashamed" to ask questions since, when they do, the teacher scolds them for not knowing anything or for being impudent. Through the common experience of verbal insults or through conversation they have overheard, people in the Visayan Area are also aware of a range of demeaning terminology that the burgis may use to describe them. Sometimes the residents of squatter settlements are simply described as *basura* (rubbish). The very term "squatter" or *iskwater*, which until recently described the legal status of most residents in Tatalon, carries a strongly pejorative meaning and is used widely in this sense. Residents of Tatalon are sometimes referred to as *palaboy* (tramp, vagrant), *ignorante* (ignorant) or "no read no write." One of the most insulting terms of address encountered by the poor is *patay-gutom*, meaning literally "dead hungry," denoting a person who is utterly hopeless and destitute; someone who lacks even the most elementary of human attributes. What all of these terms have in common is the denial of human dignity and valued social identity. In short, they are shaming terms.

This behavior and language by the rich is encountered by the poor in various social settings—at work, in shopping centers and churches, on ceremonial occasions and in daily encounters on the streets. However, most people of the Visayan Area have only limited personal contact with the rich, partly because of the different class worlds into which their existence is structured, and partly out of the mutual desire for avoidance. Indeed, it is more often the condescending body language and aloof manner of speaking than the explicitly derogatory terms that people in Tatalon encounter when they have contact with the burgis.

Nevertheless, direct abuse and ill-treatment are experienced most frequently in employment, and though particular individuals may not have been victims, they know about such incidents through family members or neighbors who have been. Many women in the Visayan Area, for instance, work or have worked as maids for wealthy families and often tell of the humiliating manner in which they have been treated.[17] Such stories are a part of common knowledge in Tatalon and help to generate widespread disaffection with the rich.

These various forms of shaming behavior on the part of Manila's rich often arouse intense feelings of class anger in Tatalon. Because of the fear of the consequences, particularly during the era of Marcos's rule, this anger is rarely voiced openly, but it does find expression, both in words and action. However muted these expressions may be, they form part of a tradition of protest and resistance in the Visayan Area and among the working class generally.[18] Against the burgis stereotypes of the poor, the people I lived with commonly looked upon the rich as arrogant and unsociable, and were quick to condemn others in the community for behaving in the same way. In conversation, they often coupled the word for rich person with the rhyming word for boastful, hence "*mayaman mayabang.*" The term "burgis" itself carries the same connotation, as does the word *high-hat*, which is also frequently used to describe rich people or those emulating them. *Mata-pobre,* a term mentioned earlier, is likewise used as an insult to describe people who mistreat the poor. Thus, just as the rich have a vocabulary that is demeaning to the poor, so do the poor have their own vocabulary to be used pejoratively against the rich. Indeed, among individuals within the Visayan Area, these two sets of terms are often played off against each other as the principles of status and egalitarianism, spoken of earlier, come into conflict.

Aside from using these expressions and speaking critically among themselves about the behavior of the *burgis,* people in Tatalon also act out their class resentment in other ways—notably at work through go-slow labor practices, absenteeism, minor sabotage of property, pilfering, and so forth. Local values of resentment against the rich, and employers in particular, are such as to lend community legitimacy to this kind of behavior. Being able to deceive or annoy the rich, without being caught, is often a matter of some enjoyment. For example, some children and youth in Tatalon take delight in disposing of their rubbish and excreta by throwing it into the yards of rich people who own houses nearby.

That such attitudes and practices can be maintained at a collective level owes much to the extensive relations of mutual help and sense of community that prevail in the Visayan Area.[19] Moreover, while values reflecting the wider status hierarchy are deeply embedded in the community, there are also elements of a counterideology that go beyond simple class hostility. People in the Visayan Area sometimes look upon the way the rich live, most notably their perceived individualism, as unattractive and disagreeable. Furthermore, in advancing their criticism of the burgis, they commonly invoke the principle of human equality against their experience of social inequality.[20] One common saying along these lines is as follows:

Parehong kalansay ang labas natin sa hukay.

In the grave we all turn out to have the same skeleton.

In some contexts, there also emerge elements of a "subsistence ethic," but they do not constitute a coherent value system or world view.[21] Rather they coexist as part of a fragmented, largely contradictory set of attitudes, variously invoked, depending on the situation at hand. There is, however, a principal line of tension that runs through thought and action in Tatalon, namely the tension between accommodation and resistance to the prevailing social order. This is most evident in the feelings and practices surrounding the concept of shame.

In essence, the feeling of shame involves a sense of social inadequacy in the face of public disapproval. To varying degrees this disapproval is both institutionally or structurally based, as described in the previous section, and actively demonstrated through particular forms of shaming behavior, as indicated above. In general, disapproval that is perceived to emanate from particular institutions or situations—evident, for example, in one's lack of formal education or secure employment—does arouse inner feelings of inadequacy and shame. Though it also arouses discontent and resentment, these feelings do not focus on the rich or the burgis. Such a perception of disapproval lends itself most to accommodation to the existing social order. Conversely, disapproval that is perceived primarily in the form of active ridicule or condescension on the part of particular actors tends not so much to arouse inner feelings of shame or inadequacy as it does to arouse anger and resentment, in this case focused on the main perpetrators—the burgis. Of course, institutionally based shame and shaming behavior often arise together. Thus, in the statements—"nahiya ako," "nahiya kami," and "nakakahiya"—discussed earlier, one can sometimes detect contradictory feelings of, on the one hand, shame and, on the other, sarcastic condemnation of the rich. Thus, not only is it possible to observe practices of both accommodation and resistance among the people of Tatalon, but elements of both may arise simultaneously within the same practices.[22]

Shame, Inequality, and Communitas

To a large extent, the response of people in the Visayan Area to the Marcos government, to their employers, and to the burgis generally, has been one of pragmatism and opportunism. While daily experience impels them to accept their subordinate status and acknowledge the superiority of the rich, it also engenders in them feelings of discontent, dissatisfaction, and class anger. Thus, in the absence of credible alternatives, their approach to politics has been largely one of cynicism and skepticism. This is the way in which most people initially approached the presidential elections of February 1986. However, as I have argued elsewhere, the circumstances surrounding the election and, in particular, the emergence of the Aquino-led opposition, were highly unusual and saw significant short-term changes in social relations between the *burgis* and the *masa*.[23]

Alongside the division of interests and sentiment between classes in Manila, the Marcos years had opened up an opposition between State and people. This became especially marked following the assassination of Benigno Aquino, Jr. in 1983; it was not only the poor who suffered at the hands of the regime but also many of the burgis. In one campaign leaflet, for example, the names of squatters killed by government troops in Tatalon were listed alongside those of Aquino and other prominent personalities killed by the regime. All had stood in opposition to the Marcos government and all had been victims of its brutality.

The sociopolitical division between State and people was widened further by the Marcoses' virtual monopoly over State resources and largesse. Unlike the opposition parties of pre-Martial Law times, the movement led by Aquino had little in the way of an effective political organization capable of mobilizing established networks of reciprocity. The Aquino campaign thus had to rely heavily on the initiatives and limited resources of ordinary people. In contrast to the tightly orchestrated campaign of the government, the Aquino party communicated much of its message through word of mouth, graffiti, and a variety of cheaply produced leaflets, posters and badges. Where the Marcos campaign was expensive, centralized, patronal, and hierarchical, that of the Aquino opposition was marked by feelings of spontaneity, fraternity, and popular participation.

At first, the alliance between rich and poor in the Aquino opposition was largely one of mutual convenience. For many in Tatalon,
the moderate opposition provided a convenient and relatively safe
vehicle for expressing longstanding dissatisfaction with the Marcos
regime. For the more privileged, an alliance with the poor was a
necessity, given the lack of customary patronal resources and an
established political organization. Opposition leaders could not appeal to traditional values of patronage; they had to draw instead on
popular participation and fraternity, in short, on People Power. In
doing so, however, the opposition campaign shifted the arena of
political values and debate, thereby further undermining the logic of
the Marcoses' authority. Increasingly, political power seemed to rest
not in structure and hierarchy but rather in commonality and com-
munion. As opposition forces mounted in the election aftermath,
participation was not just a question of common purpose; it was also
one of common capacity. What mattered over the final days especially was not so much one's attire or speech or educational skills;
rather it was one's bodily presence and in that, burgis and masa
appeared equal. The signs and symbols of hierarchy, inequality, poverty
and subordination seemed to have lost their efficacy, and thus so too
had shame.

The political movement that culminated in the February Revolution
had much in common with the undifferentiated ritual state of communitas described by Turner.[24] For an historical moment, it seemed
the Filipino people were one, the State appeared to be crumbling, and
the order and division of civil society seemed to dissolve as rich and
poor, burgis and masa, stood together in defiance, in danger, and
finally, in victory. Apart from those favoring the miraculous intervention argument, most commentators have explained the mass participation in the EDSA uprising in terms of instrumental goal-oriented
behavior. Filipinos had finally had enough of the corrupt dictator
Marcos so they would now go to any length to remove him. Alternatively, Filipino voters of all persuasions were so indignant at the
flagrant cheating that occurred during the elections that they were
now prepared to risk their lives in order to restore electoral democracy. However, as I pointed out earlier, these were generally not the
kind of explanations that people from Tatalon gave for their participation. Indeed, their accounts did not stress reasons so much as the
occasion itself—the huge crowd, the feeling of enjoyment and pride,
and, above all, the spirit of camaraderie. Although support for Aquino,
the desire to remove Marcos, and the call of the Catholic Church were
important, what mattered most were these feelings. For a time, the
EDSA uprising and the state of communitas that it embodied had

enabled the people of Tatalon to command recognition, to stand in the presence of the rich without having to contend with the power of shame. It had enabled them to experience the principle of human equality, and it had enabled them to effectively act out the resentment they felt over the way they had been treated under the Marcos regime. Paradoxically though, EDSA had also elicited their renewed consent to burgis authority which, though diluted and vulnerable, remained undissolved in the liminal state of people power. In short, the extraordinary circumstances that marked the popular uprising of February 1986 had enabled the people of Tatalon to deal with shame in each of its contradictory dimensions; it had provided them with the opportunity both for resistance and accommodation.

While the people power uprising had the highly significant effect of removing Marcos from office, in terms of the wider sociopolitical order, it was largely an expressive, cathartic event. Not surprisingly, the state of communitas has passed. Once again, the structures of social inequality govern day-to-day existence; once again, the symbols of wealth and poverty have gained ascendancy, and once again, the power of shame intrudes into Tatalon. As one young man who participated in the barricades outside the military camps said to me, "At EDSA rich and poor came together, but now it is as it was before—they can't be bothered with us."

ALEX BELLO BRILLANTES, JR.

National Politics Viewed from Smokey Mountain

The essence of the quotation below was repeated to me a number of times by many residents of Barrio Magdaragat, also popularly referred to as "Smokey Mountain."[1]

> Pangarap namin na balang araw, titingnan kami ng mga taga-labas na kapareho nila. Sa ngayon, kapag nalaman nila na sa Smokey Mountain ka nakatira, parang one-step na mas-mababa ang pagtingin nila sa iyo, dahil sa ikaw ay nakatira at namumuhay sa basurahan. Basurero ka lang.

> Our aspiration is to one day be regarded by the people out there as no different from them. Now, if they find out that you live in Smokey Mountain, they immediately look down on you as "one-step down" because you live on and make a living out of garbage. You are only a scavenger.

Basically, residents see themselves as different from the people outside (*tagalabas*) and the rest of society, because of their poverty, and the popularized notion that they all live on, and off, garbage.

This essay discusses political matters important to the people of Smokey Mountain. It then looks at how residents viewed the EDSA "revolution," the change from Marcos to Aquino, and the various elections thereafter. From a national perspective, such events have been seen by many observers and participants as watersheds in Philippine political history. My concern, though, is how do the people in this specific locality, usually lumped with the "urban poor" sector, view those episodes?

The Locality

"Smokey Mountain" covers some 15 hectares and is composed of two barrios—Magdaragat and Looban—in Balut, Tondo, on the fringes of Manila near the fishing town of Navotas. The two barrios are bounded by E. Rodriguez Street (formerly Vistas), Marala River, Honorio Lopez Boulevard, and the Marcos Highway.

Since 1954, the area has been the dumping site for garbage from many areas of Metro Manila. Today, approximately one-third of Metro Manila's garbage is taken to this *tambakan* (dumpsite) which now is some twenty meters high. The smoke emitted by the mountainous pile of garbage is actually methane gas produced as a natural result of the decaying process.[2] With the smoke continuously emitting from the garbage dump comes an overpowering smell.

The people in Smokey Mountain live in makeshift huts made of old wood, rusting galvanized iron, and cardboard. Worn out tires adorn the thatched roofs of the huts to keep them from being blown away. There is no electricity in Smokey Mountain. Most people use gas lamps. A number of households, though, have illegally tapped into the city's electric lines. Some enterprising people in the area illicitly tap lines for others for a fee. Some residents told me that these same people create demand for their skills by purposely cutting the power lines of certain residents. These enterprising people are then hired to reconnect the disconnected lines.

When I began my research in November 1987, the area had no regular water source. Some residents made a living selling water from 1.25 to 2 pesos per plastic container, depending on the location of the house where the water is to be delivered. By August 1988, the city was providing running water, a result of the initiatives by residents with assistance from these nongovernment organizations: Tulungan sa Tubigan (roughly translated "Assistance for Water"), Assissi Foundation, and Youth With a Mission. Residents did much of the labor to install seventeen outlets with running water in strategic locations. The water system is operated on a cooperative basis, with each person paying for a container of water drawn from the faucet. Each water station has a "watcher" who collects ticket stubs for the water.

Approximately 3,000 families live in Smokey Mountain, with a total population of 20,000 individuals. Many of the people are long-time residents, some for nearly thirty years (except for the brief interlude from 1983 to 1985 when they were relocated to Cavite). According to a National Housing Authority survey, 58 percent of the people in Smokey Mountain have lived there for over ten years, 17 percent between six to ten years, and 21 percent between one to five years. Only 4 percent of the residents are new settlers, having been there for less than a year.[3]

A typical household has between eight to twelve members, occupying an area of about two by three meters. Smokey Mountain has a very young population. Children between the ages of ten to twelve comprise 15 percent of the total population, while those between thirteen to eighteen comprise 25 percent. Many of the children in the area suffer from gastroenteritis, pneumonia, dysentery, cholera, and worms. Tuberculosis and peptic and gastric ulcers are also prevalent. The community has no health facilities like hospitals or clinics, although some civic organizations provide health services to the residents. The Department of Social Welfare and Development has a feeding program for children during weekdays and a program that provides free medicine and vaccinations to needy residents.

Livelihood

When the trucks arrive at the Smokey Mountain dumpsite to disgorge refuse, scavengers, armed with their picks and baskets, all rush to rummage through it. An associate who was with me during one of my visits described this scene as being similar to harvest time. Young and old alike work side by side, feverishly sorting the garbage, searching for any reusable or recyclable item, from plastics and tin cans to bottles and bottle caps. I saw children, some as young as four years old, "harvesting" the piles of garbage.

Most scavengers work up to twelve hours a day to earn from 15 to 25 pesos (approximately $0.75 to $1.25) each. Thus, a family of five—including children—rummaging through the garbage for twelve hours, is able to earn at least 60 pesos ($3.00) a day. The slogan of the scavengers might as well be "there is cash in trash," according to one government agency working in the area.

The following is a list of the many items that the scavengers search for and sell to their buyers in order to convert to much needed cash.[4]

Broken glass: 10 centavos (ctvos) a kilo
Crushed tin cans, tin: 15 ctvos a kilo
Softdrink bottles, bottles: between 5 to 15 ctvos a kilo
Paper, all kinds: 10 ctvos a kilo
Cardboard: 25 ctvos a kilo
Milk cans: 2 pesos for 100 pieces
Iron: 30 ctvos a kilo
Rubber (referred to as *hangten*, as in slippers): 1.50 pesos a kilo
Plastic cellophane: 1 peso a kilo
Other types of plastic like pitchers, bowls, toys, containers, and the like: 2 pesos a kilo
Bones: 50 ctvos a kilo
Yellow copper (*tansong dilaw*): 3 pesos a kilo
Red copper (*tansong pula*): 9 pesos a kilo
Aluminum: 7 pesos a kilo

The last three kinds of metals have to be sold by the kilo. Scavengers, therefore, have to accumulate them first because buyers do not buy less than a kilo. Sometimes, it takes a week to accumulate a kilo's worth of these metals.

Another way of scavenging is what the residents call *pangangariton* (pushing carts). The *nangangariton* (those who push the carts) spend the whole night (usually from dusk to dawn) rummaging through trash cans and piles abundant in the city of Manila. Their kariton (pushcarts) are provided by buyers who buy their scavenged materials. After a day's (or night's) work of scavenging in the dumps or going around with their kariton, people sell whatever they have scavenged to their respective buyers. There are about twenty buyers residing in Smokey Mountain, with each buyer having around thirty *tauhan*, people who regularly sell to them. The buyer is the capitalist providing the kariton and guaranteeing purchase of the scavenged materials. In times of illness or emergencies, the tauhan run to their respective buyers for help, usually in the form of loans or cash advances. In exchange, each tauhan sells only to his or her respective buyers. If a buyer discovers that one of his tauhan sells to other buyers (who may offer higher prices for the scavenged material), that person is "blacklisted" by his buyer. When the buyer's help is needed by the tauhan in times of emergencies, "doon kami nakakabawi" (that is when we get back at them), as one buyer told me. "Getting back at them" means not extending the necessary help to the tauhan during times of emergency. I asked a tauhan why he does not sell directly to the "big" businessmen who buy from his buyers. He replied:

> Kailangan naming mangipon. Kailangan namin ang kapital. Hindi naman kami makakaipon sapagkat wala kaming kapital.

> We need to gather large amounts of the materials first before we can sell. And in order to gather large amounts enough to sell directly to the businessmen, you need capital. And we don't have that.

Not a few of those I talked to shared the feeling that there is some dignity in Smokey Mountain. *Bakit kami mahihiya?* (Why should we be ashamed?) they asked. "They are a proud people," observed one of the community leaders. After all, they are making an effort to live honest lives, away from petty crime and thievery. One resident asserted that Smokey Mountain, seen by the rest of society as a symbol of the poorest of the poor, should instead be seen as an example of how a community struggles against the odds and yet manages to survive:

Mas mabuti na lang ang kumuha sa tambakan at mangariton, kaysa sa magnakaw. Ang iba, ang tingin nila sa Smokey ay kahirapan. Ngunit ang tingin namin ay mas mabuti na lang ang maghirap at makapaghanapbuhay kaysa sa magnakaw. Kahit na anu man ang sabihin ng iba, kahit papaano, mayroon pa kaming kaunting karangalan.

It is better to make a living among the garbage dumps than to steal. Others see only the hardship and poverty in Smokey. But we feel that it is better to live in poverty and make an honest living than to steal. Whatever others might say, we manage, however difficult, to have some dignity.

They nevertheless emphasized their desire to one day have a regular, "normal" (i.e., not garbage-based) means of livelihood that would provide both financial security, and greater dignity.

History of Smokey Mountain

Former barangay captain Isaias Dollente, 70 years old, who traces his roots to the area, says that it used to be a fishing village.[5] His own father supported his family by fishing in Manila Bay. Earlier settlers, too, were mostly fishermen; hence, the area was initially referred to as "Barrio Magdaragat." Today, only a few fishermen remain. Dollente still vividly remembers the times when the area was all part of what is now referred to as Manila Bay. He also remembers President Manuel L. Quezon actually promising to give them the land where their houses stood.

According to Dollente, the owners of the area in the 1930s and 1940s were Tomas Cabangis and Simeon de Jesus. However, both Cabangis and de Jesus sold the land when they heard that President Quezon was going to turn it over to the squatters. Cabangis sold to a certain Mr. Green, an American, who converted the area into a subdivision. Simeon de Jesus sold his land to Ike and Berkin Cutter, also Americans, who likewise converted it into a subdivision. Consequently, the residents of the area—including the family of Dollente—had to leave. In his words, "Naitapon kami" (We were thrown away).

The Dollentes relocated to Navotas. After the Second World War, many people returned to the area that is now Barrio Magdaragat. They came upon the structures built by the Americans, referred to as "konset" (prefabricated portable quonset huts used by the occupying American forces in the Philippines). As their numbers grew, the people developed a community. Nothing symbolized this more than their project to build their own chapel. They also had electricity installed.

Dollente's elder brother became the *kapitan del baryo* (barangay captain). During the administration of Mayor Arsenio Lacson of Manila, there was a threat to demolish the increasingly numerous squatter structures in Barrio Magdaragat. However, with the last-minute intervention of then President Macapagal, the planned demolition of the area was averted.

Dollente recalls that during the administration of Mayor Antonio Villegas, the area began to become a dumping site. The continued pounding of waves upon the shores carried the garbage deeper and deeper inland until the garbage not only was scattered, but began to build into an unplanned "reclamation" of the marshes. The area gradually increased in size.

During this time the residents of the barrio assumed a legal personality as an association when they were registered with the Securities and Exchange Commission as "Nayong Magdaragat."

With the death of the elder Dollente, Isaias Dollente was elected as a councilor of Barrio Magdaragat in 1972. He was given authority by the new barangay captain, Francisco Maglupay, to take charge of the improvements of the deteriorating chapel. Dollente later became the barangay captain after Maglupay. One of his major accomplishments, according to him, is the recognition of the "Barrio Magdaragat Homeowners' Association," duly registered with the government, with the general objective that members be given titles to the lands they were occupying.

By then, the volume of garbage had increased drastically. The peace and order situation in the area had also deteriorated. At the same time the incidence of diseases, occasioned by unsanitary conditions, increased, causing critical health problems in the barrio.

In 1983, the National Housing Authority began to demolish the houses in Barrio Magdaragat and relocate the squatters. On 23 February 1983, barangay captain Dollente petitioned the National Housing Authority to halt the demolition "until such time that they are ready to present their case with their claim of the lot." He argued that the houses were not illegal because they were some 200 meters away from the dumpsite. He filed a similar petition to then Manila Mayor Ramon Bagatsing to stop the demolition. The petitions were ignored and the demolition and relocation continued.

The people in Smokey Mountain were relocated to a resettlement area in Bulihan in Cavite, some 30 kilometers out of Metro Manila, an hour's commute away from the city. For those working in Manila, it was expensive to live in Bulihan. Travel fare cost as much as sixteen pesos, round trip, nearly one-third of a typical day's earnings.

In Bulihan, the residents were given a small piece of land, four walls and a toilet. Many people, however had no livelihood at all. As early as three months after their relocation, many started going back to the dumpsite, preferring to live among garbage where they could at least eke out a living as scavengers. Many residents told me they left Bulihan because, "Aanhin ang kubeta kung wala namang itatae doon" (Of what use is the toilet bowl if you have nothing to defecate). Another common explanation was expressed this way:[6]

> Paano, maganda nga ang bahay. Wala namang tubig. Hindi lang 'yon. Wala kaming makain. Walang mapagtrabahuan. Sa Smokey Mountain, kahit puro basura sa paligid, may hanap buhay. May laman and tiyan ng mga anak ko.

> The houses may be nice. But there's no water. There's no food. No work. In Smokey Mountain, even if we're surrounded by garbage, there's livelihood. My children's stomachs have food.[6]

In the beginning, many of the former residents of Barrio Magdaragat actually commuted from Bulihan to the dumpsite where they did their scavenging. They set up makeshift shelters but went home to Bulihan during the weekends. Because the commute to and from Bulihan became very expensive, many decided to settle back in Barrio Magdaragat again. During this period, the residents heard that Metro Manila Vice Governor Mel Mathay issued an order to simply burn all the shacks in Barrio Magdaragat. Dollente, already barangay captain, approached Vice Governor Mathay to protest the latter's plans by asking, "Yung bang mayayaman, tao, at ang mahihirap, hayop?" (Are only the rich people human beings, and the poor people, animals?") Before Mathay's orders were implemented, Dollente was able to get an order from then Manila Mayor Ramon Bagatsing preventing the demolition of their shacks. With the aborted demolition, many former residents of Smokey Mountain who were relocated to Bulihan decided to return permanently to the area.

Because of the residents' unfortunate relocation experience and their perception that the barangay captain did nothing to protect their interests, a number of residents petitioned for his removal. Some residents alleged that he was bribed not to oppose the demolition. Others claimed that the barangay captain was a "do-nothing," an ineffective local leader. Most faulted him for inadequately protecting their rights. The petition did not prosper in the Manila Barangay Office. In March 1988, petitions to unseat Dollente as barangay chairman once more resurfaced.

Dollente brushed aside efforts to remove him saying that he had done his job as barangay captain. He pointed to the peace and order situation in the area. He showed me a number of certificates of participation in seminars for barangay captains and leaders. Dollente also pointed to the water tank construction project of the Christian Youth With a Mission (YWAM) group claiming he was instrumental in the approval of the project. Dollente vehemently denied that he was remiss in his duties as barangay captain. On the contrary, Dollente claimed that he actually protested the 1983 relocation.

Dollente's term as barangay captain officially ended in March 1989 when elections for barangay officials were conducted throughout the country.[7]

Politics in the Area

Smokey Mountain residents are detached from national politics in general. Such detachment can partially be explained by the fact that the closest the government ever got to them was through their relocation experience in 1983. The government was then seen as the villain whose only interest was to "throw them away" (*maitapon kami*), they being squatters with no right to the land they were occupying. As such, they were deemed not entitled to any basic health and sanitation services as well as other government services. Additionally, there was the common perception that the local government official—the barangay captain—did not protect their interests. On the contrary, the relocation experience brought out what they felt was betrayal by the government at both the barangay and national levels.

The general attitude toward national political developments among residents in Smokey Mountain is summed up by the following statements culled from the many conversations I had with many people in the area:

> Mas maraming mga bagay na mas mahalaga sa amin. Kailangan naming maghanapbuhay. Kumain. Nasapaligid-ligid lamang kami. Kaya kami ay sumasama lamang sa anuman ang desisyon ng mga matataas na opisyal. Maliban lamang kung kami ay apektado— kagaya ng demolisyon. Tututol kami riyan.

> There are other more important and basic things that concern us. We need to make a living. We need to eat. We are in the periphery. Hence, we go along with whatever the national officials decide. Except, of course, in matters that concern us directly. Like demolition. We will resist it.

I talked to community leaders in the area who represented three major groupings: the government; the Church; and a community-based leftist organization. In separate conversations, the leaders of these sectors summarized what they felt were the attitudes of the people toward national events and developments.[8] The local Catholic priest said:

> Wala ang national politics sa kanila. Parang ghetto, parang island ang Smokey Mountain. Hindi sila naliligalig, except in issues that directly affect them. Kagaya ng forced relocation at basura which is their source of livelihood.

> National events are nothing to them. Smokey Mountain is like a ghetto, an island. They are not bothered except in issues that directly affect them—such as forced relocation and garbage which is their source of livelihood.

A leader of a Smokey Mountain community organization perceived to be leftist said:

> Hindi masyadong pinapansin ng mga tao kung sino ang nasa itaas. Hanapbuhay ang kanilang iniintindi. Ngunit kapag may mga bagay bagay na sila ay apektado na mismo—kagaya ng mungkahing gawin ang Smokey na isang industrial site, o relokasyon, kaya ng mga taong magkaisa at mag-organisa.

> The people in the area do not really care much about who is up there, in power. Their main concern is their livelihood. However, when it comes to issues that directly concern them, such as the proposal to convert Smokey Mountain to an industrial site, or relocation, the people are capable of uniting and organizing themselves.

For his part, the former barangay captain said:

> Pagdating sa gobyerno, tayong maliliit, natatakpan ang boses.

> When it comes to the government, the voices of the little people are not heard.

In trying to ascertain the people's perspectives of national events and how they were affected, I looked at two major areas: the first pertained to the involvement of the people in local political issues that directly affected them, specifically the relocation issue, and second, the people's involvement in a number of national elections.

The Relocation Experience and Community Organization

If there is any issue that binds the residents of Smokey Mountain together, it is the issue of resistance to relocation. I perceived a strong sense of vigilance and an increased sense of community among the residents when they discussed issues that concerned them most. These included:

No forced relocation: they want to remain in the *tambakan* (dump), for it is there where their source of livelihood is;

Urban land reform: they want the land where their houses are standing to become rightfully theirs;

Livelihood: they want proposals for the use of technology to recycle the garbage to be further studied so as to generate income for the people.

Many of those I talked with said that the only reason they consented to being relocated to Bulihan in 1983 was the threat that the army might be used against them had they resisted. However, after the experience of being "thrown away" to a place with no support from the government and far from their livelihood, they decided to return to the dumpsite. Their resolve was strengthened by the fact that their sense of community was increased by their resistance to the government and its efforts to relocate them once more. As far as they are concerned, demolitions are a thing of the past, while the 1983 relocation experience remains fresh in the community's collective memory.

The sense of community among the people was noted by a study conducted by an interagency committee preparing a comprehensive development plan for the area. The people do not wish to be relocated even if the area is no longer a dumpsite which essentially serves as the source of livelihood of many residents. According to the document:

The scavengers would like to stay in the dumpsite even if garbage is no longer dumped in the area. The main reasons they give are: the sense of belongingness they feel among community members (Smokey Mountain has a relatively low crime rate compared to other areas of Tondo); sentimental attachment to the land where many of their children have died (run over by bulldozers or decimated by disease); and the relative ease of finding odd jobs in the vicinity, like working as stevedores in the nearby docks. The scavengers are willing to pay for low cost housing units if these are built in the area.[9]

Fr. Benigno Beltran, a local Catholic priest who has worked there since 1978, played a key role organizing the residents of Smokey Mountain as a community.[10] He was instrumental in building the church in 1986. It is adjacent to the playground that was cemented through the efforts of a local organization, also under the leadership of "Father Ben," as he is known to residents. This church was renovated and enlarged in 1989. Expenses for church construction were raised mostly by Father Ben. Residents contributed their labor.[11]

The Church also provides social services to the area. This includes free medical services for the residents, a feeding program for the children on Sundays, and livelihood training (such as sewing) for women.

There are a number of sociocivic community organizations in Smokey Mountain. One is the Sambayanang Kristiyano, which is affiliated with the local Catholic Church and was organized in 1985. Among its notable achievements was the construction of a concrete basketball court adjacent to the church. The Welcome Friends organization was set up in 1985 with the specific purpose of "welcoming" new residents to the area. The Samahang Magkakapitbahay, composed mostly of housewives, was also organized in 1985. It assists in the weekend feeding programs of the church. In 1986, a number of other organizations with generally sociocivic objectives were organized. That same year, noting the proliferation of many organizations in Smokey Mountain, Fr. Ben pulled them all together under one umbrella organization called the Katipunan Para sa Pag-unlad ng Smokey Mountain (Movement for the Development of Smokey Mountain).[12]

Fr. Ben serves as the Executive Director of the Katipunan. When asked why he assumed such a position considering that he was already the parish priest of the area, he replied that that was precisely why he agreed to head the Katipunan. As a priest, he commanded more respect than anyone else. However, he added that when consolidation of the various organizations is done, and when they have developed more self-reliance, he would give up the position. Indeed, many of those I talked to recognized Fr. Ben's role in developing the community's sense of spirit and oneness.

Fr. Ben said that residents *do* get politically involved when something threatens their own rights and the community. For instance, in November 1988, newspapers reported that Metro Manila's acting Governor Elfren Cruz said that Smokey Mountain will be levelled. Immediately, residents sent a delegation to Cruz and got his assurance that they will not be relocated. Pictures of Smokey Mountain residents under a banner of the Katipunan declaring their resistance to any proposed demolition or relocation were published in the Manila dailies.

The residents extracted a similar commitment from Manila mayor Lopez, who has said that the city planned to level the Smokey Mountain garbage dumpsite. Upon asking him for a clarification, the Mayor said that the plans did not involve the relocation of the people from the area but only levelling, in his words, "this smelly mound of earth." But that would destroy the residents' primary source of livelihood. In anticipation of their objection, Mayor Lopez, promised that residents would be provided with other forms of livelihood, especially cottage industries. They would be equipped with basic skills by the Manila Social Welfare Department preparatory to providing them with raw materials for production. Other plans include the training of scavengers in sewing for the garment industry.

Fr. Ben himself met with President Aquino in Malacañang and got her commitment that the people in the area would not be forcibly relocated. Such a commitment was reiterated during a "Magtanong sa Pangulo" ("Ask the President") radio program, when the residents actually called in during the radio program and appealed for compassion from President Aquino.

In 1989, the residents, through the leaders of the Sambayanang Kristiyano, eagerly accepted the invitation of television host Luis Beltran to appear in the program "Straight from the Shoulder" for an opportunity to directly question the National Housing Authority head about the agency's plans for the area.

The above demonstrate the continued vigilance of the people on certain issues that affect them directly. They will not hesitate to demonstrate, take to the streets, call attention of the mass media, etc., if they feel that their rights—specifically in terms of their right to the land they have been living on—are threatened or violated.

The following section focuses on the people's involvement in issues beyond the boundaries of Smokey Mountain. The people of Smokey Mountain are indeed politically involved in issues directly affecting them, like relocation, urban land reform, livelihood concerns. However, are they directly involved in issues of national concern such as the EDSA Revolution and the elections for national officials, like President and Senators?

The 1986 Snap Presidential Elections

During the February 1986 presidential elections, the voter turnout in Smokey Mountain was extremely low: Less than 400 (24%) out of the approximately 1,600 voters in the principal barangay of Magdaragat.[13] Marcos received 242 (63%) of the 384 votes cast; Cory Aquino had 142 (37%). The same pattern held true for the vice presidential elections. Marcos's running mate, Arturo Tolentino, won over Salvador Laurel and Eva Estrada Kalaw.

I asked many people why there was such a low voter turnout. Most (including buyers, tauhan, those involved in the local Catholic Church, and those occupying positions in the local barangay council) gave similar replies, such as

> Wala silang pakialam sa eleksiyon kasi alam na nila na mananalo si Marcos sa pandaraya. At kailangan nilang maghanapbuhay.

> They couldn't care less about the elections because they knew that Marcos will win anyway. He will cheat. Besides, they need to make a living.

Others said that they did not vote because their vote would not matter anyway. They would go along with the tide and follow whatever decisions are made as long as they can survive. One resident remarked, for example,

> Kung saan ang agos ng tubig, naroroon ako. Basta makakain lang ng tatlong beses isang araw, makabili ng bagong damit dalawang beses isang taon.

> Wherever the tide is, I will be there. As long as we can eat three meals a day and buy new clothes at least twice a year.

To a certain extent, such national events hardly mattered to them. However, such an observation has to be placed within the proper context of the times. Marcos had been the dictator of the country for almost a decade and a half. The way he manipulated the people's will through the conduct of managed elections and referenda was widely acknowledged. What was so different about the 1986 presidential elections?, residents asked themselves. It would only be a waste of time to cast a vote that will not be counted anyway.

I asked Alex Caballero, head of the People's Committee for Smokey Mountain (PCSM), about the people's views of the February 1986 snap elections and the EDSA Revolution.[14] Caballero asserted that between 30 to 40 percent of the residents in Smokey Mountain boycotted the elections. However, whether the qualified voters really intended to boycott, or whether they were simply not interested in the national elections perhaps cannot be definitely determined. A common opinion, though, was that "Kahit sino ang ilagay nila sa itaas, sasama kami. Maliit lang kami." (Whoever is placed up there we will follow. We are only little people.) The general impression I have from numerous interviews is that people did not vote because they were not interested.

To those who voted, I asked: Why did Marcos win? "Binayaran lang sila!" (They were paid!) was the gist of a common reply. However, some people admitted that they freely chose to vote for Marcos. They had apprehensions that Aquino was a communist, that she was inexperienced, and that being a woman, she could not do the job. These are the very same propaganda points raised by Marcos against Aquino during the campaign. But residents hastened to add that they were no great fans of Marcos either, and that they could live with an Aquino presidency:

> Kung siya ang inilagay ng tao doon, di sangayon na kami. Sino ba kaming mga maliliit na tumutol sa pasiya ng bayan? Kailangan magpatuloy ang buhay.

> If she were the one placed by the people there, then we have to accept it. Who are we small people to resist the people's will? Life has to go on.

The EDSA Revolution

The extent of involvement of Smokey Mountain residents in EDSA in February 1986 was mainly monitoring events as reported on radio and television. Hardly anyone I talked to from the area actually went either to Malacañang or to EDSA to participate. When I asked people whether or not they knew anyone who went to EDSA, the usual reply was: "Walang nagpunta sa EDSA" (Nobody went to EDSA). One resident told me that all he and others did during those critical times was ponder upon the issue of why Filipinos are fighting Filipinos. They likewise prayed for a speedy and peaceful resolution of the problem. But they did not feel the need to go to EDSA, the calls of Cardinal Sin notwithstanding.

At least one resident, however, went to EDSA. This twenty-year-old man went not to lend his presence in response to the call of Cardinal Sin but simply to see what was going on: "Naki-usyoso lang ako" (I was just curious to see what was going on).

I was informed that they did not go because they did not feel that they, as a community, were directly threatened. EDSA was for them an event that was occurring somewhere else and their presence hardly mattered. Looking back, they still feel the same way, saying that even if they were there, things would have turned out the same way anyway. So they felt that their presence through prayers was their best contribution to the EDSA Revolution.

EDSA is around 30 kilometers from Smokey Mountain. In order to go there, one would have to commute and take two jeepney rides and a bus. However, such a factor does not explain their nonparticipation in EDSA since physical distance is not much of a deterrence to the people's participation in events that directly concern them, as manifested by the times that the people participated in protest actions and demonstrations at the National Housing Authority, the Presidential Commission on Urban Poor, or even at the premises of Congress, all of which are farther than EDSA, relative to Smokey Mountain.

1987–1989 Elections

In marked contrast to the snap elections called a year earlier, voter turnout during the February 1987 plebiscite for the ratification of the proposed constitution was heavy. As reflected in the annnex, approximately 82 percent of the voters in Barrio Magdaragat voted. This was even higher than the national average of 70 to 75 percent. The reason for the increased participation in the 1987 plebiscite, according to some residents, is that this was supposed to be the first free elections after many years under a dictatorship. After years of manipulated elections and questionable results, these elections were supposed to be held in the "democratic space" provided by the Aquino administration. Others said that they participated simply because they were available and had the time at that moment, and not for any overarching ideological reason. The results of the 1987 plebiscite were similar to that of the snap elections called a year earlier: people voted for the administration. Specifically, 85 percent of the votes cast were "Yes" votes in favor of the proposed Constitution which President Aquino campaigned very hard for.

Voter turnouts for the next three elections went down. In contrast to the plebiscite's turnout of 82 percent, turnout for the May 1987 congressional elections was 74.3 percent; January 1988 local elections, 61.2 percent, and the March 1989 barangay elections, 75.2 percent. People had become accustomed to a number of electoral exercises over a short period of time, and the novelty for participation in elections had worn off. As in the case of previous elections, some residents lost interest, believing that their participation did not really matter anyway. Only those who had a direct stake at the elections—like the candidates themselves and their circle of supporters during the barangay elections—and those who had the time, cast their votes during the elections.

In the May 1987 elections for senators and congressmen to the national legislature, radio and television personality Orlando Mercado and movie actor Joseph Estrada topped the senatorial slate among Smokey Mountain residents. Those who voted for Mercado and Estrada cited the former's popular sociocivic program, *Kapwa Ko Mahal Ko* (roughly translated, "I love my neighbor") that caters mainly to the poor in terms of rendering free medical assistance and advice. Residents favored Joseph Estrada because of his movie image as a champion of the poor, oppressed, and downtrodden.

Voter turnout during the 18 January 1988 local elections dropped significantly, down to 61.4 percent from 74.2 percent during the congressional elections. The results in Smokey Mountain were similar to the overall election results: incumbents Mayor Lopez and Vice Mayor Lacuna were reelected by large margins over their three competitors.

Seventy-five percent of the voters turned out for the March 1989 barangay elections, still lower than the plebiscite turnout. A total of forty-one candidates run for the seven elective positions for the barangay council. Acting barangay officer-in-charge Ben Ignacio was elected with the highest number of votes. Former head of the Sambayanang Kristiyano Pablo Borja also ran. He received the third highest number of votes. Both Ignacio and Borja were acknowledged leaders of the area, with their leadership stemming more from their popularity (in terms of name-recognition and visibility due to official position or involvement in community projects) rather than from doling out favors to the people. Ignacio was the former vice chairman of the barangay and took over as officer-in-charge when Dollente left. Borja was the head of the Sambayanang Kristiyano that is closely affiliated with the Catholic Church and Father Beltran. Additionally, one was a buyer.

On a number of occasions, I separately talked to the two of the above elected councilmen. During our conversations, we discussed how elections are won and lost and why people vote as they do. Each man said his capacity to influence voters is limited. Neither believed it possible to line up a large number of voters on the basis of personal relationships. One said, for instance, that if a buyer told his tauhan how to vote, he could expect to be told by the tauhan, "Naloloko ka ba?" (Are you crazy?). They recognized that voting is not as simple as the lider telling the tauhan how to vote. One has to appeal to issues that concern people such as the generation of livelihood, the resistance to relocation, the eventual development of the area into a possible industrial site, offering a hope to the residents that they shall one day rise above the garbage dumps, and eventually be regarded by the people outside as no different from themselves ("titingnan kami ng tagalabas na kapareho nila"). To demonstrate his point, one elected councilman told me that same wealthy buyers who ran during the barangay elections did not win even though they had many tauhan.

It is in this general sense that voting behavior patterns, as perceived by residents, including community leaders themselves, do not seem to be determined by factional and patron-client arrangements (in this case, buyers determining how their tauhan vote) but rather by issues that have direct bearing on their survival and ultimately, their dignity as a people.[15]

Life Since EDSA

The general concern in Smokey Mountain is that "Walang pag-babago" (There are no changes) since the change in the national government. Most of the residents I talked to said that life now is even more difficult for them than it was during the time of Marcos. A major reason is higher prices for basic commodities, yet prices they receive for scavenged materials have remained the same, or even declined. Others say that life today is the same as before. In other words, the EDSA Revolution did not seem to improve their living conditions. For instance, one housewife who is a volunteer for the weekly feeding program of the Church said:

> Mas mahirap ang tao ngayon. Noon, kahit naghihirap ang tao, hindi gaanong halata. Noon, dati singkuwenta pesos, kumakain nang masarap. Ngayon, hindi . . . Mas marami ngayong programa pero mas mahirap ngayon.

> People are having a more difficult time now. Although people were having a hard time before, it was not as obvious. Before, with fifty pesos you could eat good food. That is not true today. There may be more programs today, but life is more difficult.

A similar observation was made by a resident community organizer:

> Mas matindi ngayon ang hirap kaysa noong panahon ni Marcos. Noon, ang mga tao ay nakakain isang o dalawang beses isang araw. Pero ngayon, mas mahirap ang situasiyon. Malaking bagay ang pagtaas ng presyo ng krudo. Ang mga presyo ng mga nakukuha namin sa tambakan ay bumababa pa! Halimbawa, ang bubog noon ay treinta sentimos isang kilo. Ngayon, ito ay bumaba sa beinte. Ang presyo ng plastik din ay bumaba mula sa tatlong piso sa dalawa. Mas matindi ngayon ang buhay.

Life is much more difficult now than it was during the time of Marcos. Before, people could at least eat once or twice a day. But now, the situation has deteriorated. The increase in oil prices is a big factor for these developments. And coupled with these, the prices of the scavenged materials have gone down. For instance, broken glass before cost 30 centavos. It has gone down to 20 centavos. Prices of plastic too have gone down from 3 pesos to 2.50 pesos. Life is really much more difficult now.

Many of the people also said that they harbor no illusions about the change in government. There may be a new government "up there" (*sa itaas*) they said, but the "mayayaman" (rich) continue to dominate the government and the society.

Indeed, the people in Smokey Mountain continue to feel removed from the national government inspite of the changes (no matter how seemingly dramatic as in EDSA) in the national leadership. They have learned to live with such a situation because they feel that, based on their own local history and experience, and based on the fact that life is really getting more difficult for them, the poor, they have no compelling reason to expect much good from the national government anyway.

Conclusion

The people of Barrio Magdaragat (Smokey Mountain) are generally detached from national political events and developments. This is best illustrated by their general nonparticipation in the EDSA Revolution and their declining participation in national electoral politics since then. However, nonparticipation in the EDSA Revolution, an event widely regarded to be a watershed in Philippine political history, should not be interpreted as a general lack of involvement of the people in political matters. On the contrary, the history of the area has demonstrated the people's active political involvement in issues that directly concern them. The people resisted the government's efforts to relocate them. They organized demonstrations, protested relocation, and demanded livelihood. On their own initiatives, they formed community organizations to respond to their own needs, such as water and livelihood generation projects. The general attitude seems to be that if the government provides, well and good. But if the government does not, then they are capable of standing on their own, with minimal help (or interference) from the government.

The people's detachment from the national government can be better understood if we take into consideration their relocation experience in 1983, when they felt that they were betrayed by the government at two levels: at the national level, where the government decided to summarily relocate them to Bulihan without providing the necessary support in terms of livelihood opportunities; and at the barangay level, where they believed that the local barangay official betrayed their trust by not taking the lead in resisting relocation. In defiance of the government, many residents returned to Smokey Mountain and their livelihood there. They set up some permanent structures in the area, communicating to the government that "never again" shall they be relocated from the area. They continue to demand that the land on which their homes are standing be parceled out and that titles be awarded to them. And there they are determined to stay until their rights as citizens are recognized and their dignity acknowledged, with or without government assistance.

APPENDIX

Voter Turnout during the 1986 presidential elections, 1987 plebiscite and 1987 congressional elections in Barangay 128, Barrio Magdaragat, Balut, Tondo, Manila (Base figure is total number of qualified voters in Barangay 128: 1,642)

Significant National Political Event	Voter Turnout	Voter Turnout as Percentage of Qualified Voters
1. February 1986 presidential elections	384	23.3%
2. February 1987 plebiscite	1,347	82.0%
3. May 1987 congressional elections	1,221	74.3%
4. 18 January 1988 local elections	1,015	61.2%
5. 28 March 1989 Barangay Elections	1,235	75.2%

SOURCE: Table constructed from Commission on Elections
(February 1988, May 1989)

WILLEM WOLTERS

New Beginning or Return to the Past in Nueva Ecija Politics?

Political developments in Nueva Ecija province from 1985 up to the local elections of 1988 are assessed by this essay, which shows why the efforts of some within the new government to bring about a "cleaner" and more "open" political system failed.

The EDSA Revolution was a drama on the central stage of the nation watched by people in the provinces who hardly participated even though many sympathized. The new government of President Cory Aquino could undoubtedly boast of a large popularity. Aquino probably won the snap elections and, if the Social Weather Station surveys are correct, even with a sizable majority.

The Aquino government started with an ambitious program: restore democracy, make government clean and transparent, exorcise the Marcos influence, repair the economy, and introduce socioeconomic reforms. It had to implement this program under a set of constraints, the most pressing of which were the organizational limitations of the new ruling group.

One of the first policy acts of the new government was to replace sitting political functionaries with newly appointed OICs (Officers-in-Charge) who favored the new administration. To implement this, the new ruling group sent to the provinces trusted emissaries, generally called "political kingpins," who had broad powers to change personnel. Although the shake up was supposed to replace the bad guys of the old regime with good people of the new administration, the moral worth of the new Officers-in-Charge became a major political issue.

The Nueva Ecija Economy

Nueva Ecija, situated in the Central Luzon plain, comprises about 380,000 hectares of agricultural land, most of which is used for wet rice cultivation. The region is known as the rice bowl of the Philippines. Since early this century, its large rice surplus has flowed into the national market.

According to the 1980 census, the population was more than one million people. The population density, 202 persons per square/km, is higher than the national average of 122. A large part of the population lives in rural areas. Cabanatuan City is the regional center for trade, finance, and education. It has been an important transit market for rice since the beginning of this century. During the 1970s, its economy expanded from that of a small agriculturally-oriented town to a booming business center.

The Stakes in Traditional Politics

Why do politicians want a government position? They spend one million pesos during election campaigns for a congressional seat and five to ten million for a governorship. These expenses cannot be recovered from official salaries attached to these positions. A large part of the answer lies in the numerous informal remunerations and incomes which they receive, often of a corrupt nature. This means that many politicians have a hidden agenda behind their public promises: They are set to tap these other sources of income for themselves and their political allies. These motives and activities are neither publicly discussed nor openly admitted. But they are the topic of rumors and gossip. The degree of moral standing and the reputation of political candidates are constantly discussed.

Various advantages accrue to political powerholders. First, public office offers the chance to use government funds for private purposes. Both provincial and municipal officials are accustomed to take cuts from the budget allocation of the Department of Public Works for roads and bridges. To do this, they make sure that they get people of their own choice appointed to the crucial positions of district, provincial, and city engineer. Other budget posts can be tapped for private use, but Public Works is by far the biggest one.

Second, nonofficial sources of income can be tapped, by providing protection to such illegal activities as gambling and prostitution dens. Politicians can also make money by helping, for a fee, individuals and companies to secure licenses required for jeeps, trucks, market stalls, and other business needs.

Third, business people have to engage in politics or support politicians to protect their businesses. To control a political position or have the right connections, a politician can be vital to obtaining a business license without delay or harassment, preventing informal extortion by policemen, and getting lenient treatment from tax collectors.

Fourth, political powerholders can allocate business opportunities to business friends, such as allotting public works projects to contractors and logging concessions to provincial entrepreneurs. The political powerholder can get his share from the contracts transacted with the entrepreneurs.

Fifth, political powerholders can try to create a thicker protective umbrella by entering into an alliance with higher level politicians, using the usual transaction of delivering votes in exchange for political favors.

This enumeration does not imply that all politicians engage in these activities. Because such activities are carried out behind the scene, it is usually difficult to determine whether or to what extent politicians have become involved in self-interested transactions. Although the evidence can not always be mustered, the informal side of political ventures has to be taken into account in order to depict this system realistically.

Traditional Politics in Nueva Ecija Before 1986

The postwar political scene in Nueva Ecija can be depicted in traditional terms as a power struggle between several competing political clans: Joson, Diaz, Concepcion-Perez, Garcia, and a number of others. None of these families controlled a sizable chunk of the provincial economy, as wet rice production and trading are too dispersed to allow for the buildup of permanent monopoly positions. Since the postwar years, political leaders often used violence, with the help of private armies, to help win and maintain public office. An outstanding example of this brand of provincial politicians was Governor Eduardo L. Joson.

Joson came from a landowning family in the town of Quezon. During World War II, he joined the American guerrilla organization in Central Luzon and formed his own squadron, which continued to serve him as a political machine after the war. In 1947 he was elected mayor of Quezon, where he served three terms. In 1959, he ran for governor and won. He was reelected in 1963, 1967, and 1971, each time with a comfortable majority. Up to 1972, Governor Joson belonged to the Liberal Party. He was compadre of the Benigno Aquino family and he followed Aquino's line vis-à-vis the threat that President Marcos would proclaim Martial Law. However, when Martial Law was proclaimed in 1972, Joson made a deal with Marcos which enabled him to stay on as a governor. In the late 1970s, when electoral politics was restored, Joson was made provincial chairman of Marcos's Kilusang Bagong Lipunan (KBL).

Over the years, Governor Joson gradually built a network of followers and political leaders (*lider*) down to the barangay level. These retainers assisted in disbursing patronage and favors to constituents and in winning votes during elections. Joson earned the gratitude of many people in the villages with his program of free medicines and hospitalization to indigent citizens. Joson's organization also provided free coffins to indigents. One of Joson's other programs promoted education for barangay children, providing them with loans for tuition fees for schools in Manila that are paid after graduation. In addition, the governor offered free room, tuition, and medical insurance to nearly 700 students from throughout the province studying in colleges in Cabanatuan City. People who benefited from these programs often felt *utang na loob* (gratitude) toward the old politico, and they did not ask whether these benefits had been paid by Joson personally or out of government funds. In fact, the governor could use the provincial budget to keep his program running.

The Joson faction had a private army of probably 200 men who were paid from provincial government payrolls. Aside from performing security tasks, they acted as enforcers at the local level, thus maintaining the governor's sphere of influence.

The May 1984 elections for the Batasang Pambansa brought together the Joson and the Concepcion-Perez factions under the KBL banner. Four assembly members were to be elected for Nueva Ecija, but the elections were province-wide rather than by district as in the past. The four candidates on the KBL slate were Edno Joson (the governor's son), Angel Concepcion, Mario Garcia, and Narciso Nario. Assemblyman Leopoldo Diaz, who had been a KBL politician, was not included in the ticket and decided to run as an Independent. Other opposition candidates included Noli Santos and Virgilio Calica for PDP-Laban, Sedfrey Ordoñez as an Independent, and Rebeck Espiritu for UNIDO. In the polls, three KBL candidates—Edno Joson, Angel Concepcion, and Mario Garcia—and the Independent Leopoldo Diaz won, but opposition candidates charged that there had been widespread fraud and intimidation.

The Snap Elections in Nueva Ecija

The campaign for the snap presidential elections started early December 1985. An editorial in a local newspaper in Nueva Ecija said,

> The battle lines have been drawn. The combatants are now clearly defined, Marcos-Tolentino versus Aquino-Laurel. Their campaign programs are defined: "impeccable performance" by the KBL and

"return to the basics of morality in government service, sincerity, justice and a government the people can identify with" by the opposition.[1]

The KBL machinery in Nueva Ecija was fully in place, although the party was divided in two seemingly irreconcilable camps, the Joson faction and the Concepcion-Perez faction. Both had networks of followers down to the barangay level. In addition to this there was large scale vote-buying. Long before the election, the Marcos forces also saw to it that large amounts of money were disbursed to farmers.

The opposition had neither a network of *lider* at the barangay level nor the financial resources to buy votes. Its main hope lay in a groundswell bandwagon effect, based on the Aquino magnetism. In December 1985, the Aquino team made a stumping tour in Nueva Ecija with political rallies in four towns, which drew large crowds of several tens of thousands of people.

Election day, according to a local newspaper was "relatively peaceful in the sense that there was no bloodshed as had been widely feared, but it was definitely disorderly and chaotic and admittedly not clean."[2] In a number of precincts the names of many voters were missing from the Comelec official lists. In many precincts, voters showed up bearing handwritten "certifications" to vote, allegedly signed by the Comelec registrar. The registrar publicly denied having issued them. NAMFREL volunteers reported from various places that barangay captains conspicuously supervised polling places as if suggesting to the voters that their votes were being monitored. Several barangay captains allowed no opposition party watchers and inspectors to enter the polling centers.[3]

According to the official Comelec returns for Nueva Ecija (minus Cabanatuan and two other cities, which were separately submitted) Marcos got 222,095 votes and Aquino 131,814 votes, respectively 63 and 37 percent. Although Comelec returns are unreliable, it is plausible that Marcos won the elections in Nueva Ecija but by a much smaller margin than officially reported. The land reform program and the Masagana 99 credit program in the 1970s had earned Marcos a certain amount of goodwill among the farming population.

New Leaders and a New Vision

Although the "EDSA Revolution" did not spark similar demonstrations in Nueva Ecija, there was definitely a sense of relief among a large part of the population in the province. At least 37 percent of the people had voted for Aquino. In articles on "People Power" and about the need to restore honesty in the government, local journalists urged President Aquino to proclaim a Revolutionary Government.[4] Several media people warned that the government should not betray the people's confidence. Local officials were exhorted to resign from office and there were warnings against "recalcitrant KBL holdouts." Both journalists and professionals hailed the "rebirth of the media, which were no longer subservient to political masters."

The political philosophy of the new administration was that the old type of morality had to be changed. In the words of one of Cory Aquino's active supporters in Nueva Ecija:

> Since this was a new administration we had to change the old type of morality. That was the instruction, not only from Sedfrey Ordoñez, but also from Aquilino Pimentel, the Secretary of Local Government. I believed that it was really possible, because we had been appointed, not elected, so there were no election expenditures which had to be recovered. Noli Santos, myself, the board members, all of us were idealists at the time. We tried to implement this new vision: a new morality in the government, closer ties between the citizenry and the public officials, clean government, that was the clamor of the citizenry. We were not able to succeed, because of various reasons, and also because of financial constraints.[5]

To implement this vision, Aquino's government had to cleanse the political system of the Marcos past and to redirect that system toward the new political morality. There were, broadly speaking, two extreme options. Some people around Aquino favored a radical cleanup of the government apparatus, replacing not only elected officials, but also the top-level of the bureaucracy which had been deeply involved with the Marcos regime. Others advocated reconciliation as the guiding spirit of reforms, avoiding a total overhaul of the existing apparatus and working along the line of gradualism. The moderate approach soon got the upper hand.

Still, even moderate change required replacing Marcos followers with officials imbued with the EDSA Revolution spirit. The central leadership in Manila decided to give a political kingpin in each province the task of supervising the political transition. The person selected for Nueva Ecija was Sedfrey Ordoñez, a lawyer from a farming family in the town of Laur.

Ordoñez had worked in Jovito Salonga's law firm in the 1960s. In 1970, he ran for the Constitutional Convention on a progressive ticket and won. He was one of the few Con-Con members who voted against the Marcos-inspired constitution, which was later ratified after Marcos declared Martial Law. Ordoñez was one of the lawyers of Ninoy Aquino and a trusted friend of the Aquino family.

After the EDSA Revolution, President Cory Aquino offered Ordoñez the dual position of Solicitor General and governor of Nueva Ecija. Ordoñez refused, arguing that the previous Solicitor General, Estelito Mendoza, had combined his position with too many other posts. Ordoñez thus accepted only the position of Solicitor General. But he was also PDP-Laban chairman for the province with the responsibility for replacing incumbent officials and recommending new Officers-in-Charge (OICs) for appointment by the Local Government Minister Aquilino Pimentel. In February 1987, Ordoñez was made Secretary of Justice.

As Aquino's political kingpin for Nueva Ecija, Ordoñez sought to replace corrupt officials of the old regime with morally clean and impeccable new persons. Ordoñez also wanted to have a political machine in the province, not for personal ambition nor greed but to have a following, probably realizing, in the words of one political observer, that "a cabinet member here in the Philippines without a political base is nothing; he can be removed or replaced with gusto, if the situation so permits."[6]

Despite Ordoñez' reputation for honesty and integrity, his political measures were controversial almost from the beginning. In May 1986, supporters of President Aquino in Nueva Ecija expressed disgust over Ordoñez's recommendations for OICs, accusing him of nepotism, of totally ignoring them, and of sacrificing public welfare for personal considerations. Out of thirty-two recommendations for top OIC positions in the province, nine candidates were directly related to Ordoñez by blood or by affinity. Many of the others were connected to him by personal friendship. The recommended OIC mayor of Cabanatuan City, for example, was Atty. Cesar Vergara, Ordoñez's brother-in-law, who, critics said, had no political base and had not campaigned for Aquino.[7]

Nueva Ecija Under Governor Noli Santos

In May 1986, Emmanuel "Noli" Santos was appointed OIC Governor of Nueva Ecija upon the recommendation of Ordoñez. Imbued with the more radical political ideas of Ninoy Aquino, Santos had been a candidate in the province twice, but he had not built a power base. Coming from a business family in Cabanatuan City, Santos had studied law and had worked in a law firm in Manila.

In 1970, Santos was elected to the Constitutional Convention on a left-of-center political program. In 1973, he voted tactical "yes" to the latest version of the draft for the new constitution, a version which bore Marcos's imprint, on the promise that all those who approved the new constitution would automatically become members of the Assembly which President Marcos was to convene later. This expectation did not come true. In the 1977 elections for the Interim Assembly (Batasang Pambansa), Santos ran on the oppositionist ticket of Laban ng Bayan, Ninoy Aquino's party in Metro Manila. He had joined that ticket, he said, because it would provide him with a chance to "reawaken the democratic spirit in this country." Amidst electoral fraud, this ticket was doomed to lose. In May 1984, Noli Santos ran in the Batasang Pambansa elections in Nueva Ecija on a PDP-Laban ticket. Although he finished only seventh, he had presented himself to be a staunch PDP-Laban supporter. This gave him an important political qualification in the post-Marcos era.

As a newly appointed governor, Santos faced several tasks: implement the new political philosophy of the Aquino government, create a clean government, and build his own political power base. He was also expected to help with the economic recovery of the province and initiate new development projects. He had to pursue these objectives under conditions fraught with political rivalry and controversies over policy directions.

The relationship between him and Sedfrey Ordoñez evolved from hidden rivalry to open conflict. Aside from personality differences and possibly old scores to settle, the two politicians competed for political support. Ordoñez, trying to gain a foothold in the provincial bureaucracy, agreed to Santos's appointment as OIC governor on the condition that his own men would be appointed to the sensitive positions of provincial administrator (i.e., the head of the provincial bureaucracy) and provincial engineer. Santos only consented to the first candidate; he put his own man in the second position.

During the first few months of the new provincial government, a conflict arose over the proper policy toward the sitting members of the provincial bureaucracy. The new provincial administrator wanted to remove the department heads in the provincial office and replace them with his own followers. Governor Santos opposed. He wanted to follow a policy of reconciliation, in an attempt to win the bureaucrats over to his side. He probably also feared that Ordoñez people would be appointed to these positions. The conflict mounted until Santos dismissed the provincial administrator after three months in office.[8]

One of the few department heads dismissed was the head of the provincial planning office who had been involved in anomalies. He was replaced by Manuel Tobias, a civil servant from the central NEDA office. Tobias started an investigation into the anomalies of the previous administration. This was apparently resented in some circles because in November 1986 Tobias was assassinated, presumably by people connected with the previous administration. The killing has never been solved. In May 1987, another key Santos man was killed: the contractor Feliciano "Fely" Samaniego whom Santos had made executive assistant for projects. Samaniego's department, the project management office, was responsible for the bidding of contracts for development projects in the province. Samaniego initiated Governor Santos into the world of the contractors and their practices. Apparently some people in the province decided to stop this by having Samaniego killed. Again, this crime has not been solved.

Santos was not able to control the sensitive position of district engineer, the provincial-level official of the Department of Public Works. He knew that the Ordoñez faction was trying to get their own person appointed. Although he tried to prevent this, complaining to President Aquino that "the perception of the people of Nueva Ecija is that there are two governors of the province, one de facto and one de jure," the Ordoñez faction succeeded through direct connections with the Palace.[9]

Santos attempted to improve the level of welfare in the province by carrying out infrastructural works and promoting the construction of roads and bridges, schoolbuildings, and the installation of water pumps. He claims to have channeled loans to more than 3,000 farmers and to have created a number of livelihood projects. He continued the practice of providing free hospitalization to people through two hospitals in Nueva Ecija. The governor also organized vocational training courses, seminars, and workshops and disbursed more than 800 scholarships to deserving students of Nueva Ecija.

Santos described himself as ideological rather than personalistic in orientation.[10] He vigorously criticized politicians and military who still favored Marcos. He strongly opposed any form of military rule, organized rallies in Cabanatuan to commemorate the 1972 proclamation of Martial Law as "shame of democracy day," and later chastised the attempted coup by Col. Honasan. He held regular "people's dialogues" in various places around the province and installed "suggestion boxes" at the lobbies of the provincial capitol. All of these earned him the reputation in some circles of being "left-leaning."

His relations with the military were strained, at least until the middle of 1987. The provincial PC Commander publicly accused Santos of being partial to the left and to critics of the military and of openly encouraging rallies staged by leftist organizations.

These military-civilian controversies took place against the background of frequent encounters in the province between the New People's Army and the military, causing casualities on both sides. In addition, the Army and associated vigilante groups committed human rights violations, the most infamous being the 10 February 1987 "Lupao massacre" when an Army patrol, after a brief encounter with NPA rebels, continued to fire at village huts and people, killing seventeen unarmed civilians.[11] Noli Santos was horrified and accused the military of wanton violation of human rights.

During 1986 and 1987, the political atmosphere gradually changed, both at the national level and in the province. The euphoria of the February Revolution petered out and the Aquino government lost its momentum to initiate structural changes. Increasingly people realized that the new administration was not able to fulfil its promises. An editorial in a local newspaper lamented that

> President Aquino had advocated the concept of "transparency in government" under which the people are supposed to know what those in government are doing to merit public trust. The concept, however, seems alien to most government functionaries, both in the higher echelons of power and in the petty bureaucracy, who generally regard government and their respective realms as their private preserves. . . . government engineers and local administrators fake public biddings of government projects in favor of negotiated arrangements with contractors where they dictate their demanded kickback now euphemistically referred to as SOPs.[12]

Initially, after Aquino had just taken office, many political leaders had the feeling that they could "start a new beginning" for an improved government and society. Later, the August and November 1986 coup attempts made clear that there was a strong opposition against the Aquino administration. The new government, they concluded, must consolidate its power and increase its legitimacy by resurrecting democratic procedures and approving a new constitution.

The Plebiscite

The campaign to ratify the new constitution started late November 1986. Solicitor-General Ordoñez actively participated in rallies and other campaign activities in Cabanatuan and elsewhere, as did the OIC officials in the province. At the largest demonstration in early January, a number of former KBL officials pledged their support to the charter. Former Governor Eduardo Joson, particularly, announced his support which in turn brought many of his followers to the side of the administration. Leaflets were circulated citing reasons why the people should vote Yes. But the strongest argument for ratification of the constitution, as one local journalist remarked, was the popularity, integrity, and honesty not of any local leader, but of President Aquino.[13]

Three groups opposed the ratification. First, some old KBL loyalists led by former Cabanatuan City Mayor Honorato Perez criticized the "questionable circumstances" surrounding the charter's formulation.[14] Second, certain leftist organizations opposed the new constitution. In January 1987, at a rally in Cabanatuan City—organized by Bagong Alyansang Makabayan (BAYAN), the Partido ng Bayan (PnB), the farmers organization Alyansa ng mga Magbubukid sa Gitnang Luson (AMGL), and the youth organization Kabataan para sa Demokrasya at Nasyunalismo (KADENA)—speakers took turns in lambasting the ratification exercise, calling it a "solo presidential election."[15] Third, a number of heavily armed NPA guerrillas campaigned against the draft constitution. They told the villagers that if they voted "no," they would have better chances of eventually owning the land they were tilling, whereas if they voted "yes," they would have no chance at all.[16]

The poll itself was quiet and orderly. Of the registered voters 82 percent actually voted, a normal turnout. Of the votes, nearly 70 percent were yes, 30 percent no, and 0.5 percent were abstentions. The "Yes" vote for Nueva Ecija was below the percentage for Region III (Central Luzon), which was 81 percent, and the national average of 76 percent. Cabanatuan City with a voter turnout of 81 percent had 65 percent "Yes" votes and 35 percent "No" votes, even farther below the national average.[17]

Congressional and Senatorial Elections

Immediately after the plebiscite, preparations for the May 1987 senatorial and congressional elections shifted to a higher gear. Political leaders and factions were busy organizing their networks of followers, planning strategic moves in the selection of candidates, and wooing potential allies. Because vote-buying was likely to be a major strategy, preparing sufficient campaign funds was of utmost importance for future candidates.

The burning question was which of the main political factors would be decisive in these elections: the traditional political machinery with networks down to the village level; large amounts of money; or the new clamor for honesty and clean government among the public.

The pro-Aquino PDP-Laban had not not been able to build up a strong party organization in the province. In 1984, the PDP-Laban candidates for the Batasan all campaigned on an individual basis, trying to build up their personal networks of followers. During the campaign for the snap elections, only a small number of political figures in the province had dared to campaign openly for the Aquino-Laurel ticket. After the February Revolution, PDP-Laban provincial kingpin Sedfrey Ordoñez had difficulties finding suitable candidates for OIC positions. By the end of 1986, the party had councils in only eight of the twenty-nine towns and in one of the three cities. The party's provincial and Cabanatuan City councils were in the hands of people identified with Governor Santos, rather than with Ordoñez.[18] Below the level of the councils were personal followers of the politicians, but no party organization.

PDP-Laban's rudimentary provincial party organization was not allowed to select or even to discuss the candidates for these elections. It was the party's national level committee, consisting of Jose "Peping" Cojuangco, Ernesto Tiopaco, and Sedfrey Ordoñez, which made these decisions. Ordoñez was the key figure and he consulted with a handful of advisers and trusted friends from the province.[19]

The changing political atmosphere in the Philippines was clearly reflected in the arguments used by Ordoñez and his advisers in their deliberations on suitable candidates. Prospective candidates were judged, on the one hand, on the basis of their moral standing and their reputation for honesty and reliability and, on the other hand, on the basis of their capacity to attract votes and to win the elections. Ordoñez rejected seasoned politicians on the argument that they had cases in court and criminal records. But some of his advisers argued that honest and clean persons would surely lose the elections, because they were too soft and inexperienced. In closed door meetings, the advisers often clashed over these conflicting viewpoints.[20]

A related issue was whether PDP-Laban/Lakas ng Bansa should have as its official candidates politicians from factions that had played prominent roles in President Marcos's KBL. President Aquino's brother, Peping Cojuangco, had no qualms about making political deals with former KBL politicians and on his instigation, Lakas ng Bansa put a number of former KBL stalwarts on the ticket. The national-level party leaders also tried to recruit former Supreme Court Justice Hermogenes Concepcion as a congressional candidate in Nueva Ecija. Sedfrey Ordoñez did not consent to this because the Concepcion family (including former Cabanatuan City Mayor Honorato Perez) had been staunch Marcos supporters and some still opposed the new constitution.

Ordoñez had to talk personally to President Aquino to have Concepcion removed from the list.[21]

The PDP-Laban committee had difficulties deciding on its official candidates. For the first district, it chose former Assemblyman Leopoldo Diaz who had been a KBL and Marcos loyalist for many years but who had run as an Independent in the 1984 elections and had always had good relations with Sedfrey Ordoñez. Diaz had his own political machine and he was considered to be a match for the Joson faction. In the second district, it fielded Simeon Garcia, a newcomer in politics, lawyer, and protegé of Peping Cojuangco. In the third district, the choice had been very difficult. Some potential candidates had refused and others had been rejected by Ordoñez as not being honest. Ordoñez also ruled out coopting the Concepcion faction. In the end, the Ordoñez faction chose Arturo Vergara, nephew of both Cabanatuan City Mayor Cesar Vergara and Ordoñez. In the fourth district, PDP-Laban fielded Nicanor de Guzman, Jr., often characterized as a tough guy who had his own private army.

In the third district, two candidates ran under the PDP-Laban/Lakas ng Bansa banner. Arturo Vergara was officially proclaimed by President Aquino, but Hermogenes Concepcion, who had filed his candidacy under the UNIDO party label, managed to get the official authorization from the ruling party's leadership.[22] The cleavage at the top, between Secretary Ordoñez (who had personal access to the President) and the party leadership, opened the possibility for a rival faction at the provincial level to link up with the ruling coalition.

Meanwhile, the Joson faction was preparing for the elections. In February 1987, Governor Joson became the head of a new political party in Nueva Ecija, known as BALANE, an abbreviation of Bagong Alyansa (later changed to Bagong Lakas) ng Lalawigan ng Nueva Ecija (New Force of the Province of Nueva Ecija). Joson and others decided to ignore the old national parties, including KBL, because those were, as Joson said, "luma at kupas na" (old and passé).[23]

The "new morality" issue cropped up again in Nueva Ecija politics when civic groups accused the new political kingpin of Nueva Ecija of nepotism. In March 1987, Aquino supporters in the province mutinied against Sedfrey Ordoñez because he continued to promote his relatives in political positions.

Then in April 1987 700 professionals, students, laborers, vendors, and other diverse people in Cabanatuan lined up behind Dr. Rolando Veneracion for the third district. He, they said, was the most credible aspirant to initiate needed reforms in government.[24] The movement, called Lakas ng Sambayanan, attracted many volunteers. Veneracion campaigned on the issues of new political morality, consultative democracy, socialized medicine, and educational opportunities for the poor. His supporters claimed that "if Rolly wins, we will have proven that traditional politicians are now vulnerable, if not passé."[25]

Eventually thirty-three provincial politicians vied for the province's four congressional seats. Aside from Lakas ng Bansa and BALANE candidates, there were candidates on such other tickets as UNIDO, KBL-UNIDO, LP-Salonga, LP-Kalaw, and PnB. Several ran as Independents. Many expressed loyalty to President Aquino, or claimed that they were supported by her party. As a local newspaper commented: "The splintered minority during the Marcos years has become the fragmented majority today."[26]

The May 1987 contests did not conform to the traditional two-party system. Only in the first district did two major candidates stand out, former Assemblyman Edno Joson (son of the ex-governor) and Leopoldo Diaz. In the other districts, the fight was between at least three equally strong contending factions. This multifaction system at the provincial level reflects not only the dispersion of power among the provincial elite but also the fact that the national party system was still so unstable that many provincial politicians and factions tried their luck to get access to central institutions. The large number of candidates and the widespread uncertainty over the outcome of the contest showed that people were not sure about the rules of the game.

Ultimately, three PDP-Laban candidates won. Simeon Garcia won in the second district. Nicanor de Guzman, Jr., won in the fourth, although his victory was contested by two other candidates who accused him of fraud and intimidation. Of the two PDP-Laban candidates in the third district, Hermogenes Concepcion came in first, and Arturo Vergara, Ordoñez's nephew was second.

The results for Eduardo Joson's BALANE party were disappointing: only his son Edno Joson (first district) was elected. The outcome was also disappointing for the civic movement of Rolando Veneracion: he ended as number four in the third district. The only left-wing candidate in the congressional competition, human rights lawyer Vidal Tombo, running in the third district, was equally unsuccessful in the polls, ending as number five on the list.

The results of the congressional elections revealed the relative persuasive powers of provincial politicians. That was not necessarily true for the Senate race. In the senatorial elections, the voters had to select twenty-four national candidates. In Nueva Ecija, sixteen in the pro-Aquino coalition, seven in the Grand Alliance for Democracy, and one Independent won, significantly different from the national outcome of twenty-two pro-Aquino and two GAD winners. GAD candidate and popular movie star Joseph Estrada was number one in the

Nueva Ecija count (227,137 votes) but number fourteen nationwide, while Juan Ponce Enrile was number twelve (176,749 votes) but number twenty-four nationwide.[27] The large number of GAD winners in Nueva Ecija shows the strong influence of rightist forces in the province. One can surmise that the Joson party machinery actively worked for the GAD candidates.

Candidates from the PnB, BAYAN, and Volunteers for Popular Democracy, who presented themselves under the banner of the Alliance for New Politics (ANP), had a poor showing in the province. The human rights lawyer and former LABAN activist Atty. Romeo Capulong, who hailed from Nueva Ecija, ended as number forty on the senatorial list with 74,549 votes. Others were in the fifty to seventy bracket (with about 20,000 to 25,000 votes).[28] As one political observer remarked: the vote for Capulong was *pakikisama* (friendly relationship) from Novo Ecijanos; the support for the others showed the real electoral following of the left.

The Local Elections of January 1988

After the May elections Ordoñez's political position had weakened. The PDP-Laban candidates who had won were protegés of Peping Cojuangco and other party leaders, not Ordoñez's. Testimony to his weakness, in the eyes of many Novo Ecijanos, was the defeat of his nephew, Arturo Vergara. Vergara's fate had become a matter of family honor and, prior to the poll, there were rumors that Ordoñez would resign if Vergara lost. However, he stayed on and continued his attempts to get a foothold in Nueva Ecija politics, readying himself for the local elections, originally scheduled for November 1987 but later postponed to January 1988.

Political relationships within the ruling party had become more complicated. Political kingpin Ordoñez was no longer the only one deciding Nueva Ecija affairs within the party leadership. The Concepcion faction had again become a political force to reckon with.

As soon as the new Congress convened in July 1987, Congressman Hermogenes Concepcion entered into an alliance with other former KBL politicians who had made their comeback to the national political scene. He formed a group with a voting capability of twenty-four votes, and he pledged the support of this group to leaders of the ruling party, in exchange for the chairmanship of a congressional committee. The deal worked: Concepcion became chairman of the newly created Committee on Crimes, Fraud and Corruption in Government. Well-entrenched at the national level, Concepcion then started to assert his influence in Nueva Ecija provincial politics.

During a meeting in September 1987, called by PDP-Laban national chairman Peping Cojuangco, Nueva Ecija political leaders discussed candidates for the 1988 provincial and municipal elections. Hermogenes Concepcion warned Ordoñez to stop interfering in local politics, as this would not be proper to his position as Secretary of Justice.[29] In the same meeting, differences of opinion concerning political candidates came into the open.

The competition for the governorship was the most debated issue in the local elections. In July 1987, the two main contenders for the governorship were already known. Former Eduardo Joson announced his plan to return as supporters carried his picture and the slogan: "Ako'y babalik" (I will return). Governor Noli Santos announced that he was running with the blessing from above, presumably from the presidential palace. Santos issued his own slogan against Joson's challenge: "Di Kami Papayag na Bumalik Kang Muli" (We will not allow you to return).

The number of candidates in the local elections was large. Two parties had slates for provincial government officials: PDP-Laban/Lakas ng Bansa and BALANE. Two other candidates ran for vice-governor as an Independent and a Liberal. For Cabanatuan City government, there was a three-cornered race among the Ordoñez faction (with Sedfrey's son Philip as candidate for mayor), the Concepcion faction (with Honorato Perez), and the Garcia faction (with Mario Garcia).

In the province's two other cities and twenty-nine towns, as many as seven candidates ran for mayor; the average per municipality was 4.4 candidates, of which three or four were often strong contenders; rarely were there only two.

The campaign included rallies and candidates talking to villagers. Rumor had it that there was vote-buying on a large scale. The Joson faction, especially, disbursed money—allegedly ten million pesos—to its followers and prospective followers a few days before the poll. The Santos faction apparently could not match these efforts, the money given by Peping Cojuangco amounting to less than half a million pesos.

In the days after the poll, tension built up in the province. Santos, noticing that he was losing in the canvassing of votes, accused the Joson faction of "massive terrorism, fraud and intimidation" and filed a complaint with the Commission on Elections. The canvass of election returns was suspended for some time and transferred to the Comelec Central Office in Manila. Santos said that "the canvassers' board was being allegedly intimidated by the presence of Joson's armed followers."[30] However, both the Nueva Ecija provincial election supervisor and the PC provincial commander attested that no violent incidents had been reported to them.[31]

Eduardo Joson won the gubernatorial race against Noli Santos, 282,303 to 188,504. In the provincial board, the division between PDP-Laban and BALANE members was six to four. At the level of municipal mayors, the PDP-Laban coalition fared better: in the thirty-two towns and cities, twenty-four PDP-Laban mayors, seven BALANE mayors, and one Independent mayor were elected.[32] In Cabanatuan City, Honorato Perez won over Philip Ordoñez.

Following the January 1988 elections, the Joson family now occupied a number of strategic elected positions: Eduardo Joson was governor again, his sons Edno, Thomas, Eduardo "Danding," and Boyet had been elected congressman, provincial board member, vice mayor of Cabanatuan City, and mayor of the town of Quezon respectively. Although the Josons had a strong political machinery in Nueva Ecija, they were still isolated in the country: BALANE was not affiliated with any of the national parties. It was only toward the end of the year 1988 that the Josons finally decided to join forces with the Enrile-Laurel camp.

One useful way to understand the outcome of the gubernatorial race is Adrian Mayer's action-set and social network concepts. An electoral action-set is the purposeful mobilization of a set of persons to achieve the goal of getting the candidate elected to political office. A network is a series of relations or links between persons, which may lie dormant for some time. Mayer argues that one should distinguish between the potential material of network links and those links which are actually used in the action-set's constitution.[33] In his analysis of election strategies in India, Mayer uses these concepts to make a distinction between "hard" and "soft" campaigns. In a hard campaign, an extensive network serves as the basis for the construction of an action-set with shorter paths using personal relationships between the candidate's faction and the voters. In a soft campaign, longer paths are used, often of an impersonal nature, to recruit voters. In the Philippines, these different approaches are usually discussed under the labels of "the personal approach" versus "general campaigning," with the first as being considered far more efficient.[34]

In the gubernatorial race discussed here, the Joson faction used the personal approach or "hard" campaign. The Joson action-set could mobilize an organization of probably a few hundred men, who could contact and reactivate an old network of followers and supporters in each municipality down to the barangay level. Families who had received past favors could be persuaded to vote for the candidates of the Joson faction. The persuasive power of the Joson action-set was backed up by money to buy votes. The organization's enforcers saw to it that barangay captains and *lider* who had committed their support were actually working for the candidate.

Noli Santos followed the soft campaign, using the style of general campaigning with rallies, shaking hands with the public, and touring the province with an election caravan. Santos did not have an organization of his own and was forced to depend on other politician's political machines. Looking back at the elections, Santos attributed his defeat to a number of factors, the most important of which was the fact that he had not been able to form a strong cohesive political organization in the province.[35] In addition, he complained that he did not receive sufficient support from the ruling party: he was not given enough campaign funds, only less than half of a million pesos shortly before the elections. The conflict with Ordoñez meant that Santos did not receive the full support of the Ordoñez faction and of other politicians who were primarily allied with the Secretary of Justice. Santos also pointed out that he clung too long to an inappropriate political style, modeled after the People Power movement at EDSA, without realizing that "starting new politics in a traditional setting does not work."[36]

Even though the odds were heavily against Santos, it is remarkable that he still got 40 percent of the votes. If it is true that the personal approach is far more effective than general campaigning, then Santos's electoral support can partly be considered as a conscious vote for a candidate backed by Aquino and associated with the promise of political renewal.

Conclusion

The outcome of the elections in the years 1987 and 1988 has been characterized as a return to the pre-Martial Law political system, i.e., an elite democracy based on political patronage. Political developments in Nueva Ecija to a large extent corroborate this picture. Focusing on the provincial level enables us to analyze in more detail the factors leading to this outcome, i.e., the lack of political renewal under the Aquino administration and the resurgence of traditional politics. This outcome can be explained as a result of the interaction between political developments at different levels, i.e., at the national, provincial and local levels.

At the national level, the Aquino administration did not initiate determined action to introduce structural reforms within government and society. The new administration envisaged political renewal in personalistic terms, as a change in morals and personnel rather than as a change of the rules and regulations of policy-making. Absent was a conception or vision of structural change. Aquino's emissaries to Nueva Ecija also had no program of changes nor a strategy for building grassroots support. The leading politicians were unsure of the rules of the game until the first few months of 1987, wavered in their election-strategy, and, lacking a plan to build up the PDP-Laban Party organization in the province, fell back on personal followings and networks of seasoned politicians.

Leaders of old political clans were eager to reenter politics for various reasons. Aside from family pride and the proverbial lust for power, they sought to use public office for private purposes. Such elite behavior in politics both fosters corruption and allows political entrepreneurs to finance armed retainers and to buy influential leaders at the local level. In Nueva Ecija, former KBL politicians were admitted to the ruling group and became more influential than Cory's original emissaries.

Election politics did not provide much space to articulate principles, programs, and policies. Former opposition parties such as PDP-Laban had fought the Marcos-regime with an ideology and political platform, but after the Aquino takeover, the ruling coalition returned to traditional politics. Leftist parties such as PnB and other groups under the banner of the Alliance for New Politics, following the strategy of general campaigning and presenting a political platform based on an ideology, drew only small numbers of voters. Independent candidates campaigning with a platform of moral and social reforms were equally unsuccessful.

Programmatic politics could be stimulated if segments of the population would be able to organize themselves and articulate their interests vis-à-vis politicians at the higher levels. However, Philippine rural society is characterized by a weakness of organized interest groups or categorical organizations operating on a region-wide or province-wide basis. There are peasant unions and active nongovernment organizations, but these are small and have a network structure which is limited to a few villages. These groups are not strong enough to present themselves in election politics.

An explanation for the weakness of class or categorical organizations should be sought outside the sphere of electoral politics. The social structure of Central Luzon's population has been deeply influenced by a number of interrelated processes. The Green Revolution and the Marcos land reform have led to a pronounced differentiation among the peasantry, which has bifurcated into strata of better-off farmers, on the one hand, and landless, on the other. This process of differentiation blocks potential links of solidarity and contrasts strongly with the historical experience of the 1930s and 1940s when peasant organizations were very strong in Central Luzon.[37]

Provincial outcomes and emerging structure can thus be situated between national level developments and emerging structures at the provincial and local levels. At the center, the ruling coalition, driven by a desire to consolidate its power, entered into coalitions with provincial political clans driven by personalistic objectives who dispense particularistic patronage in order to enhance their personal position. At the local level, rural people have unlearned the politics of collective action.

BENEDICT J. TRIA KERKVLIET

Understanding Politics in a Nueva Ecija Rural Community

Distant spectators to the climax of the February 1986 presidential elections were not limited to people in foreign countries. In the Philippines, too, many followed the story through the mass media. Among them were the 1,500 people of San Ricardo, a lowland village in the middle of the Central Luzon province of Nueva Ecija. Asked what they did or thought while throngs of fellow Filipinos camped out at EDSA, residents of San Ricardo typically replied, "We listened to the radio, discussed it among ourselves, and hoped that the situation wouldn't become bloody."[1]

Meanwhile, people went about their business, especially preparing fields for the dry season rice crop and repairing their houses, which had been damaged by a hurricane the previous October. No one knew anyone from the village who journeyed to Metro Manila (four hours away by bus) to join the "EDSA Revolution," as San Ricardo people generally refer to the final event that brought down Marcos and ushered in Aquino. Nor did any demonstrations for or against the two contenders occur in the San Ricardo vicinity. The only abnormal activities at the time, aside from residents being more attentive than usual to the radio, were a few wealthy villagers sending donations to the throngs on EDSA and several folks holding a vigil in the local Catholic chapel to pray for peace.

Villagers were not deeply engaged in EDSA. Moreover, 69 percent had actually voted for Marcos and only 31 percent went for Aquino. Marcos also won by a large majority in one neighboring village. Aquino won by a slender 52 percent in a second.[2] For the whole municipality of Talavera, Marcos won with 59 percent of the votes.

Many Marcos voters in San Ricardo believed in February 1986 that he actually had won nationwide but was prevented from staying because the military's leaders tried to pull a coup. During the resulting confusion, Aquino's supporters poured into the streets of Manila because, as one villager said, "they could not accept that Cory [Aquino] had lost."

Many residents, both Marcos and Aquino voters, credit Marcos for preventing bloodshed. Marcos, they say, could have bombed the two military camps and demonstrators. "Instead," said one Aquino voter, "he took pity on the people and the country," ordering that no guns be fired. "Our prayers were answered," recalled a woman who was among those who joined the vigil at the village chapel to pray that the "disorder" (gulo) not spread and that "calm" (tahimik) be restored. Like several of the worshippers, she had voted for Marcos, but she was asking Jesus and the Virgin Mary to prevent him from "causing Filipinos to kill Filipinos" and for San Ricardo to be spared from the trouble in Manila.

What is the explanation for the election results in San Ricardo? Who voted for whom and why? I am particularly interested in seeing whether the widely used factional model of Philippine electoral politics works well here.[3] I also put this election into the context of political-economic life in the village prior to and shortly after the event. Doing that reveals an interaction between national policies and local problems and illustrates the important point that elections are but one facet of village politics.

Village Society

Settled at the turn of this century, San Ricardo was, until recently, composed primarily of peasant households—mostly share tenants farming the land of a small number of large and medium-sized landowners who often were the tenants' creditors, patrons, and principal abusers. By the mid-1970s, however, less than half the households had fields. About 35 percent of those still with land were owners; nearly all the remainder were leasehold tenants or scheduled, by land reform, to become owners. Forty percent of village households are landless, most of them poor seasonal agricultural workers. A few have intermittent employment beyond the village, usually as construction workers. Several peasant households also have or have had members, both men and women, working outside the village, some as far away as Saudi Arabia.

Wage labor, capital intensive agriculture, rising landlessness, and villagers coming and going in search of work are obvious manifestations of accelerating capitalism since the 1950s. A generation ago, a chief concern of peasants was avoiding eviction by their landlord. Nearly a fourth of today's landless were victims in the 1950s-1960s of one phase in the spread of capitalism when landowners replaced tenants with machinery and hired laborers (recruited primarily from other regions). Today, a chief problem for peasants is scraping together enough capital to put in a crop. For workers, it is finding employment.

Two-thirds of San Ricardo's 240 households are poor. They have little or no cash beyond the bare necessities, eat primarily rice, live in houses made of the least expensive materials and cannot support their children's schooling beyond elementary grades. Half the poor are landless workers; the other half are peasants and petty traders. About a quarter of the households have what many villagers regard as an "adequate" status or standard of living; most are the better off peasants. The remaining tiny percentage are the rich, composed of a few peasants and the capitalists.

Most household heads are preoccupied with securing a livelihood, improving their living conditions, and giving their children a better start than they had. Land, employment, and education are the principal resources people try to acquire. To get them, people act individually and in nuclear families. They also cultivate strong connections with others, especially with those controlling more resources. The same villagers will also join fellow class and status cohorts to struggle for shared goals and against common antagonists.

Consequently, an ongoing major dynamic of village politics is two different forms of class and status interaction. One is building and maintaining networks among people in different classes and statuses. The other is conflict, often subdued and indirect but occasionally blatant and confrontational, between people and groups in contentious class or status relationships. Entwined are prominent political and economic concerns, particularly prices paid and received, land distribution, and peace.

The 1980s Under the Marcos Government

Rapid inflation, falling real incomes, inequality and poverty were salient features of the Philippine economy during the first half of the 1980s.[5] In San Ricardo, many who had worked in the late 1970s and early 1980s on distant construction sites and in Metro Manila factories were unemployed in 1985-86, victims of the downturn in the nation's industries. Back in the village, they competed with landless workers and others for agricultural work. The abundance of people wanting to harvest contributed to a 30 percent drop in harvest payment between 1979 and 1985.[6] Meanwhile, local prices for basic food items rose 3.3 times.

Worsening economic conditions aggravated tensions among villagers. Theft of chickens, grain, and equipment increased. Culprits were usually among the poorest in San Ricardo and neighboring villages. They justified their actions in terms of their families' desperation and, frequently, their criticism against those from whom they took. Peasants, looking for angles to cut farming expenses, eschewed paying irrigation fees and haggled to lower wages paid for planting, weeding, and harvesting.[7] Agricultural workers, in turn, often pilfered from the harvest, prolonged tasks in order to increase their earnings, and boycotted landholders known to be stingy and rude.

Some villagers blamed the declining economy on greedy merchants and companies. Others faulted Marcos's government—particularly corruption and the assassination of Benigno Aquino, Jr. (for which most thought someone very high up was responsible), both of which, they said, caused business to plummet.

In 1985, three to six thousand peasants and other people mostly from Central Luzon (including ten from San Ricardo) camped for days in front of the Ministry of Agriculture and Food in Quezon City. Organized by the young Alyansa ng mga Magsasaka sa Gitnang Luson (AMGL; Alliance of Central Luzon Peasants), the demonstrators demanded that pesticide and fertilizer prices be reduced to 1983 levels and that price supports for *palay* (unhulled rice) be strengthened without increasing the price for *bigas* (hulled rice). After ten days, by which time the number of demonstrators had dwindled to 500, the government replied by sending police and fire fighters with guns drawn, batons flailing, and water cannons blasting. Some fifty people were seriously injured.[8] That in turn provoked a wave of protests in Metro Manila, which intensified pressure on Marcos to announce an early presidential elections.

Despite the government's unsympathetic response to peasants' concerns and the atrophying economy, a significant reservoir of support remained for Marcos in 1985, albeit more shallow than five years earlier. Marcos's popularity among peasants came primarily from land reform done in the 1970s.

Land tenure and related conditions had been contentious in Central Luzon, including San Ricardo, for decades and figured prominently in the Huk rebellion (circa 1946–54), which had involved most San Ricardo families. Two demands that persisted into the 1960s were security of tenure and lower rents, if not outright ownership of the fields they farmed.

By the late 1970s and early 1980s, both of these demands had been met to the satisfaction of most tenants.[9] Not since the early 1970s had any tenants been evicted. As for rent, the typical amount in the 1960s of 40-50 percent of a tenant's crop had virtually disappeared. By 1979 half of all nonowner peasants were leaseholders, paying small fixed rents averaging eight to ten sacks (*kaban*) per hectare. All but a few of the remaining half were in varying stages of becoming owners of their fields under the government's Operation Land Transfer program.

While many villagers say that these improved tenure conditions are the "fruit of seeds planted" by previous peasant organizations and the Huks, they also credit Marcos. A common characterization even in 1985 was that no other president had done as much for peasants as Marcos had.

Land distribution remained contentious, however, for landless families, who did not benefit from land reform. Yet from their perspective, over 300 hectares lay right outside their doors that should be farmed by them. The area constituted parts of two haciendas—owned by two branches of the wealthy Tinio clan—that agrarian reform laws had exempted because the owners had mechanized in the 1950s-1960s (by evicting families who now are among the landless). Moreover, both haciendas were practically idle between 1978 and the early 1980s.[10]

The long history of animosity between the owners and the residents of San Ricardo and neighboring villages continued during the 1970s. By the late 1970s, some landless villagers toyed with trying to take over idle Tinio fields. More followed the lead of a local Sama-hang Nayon (Village Association) officer to petition the government to redistribute both haciendas among landless residents. The government answered that it had neither the authority nor money to do that.

In 1981, when the owners of the Vivencio Tinio (VT) hacienda leased it to a contractor who began farming rice with machinery and non-resident laborers, many landless people figured they must act quickly to insist on their claim. If anyone was going to become tenants on that land, argued eighty-four villagers in a letter to the municipal mayor and provincial governor, it should be poor landless people in the San Ricardo area, not a wealthy farmer. Subsequent discussions with those officials gave the impression that the mayor and governor supported their claims (a sentiment both men later denied).

In May 1981, members of more than 100 San Ricardo households began dividing up and plowing 70 hectares of the VT hacienda. Their actions emboldened hundreds more in neighboring villages to plan the same for other parts of the VT as well as the adjacent Manolo Tinio (MT) hacienda. On the fifth day of the takeover, however, soldiers and policemen ordered the "trespassers" off the land. Unprepared to resist an overwhelming force, the people had to leave. But their desire for land remained, as we shall see.

Peace is another chief concern in San Ricardo. Many had welcomed Martial Law because by the early 1970s violence was getting out of hand. They credit Marcos with disarming politicians' guards (who bullied and threatened opponents' supporters during elections), stopping carabao rustling, and ending the connivance between the police and provincial crime syndicates. Until the early 1980s, conditions remained peaceful. Unlike many other parts of the nation, villages like San Ricardo in Nueva Ecija's lowland had not been disrupted by logging, mining, and agribusiness corporations nor by destructive government projects. They were also unaffected by rebellions elsewhere in the nation.

By 1985, however, anxiety was high in San Ricardo about the spreading civil war. Fighting between the New People's Army and the military had sporadically occurred in nearby municipalities, military troops roamed where they had not gone before, and soldiers on occasion had rounded up and shackled young men in nearby villages in their efforts to locate NPA organizers. Many stories circulated about the military killing innocent people.

The Election

As a rule, most villagers do not get terribly excited about elections. From experience, they know that government has long been dominated by and is mainly for the wealthy. Most politicians themselves are rich, arousing many villagers' suspicions because rarely are the rich genuinely concerned about their problems. An opinion that cuts across much of San Ricardo society, from the poorest to the moderately well off, is that politicians will promise anything to get votes; but once elected, they promptly forget the rural people. Consequently, to many residents, elections are basically a way to determine who among the wealthy will have the opportunity to take advantage of government resources. In so far as elections resolve this question in a peaceful way, people do acknowledge that they serve a purpose. Campaigns, though, have been known to become hostile, even violent.

Elections may materially benefit some voters. Several residents recall accepting during one campaign or another money and gifts from candidates or candidates' supporters in exchange for their votes and those of relatives and friends. This, many say, is practically their only opportunity to get anything from people in government.

Such was the milieu in San Ricardo as the 1985-86 election campaign proceeded. Because of their general cynicism about government and elections, numerous residents paid it little attention. Many of these were among the 35 percent who did not vote.[11] A few people voted for Aquino on the grounds that Marcos had been in office for twenty years—"time to give it to another rich person," as one man said sarcastically. Many more villagers, however, voted for Marcos because he seemed likely to win anyway. They figured it was wise to be on the winning side.

In early 1985, when already there was considerable speculation that Marcos would announce an election, the prevailing opinion in San Ricardo was that Marcos would only do so when he was confident of winning, especially since the opposition was divided. Even after opponents rallied around Aquino and Laurel in late 1985, most villagers could not imagine Marcos losing. If nothing else, many speculated, he would win by "extensive cheating" (*pandaraya*).

The likelihood that Marcos would win argued for prudence on the part of those inclined toward Aquino. Many worried that, because the election seemed so "important" and "serious" (*delikado, malubha*) to Marcos campaigners, particularly to local government officials, Aquino advocates might be harassed during the campaign or afterwards. Others wanted to avoid being tainted as strong Aquino backers in order to maintain good relations with relatives and local officials who favored Marcos.

This atmosphere certainly dampened potential enthusiasm for "Cory," as everyone calls her. Scarcely anyone in the village openly urged people to vote for her. And no outsiders visited San Ricardo to speak publicly for her. Pro-Cory discussions were confined, as several residents put it, to "whispered conversations" (*bulung-bulong*). Meanwhile, village and municipal government officials were openly campaigning for Marcos.

Thus Marcos's incumbency and reputation for winning was a definite advantage for him. It influenced some disinterested residents to vote for him, meant that local politicians supported him, and constrained the behavior of those who were partial to Aquino.

Factional and family alliances also played a role. Talavera Mayor Marcelo Diaz was the local cog in the Marcos political machine. He owed his position to Marcos, who had removed the previous mayor and appointed him perhaps as a favor to his older brother and Marcos supporter Assemblyman Leopoldo Diaz. Many of the municipality's barangay captains, in turn, were linked to Mayor Diaz, who had helped them to be elected in 1982.

One was the incumbent San Ricardo barangay captain, Fidel Lorenzo. In 1982, Mayor Diaz had helped Lorenzo and his handpicked barangay council candidates to avoid having any opponents by giving would-be competitors the run-around when they tried to file candidacy papers.

When Lorenzo died in 1985, he was succeeded, with Mayor Diaz's approval, by Victor Bruno, one of the councilors who had been elected in 1982.

Bruno made use of his position and his family and ritual kinship connections to lobby for Marcos. Assemblyman Diaz and Mayor Diaz, too, urged their *kumare* and *kumpare* in San Ricardo to campaign among their relatives for Marcos. Money helped to reinforce these linkages as a couple of Marcos proponents, including Barangay Captain Bruno, distributed 100-peso bills to some undecided voters in the final days of the campaign.

There is no evidence that any votes for Aquino were bought. But alliances did figure in the support that developed for her. Romeo Maliwat, a prominent physician in Talavera town and former mayor (1964–67), strongly favored Aquino. Maliwat had known Ninoy Aquino and had run on the PDP-Laban ticket for assemblyman in 1984. (He lost, supporters claim, because of cheating in Nueva Ecija at the time.) His association with the Aquinos and his conclusion years earlier that Marcos's rule was "ruthless" and "ruining the country" were major reasons why Maliwat favored Cory. Another one was the Maliwat family's long-time rivalry with the Diazes.

Maliwat and several of his wealthy relatives and friends solicited endorsements for Aquino among their kin and acquaintances throughout the municipality. Maliwat himself visited some San Ricardo residents, including former Barangay Captain Lando Cruz, whose daughter had been a nurse in Maliwat's clinic. Maliwat was a godparent (*ninong*) at the daughter's wedding in 1982, making Cruz and Maliwat *kumpareng buo* (close ritual relatives).

Cruz, not rich though one of the better off peasants in the village, became one of the few in San Ricardo who spoke openly on behalf of Aquino and against Marcos. Two additional Aquino supporters were Ipe and Toyang Trinidad, one of the village's wealthiest couples. Ipe is a civil servant in a distant government office. Toyang runs the couple's granary, manages their 20 hectares of ricelands, and is the area's largest moneylender.

Lando Cruz and Ipe Trinidad were prominent figures in one of the village's two major political factions beginning in the 1960s. The heart of the faction was the Cruz family's extensive network, especially in the heavily populated part of the village lining the highway. In 1968, Lando Cruz became the first person to win the village captaincy who was not backed by the Gregorio-Castro families.

The Gregorios and Castros were the center of the other significant election alliance. Concentrated in another principal part of the village, these two interrelated families trace their roots back to turn-of-the-century settlers in the area. From 1953 until 1967, a Gregorio, a Castro, or someone supported by this Gregorio-Castro "side" (*panig*) had been barangay captain and controlled San Ricardo's government. The most influential individual in this alliance was Tomas Gregorio, who was himself barangay captain from 1958 until he stepped down in 1967. Like Ipe Trinidad, Tomas Gregorio was one of the village's wealthiest landowners, a similarity which many villagers claim accentuated the rivalry between them during elections.

Although the Gregorio-Castro side lost the captaincy in 1968, it regained the position in 1972. Its candidate was Fidel Lorenzo, another large landowner (18.5 hectares), whose opponent was Lando Cruz, seeking reelection with the backing of the Cruz-Trinidad faction. Cruz lost by eight votes. While bitterness persisted between some leaders of the two factions, it was mollified by numerous linkages among families on both sides. Cruz and Lorenzo themselves were brothers-in-law.

Thus far in the analysis, the 1986 campaign for president appears to have piggybacked on the longstanding rivalry between San Ricardo's two major factions. Lando Cruz and Ipe Trinidad favored Aquino while Barangay Captain Bruno and village council members, all close to Fidel Lorenzo and by implication allied with the Gregorio-Castro faction, campaigned for Marcos. This would seem to be considerable evidence for the factional model.

But the situation is more complicated. One complexity is that by 1982–83, the Gregorio-Castro-Lorenzo alliance had virtually dissolved. Lorenzo's poor performance as barangay captain had alienated many in the Gregorio-Castro network. "All Captain Lorenzo did," said one elder in the Castro family, "was look out for number one; he did nothing for the village." Tomas Gregorio had urged him not to run again in 1982. When Lorenzo ignored that advice, many in the Gregorio-Castro faction disassociated themselves from him. Several were especially disgusted at the shenanigans Lorenzo pulled to prevent potential challengers from registering their candidacy papers. That opposition to Lorenzo and his slate was widespread is indicated by the 1982 election result. Although they easily won in the balloting, two-thirds of San Ricardo's 649 registered voters did not vote, an exceptionally low turnout for such contests.[12]

After Lorenzo died, the new barangay captain, Victor Bruno, had meager linkages to the Gregorio-Castro faction. And Lorenzo had left no sizeable following for him to inherit. Bruno himself had little support in the village. Many believed that he did not deserve to be barangay captain. He was known to be rude and was frequently drunk, which is why many residents nicknamed him, behind his back, "Kapitan

Bote" (Captain Bottle). Having scant respect or backing, Bruno and his associates were incapable of being effective advocates for Marcos.

Meanwhile, the Gregorio-Castro faction was divided on the presidential candidates. No one had emerged to replace Tomas Gregorio, who had died in early 1985, as its principal leader on election matters. Several Gregorios and Castros, including Tomas's only child, voted for Aquino whereas others, such as Tomas's brothers, went with Marcos.

Marcos won twice as many votes as Aquino, therefore, even though he had no solid factional support within the village and his most prominent advocates had little credibility.

On the other hand, Lando Cruz and Ipe Trinidad, principals in the village's second faction, were united for Aquino. Yet they had great difficulty lining up people in their networks to support Aquino. At least one of Lando Cruz's sons, for instance, voted for Marcos as did several other close relatives. Two men who previously had been among Lando's key advocates during his races for barangay captain not only voted but campaigned for Marcos.

Personal connections often tug in different directions. Two examples are Nora Dison and Cardo Buwan. Dison, a well-respected sixty-one-year-old, has long been active in local and national peasant organizations and is a former municipal councilor. Because she likely could influence other voters, she was approached by Romeo Maliwat as well as by Leopoldo Diaz, each asking her to favor his respective candidate. Both men are her *kumpareng buo*, one a godfather to her son and the other to her daughter. Cardo Buwan, a poor worker living in a section of the village where many landless people live and among whom he is well liked, was approached by one of his *kumpare* to support Aquino. But another man, also his *kumpare* and to whom he is equally close, asked him to vote for Marcos. Many other residents had linkages equally strong to individuals favoring Aquino and to others favoring Marcos.

Both Dison and Buwan voted and like most residents, they arrived at their choices through discussion, the content of which was not limited to the incumbency of Marcos, which candidate was likely to win, and who was supporting whom. The picture I get from conversations about why people voted as they did and what was going on in the village as election day approached is hundreds of small discussions covering numerous issues. Those discussions—typically occurring as people washed clothes, walked to their fields, bought vegetables at village stalls, fixed their houses, and performed other tasks—helped people to decide whether to vote and for whom. Along with whatever obligations they felt as a result of personal relationships, they assessed the arguments and observations they heard and chewed over.

Gender was an issue because some worried that a woman president would be ineffectual. That Aquino is a widow was also an issue—in her favor, because several argued that her husband was killed by Marcos's soldiers and Marcos himself was quite possibly involved in the crime or its cover-up. The broader issue of human rights violations was also raised against Marcos, as was the spreading civil war. People feared peace was fast being overtaken by turmoil. Some thought Marcos could better restore calm; others argued repression during his term was a principal cause, so a new leader was necessary. Qualifications, too, were debated. Marcos, noted many, was experienced in government, suggesting that Marcos was the better candidate. Others, though, cited his longevity in office as precisely one reason to vote against him and for Aquino. The time had come to end, as several put it, "the Marcos dynasty."

Two issues more than any others, however, permeated village discourse in early 1986. They are land reform and corruption. And where people stood on each was noticeably, although not uniformly, associated with their class.

A large majority of peasants favored Marcos because of land reform. This sentiment was especially pronounced among land reform beneficiaries, many of whom reasoned that a vote for him was a "thank you" for improving tenancy conditions and redistributing land and for not sending government authorities to pressure them to pay annual installments on fields that had been awarded to them. Moreover, many worried that were Marcos to lose, the next government might return the land to previous owners. They knew that many former landowners were waiting for Marcos's demise in order to challenge the legality of his government having forced them to sell their lands.[13] Corazon "Cory" Aquino may be very sympathetic to such a claim, it was suggested, because she and her family are themselves huge landowners.

Nora Dison, whose vote had been solicited by backers of both candidates, made land reform her primary consideration and decided to favor Marcos. Besides what had already been achieved, she and others calculated, there was more chance of expanding land reform under Marcos than under Aquino. Marcos had a record of, at least, some accomplishments; Aquino had none and was inexperienced in governmental affairs, besides.

Focusing on the same issue, Cardo Buwan, the landless worker who had also been solicited by both candidates' campaigners, decided in favor of Aquino. Like many poor landless people, he had long wanted to farm. He was among those claiming rights to the two Tinio haciendas. The Marcos government, however, had spurned them, clearing the way, in the view of many poor landless villagers, for the owners of the VT hacienda to sell the land in 1985 at an outrageous price of thirty thousand pesos per hectare. "Only those with cash, not poor folks like me," scowled an angry seasonal laborer, "got the land." Indeed, half of it was purchased by rich capitalists and the other half by better off peasants. No poor landless villagers were able to buy even a fraction of a hectare.

Many landless people, consequently, hooked on to Aquino's promise of a "real land reform program" that would benefit poor agricultural workers throughout the nation. This was a major theme in their understanding of what they heard her say on radio and what advocates said about her. Certainly not all landless villagers supported Aquino, but about half did with expectations of a better agrarian program being a significant consideration. As Cardo Buwan explained, "My family and I figured Cory could help us get those haciendas. That's one big reason we voted for her."

Manifested in the campaign, therefore, was some of the tension in the village between landless workers and the peasants and capitalists they work for. Many landless people favored Aquino in part because she might help them and because Marcos had not. Meanwhile, many beneficiaries of land distribution of recent years, including some of those capitalists who had purchased several hectares of the VT hacienda that had been sold, favored Marcos.

The alignment, though, is imperfect because considerations cited in earlier pages influenced people's choices. An additional consideration was corruption.

Most local capitalists (about 7 percent of the population) wanted Marcos out. Extensive graft and corruption of the Marcoses, Romualdezes, and others close to the ruling circle was their consistent reason. Related to it was the pronounced fear, as one landowner and businessman said, that should Marcos stay, "the country would be overrun by communists within two or three years." The Marcos government's "extensive corruption" and human rights abuses, he said, were driving people to the NPA.

The corruption issue had mixed effects on peasants. Some set aside inclinations to support Marcos (due to land reform or persuasion by relatives and neighbors) because they had concluded that corruption overwhelmed all other considerations. But the majority downplayed the corruption.

All politicians are corrupt, they said. At least Marcos, unlike his predecessors, did some good for peasants and rural people generally. Here, peasants always cited land reform. Other accomplishments attributed to him include improved irrigation, electrification, and new roads and bridges. Besides these projects' long-term benefits to villagers, people pointed out that many in San Ricardo had earned incomes during some of those years by working on those projects. Also to Marcos's credit, he had recognized the Hukbalahap for having been a genuine anti-Japanese guerrilla organization. That recognition, which no previous president would give, legitimated at last an important part of the lives of many villagers who had joined and supported the Hukbalahap during the Japanese Occupation.

Having seen the 1986 election outcome as more complex than what the factional model allows helps us to understand also the interaction between local political currents and the new Aquino government while it was being established.

The Aquino Government's First Year-and-a Half

Immediately upon forming a government in late February 1986, Cory Aquino gave high priority to perpetuating People Power by "restoring democracy." The resulting democratic space permitted numerous rural-based organizations to blossom, several emphasizing the need for a "genuine land reform."

To the relief of many San Ricardo residents, Aquino did not invalidate the Marcos-era land reform and no former landowners attempted to retrieve their land. News in late 1986 that the forthcoming constitution would require a redistribution of land to agricultural workers was encouraging to that sector of the village. Large landowners who relied on hired laborers, however, worried how this might affect them.

Meanwhile, in San Ricardo and the neighboring village of Bagong Sikat, several poor landless families began to move in that democratic space. And in mid-January 1987, they unilaterally began to farm 27 hectares of the MT hacienda.

Several considerations influenced their action. The immediate stimulus was the sudden vacancy of those 27 hectares when the subtenant of the contract farmer who had the lease to the whole hacienda was killed in late 1986.[15] Immediately, numerous landless villagers reasoned that they should be the ones to farm that area. This made sense not only because of their desire to farm, but also because of "Cory's promise" to help the poor get employment and land. Some even said that their takeover would "help Cory do what she claimed she wanted." An additional influence was word from Department of Agrarian Reform provincial offices that the MT hacienda would likely be included in a new agrarian reform. To whom the land would be given,

PACKING LIST

PACKED BY	DATE	NO. CTN.	INVOICE NO.
			512541

University of Hawaii Press
2840 KOLOWALU STREET
HONOLULU, HAWAII 96822

WAREHOUSE CODE

however, was vague. Certainly, people figured, not all 200 hectares would be awarded to the contract farmer and his few subtenants. Were others to farm it, they would earn priority to receive fields. This interpretation heightened the enthusiasm to take over the vacant 27 hectares. A third significant consideration was "the different climate" (*ibang panahon*) in the country. The proliferation of peasant and worker organizations contributed to the perception in San Ricardo that conditions were ripe for "the little people" to take concerted action to improve their lives. The NPA was also considerably more active in the vicinity.

This combination of factors, recalled one landless participant, pushed "the government to be more sympathetic" to the villagers, less so to the landowners, and "more scared" to send soldiers to "drive us away." Sending troops could end in "a lot of blood, many dead" because dozens of people were determined to stay and had the support of "hundreds more." There was also the possibility, "because no one knew for sure," that the NPA supported these people and would attack the soldiers.

Although several landless households decided not to join because they feared that possible NPA backing could provoke violence, over sixty people from San Ricardo and nearby Bagong Sikat in November 1986 formed SAMAKA (Samahang Magbubukid sa Kanayunang Hacienda Tinio, Association of Peasants in the Villages of the Tinio Hacienda). The organization had grown to 160 members when the takeover began in mid-January 1987.

Membership fees plus loans from several organizations enabled SA-MAKA to purchase seed, fertilizer, and other inputs. The Nueva Ecija chapter of AMGL also put SAMAKA in touch with lawyers and Department of Agrarian Reform officials who were sympathetic to their cause.

Not wanting to violate the law, SAMAKA leaders approached both the previous subtenant's widow and the man who was leasing the MT hacienda. Both agreed to the organization's request to farm the 27 hectares. In letters to owner Mario Tinio, members claimed the right to farm the land as tenants, for which they would pay the 17 sacks per hectare specified in the contract farmer's lease, although they could not pay the rent in advance as that contract stipulated. They would pay after harvest, a method which attorneys assured them was entirely legal.

Tinio never responded to SAMAKA's letters or requests for a meeting. Finally, on New Year's Day, SAMAKA leaders wrote to him that they would begin to farm the 27 hectares on 12 January 1987.[16]

That day, many recalled later, "was like a fiesta"; the 27 hectares were filled with people talking and laughing while they worked.

Besides SAMAKA members and their families making dikes and plowing, many others from San Ricardo, Bagong Sikat, and elsewhere helped and watched. It was the first of many days, for SAMAKA succeeded in farming the land through harvest the following May. After the harvest was in, members were paid, at higher than average rates, according to how many days they had worked. After all expenses and loans had been settled and rent for Tinio (who had yet to respond) had been put in the bank, SAMAKA still had a surplus to apply toward expenses for the next season.

Why were no soldiers sent to remove these people like what happened in 1981? Basically, SAMAKA participants' assessments proved to be correct. In the context of the new climate, their timing was right.

The new mayor was Romeo Maliwat, who said he feared that "terrible bloodshed" would result were he to allow the Constabulary commander in Cabanatuan City to send in troops. "Several hundred" people were in the fields, many apparently bent on staying, he concluded, and "there was a strong possibility" that they had "supporters who were armed." Also the Aquino government with which he closely identified had said that landless people should get land. Consequently, although what those villagers did was "illegal," he said, he decided to leave SAMAKA alone for the time being. He even supported a municipal council resolution urging the national government to subject the MT hacienda to land reform.

SAMAKA members wanted to farm the 27 hectares again in August 1987, but the political climate had become decidedly less auspicious. Mario Tinio had met with SAMAKA leaders, refused to accept the rent they offered him from the first crop, and threatened legal action if they tried to farm again. Mayor Maliwat informed them that he could no longer guarantee that no troops would be sent. And the Nueva Ecija Constabulary commander warned SAMAKA leaders that definitely troops would be sent were they to resume farming.

This change reflected the national government's hardening stance against "land invasions" and other "unauthorized occupation" of land. In 1986 and 1987, some 50,000 organized villagers across the Philippines had taken over 70,500 hectares, alarming government officials as high up as President Aquino herself.[17] Her executive order on agrarian reform in late July 1987 "permanently disqualified from receiving benefits" of the reform all who "prematurely occupy" land.[18] Clearly, now the ruling elite did not look kindly on local initiatives by the masses.

Those in San Ricardo who knew about this exclusion were angry. Aquino's entire pronouncement on agrarian reform disappointed many poor landless villagers who had voted for her. Said one SAMAKA leader, it "evades major issues" like what lands are included and how much landowners may retain "and passes them to Congress; but Congress is filled with big landowners" who are unsympathetic.

An earlier letdown for those who hoped that the Aquino government was at least moderately concerned about land use problems was "Mendiola." Although "EDSA" had been a distant event for San Ricardo residents, "Mendiola" a year later was near. Organized by AMGL's Nueva Ecija leaders, numerous villagers had joined a few thousand demonstrators at the Kampong Magbubukid para sa Lupa, Kapayapaan, Kalayaan, at Kasaganahan ("Peasant Camp for Land, Peace, Freedom, and Prosperity") in front of the Department of Agrarian Reform in Quezon City beginning 15 January 1987.[19] "The purpose," recalled one participant, "was to remind Cory of her campaign promise about agrarian reform." After a year in office, "nothing had happened; we thought she had forgotten." For days, the demonstrators' representatives tried unsuccessfully to meet with high level officials. On 22 January the crowd walked to Malacañang, where President Aquino held office. Arriving at Mendiola Bridge, 300 meters from Malacañang, the road was blocked by soldiers who shouted that the marchers should proceed no further. The marchers continued. Gunfire began. At least eighteen people were killed, and over ninety were wounded. A government investigation blamed some police and demonstrators. A strong feeling in San Ricardo, however, was that the government was at fault for failing to listen to the landless people and provoking the bloodshed.

Besides land, prices and peace remained major concerns to people in San Ricardo in 1986–87. Inflation had tapered by late 1985 and there had actually been a modest deflation by mid-1986. A year later, July 1987, consumer prices averaged only one percent more than the year before.[20] Meanwhile, the negative Gross National Product rates for 1984 and 1985 had been turned around to positive 5.5 by early 1987.

These trends were reflected in San Ricardo by stable prices for essential food items and a 15-20 percent decline in fertilizer and tractor fuel prices since 1985. Meanwhile, prices peasants received for their *palay* were about the same as two years before. Many of the construction workers laid off in 1984–85 were working again. Although life remained hard for most, complaints about worsening economic conditions were less shrill than a few years earlier.

While the economic situation in the nation was no worse and in some respects better than during the last years of the Marcos government, peace remained precarious. Battles between rebels (MNLF, NPA, others) and government soldiers continued in many regions. Attempted coup d'etats, threats of coups, and constant rumors that Marcos was returning to seize power heightened the turmoil.

Most villagers feared that the country, and specifically their area, would be engulfed in bloody fighting unless decisive steps were taken to bring "peace" (kapayapaan) and "calm" (tahimik). That concern was manifested both by their 74 percent "Yes" vote for the country's new constitution in the 2 February 1987 plebiscite and the nearly 80 percent voter turnout. A pronounced sentiment across all classes—and whether previously for or against Marcos—was that approving the constitution would help to end the turmoil and civil war. At the very least, many believed, disputes about the Aquino government's legitimacy would diminish. Similarly, 75 percent of San Ricardo voters cast ballots in the May 1987 congressional elections, most distributing their votes among senatorial candidates on both Aquino's slate and that of the major opposition (Grand Alliance for Democracy). One villager made this point in a cynical remark: "If politicians on both sides are well-fed [from government resources], things will be more peaceful."[22]

The NPA's increased presence was another potential threat to peace in San Ricardo. Beginning in 1984, NPA organizers had become active in the area and made clear that they sided with the poor and powerless. They advised peasants to pay no more on fields awarded to them through agrarian reform; they asked rich families for regular contributions; and they told moneylenders to lower interest rates. They also warned people who had been abusing fellow villagers to stop and executed five people in the area who failed to heed the warnings.[23] While many villagers appreciated what the NPA was doing, they simultaneously perceived that the NPA threatened tranquility in two ways.

First, government soldiers may one day swoop into the area searching for NPA members who moved in and out of the village. Worse still, there could be gun battles, killing and wounding villagers caught in the crossfire. People worried, too, that government troops will regard all villagers as NPA members and therefore abuse, if not, kill them.

Second, people wondered whether the NPA would remain benevolent and helpful. While they did not mind the NPA guerrillas executing "those who have a record," they began to ask what would prevent these gunmen from killing people without bad reputations? Similarly, they worried that the NPA could become abusive and impose onerous demands on everyone. Behind this apprehension is the widely believed allegation that the NPA is communist, a label most villagers associate with repression in Russia, China, and Kampuchea, which they know about from news reports.

Conclusion

Let me return to the EDSA Revolution of February 1986. We can now better understand why San Ricardo people were not active in that major event in recent world history. They neither went to Manila to participate nor did anything in the village to show strong support for either side. Although a majority had voted for Marcos and many thought he had actually won, they made no effort to support the Marcos position. Nor did the sizeable minority of Aquino voters do anything for her.

No doubt poverty is part of the reason. Few could afford to spend twenty-five pesos for a bus ticket to Manila. Besides, fields had to be tended and houses repaired. Yet many had made time and even spent money in 1985 and 1987—a year before and a year after the EDSA event—to join demonstrations in Metro Manila regarding prices and land reform.

The difference is those issues were significant to many villagers— and not just as individuals but as members of peasant and landless worker organizations. EDSA, on the other hand, was an extension of an electoral contest between rich politicians, hardly a matter for most villagers to get terribly worked up about. After all, the national government has never been particularly generous to San Ricardo.

What did concern most villagers about "EDSA" was the possibility of turmoil there spreading, perhaps even to Nueva Ecija. *That* they worried about and is a major reason why most monitored what was happening. Symbolic of this concern is that the village's only group activity related to the event was a prayer vigil at the local chapel where Marcos and Aquino voters prayed together for peace.

During the 1980s, people had become increasingly worried that civil war was engulfing the country. How to head it off was widely discussed during the 1986 presidential campaign, although no consensus emerged as to which candidate was more able to accomplish the task. A similar concern guided villagers to welcome Marcos's Martial Law in the early 1970s and to commend the NPA's efforts to bring peace in the mid 1980s. "Rightist" or "leftist," it seems to make no difference to San Ricardo folks so long as someone, something keeps the peace—and so long as those peacekeepers do not turn into abusers, as happened later under Marcos and as some worry might evolve under the NPA.

Other issues, too, are prominent in village politics. One of the most crucial is land distribution. Who can use what land and under what conditions? These questions have been controversial and often hotly contested for as long as most villagers can remember. Where one stands depends in part on one's class. In the 1980s, the struggle over land emerged as a major issue during the presidential campaign and culminated in two attempts, locally initiated and led, by groups of primarily poor landless workers to take over large chunks of riceland.

Opposing the land takeovers have been the state, local government officials, landowners, and capitalists. These formidable opponents quickly subdued the first attempt in 1981, but they could not do the same in 1987. Conditions that year were more favorable to the underdogs. The hands of the new national and local government officials were restrained by the freshness of their People Power victory, their rhetoric about land to the landless, and the hidden illegal armed forces supporting the poor. Maybe who won in 1986 made a difference after all, at least this once.

By August 1987, though, after eighteen months in office, the Aquino administration had done little to impress most San Ricardo residents. It lost a chance to become legendary when it failed to assure that large mechanized lands would be turned over to the landless poor. Not only would the direct beneficiaries have been pleased but so would numerous others in the village because redistributing those fields would considerably relax social tensions growing from the prevalent poverty and underemployment.

In any event, recent political history of San Ricardo is certainly much more complicated than that suggested by the factional model in which rich candidates and their campaigners jerk on their lines connected to poor villagers and haul in votes. Elections themselves are not nearly so straightforward. Lines are often crossed, linking individuals and families to campaigners and candidates on different sides, effectively leaving voters free to decide on other grounds. Public issues are prominent in discussions as people consider not only who to vote for but whether to vote at all. The whole process occurs in an atmosphere of cynicism. Politicians, say many, are not genuinely concerned about villagers' problems but instead are preoccupied with competing against other rich people to control government resources.

This is not to say that linkages between people in different classes and statuses are unimportant. They are, indeed, a significant aspect of political life. And elections are a time when such networks are particularly likely to be manifested. Because candidates and their supravillage campaigners are usually from the better off layers of society and they cannot win with votes only from people like themselves, it is a prime time to activate their linkages to people in lower statuses.

Precisely because linkages are likely to be pronounced in election campaigns, it is unwise to generalize from them about other aspects of village politics and class and status relations. Previous studies have erred by concluding from the multiclass factions active during elections that there is no significant conflict along socioeconomic lines in Philippine politics.[24] In San Ricardo, this has simply not been the case.

A final conclusion about politics in San Ricardo is that generally villagers have a keen sense of their political environment. In the first place, they accurately perceive that the central government is not greatly concerned about the welfare of rural people like them. A village like San Ricardo is not powerful in the nation-state system. As one peasant put it in 1987: "Definitely the national government is one thing, our situation and problems in the village are another. To those at the top—the officials and rich—we're nothing; they forget about us except at election or if we cause them trouble."

Villagers are also well aware of status and class differences and each person knows where he or she stands vis-à-vis others. There is also considerable shared awareness among people in the same class or status. Peasants talk about "our problems" such as high farming costs, insubordinate wage laborers, and low prices for "our grain"; workers complain in numerous ways about "low wages *they* pay *us*"— the "they" being peasants and capitalists for whom they labor. And the poor frequently contrast "*our* hard life" and "*our* poverty" to the "good life of *the rich*." The rich frequently say "*the poor* have only themselves to blame" for their condition, a view not widely shared among the poor. Indeed, causes for inequality and how the people in one class or status should relate to people in other socioeconomic positions are contested issues in local political life.

In the 1980s, the political awareness and dexterity of poor villagers was striking. During the 1986 presidential campaign, they frequently deliberated over which candidate was more likely—or the least unlikely—to be of some value in their struggles to improve their conditions. They reached no consensus. Poor peasants often voted for Marcos because of gains they had made from his government's land reform and some concern that a different president might retract those advances. Poor landless workers tended to support Aquino because she promised to get them land.

Earlier in 1981 and again in 1987, poor villagers from San Ricardo and vicinity collectively took bold steps to claim some of the land owned by wealthy families. They were not limiting themselves to elections to express their political interests and preferences. Indeed, these land takeovers were only the most dramatic of numerous acts grounded in the same political contention: they had a right to farm the land. What was different in 1981 and 1987 were openings created by local and national events that villagers astutely recognized.

Each takeover was preceded by considerable investigation and analysis of the land, the owners, and the larger political context. People tried to assess how much latitude they had and their chances of success. They wanted to stay within the law but knew they were moving in nebulous legal territory dangerous to the poor and powerless. For protection, they sought support from others more powerful and higher placed than they. In 1987, they also reached out to other peasant and landless worker organizations.

The underlying justification for the takeovers was not a millenarian or apocalyptic vision beyond the comprehension of all but a chosen people. Nor were poor people making the radical claim that they were the rightful owners of the land, rather than those holding title to it. In this sense they were not rejecting the dominant ideology codified in private property laws. But in another sense they were challenging that ideology and the wealthy landowners and the state upholding it.

In their view, everyone is entitled to livelihood and dignity. When these basic rights conflict with the right to private property, they argue, their rights take precedence. The wealthy landowners in these cases were supposed to give way to poor villagers who had no or too little land from which to earn a living and no viable alternative ways to make a living. Having a livelihood would itself be a step toward dignity because one of the hardest aspects of being without a satisfactory way to provide for one's family is the loss of, or at least constant challenge to, one's sense of worth. Poverty also threatens, if not destroys, dignity because the better off frequently regard the poor as less than human. Consequently, asserting the right to livelihood and dignity ultimately challenges the gross inequalities in society and puts a claim on the resources of the wealthy.

RAUL PERTIERRA

Community and Power
in an Ilokano Municipality

The extraordinary events of February 1986 leading to the
exile of Ferdinand Marcos and the political victory of Corazon Aquino
focused world attention on the Philippines. The peaceful removal of
a corrupt regime provided international viewers with a welcome change
from the violence normally associated with such events. A similar
experience characterized the early days of the establishment of Solidarity in Poland.[1] In both cases, it seemed that a corrupt and authoritarian political structure would yield to the moral claims of its outraged citizens. The strategic use of nonviolent protest has a long history
but the cases above represent unusual challenges to the use of force
by contemporary nation-states. Both Aquino supporters and Solidarity members were claiming their civil rights over, on the one hand,
the corrupt interests of a regime and, on the other, the authoritarian
tendencies of a State. The extent and nature of these rights and hence
the perceived limits of the legitimate powers of the State have been
a major concern of social theory.

In this paper I explore the notions of community and its correlate
in systems of action ultimately constituting structures such as the Philippine state. My purpose is to examine the links between, on the one
hand, territorial or ideological notions of community and, on the other,
structures of collective actions represented by entities such as the state.
I shall explore how notions of community and local structures of action
constitute and are sustained by external structures resulting both in
the shifting and the stable features of Philippine social life. I shall also
show that the elections during the transition from Marcos to Aquino
provoked a range of responses reflecting several models of community and society in an Ilocos municipality.

National Politics and Local Society

Anthropologists study how national cultures manifest themselves at the village level.[2] I would add that anthropologists also study how village life contributes to the constitution of national society. Just as it is impossible to understand village life outside the context of the national structure of which it is a part, it is also impossible to understand national society without considering the values and routines of village life which help constitute it.

In the Philippine case, we can see how an understanding of village politics in the contemporary period is only possible after looking at how Marcos appropriated for his personal use the nation's political structures. However, one can only understand Marcos's appropriation of national politics by seeing how local and regional politicians themselves help constitute national politics. Marcos's and Aquino's political legitimacy depend on the extent to which each consistently reproduce appropriate political behavior for people at the local level. My view assumes that macrostructures, be they economic, political or cultural, are ultimately constituted and reproduced by local actors. This view does not reduce macrostructures to their microbases, but simply insists that any explanation for macrostructures depends on an adequate understanding of local actions. It demands that Marcos's and Aquino's appropriation of national politics be seen in the context and in terms of local political behavior.

In taking this position I am not denying that the forces affecting local community are often externally generated, unintended in their consequences, and whose sources are unknown to those affected. Thus local economic, political, and religious practices are often responses to influences from outside the community. Nevertheless, the responses to all these externally based structures are generally meaningful in local terms, the consequences of which in turn help constitute, in varying degrees, the national structures. The task of anthropology is to understand how local actors experience external structures and how their responses reconstitute external structures.

The Municipality of Zamora

Zamora (not its real name) is a rice and tobacco growing municipality in the province of Ilocos Sur some 350 km. north of Manila. I have been conducting research there since 1975-76, returning yearly to follow political developments. My last visit was in 1989. I was present in Zamora for the 1986, 1987, and 1988 elections.

Zamora's inhabitants mainly speak Ilokano and live in twenty-six villages whose population range from 88 to 850 people. These villages are generally separated from one another by fertile fields that lie on either side of the river which effectively divides Zamora into its two major sections. Although the municipality sees itself as predominantly Ilokano, several villages retain close linguistic, cultural and kinship ties with non-Ilokano communities to the east of Zamora. Despite the long-term presence of Catholic missionaries in the area (from 1760), Zamora retained much of its pre-Christian culture, including its political institutions, until the first quarter of this century. Having rejected Catholicism, villages in Zamora accepted various forms of Protestantism soon after the imposition of American rule (1902–1946). However, when independence was achieved and mass-based political parties with national structures were introduced, Zamoran leaders and many of their followers switched their religious allegiance to Catholicism, the major religious denomination in the Philippines.[3]

Apart from the presence of the Augustinian missionaries and the occasional visit of an official, state structures had not effectively penetrated Zamoran life for most of the period of Spanish colonization (1521–1898). Even the imposition of Spanish surnames in the 1850s to facilitate record-keeping had little practical effect in Zamora until the 1920s when the Americans introduced village schools. The American period (1902–1946) saw an increased penetration of state structures into local society. Literacy was expanded, mass-based political parties begun to recruit members in Zamora and an increasing number oriented their activities toward the cash economy. However, until the 1950s when Virginia tobacco was introduced, Zamora retained its primarily subsistence economy despite significant changes in its ideological structure brought about by schooling and a strongly proselytizing Protestantism.

Like many other Philippine municipalities, Zamora is divided into two major sections characterized by geographic and cultural elements and each headed by a different, influential family or faction.[4] The southern section centers around the village of Luna, while the northern one is headed by the leading families of Macaoayan, a prosperous and culturally distinct village. The competition between these two factions and sections determines much of local political life and has repercussions for the linkages between Zamora and the rest of the country. Even before the time of its formation into a municipality in 1919, Zamora had been divided into two main sections. This division is expressed at two levels. The first involves a coalition of villages and the second, the leading families who are responsible for determining the political and social affairs of the municipality and who generally live in its principal villages. While these leading families determine the configuration of personal alliances constituting each faction, the first level of this division (i.e., coalition of villages) exercises constraints in the range and stability of their choices. Apart from the geographic nature of this division (north vs. south) certain cultural differences also enter into its constitution. The northern section is dominated by non-Ilokano villages, while the southern one is predominantly Ilokano.

From the time of its formation as a municipality in 1919 until 1964, each section in Zamora was closely associated with a major party (the northern faction with the Liberal Party, the southern faction with the Nacionalista Party) but in 1964 Marcos switched from the Liberal to the Nacionalista Party. This change caused a complex reworking of local political networks and since then party affiliation no longer clearly reflects sectional groupings. This meant that during the twenty odd years of Marcos's rule sectional disputes did not manifest themselves primarily along party political lines. Marcos supporters were found in both sections, all of whom attempted to maximize their links with their respective political patrons. The resources obtained, however, tended to flow along factional lines. In the last presidential elections Aquino received her strongest support in Macaoayan and Luna, each of which is a core of a section. In the 1987 constitutional plebiscite, only Macaoayan supported Aquino. The point is that political support which had earlier mainly been expressed along clear sectional lines is no longer reflected directly. In other words, while national politics continues to affect Zamora both during Marcos's days and now under Aquino, this impact does not work primarily through the traditional sections as it had done until 1964. The result is a much less predictable and a less stable set of local political alliances since these now cross what are still significant structural divisions. It remains to be seen whether these crosssectional political alliances diminish the traditional divisions or whether the old sectional loyalties reimpose themselves on the new politics.

Multiple Models of Local Community

No single set of characteristics such as north-south or Ilokano-non-Ilokano indicates the complexity and difficulty of describing the often shifting alliances and boundaries between local village communities. It would be as valid to say that each of the twenty-six villages composing Zamora sees itself, to some extent, as an autonomous unit in opposition to all the others. The binary model of factionalism earlier described is commonly employed by members of the leading families who are primarily responsible for constituting, maintaining and reproducing this particular view of Zamoran politics and society. This binary model accurately describes the main networks linking the elite families as well as the major class divisions in Zamora. From the elites' perspective the model is both empirically and normatively valid. The conflation of descriptive and prescriptive elements in local models of community allows Zamorans to have a view of their society while simultaneously taking a position in it. Instead of the binary model of Zamoran factionalism stressed by its elite leaders, however, a poor tenant could just as validly emphasize the ternary status divisions present in all villages (e.g., rich-middle-poor; *baknang-kalkalaingan-napanglaw*) and extend this view to the whole of Zamora. Finally, a member of an aggressive village-gang (*barkada*) is likely to view his village as surrounded by hostile villages containing other predatory gangs.

All such models of Zamoran life coexist, if not happily, at least contingently in most people's perception of local society. Which model they give primary credence to and base their actions upon depends both on the given context and the interests of the persons concerned.

While loyalty to one's village is strongly felt in Zamora, other ties compete for the individual's attention. These ties often extend beyond the village, creating a network spanning several villages in and often outside the municipality. In many cases, these networks are directed along certain directions (e.g., Macaoayan and Lucaban have strong kinship ties) or stress particular aspects (e.g., Macaoayan landowners and their Taliao tenants). Villages may share common interests (e.g., Luna and Balugang's involvement in the Catholic Church) or alternatively view themselves separately (e.g., Dirdirig's distinctive religious membership). All of these diverse and complex factors enter into the final constitution of Zamoran's perceptions of themselves as members of distinct yet contiguous, separate yet consociate local communities.

At times, Zamoran conceptions of community stress an element such as territoriality while at other times elements like kinship and status. In other words, even when a particular model of community prevails, other views are at hand to counteract or prevent a simple practical response within any given model. This is nicely illustrated at dances where the young men of each village group dance as a cohort. On these occasions, other cohorts or categories are also called out to dance, such as old men and women; recently married men; specific kin of the hosts; distinguished and/or distant visitors; internal (but not status) divisions within the village such as the southern or northern sectors. Normal formalities are also reversed by announcing "ladies' choice" when the usually reticent young women choose their

dancing partners. All these proceedings, while done in jest, nevertheless express the existing conceptualizations of local society and its
relationship to individual identity. Territorial units, generational
distinctions, status hierarchies, ego-focused networks, internal and
external boundaries and gender differences are all referred to explicitly during these occasions. Finally, "a dance for all" is always announced and the proper balance between stressing specific categories
as against general ones requires considerable skill, local knowledge
and an equitable judgment.

A dance is usually only a phase in an ongoing social event during
which different aspects of community may be emphasized. The
interactions in a dance reflect the context of which it is a part. Hence
the example above generally occurs during dances held at weddings,
funerals or fund-raising occasions. In contrast a dance held to commemorate the municipal *fiesta*, attended by the local elite and marked
by extreme formality, is characterized by its restricted participation.
Although all dances are nationally open events, the latter occasions
stress status hierarchies to an extent that excludes other interested
participants. In this case, a dance serves to express the restricted
relations present in the community rather than celebrating the relatively open and equalitarian aspects. Although a public dance is not
normally seen as an instance of ritual, many of its features point to
its function as ritual. Besides a dance constituting a part of the formal
rituals of marriage and death, the earlier description illustrates the
way in which significant relationships and categories are expressed
and articulated at a dance. However, as E. Leach has argued "if we
accept the Durkheimian view that religious rituals are representations
of the solidarity of the participating group, we need clearly to understand that the solidarity need exist only at the moment at which the
ritual takes place; we cannot infer a continuing latent solidarity after
the ritual celebrations are over."[5] While public dances may indeed
have solidary effects, what better characterizes such occasions is the
range of articulated models of community which they manifest. These
models of community are generally participatory except in the case
of dances involving major status divisions. Significantly the only major
categories not called out at dances are those referring to internal status
hierarchies. This indicates that the notion of community is distinguished
from the understanding of structure, which is also present.

Boundaries of Community

The comments above indicate the impossibility of delimiting the
boundaries of community, since this notion is both polysemic and multi-

referential. The most bounded notion of community is based on territoriality such as a village, its internal sectors or external alignments.

Other notions such as parentation (*kabagian, kaputot*) or association
(*agkasukob, kagayyem*) are also used to refer to nonterritorially constituted communities all of whose members recognize moral obligations
to one another. Zamorans also recognize membership in nationally
constituted bodies such as religious congregations and other associations whose members are often unknown to one another but who
nevertheless acknowledge a common commitment to a set of ideals.
Finally, like other Filipinos, Zamorans are increasingly conscious of
belonging to a national polity even if its communal obligations are still
difficult to specify.[6]

These notions of propinquity, parentation and association can take
on varied and significant aspects which allow Zamorans to adjust
their actions to the appropriate situation. In everyday life, the village
is the focus of these notions of locality, parentation and association.
However, Zamorans also interact frequently outside the village context and in such cases either extend or accentuate different notions.
The tobacco economy obliges Zamorans to develop ties with outside
buyers on a regular basis; travel to Manila and other centers for
educational and other purposes require Zamorans to establish stable
networks outside the village; membership in a range of associations
obliges them to extend their interests correspondingly. All of these
extravillage orientations themselves arise in the context of ordinary
village life and for this reason Zamorans at times willingly and at
others, reluctantly leave the village in order to pursue them. In many
cases, such departures result in their permanent separation from their
village community but just as often, and despite the considerable effort
and expense, many Zamorans return regularly to renew village ties.

Apart from the intensity with which village life focuses propinquity, parentation and association, these separate dimensions for basing
social relations and for generating distinct models of community and
society equip Zamorans adequately for their increasingly more regular dealings with national and international life. Whenever Zamorans
deal with outsiders, whose normative framework clearly lie beyond
the structures of village life, they tend to develop the relationship
along specific unidimensional lines. Converts to the Iglesia ni Kristo,
an exclusive and demanding religious denomination, frequently point
out the difficulties of maintaining orthodoxy in the context of village
life, with its generalized demands of kinship and locality, and contrast
this with the relative ease of meeting the heavy but specific expectations of Iglesia membership in Manila and other urban centers. Iglesia
members often converted to this religion during their stay in Manila

because membership was seen as providing a sense of community in an otherwise anomic environment. However, their attempts to maintain this membership in Zamora often clashed with the loyalties due to non-Iglesia kin and neighbors. These distinct models of community have appropriate modes of consciousness as well as corresponding potentials for the structures of action. The link between cultural and societal integration is differently constituted for each of these models of community.[7]

Power, Legitimate Authority, and Structured Action

So far I have been discussing the variety of models or views of community held by Zamorans. I have indicated that while particular models of community are more prevalent in some situations, no situation is exclusively defined by a given model. Any given situation includes multiple normative models for action reflecting the variety of interests and perspectives of social actors. To the extent coordinated action is required, participants have to reach a sufficiently common understanding to proceed.

The notion of power differentials is, within certain limits, included in local notions of community. The recognition of legitimate authority is highly developed in Zamoran society although the process of its implementation varies from one context to another reflecting the overlapping nature of the models of community referred to earlier.

Local notions of legitimate authority are sometimes opposed to the structures of the state as in the following case. Kamlon, a young and clearly troublesome man from Luna, eventually had to flee the village pursued by the police for having raped a woman from a neighboring town. For several years, aided by his family, he managed to elude capture. On the sudden and unexpected death of his young wife in Luna, his kin sent for Kamlon to return in order to fulfil his mortuary responsibilities. He complied but early the following day was confronted and killed by the police. When asked why Kamlon had knowingly risked his life by returning, the frequent response by people in Luna was that he had no choice. Either he fulfilled his mortuary duties or he no longer considered himself a full member of his kin-group. The latter possibility was just as unsatisfactory since he would no longer receive their support against the police. An informant suggested that a third possibility would have been for Kamlon to have broken his kin ties and join a criminal gang in Manila. This rather grim choice was largely the result of his kin-group's assessment of Kamlon's basically recidivist nature.

This example indicates that Zamorans have a rich range of normative models of community that allow them to deal flexibly with the interactions of daily life. Apart from recognizing the normatively defined nature of social life, Zamorans are also well aware that the structures of interaction are not exclusively nor perhaps even primarily based on these normative models. Conflicts of interests occur which not only bring into question particular normative understandings but their resolution is not always necessarily based on a fixed consensus of the normative basis of conflict.

Structures of action in Zamoran society are generated by the confluence of a range of models (normative, cognitive and expressive) on a variety of interests and perspectives along particular dimensions of power. An agricultural economy based on rice for subsistence consumption and on Virginia tobacco for access to the world of cash goods sets fundamental limits on the structures of actions. Moreover, the increasing effects of State institutions such as schooling, the police, the media, health and other public services expose Zamorans to a world to which they are attracted but which they know is not based on local notions of community. Finally, for at least a generation Zamorans have had the opportunity of overseas employment, initially as agricultural workers in Hawaii and more recently as domestic workers in Europe, the Middle East and Hong Kong.

Although I have stressed the local basis of community because many of the daily routines of village life are still significantly determined by these local relationships, the State has also increasingly penetrated local life although often its effects are reinterpreted to suit local needs. Thus, when Kamlon was killed by the police, the local constables were conspicuous by their absence. Village solidarity is still sufficiently strong to discourage collaboration with outsiders even in enforcing the law.

It is perhaps in the area of culture where the external world has most visibly affected local life. Since the introduction of electricity in 1975 many families have acquired TV sets which allow them to watch national and international programs. Many years earlier radios became widely dispersed throughout the municipality. As illustrated by the willing acceptance of Protestantism early this century, Zamorans have never been reluctant in accepting outside influences whenever the conditions are appropriate. This rapid conversion to Protestantism had been preceded by a stubborn resistance to Catholic conversion despite their extending hospitality to visiting Augustinian missionaries from the neighboring coastal municipalities. The acceptance of outside influence at one level while simultaneously preserving traditional orientations at another level has characterized Zamoran culture and society since its formation was historically recorded in the late seventeenth century. These external cultural influences have not been passively imposed on local life. Zamoran adolescents, like other Filipinos eagerly absorb the latest fashions in dress and song which they display to their suitably impressed audiences. However, in important aspects of village life such as courtship, these same adolescents orient their behavior, if not their songs, to the prevailing local norms which are often diametrically opposed to western sentiments.

The structures of action in Zamora result from the systematic enactment of cultural models reflecting a variety of interests and perspectives along particular dimensions of power. Thus, for example, the binary view of factional politics is a very prevalent model of Zamoran society exemplified in various areas of local life such as the constitution of political parties, religious congregations and the intensity of competitive encounters. This view is also consistent with certain political interests and perspectives of village life, allowing the local elite to determine the major alignments of Zamoran politics through their control of local political loyalties. It comes as no surprise that the major lines of tension reflecting this binary division involve villages many of whose inhabitants are tenants of wealthy families heading each faction. I am not suggesting a functionalist explanation for the binary model of Zamoran politics but simply pointing out the reproductive consequences of systematic tensions for the maintenance of communal boundaries. These same tensions prevent the conscious articulation of a class ideology which is conspicuously absent in notions of local community despite people's developed awareness of social inequality.

Apart from these locally based notions of community, Zamorans are highly aware of external structures impinging and shaping the daily routines of village life. The tobacco economy as the basis for access to the market and the various national agencies are the main forces affecting village life and over which Zamorans have at most a limited control. Their strategies in dealing with these latter situations are often markedly different from those used with co-villagers (*kailian*), kin (*kabagian*), or close friends (*kagayyem*). The possibility of discursive will-formation or of reaching an understanding in dealing with outsiders is not as highly developed. Instead resort to purely strategic activity, where only the means and not the ends are in dispute, is the preferred mode of interaction. This may involve instrumental action such as market exchange with Chinese and other tobacco buyers or political alliances with regional and national wielders of power. In neither case do they assume, however, membership in a common moral universe where interaction consciously acknowledges the other as significantly entering into the constitution of one's self. Thus, the notions of locality (*ili*), parentation (*kabagian*), and association (*kagayyem*) are not just descriptive appellates but prescriptive performatives. They refer to co-subjects with whom one shares a common world as opposed to others whose existence is recognized as co-agents inhabiting a life-space overlapping one's own but not entering into its constitutionality.

Zamoran Notions of Community during the Transition

The February 1986 election in Ilocos Sur was unusually quiet and peaceful.[8] Marcos's KBL Party through its major supporters such as Governor Chavit Singson and ex-congressman Dr. G. Reyes confidently predicted victory, a feeling shared by most people in Zamora. Nevertheless, it was widely rumored that Marcos was pouring money into the campaign and that provincial as well as local officials were keeping most of it instead of distributing it to the people. This was interpreted by Zamorans as indicative of Marcos's precarious grip over the electoral process. He had to buy his support and was cheated for his efforts. While vote-buying is an almost acceptable practice in Zamora, as it seems to be elsewhere in the Philippines, locals claim that a candidate who relies primarily on this strategy as opposed to one who possesses a charismatic personality or is supported by an effective alliance network, runs a great risk of impoverishment and derision. Admittedly, Marcos's resources seemed limitless, but his reliance on a vote-buying strategy indicated a weakening of his earlier seemingly invincible influence and support network.

However, in Zamora as in the rest of Ilocos Sur, the opposition was even weaker. Rogelio Fabrigas, a young lawyer and follower of Pablito Sanidad, the provincial convenor of UNIDO, campaigned hard for Aquino and Laurel fully aware that their chances were minimal. Zamorans listened to his campaign speeches, mused over the possibility of having a woman as president (particularly one whose moral claims seemed undeniable), but in the end—and not just due to vote-buying—overwhelmingly voted for Marcos. The reasons for their support of Marcos consisted of variations on the theme of "better the devil you know than the one you don't." The country was obviously undergoing difficult times and in such circumstances one should have an experienced politician like Marcos, despite his faults, rather than an inexperienced woman, whatever her moral qualities. Moreover, many Zamorans openly questioned whether Aquino would have the ability and the inclination to bring about basic structural change as opposed to simply replacing one set of self-serving and corrupt officials by another similarly disposed set.

Aquino received 25 percent of Zamoran votes and Laurel around 30 percent. They actually won in Macaoayan (56 %), just lost in Lesseb (46 %), and acquitted themselves well in Luna (30 %). Governor Singson sent a terse message as soon as he heard of the Macaoayan result but most Zamorans explained this in terms of Macaoayan voters sending a clear message to Mayor B. Filaart that he could not presume their support—that Macaoayan voters would not necessarily support Mayor Filaart's candidate. This snub to the mayor was made knowing that Marcos would nevertheless win in Zamora. The result in Lesseb was interpreted as the consequence of kin-loyalty since Fabrigas came from this barrio. The support for Aquino and Laurel in Luna is due to several causes. This barrio belongs in the section currently out of power and has resented for some time its lack of political influence. There were a few strong Aquino supporters in Luna and they waged a successful campaign among their close friends and kin. However, apart from these interesting exceptions, Zamorans had clearly supported Marcos, despite certain misgivings both about Marcos's own viability and that of his party.

Just as Zamorans are clearly aware that the structures of action in the village resulting in the status hierarchies mentioned earlier are not consistent with prevailing models of an egalitarian community, they are also aware that the notion of community may be expanded to coincide with the wider structures of action affecting the village. In ordinary interactions, kinship terms are extended to include all Ilokano speakers. While it is not expected in practice that Ilokano speakers unknown and unrelated to one another behave as members of a common moral universe, this linguistic usage indicates that such a community is at least theoretically possible. The clannishness of Ilokanos is frequently commented on by other Filipinos and Marcos's practice of appointing Ilokanos to senior positions in the military is cited as an example.

However, during the 1986 elections what struck me was the re-peated distinction Zamorans made between their sympathies for Aquino and their support for Marcos. The first referred to an acknowl-edgment of her moral grievance. Whether or not Marcos himself directed her husband's death, he was morally implicated in the event since it served his interests. The second involved a sober assessment that effective leadership need not always be normatively based. Thus, the grudging respect due to a village *baknang* by his status inferiors need not assume a normative consensus on the part of both parties. A *baknang*'s position in society does not always reflect his position in the idealized notion of community. In the presidential election, a significant proportion of Zamorans (25 percent) voted for Aquino indicating that for some her moral stance was seen as a basis for political support. The 1986 presidential elections elicited a range of responses in Zamora reflecting the varied notions of community and society present in the municipality. For many people, despite a considerable sympathy for Aquino's moral grievance, political support consists of strategic and instrumental action toward a given set of ends, while for others the ends themselves enter into the constitution of the viability of the means. The former view separates the structures of action from their normative aspects and is solely concerned with the viability of instrumental means to a given set of ends. The latter sees the means in themselves being constituted by the ends. It is, in other words, a morally guided view of instrumental or technical action. It is this latter view which is consistent with the egalitarian models of community referred to.

The result of the elections clearly indicated that to the extent that Zamorans participate in a national politics, the majority see this action largely in instrumental terms, similar to the attitude they take in dealing with the powerful economic and other interests impinging into village life and whose moral base lies outside their control. Now that Aquino is in power, Zamorans have no difficulty in adjusting their strategies to the new political masters. A new set (1987–88) of provincial and local officials are in power and like the old set, the new are busy establishing networks to ensure continued political support. The rise and fall of many Zamoran political leaders reflects the fact that the basis of external alliances and of internal support are not consistent. The strategic and instrumental gains of political office are unable to satisfy the moral claims of local constituents. For this reason Zamorans are careful to distinguish between occupants of political office and people of influence and authority in the village. The former are generally seen as primarily interested in cultivating political ties with powerful external patrons whose benefits may well be partially redistributed among local supporters. This relationship is primarily instrumental and quid pro quo on the part of all parties. While this fact is not in itself objectionable and indeed is characteristic of many relationships within the village (e.g., a stingy landowner who insists on a strict allocation of harvest shares), it is contrasted with the understanding and sympathy shown by a village *baknang* who is willing to compromise or be persuaded by the overall merits of a particular plea or dispute. Influence and legitimate authority are ultimately founded on the uncoerced acceptance of the prevailing notions of community and distinguished from an agreement achieved through superior force. Enough examples of the latter are also encountered in village life but the requirements of close consociation and the relative absence of repressive apparatuses necessitate some attempts at achieving mutual and uncoerced understanding.

In contrast, external political ties are assumed to involve only adjustments to existing power differentials where each party obtains power in proportion to the resources they bring into the relationship. Market exchange and political power are the most explicit arenas for such relationships since interests are clearly delineated, whereas in the domain of kinship, interests are to some extent conflated.

After Aquino came to power, Rogelio Fabrigas was appointed officer-in-charge of Zamora. Unfortunately ex-Governor Singson had by then organized his own version of "people power" in Ilocos Sur and with the support of many local officials managed either to thwart the appointment of many OICs or to have incumbent KBL officials reinstated, some of whom had quickly joined PDP-Laban. Singson's wife Evelyn, who during the presidential elections was reported to have supported Aquino, was appointed Vice-Governor of Ilocos Sur and later acting Governor when the provincial O.I.C. Jose Burgos ran for the Senate. Fabrigas's mentor/patron, Pablito Sanidad, was appointed briefly as Assistant Minister of Labor but soon after lost favor with Malacañang. Sanidad's loss of political influence left local supporters such as Fabrigas without the necessary backer required for recruitment to the network of Aquino appointees in provincial and local government. Fabrigas retired from political activism to nurse his wounded pride and plot his political future.

When the plebiscite for the new constitution was held in early 1987, among its strongest supporters were former KBL members who had quickly shifted their support to the PDP-Laban Party. Although many of them gained short-term political rewards such as O.I.C. appointments, the results of the plebiscite in Ilocos Sur showed that the majority of the electorate (68% voted No) did not respond to the advice offered by such officials. In Zamora, again with the exception of Macaoayan (56% voted Yes), the new constitution was rejected (63% voted No). The results in Macaoayan showed that the earlier support for Aquino was not entirely due to local factors. In Luna the new constitution received a result consistent with its earlier support of Aquino. These electoral and plebiscite results reflect the complex ways in which local factors, including kinship, ethnic, class and factional affiliation combine to determine the final results. These results, unless interpreted in terms of local interests, often disguise significant factors. Thus the support for Marcos was much less than might be assumed by the 1986 presidential elections and similarly the rejection of the 1987 plebiscite did not entirely reflect Aquino's popularity.

The difficulty in interpreting these results is a consequence of the underlying empiricist and nominalist assumptions associated with elections. Each vote is assumed to signify a definite intention, determined by the formal political structure. But since formal political structures are often reinterpreted in local contexts, one cannot assume an unproblematic link between a local electoral choice and its national consequences. Thus a vote for Marcos or Aquino is just as indicative of political choice at the local level as it is of political choice at the national level. The notion of unintended consequences of political action in societies such as the Philippines where the integration of local and national structures cannot be unproblematically assumed should be kept in mind.

To illustrate the complex reinterpretation of national structures in local contexts, let us consider the case of Rogelio Fabrigas, the young lawyer who was the principal supporter of Aquino and Laurel in the 1986 election but whose political career was blocked by the astute machinations of ex-Governor Singson, following the downfall of Sanidad, Fabrigas's major backer. Despite his letter of appointment as acting Mayor of Zamora, Fabrigas was initially prevented from taking up the position as a result of the continuing influence of KBL officials in Ilocos Sur. Peeved by this injustice, he refused to support the plebiscite and instead developed political ties with the still powerful KBL network led principally by the Singsons. This strategy proved more successful and when the Singsons regained political power in the May 1987 congressional elections, Fabrigas was in a stronger position to pursue his case. He was eventually appointed acting Mayor of Zamora in 1987 which allowed him to amass political resources for his bid to run for this office in 1988. Having learned from his earlier experience, Fabrigas managed to obtain at least the implicit support of the Singsons. However, two other candidates presented themselves for Mayor in the 1988 elections, both of whom had varying claims on Singson support. Brigido Filaart had been a loyal Singson supporter throughout his seven years as Mayor of Zamora but his popularity particularly in the influential barrio of Macaoayan was doubtful. Cesar Escobar had less direct claims on Singson support but instead had some influential local connections. In the end the Singsons supported all three candidates making it clear that each of them would be found acceptable. This meant that provincial influence was reduced and the election ultimately rested on local support and personal resources. Filaart was reputed to have spent the most, followed by Fabrigas who eventually won the elections by a narrow margin. Escobar came a very poor third and partly consoled himself by accusing the others of having spent much more. Fabrigas's electoral victory was achieved, naturally, by obtaining more Zamoran votes than his opponents. However, as I have shown, this result was partly due to his cultivation of political support outside Zamora following his earlier disappointing experience with the UNIDO Party.

The decision by the Singson power block not to interfere in Zamora intensified rather than reduced the internal tensions associated with the elections in 1988. External alignments which on such occasions normally coalesce local interests were inoperative. This resulted in bitter divisions within barrios and even within families as people, more of less idiosyncratically, supported particular candidates. The three sets of candidates (mayor, vice-mayor and local councilors) each brought with them particular kin, barrio, ethnic and alliance networks. However, each set made sure to extend its network as much as possible resulting in the bitter divisions mentioned. The usual political divisions in Zamora such as north–south, Ilokano–non-Ilokano, rich–poor, kin-nonkin were deliberately breached as each set of candidates activated its particular network. The personalistic nature of these political networks is shown by the source and the number of votes obtained by each candidate. Both Rogelio Fabrigas and his Vice-Mayor Francisco Reinante were able to attract enough votes throughout Zamora drawing on their Macaoayan and Luna networks, a strategy also but less successfully used by the Filaart team, their closest rivals. The poor showing of the Escobar team was due to their inability to attract votes outside their immediate circle of barrio supporters. The barrios of Macaoayan and Luna are not only the biggest in Zamora but are also the centers of the most extensive networks in the municipality. Fabrigas's wife comes from a wealthy Macaoayan family while Reinante belongs to one of the most influential families in Luna. Filaart also has ethnic links with Macaoayan and his vice-mayoral candidate P. Foronda comes from a very prominent family with strong ties to Luna. Thus these two barrios were themselves divided in their support for the candidates mentioned.

In the case of the eight municipal councilors, a much narrower electoral base was sufficient and as a consequence even the Escobar ticket won a seat. Whereas Fabrigas had to get at least over a third of the votes to win and therefore needed to have support in all of the principal barrios, a councilor only needed to obtain an eighth of the vote, thereby making it possible to win simply by having strong support in a couple of barrios.

The results of the recent elections (1986, 1987, and 1988) indicate the complex intercalation of local and national politics. The routines of Zamoran everyday life are primarily but not exclusively determined by factors such as propinquity, parentation, class and ethnicity. These factors have their own rationales and particular connections to national structures. A factor such as locality may pit one barrio against another but kinship and alliance often transcend the boundaries of the barrio, as do class and ethnicity. For example, Filaart activated the ethnic ties he has with Macaoayan but Fabrigas obtained more votes from this barrio through his affinal and alliance links with some of its influential families. Finally, people in Zamora exercise personal choice outside the constraints of the above factors whenever they judge that it is in their interests to do so.

The transition from Marcos to Aquino, although unexpected, did not create major breaks in the structure of Zamoran politics. Local politics still depends on the internal factors mentioned in association with external ties to provincial and national networks and structures. Apart from the replacement of Marcos by Aquino and the electoral recognition of the consequences of such a change (e.g., new networks for patronage and clientelism), the main structure of provincial and local politics in Ilocos Sur has not changed significantly. While Marcos's personal grip on Ilokano politics was waning, the 1987 elections in both Ilocos provinces indicate that his network of political alliances has largely been preserved, even if under the banner of a new party (Lakas ng Bansa) and a new leader (Corazon Aquino). At most, one could describe this change as a partial circulation of elites but definitely not as a revolutionary transformation of society. This latter change would require that national structures penetrate the organization of village life more thoroughly than has so far been achieved by a largely weak Philippine state with its fragmented economy.

Conclusion

In this essay, I have discussed local notions of community and their relationship to wider structures such as a national polity and the state. The lack of articulation between local notions of community and their external sources in the national polity creates major problems when interpreting elections as an expression of a political will. This uneven integration of national structures with local notions of community is reflected in the cultural imperative to defend kin in defiance of the law such as in the case of Kamlon as well as in the moral sympathy accorded Aquino by Zamorans while voting for Marcos. In another instance, the pattern of voting (e.g. the defeat of the 1987 constitutional plebiscite) may indicate moral disapproval of the self-serving interests of politicians.

These cases illustrate the difficulties in interpreting political behavior in a context such as Zamora where the cultural and social orders are not only poorly integrated but follow inconsistent demands. These inconsistencies and lack of articulation have both internal and external sources. Thus the notion of local society as a normatively bound, participative community also includes an awareness of inequality and exploitation. In dealings with outsiders, Zamorans assume very little normative consensus and proceed along strategic and instrumental interests. But notions of community may also be extended indefinitely including all Ilokanos, Filipinos and others as expressed in the Tagalog *pakikipagkapwa-tao*. For this reason, Zamorans recognized Aquino's moral claims even while they supported Marcos's realpolitik. Moreover, as the case of Fabrigas shows, his initial support of Aquino did not automatically assure him political patronage. On the other hand, despite Marcos's defeat, Filaart was initially able to retain political power through the intervention of regional influence. National structures are reinterpreted regionally before impinging on local structures. Fabrigas had to neutralize provincial opposition before obtaining local support.

Each level of the social, political and cultural order enjoys a relative autonomy from other levels let along other orders. Whilst Zamorans may not be theoretically aware of the complex articulations as well as discontinuities between local and national structures, they realize that social life consists of normative expectations embedded in differential structures of power. This realization is consciously elaborated at public dances and other occasions in the ordinary course of village life. However, the requirements of local consociation often tend to mute and disguise wide disparities of power. Only when Zamorans leave the village, as they are increasingly forced to do, are they obliged to distinguish inequalities embedded within a normative model of community from those based on the reality of class. Class relations exist in Zamora but the requirements of parentation, propinquity and local association transform them into status inequalities. Hence the apparent paradox of the lack of a reflexive class consciousness while acknowledging social inequality and the presence of class action (e.g., Iglesia ni Kristo members in Zamora are predominantly poor tenants who link membership in this denomination to their material position).

These multiple notions of community and their weak integration into wider structures indicate the uneven routinization of the life-world achieved by a weak state. The imposition of law and order (in both their normative and cognitive senses) over a given territory characterizing a modern nation-state has not been accomplished in the Philippines. The lack of integration of the ideological-moral spheres into the structural-coercive has prevented the Philippine state from creating in the consciousness of its citizens the conditions for its own reproduction. Hence the state's ideological reproduction is based on local structures which themselves impose constraints on the penetration of a national consciousness. This is clearly illustrated by the scores of Zamorans who, while abroad in search of economic security, strongly experience their sense of Filipino nationality without losing their local identity.

The capacity of the Philippine state to colonize the inner life-world of its citizens is limited by the fragmentation and dependent orientation of its national economy. For this reason factors such as propinquity, parentation and ethnicity continue to constrain the development of a consciousness of class in the face of increasing inequality. There are economic and ideological causes for the lack of a consciousness of class. This absence of a class consciousness is reflected in a national politics which rejects ideological alternatives. Thus, despite the constitutional and organizational changes under Aquino, the Philippines has a reconstructed system very similar to what existed under Marcos. Just as local structures transform class relations into status inequalities, national structures negate the reality of class by preventing ideological differences from entering the political arena. The electoral process distorts the perceptions of class such that people appear to vote against their own interests. Many Zamorans supported Marcos because they doubted that Aquino had the capacity or inclination to bring about structural change. In most cases, their suspicions appear to have been confirmed. What this shows is that elections have little to do with the expression of a political will and even less in relation to the articulation of power structuring class relations in Philippine society. This essay has explored some of the local reasons for this situation and has suggested how these local factors are related to broader structures constituting national life.

FERNANDO N. ZIALCITA

Perspectives on Legitimacy in Ilocos Norte

What sort of authority do barrio residents in Ilocos Norte regard as "legitimate" and how does the leadership of Ferdinand Marcos and Corazon Aquino rate under this concept? As defined by Ronald Cohen, legitimacy consists of a "recognized right" plus a people's belief in its rightness.[1] A recognized right is a set of rules, either explicit or implicit, that determines how resources are allocated among superiors and subordinates. Members of a polity may either support, tolerate or even dislike this right. As long as they do not actively oppose it, however, then it is a recognized right. By itself, a recognized right does not confer legitimacy. Superior force may give a tyrant a recognized right, but not necessarily legitimacy, for the populace does not believe in his right to this recognized right.

Several factors contribute to the formation of a recognized right: a leader's own power, a people's beliefs about the prerogatives due a person in authority, and their fears about outside enemies. Power springs from the political actor's position in the status system, his use of coercion and his own political skills.[2] These sources of power are all obviously related to each other. For instance, a person's high status may broaden his capacity for coercion and sharpen his political skills; conversely, by cleverly manipulating his followers, his status may rise. On the other hand, the mere threat of coercion subtly influences a community's beliefs about what is or is not permissible in the political order.

To examine legitimacy during a transition of power, I focus on a rural village, which I call Rangtay, in a municipality that is in the economic and cultural heartland of Ilocos Norte. I first stayed in Rangtay while doing research in 1978–79. For this current project, I made several visits in 1987-88, for varying lengths of time. My research assistants are residents of the community and have been extremely helpful because I am not a native speaker of Ilokano.

For this project I used a structured questionnaire to gather some specific data, but much of my information comes from extended, unstructured interviews that emphasized what people did and thought regarding the four elections that took place between 1986 and 1988. My assistants and I spoke with thirty-five adults, most of them from separate households in the three neighborhoods of the village and from the various classes and status groups.

Socioeconomic Context

In 1988, Rangtay consisted of around 750 people, living in 140 households in what I call Baybay, a municipality close to Laoag, the provincial capital. The villagers grew rice, garlic and tobacco.

Most of the houses were made of hollow blocks and galvanized iron and had amenities such as electricity, televisions, and hand pumps. It was not always so. In 1946, when the Republic began, only two houses were of solid materials. The rest were of bamboo and thatch, lit at night by wicks and gas lamps. What this contrast illustrates, among others, is that, over the past forty years, Rangtayans have increasingly needed cash to purchase products from outside the region.

Originally the local crops were rice for home use and native tobacco for barter. New crops during the past four decades brought in cash: garlic beginning in the 1950s and high-yielding strains of rice during the 1970s. This last improvement not only ended the frequent rice shortages of the past but also gave some households a surplus to sell.

Emigration from the village has accelerated over the past forty years: first to Hawaii, then to other countries, or else to the Metropolitan Region. Well-paved roads and daily bus trips link Ilocos to Manila. Migrants, whether temporary or permanent, send money to relations in the barangay. Villagers estimate that between 40 to 50 percent of all the households depend heavily on these remittances. Because of the inflow of cash, other important changes have become possible. Many Rangtayans have been able to pursue a college degree for a range of professions. Marcos's electrification program, coupled with available cash, has enabled two residents to open capitalist ventures: an automotive repair shop and a factory for making hollow blocks. Tiny stores are found in the various neighborhoods of Rangtay.

Money from abroad has also enabled residents to buy farmland from townspeople. Since the 1920s the number of locals who own land has increased. Most households hold title to a parcel of land, averaging about half a hectare. As a result, there is no tenancy problem of the dimensions found elsewhere in Luzon.

As Rangtay has become more integrated into the national economy, it has increasingly felt the presence of the central government. Under Marcos, the old road linking the area to the highway was filled in. Unfortunately, despite his campaign promise many years ago, it has not been paved. Electrification came in; a new strain of rice became popular; the government became the biggest customer for surplus rice through the National Food Grains Authority; and the government organized farmers, albeit not entirely successfully, into two grassroots farmers' associations. After Marcos declared Martial Law, elections in Rangtay, as elsewhere, were suspended for several years. Initially, people welcomed that because during the preceding administration of President Diosdado Macapagal, local elections in Rangtay's municipality had become increasingly bloody. A mayor, for example, was assassinated—allegedly by his rival's followers.

Economic and political changes helped to bring about new configurations in the class system and the status hierarchy. There are, of course, many ways of defining class. By class, I refer to a category of individuals occupying a similar position in the total system of production, exchange, and distribution. The economic interests of such individuals are defined by the assets they actually possess, whether this be land or capital. I use the the term "category" because members of a class may not be aware of their de facto membership.[3] Using ownership of a farm as criterion, these would be the classes in the village:

1. Pure landlords. Twenty-three households (16.4%) own farms within the locality but entrust the cultivation to others. Fourteen of the household heads are professionals: most are largely in teaching, a few others in engineering and construction. Two have the capitalist ventures mentioned above and two are pensioners from Hawaii. Some of these landlords, be they professionals or nonprofessionals, run little businesses such as neighborhood stores or vehicles for hire.
2. Owner-cultivators. One hundred and three households (73.6%) both own and cultivate their farms. Because landholdings in the Ilocos are highly fragmented, tenure arrangements vary. An individual, who cultivates a parcel he owns, might also be a landlord of another plot, and a tenant on still a third. For this reason, I call the preceding class, "pure landlord," to denote that they are not in anyway a tenant on another's farm. About fifteen of these owner-cultivators either own neighborhood stores or buy and sell vegetables in the town proper.
3. Pure tenants. Nine households (6.4%) have absolutely no land of their own and must therefore rent it from others.

4. Landless farm workers. Five households (3.6%) are not even tenants. They subsist by working for others in the locality.

Beneficiaries of remittances from migrant kin abroad are found
among all four categories: almost half in each of these.

Conflicts do occur between people in different classes. For instance,
some small landlords wanted to get rid of their tenants but were
deterred because of a law in the 1970s against evictions. Still, no social
movements of any sort have appeared to press for the rights of a class.

Unlike class, status ranks individuals and groups according to
socially defined criteria. One important criterion is the style of consumption.[4]

Villagers speak of three levels: (1) baknang, (2) napanglaw, and
(3) gagangay:

1. *Baknang* (the "wealthy"). A basic characteristic is easy access to
   cash. They generally live in a large house of cement and wood with
   modern appliances, have children in college, and may have a private
   vehicle. The two capitalists; a couple of pensioners from Hawaii;
   two farmers who regularly received money from kinspersons abroad;
   and three professionals, who owned two or three hectares each,
   were baknang.
2. *Napanglaw* (the "poor"). They suffer periodically from insufficient
   cash for basic necessities, live in small houses either of flimsy
   materials or roughly finished cement, and have a difficult time
   sending their children to school because of their meager finances.
   Landless households, who depend entirely either on wage labor
   or on pure tenancy, fall into this category.
3. *Gagangay* ("those with sufficient means"). Such households have
   just enough resources to meet their basic needs. They live simply,
   though at times may have some extra cash for modest pleasures.
   Informants would situate most villagers in this category.

Still, when villagers are asked directly where they belong, they are
always *napanglaw* in relation to somebody else who is truly *baknang*.
As Mark Turner observed in another part of the Ilocos region, an
individual's judgment of his position on the social ladder is always
relative to the position of those he compares himself to.[5] A villager
of means regards himself as poor vis-à-vis a city-dweller of similar
means.

When asked about the code of behavior between napanglaw and
baknang, a villager replied in a way that is typical:

Baknang and napanglaw meet each other in many parties, such as weddings, baptisms and birthdays. In these occasions, often the napanglaw are present in order to either help serve or take care of the guests. So that the napanglaw will not feel inhibited (*mabain*), the baknang should be the first to greet and call on those who have gathered there. The baknang should not act superior.

Note the passive, servile manner attributed to the napanglaw vis-à-vis the baknang. It seems the napanglaw have been invited to attend an important event in order to be at the disposal of others. At the gathering they act in a restrained manner before their social superiors. The baknang are therefore expected to draw out the napanglaw to reassure them that for the time being, equality is the norm.

Nonetheless, according to the same villager, though the napanglaw accept the baknang's overtures, they remain distrustful about the latter's intentions.

These baknang respect the napanglaw a great deal, for when they visit the latter they bring a gift. Most of the baknang behave properly toward the napanglaw just so the latter will help them. Yet, should the occasion arise, they will take the napanglaw's products away. Many of the baknang know how to speak to the napanglaw only when they want or need help. Only a few baknang truly have a good disposition (*nasayaat ti ugali*).

The relationship between baknang and napanglaw is significant for several reasons. First, being a baknang gives a person power. Second, although being a baknang may attract respect, it may also create resentment. Undoubtedly many of the more powerful figures respected by Rangtayans are baknang, nonetheless lower status Rangtayans have ambivalent feelings about them precisely because they are baknang. Hence, a baknang leader must take care not to act like one. Third, the continuing loyalty of many Rangtayans to Ferdinand Marcos (and conversely their hostility to Corazon Aquino) may be interpreted partly in terms of the baknang-napanglaw dichotomy. Although Marcos is baknang he is perceived not to act like one; while Corazon Aquino is a baknang and acts like one.

Power and Leadership

Being baknang may increase a person's ability to influence others. Gender is another source of power. Women are not allowed to inherit riceland at Rangtay, nor are local women allowed to participate in the rice cycle, although women hired from other municipalities can.

Another source of power is a person's ability to generate support for himself and his causes. Within recent years a distinction has been made between what I call "simple patronage" and "complex patronage."[6] The former involves the use of public funds for local projects, such as roads and school houses. This relationship is, by and large, sporadic and transactional. Complex patronage, more commonly called patron-client ties, involves a patron who has long-lasting exchanges with a subordinate where he plays several roles as protector, financier and friend. In both types of patronage the client supports the patron in time of need; however, the bonds between benefactor and benefactee in complex patronage would be stronger and more emotion-laden. Officials may use either or both simple and complex patronage to create a following.

Both sources of power imply the use of material resources. However, even without them it is possible for a fellow of average means to be influential. Responsibility in action, depth of thought, and eloquence of expression are highly regarded. In this highly oral culture, people expect a leader to give a speech extemporaneously and without notes as a sign of a quick mind. But the speech must also address the concerns of the moment. Artemio, a farmer of modest means, is always listened to in Rangtay because "his speech is full of substance" (*nabagas ti saona*). As one villager put it, "In his presence, I feel awed."

Rangtayans expect their officials to create an atmosphere of peace and quiet by promoting public order and to set a good example by following the law. Yet when their officials do break the law, they do not publicly protest, perhaps because they feel themselves powerless. When municipal officials visited the barangay sometime ago, they disregarded an ordinance by asking the locals to poison a stream and gather the motionless fish for their meal. Villagers did not publically object because the public officials controlled the police and the local bureaucracy. In private, however, Rangtayans complained about this behavior to each other.

Rangtayans also believe that officials should spend government funds to improve the livelihood of the villagers and other citizens. Yet they wink when officials pocket some public funds as long as this is not excessive. As Eduardo, a college-educated farmer, puts it, "If there are ten glasses, an official may get two for himself but not all ten." Though Freddie, the former vice-mayor, is said to be guilty of graft, another informant reasoned, "What official isn't?" Freddie's popularity remains strong in part because his graft is not exorbitant.

Moreover, he has clearly helped Rangtayans by getting them jobs in the local government, hiring them to run his jeepneys, and ordering his drivers to bring home villagers who have been stranded at night in the town proper. And he kids around with the guys.

Maleness seems to be an important requisite for leadership. Many Rangtayans, of either sex, feel that a man knows more about politics. Men also show more visible interest in the topic. Because of conditioning, the women tend to give their political views only when prodded. Local inheritance practices certainly reinforce the tendency to regard women as suited only for the home and minor jobs, rather than for high, public positions as well.

An important trait, often mentioned, is that a leader (*pangulo*) makes his followers feel good. He is understanding and is easy to approach, for he is patient. Regardless of the number of times a follower comes back to voice his complaint, a good leader does not get irritated, for he is basically humble (*napakumbaba*). In other words, if a leader happens to be a baknang, he should not act like one.

A leader must also find ways to help his fellowmen, particularly the poor, either through simple or complex patronage. Ideally, he should help them in their livelihood; but assistance in any form, when needed, is welcome. Rangtayans probably do not expect a leader to actually help each single follower who comes to him. Attending to a few suffices to create a positive public image.

A leader, villagers say, should also be capable (*nalaing*) and wise (*masirib*). He must know what he is doing and be able to guide his followers toward his goals. A clear vision, however, must be translated into firm decisions: "He should clench his molars together (*nasangi*)." Indecisiveness weakens respect.

While people from various occupations agree on the importance of these qualities, those with experience in running their own business or have taken commerce courses explicitly want a managerial leader. Thus Roberto, a farmer and owner of a vehicle repair shop, seeks an "economist" as leader. Another villager, enrolled in a business course, praises goal-orientedness and the will to check on subordinates lest they commit anomalies.

A final leadership trait expected by many, regardless of their position, is honesty. A true leader is not greedy; he does not appropriate public funds for himself and he shuns extravagance. Still, some graft and corruption in a leader is tolerated so long it as it is not excessive.

The villagers' concept of leadership represents a practical accommodation with existing power structures. Realizing their inability to influence the ways of the powerful, except every so many years through the ballot, they ask that the powerful should at least not be brazen in their dishonesty and that they should be respectful toward the lowly in face-to-face encounters.

Democracy and Elections

When asked, many farmers and housewives cannot define *demokrasya*. Those who do attempt a definition equate it with "peace and quiet," "a sound economy," "prosperity"—in other words with its possible consequences rather than such characteristics as separation of powers; freedom of the press, of assembly and of elections; or a multiparty system. A small number, largely farmers, do define it in terms of freedom (*wayawaya*). By this they mean the freedom to pursue a livelihood without anyone unduly sharing in it or giving orders on what to do. "In a democracy," says one resident, "you are free to move. You may postpone your work, you can go to the fields when you want. Under communism, there are no chance conversations (*tungtong*), no wasted days. The (communist) government comes in to order you around. In a democracy, you have time to rest."

Small farmers value their freedom to decide their own daily agenda and see this as demokrasya in action. They surely cannot be faulted for their desire for minimal government intervention in their routine. After all, as most other commentators would agree, the Philippine bureaucracy has created complicated regulations that dampen initiative and breed graft. Only a few villagers, mostly college-educated ones like teachers, define democracy as freedom of speech and conscience. Fewer still—two among the thirty-five I spoke with—see democracy in terms of economic equality. Roberto, who loves to read books and lives frugally despite his thriving vehicle repair shop, sees democracy as the elimination of the differences between rich and poor. Ramon, an administration student at a reputable college in Laoag, says that "the key is socialism, but not communism." By socialism, he means a system that eliminates differences between the rich and the poor but still respects political freedom.

Rangtayans' fondness for deciding things in concert and through elections was evident during my stays in 1978–79 and 1987–88. Villagers frequently came together to decide on issues affecting them. Examples in the late 1970s were cleaning and weeding the footpaths, repairing the bridges, or fund-raising for a victim of an accident. Decisions were taken through votes. In government elections between 1984 and 1987, voter participation was high, on the average: 92.7 percent. However, reports of high voter turnouts under Marcos ought to be treated with caution (See table 1).

Table 1. Voter Turnout at Rangtay during six elections, 1984–88

	Reg. Voters	Actual Voters	% Turnout
Plebiscite, 27 January 1984	353	288	(81.6%)
National Assembly elections, 14 May 1984	359	355	(98.9%)
Presidential elections, February 1986	401	376	(93.8%)
Referendum on the Constitution, 2 February 1987	357	344	(96.3%)
Congressional elections, 14 May 1987	369	350	(94.9%)
Local elections, 18 January 1988	361	329	(91.1%)
Average voter turnout in 6 elections			(92.7%)

Rangtayans offer various reasons for participating in elections. A cynical reason is that "they just want to be chummy (makikadua) with the wealthy and powerful"—who dole out money during the campaign. Another reason expressed, for instance, by an average farmer with just a grade school education, is that political parties can be pitted against each other so that no single group becomes too strong and therefore dictatorial. For many Rangtayans, elections matter despite the bloodshed sometimes associated with them because that is the only way they can get local officials they want. Over the past decade and a half they kept reelecting Ramiro as barangay captain and were disgusted when the Aquino government replaced him with Leoncio as officer-in-charge (OIC). The latter was reputedly a drunkard and womanizer. In past elections, they got Freddie into office as vice-mayor. Through him, Ramiro, and Leoncio, some villagers got jobs.

Villagers generally see elections as a way for a person to legitimately hold public office.

Marcos's Legitimacy

For many Rangtayans, whether farmers, teachers or businessmen, Marcos approximated their concept of a true leader. On this basis they considered him the legitimate final authority for the country. He had won in successive elections that supposedly impartial government bodies had certified. He was male, a fact stressed by propaganda about his exploits as "the most decorated Filipino war hero." And he was an Ilokano who did not act like a baknang.[7]

He returned regularly to Ilocos—at least during the early part of his rule—to meet with his people. Though this may seem trivial to the outsider, for the average Ilokano, it signified that he had not forgotten his origins. And despite his wealth, Rangtayans thought he acted humbly. Many remarked, "He cared little for meat; he liked boiled vegetables flavored with fermented fishpaste (*bugguong*)." The Ilokano's fondness for vegetables has both status and ethnic resonances. Being expensive, meat is rarely eaten by rural households. Moreover, Ilokanos in general consider their fondness for vegetables a trait that distinguishes them from Tagalogs and Visayans, whom they put down for having expensive tastes. They say the latter crave sauteed meat dishes in their daily meals. During the opulent Ilocos wedding of Marcos's daughter, Irene, he reputedly preferred a simple dish of bittermelons. Also, unlike the arrogant and haughty rich, Marcos in his palace allegedly ate with his fingers—just like an ordinary farmer.

But what about the unexplained wealth of the Marcoses that became highly visible on television especially in 1986? Rangtayans, like many other Ilokanos, blame his wife, for she is Visayan and therefore extravagant. Meanwhile, Ferdinand Marcos, by living and eating frugally and helping fellow Ilokanos, has remained within the bounds of local conceptions of legitimacy.[8]

Marcos also helped both particular individuals and the people of Rangtay as a whole. When one villager lost several fingers in an accident, the Marcoses had him flown to a Manila hospital and paid for his treatment. Under Marcos, various improvements were introduced, as indicated earlier. While dispensing favors to individuals and the community, he at the same time kept the peace. Although there were occasional rumors about members of the New People's Army, popularly called NPAs, crossing the hills or collecting protection money, the entire province of Ilocos Norte was relatively peaceful and quiet compared especially to the Cagayan Valley or parts of neighboring Ilocos Sur.

Apparently, many Rangtayans had few problems accepting Martial Law in 1972. There was no overt government interference in their accustomed way of life. They could go to the fields at their own pace, or start their own small, informal businesses. Though the new high-yielding rice strains required expensive fertilizers and pesticides, their introduction by the Marcos government had ended the rice shortages that used to plague most households. As far as peace and order was concerned, since the NPAs had not yet spread, few government soldiers were present, and their units did not abuse civilians. Finally, no cause-oriented groups had reached out to Rangtayans to involve them in the formulation of decisions affecting them or lead people to question the Marcos government.

Though elections did matter to the villagers, nonetheless they had initially welcomed a respite from the increasingly bloody municipal elections. It also happened that the barangay captain then in office was extremely popular. Still some opposition to Marcos gradually built up in the village and highlighted the importance of elections. According to an informant, 20 percent of the votes cast during several referenda in the 1970s were actually against Marcos. The Commission on Elections allegedly maneuvered to give the impression that the province was solidly for Marcos. He lost favor among a fifth of the village because their conditions did not significantly improve despite his long stay in office. They wanted him replaced. During my stay in 1978–79, I heard frequent complaints about the high prices, for which a few people sometimes blamed Marcos. It was rumored that his sister, Elizabeth Keon, then the governor of the province, made an illegal profit on the sale of fertilizers to the farmers.

EDSA as a Factional War

Many observers have said that what ultimately led to the February 1986 change in government was the assassination of Senator Benigno Aquino, Jr. in 1983. Few in Rangtay, however, saw it that way and even fewer believed that the Marcos government was responsible for the murder. True, the assassination did shock many in Rangtay. Ninoy Aquino had captured their imagination a decade earlier when, as the youngest senatorial candidate, he had campaigned in the province during the senatorial elections. He had dazzled them with his wit and eloquence—delivered in the Ilokano he had learned in Tarlac. Rangtayans also recall that shortly after the Aquino assassination, there were mass lay-offs. Relatives who were working in factories and offices in Metro Manila lost their jobs.

Yet Rangtayans say that the economic crisis after 1983 was essentially caused by the devaluation of the peso, for which they have no explanation. As the peso plunged, the price of gasoline and essential goods soared. One result, according to some Rangtayans, was that more people in other parts of the country joined the NPA.

Although Rangtayans experienced economic problems in the mid 1980s, they were probably more protected than many Filipinos because of the large volume of dollar remittances from relatives who were abroad. This helped the households pay for their farming costs, groceries, and education.

Moreover, many of my informants did not really understand the issues raised against Marcos. They seemed not to understand why the Philippines had contracted a national debt of $28 billion, nor did they blame Marcos for it. Some, like Julio, a schoolteacher, saw the debt as the accumulation of years of borrowing that had begun under previous presidents. Others said that the debt ballooned to its enormous size in 1987-88 during the Corazon Aquino government. Many did not know that the former president and his circle were accused of forcibly taking over business companies for their own gain. Few villagers thought the President was that corrupt.

When the 1986 election was announced, many Rangtayans were surprised. But few expected Marcos to lose or to have a tough campaign. Most indicated they would support his reelection.

However, a handful—Ramon, Art and Cris—openly criticized Marcos, much to the dismay of their relatives and friends. Although Ramon comes from a household with a tiny piece of land, he put himself through school because of his writing skills. Unlike other villagers, Ramon is at home in the national capital where he has many friends. Recently, he obtained assistance in finishing his studies at a prestigious Laoag college. As a member of a cause-oriented group, he became aware of the First Family's exorbitant greed and abuse of power. What further angered him was that the nephews and nieces of an old, prosperous village family had become snobbish and unfriendly ever since they started working in Malacañang. Ramon's friend, Art, was being put through the same school as Ramon by relatives in Hawaii. His family had no land. In college, he attended workshops on human rights within and without the province. Cris was a non-Ilokano who resided in the village because of his business. He lamented the lack of freedom, for people could not criticize Marcos at assemblies for fear of arrest. He did not specify whether such a threat existed outside or inside the region.

Ramon, Art and Cris had several things in common: they were single males under fifty, college-educated, potential professionals, and well-aware of the world beyond Ilocos.

A few others with similar exposure, who were neither rich nor very poor, also questioned the regime. For example, Eduardo, a college-educated farmer and rice trader, criticized the Marcoses for their greed. "If I were not Ilokano, I would not have voted for him." Also, as a married man, he probably had to consider the risks. According to Cris, "In opposing the Marcos government, you had to realize that there were many drunks. One of them might stab you 'by accident.'"

People saw no reason to join the election campaign and the National Movement for a Free Elections (NAMFREL). They figured Marcos would win regardless. None joined the Opposition's campaign. Art boycotted the elections since he did not think Aquino could beat Marcos's machinery. Besides, he doubted that Aquino would share her wealth or otherwise be a good president. Cris, at the last moment, voted for Marcos. Approached by the barangay captain and asked to cooperate, he gave in; he had no relatives to support him in case of a confrontation. And he might be "accidentally" attacked. Only Ramon voted for Aquino (see table 2).

Although about 20 percent had allegedly voted against Marcos during referenda in the 1970s and early 1980s and many residents had been fascinated, in the 1960s, with the young chubby senator from Tarlac who represented a fresh start, these matters were not translated in 1986 into votes for Cory Aquino. For some, like Eduardo, the reasons boiled down to ethnicity—they chose Marcos the Ilokano over Aquino the non-Ilokano. For others, the reasons focused on Marcos's concrete achievements, especially for them and their locality. He had done something, whereas Aquino the wife of an assassinated politician, was unknown. In this contest between two baknang, they sided with a provincemate who knew their humble ways.

The majority of Rangtayans believed that Marcos had actually won nationwide in 1986. "He had never lost an election before. Besides, the Commission on Elections certified his victory." And they distrusted the NAMFREL for being partial to Aquino.

From this understanding of the vote follows the predominant view among Rangtayans about the "Four-Day Revolt." One resident, for example, said Juan Ponce Enrile and Fidel Ramos "turned against Marcos because Cory paid them to do so. They were ambitious." Another characterized Enrile and Ramos as "leftists" who revolted. Few villagers believed Aquino could rightfully claim the presidency. As someone explained, "People Power was really an encounter between groups loyal to Marcos and Aquino. Unfortunately, the latter

Table 2. Presidential and Vice-Presidential Election Returns at Rangtay, February 1986

Presidential elections

Reg. Voters	Actual Voters	Voted for Marcos	Voted for Aquino	Voted for Canoy	Voted for Padilla
401	376 (93.8%)	375 (99.7%)	1 (00.3%)	0 (0.0%)	0 (0.0%)

Vice-Presidential elections

Reg. Voters	Actual Voters	Voted for Tolentino	Voted for Laurel	Voted for Arienda	Voted for Kalaw
401	376 (93.8%)	371 (98.7%)	4 (1.1%)	0 (0.0%)	1 (0.3%)

were poor sports, so they could not admit that their candidate lost. Also, they were Manila people who disliked Marcos, an Ilokano."

To this day, many do not understand why multitudes crowded the EDSA highway in Metro Manila. "On television, it did not look like a revolution. Many people were just there to take a look. People Power is sheer craziness," said one resident. Most Rangtayans believe that the Americans kidnapped Marcos. Other villagers said that Marcos, after seeing all the confusion, willingly stepped down from the presidency. They take this as further proof that he was humble (*napakumbaba*).

The young parish priest of another town recalls how he wept when Marcos fled, for the president was basically a good man even though he was rather stingy in his donations to the local church. He castigates Cardinal Sin and other non-Ilokano members of the hierarchy for waging a hate campaign against the poor man.

The years since EDSA have not lessened many Rangtayans' admiration for Marcos nor has respect for Corazon Aquino attained parity. Initially, she was regarded as a usurper who had come to power through a revolt. But, Rangtayans made no active move to oppose her; they did not send a contingent to anti-Aquino demonstrations after February 1986. Instead they have been content with taking occasional potshots. They measure her according to their standard of an ideal ruler and have found her wanting. In a culture that values eloquent and spontaneous oratory, she is scorned for speaking in a monotone, while using written notes (*kodigo*).

Many villagers do not regard her as kindly, helpful, decisive or honest. A favorite complaint is that she has done nothing for them. The price of first class garlic plummeted to 15 pesos a kilo in 1986–87, whereas in good times it generally was 35 pesos a kilo at harvest time. People now fault the government for not clamping down on the smuggling of garlic from Taiwan.[9] As in 1979, people complain about the increasing cost of groceries. Epifania, a housewife, says that the new government has not built any new roads to help the farmers. There was, in fact, a road that had been finished by the present government in the northern part of the barangay. Either she had not heard of it, for the village is so spread apart that months pass before she ever visits that part, or a feeder road is of less importance to her than a main road.

Another Rangtayan charges that the calamity fund that was to help them after two typhoons devastated Ilocos Norte in late 1987 did not suffice: it gave food but not loans for rebuilding houses. Nor has her administration been perceived as cleaner than Marcos's. The provincial OIC, Castor Raval, was accused of using money from construction projects for a huge mansion in Manila without doing anything for the people. Aquino does not come across as being understanding, compassionate and helpful. To many, she seems to be a *baknang* who remains aloof.

Still, Rangtay itself has benefited somewhat from the government's new infrastructure program. A concrete feeder road connecting the barangay to another was completed in 1986. Work has begun on another feeder road.

But these improvements are regarded as minor. Moreover, many Rangtayans perceive the Aquino government as disunited, confused, and weak, therefore unable to promote the peace and quiet that they seek. Epifania, commenting on television talk shows, lamented that with the return of free speech, things have become *napulitika*: there is too much politicking, not enough unity. Rangtayans find the Aquino government fickle: the position of Municipal OIC changed hands four times in less than two years. And the Aquino government ignored the people by replacing Ramiro, the barangay captain, with the unpopular Leoncio.

Above all Aquino is faulted for the upsurge of NPA activity. Communist rebels reputedly twice tried to blow up a bridge to the municipality, they attacked the town center of Piddig municipality, they kidnapped candidates campaigning in various municipalities during the 1988 local elections, and they threatened Laoag itself. During the Christmas season of 1987, soldiers manned checkpoints at the approaches to Laoag.

According to the villagers' definitions of democracy, Aquino's government is "undemocratic": it has neither kept the peace nor created new job opportunities. Moreover, it has forcibly removed two officials respected by the villagers: Marcos and the barangay captain Ramiro.

Nonetheless, not all villagers are still enthralled with Marcos. During the past two years, the villagers have been exposed to radio and television programs in which political issues are openly discussed according to differing, conflicting political ideologies. Moreover, propaganda from the extreme left has also entered through personal contacts, especially through relatives visiting from the NPA-influenced Cagayan Valley.

A small number of residents observe that the new government has organized construction projects and is making farm inputs more readily available. One resident appreciates the fact that the provincial, rather than the municipal government, now undertakes these constructions. Less is stolen in contrast to the situation under Marcos. Another, who has worked as a laborer for construction projects, is thankful that, under Aquino, he has finally received the health benefits due him, except that some official skimmed off part of it. A number of farmers also applaud the government's attempt to bring down the cost of fertilizer. Meanwhile Freddie, the previous vice-mayor who had cultivated patron-client ties with some of the young men in the village, has turned Aquino supporter. After he became the municipal OIC, he campaigned for the new administration.

This change in attitude toward the Aquino government has been translated into a few votes, although the majority still voted "No" in the constitutional plebiscite in 1987, when the catchword was "Iloka—No" (see table 3).

In the May 1987 congressional elections, the candidates of the Grand Alliance for Democracy, the Nacionalista Party, and the Kilusang Bagong Lipunan won most of the Rangtay votes. The KBL was, of course, perceived as the ex-president's party, the NP and the GAD as at least friendly to him. Aiming for the Senate, Rodolfo Fariñas, a Marcos loyalist, won the most votes (see table 4). This previous mayor of the provincial capital reaped praise for minimizing corruption in the city market and introducing free education in the public high schools. Another popular candidate was Enrile. But had he not precipitated Marcos's downfall? Well, according to Rangtayans, he was, after all, Ilokano. Besides, after Cory ousted him from her cabinet, they took pity on him for being an underdog. Only two Aquino-backed candidates won among the top 24 Senate candidates in Rangtay. Jovito Salonga, a prominent critic of Marcos and a non-Ilokano, was remembered as a capable senator before Martial Law. Another favorite was Ernesto Maceda who had served in the Marcos administration.

The last election that took place at Rangtay, during the period of my study, was the municipal and provincial election (see table 5). Beaten nationwide in the senatorial election, Rodolfo Fariñas ran for and won the governorship against Manuela Ablan, the eighty-year old mother of Roque Ablan Jr., another Marcos ally. Fariñas won handily in Rangtay and in the rest of the province. The main issue was

Table 3. Constitutional Referendum Returns, 2 February 1987

	Reg. Voters	Actual Voters	Yes	No	Abstained
Ilocos Norte	209,217	198,699 (95.0%)	27,792 (13.9%)	169,874 (85.5%)	1,033 (0.5%)
Rangtay	357	344 (96.3%)	47 (13.2%)	297 (83.2%)	0 (0.0%)

Table 4. Senatorial Election Returns at Rangtay, 11 May 1987
(The elections were for 24 senatorial seats)

	Votes		Votes
1. Fariñas (Ind.)	327	13. Bautista (Ind.)	114
2. Estrada (GAD)	288	14. Kalaw (LP-Kalaw wing)	114
3. Tolentino (GAD-NP-KBL)	261	15.Almendras (NP)	108
4. Recto (KBL)	261	16. Britanico (KBL)	105
5. Raquiza (Ind.)	224	17. Mathay (KBL)	96
6. Puyat (NP)	164	18. Tatad (GAD)	94
7. Venus (KBL)	150	19. Jalosjos (GAD)	89
8. Ople (PNP)	142	20. Magsaysay (KBL-NP-GAD)	89
9. Adaza (GAD)	137	21. Salonga (LP-Salonga wing)	76
10. Enrile (GAD)	132	22. Maceda (Lakas)	69
11. Yñiguez (KBL)	127	23. Lopez (Ind.)	62
12. Perez (KBL-NP)	126	24. Cuadra (Ind.)	69

Table 5. Gubernatorial Election Returns at Rangtay, January 1988

Reg. Voters	Actual Voters	Voted for Rodolfo Fariñas	Voted for Manuela Ablan	Voted for Castor Raval	Abstain
361	329 (91.13%)	286 (79.22%)	37 (11.24%)	3 (0.9%)	3 (0.9%)

corruption. Roque Ablan was resented for having smuggled in garlic from Taiwan and thus precipitating a fall in prices in 1986-87. Castor Raval, who had been the provincial OIC appointed by the Aquino government in 1986, was soundly defeated. He was widely satirized and criticized for profiting enormously as the provincial OIC.

The significance of Fariñas's victory has not been understood outside the province. Both he and Ablan, Jr. had been Marcos loyalists but Ferdinand Marcos preferred Mrs. Ablan because she was old. In the event he could restore his government, Marcos reportedly reasoned, and after Mrs. Ablan had passed away, Marcos could make his son, Ferdinand Jr.(Bong-Bong), governor again.[10] Fariñas won against heavy odds. Though popular, he did not have Roque Ablan Jr.'s hold over the various mayors and sections of the military and the police. A volunteer movement was launched by Fariñas' supporters to keep watch over the polls in all precincts. Unknowingly, Ilokanos created their own version of People Power. The election may have weakened

Marcos's power in his own province.[11] At the same time, it may have engendered feelings that Corazon Aquino, after all, does respect elections in that she did not block the victory of a popular Marcos loyalist.

Conclusion

Non-Ilokanos believe that Ilokanos have been stubbornly loyal to Marcos simply because he is one of them. The importance of ethnicity is certainly borne out by Ilokanos' willingness to vote for Enrile in 1987 despite his betrayal of Marcos in 1986. But the importance of ethnicity itself begs for explanation. Unlike class and status, ethnicity is a form of solidarity that does not require, at least overtly, similarities in assets and market opportunities. Instead it proposes symbols— such as language, a cooking style, a corpus of songs and dances— which mask social inequality with feelings of unity. A shared ethnicity can be one way of compelling a government official to heed the interests of a disadvantaged group, particularly if the official holds office in the remote, unfriendly, and non-Ilokano national capital. Moreover, a shared ethnicity can also signify that an official will watch out for a region's interests because he has a direct experience of its problems and perhaps, more importantly, because his kin reside there. Because of the highly centralized character of the Philippine state and the well-known inefficiency and insensitivity of its bureaucrats, it is imperative that a fellow Ilokano be well positioned to focus attention on the region. Thus, Enrile's revolt against Marcos was easily glossed over. Instead he became a counterweight to an executive reputed to be hostile to Ilokano interests.

There is another dimension to the supposedly fierce ethnocentrism of many Ilokanos. It may explain their seeming stubbornness in the face of facts about Marcos. The polarity between rich and poor, high and low, city and country crystallizes in the polarity between Tagalog and Ilokano. Tagalogs are looked upon as proud, arrogant, and citified whereas Ilokanos see themselves as humble, sensible and close to the earth. Tagalog stereotypes of Ilokanos reinforce this polarity. True, Tagalogs poke fun at the accents of Pampangos and Visayans; but they praise the former for their sophisticated cooking and crafts, and admire the latter for their gracefulness, romantic music, and beautiful women. For many Tagalogs, Pampangos and Visayans exude an urbaneness that Ilokanos supposedly do not. While ethnocentric Tagalogs grant that Ilokanos are thrifty and hardworking, they jeer at their backwardness, loudness, and fondness for raw meat. Word of these attitudes does reach the hinterlands of the Ilocos. After all, there is easy traffic between Manila and the North. But Marcos's ascent to power tipped the scales. Not only was he the third Ilokano president after Quirino and Magsaysay, rural Ilokanos proudly note, he also stayed longest in the seat of power.

This sensitivity about ethnicity may be truer of Ilokanos with little or no education or who have few or no Tagalog friends. The parish priest who accused Cardinal Sin of a hate campaign against Marcos mentioned that he does not feel at home in the company of non-Ilokanos, priests though they be. On the other hand, Ramon, who is educated and has many friends in Manila, was critical of Marcos.

Notions of ethnicity are not impermeable among Ilokanos. In particular situations, these expand to include non-Ilokanos like Salonga whom many recall was an able senator. Ilokanos do acknowledge another ethnicity, that of being Filipinos. Understandably, this is premised on the condition that their local interests be safeguarded as well. It would be interesting to find out if Salonga's popularity was due to his perceived fairness to non-Tagalogs, including Ilokanos.

A shared ethnicity, however, would not have helped Marcos's chances in the barangay if people had not witnessed some improvements or if conditions had deteriorated significantly. Recall that a fifth had allegedly cast votes against him in his referenda. For the majority, the improvements were high-yielding strains of rice, electricity and roads. Also important to explaining villagers' support is that most have a plot of land and a significant number receive remittances from abroad. While Marcos was not responsible for these, they fostered some stability which in turn made people less critical of national conditions. A vote for Marcos therefore meant affirming a far from satisfactory but stable status quo against the promises of an inexperienced widow. The events that have taken place since 1986 have confirmed the villagers' doubts about Aquino. The government forcibly removed the popular barangay captain from office, the price of garlic dropped in 1987, and the insurgency finally entered the province.

While ethnicity does color the villagers' notions of legitimacy, it is but one symbol of a broader concern: that the ruler should take care of his people by helping them materially and by respecting their lowly status. Through simple patronage, a crafted public image, and censorship, Marcos has lived up to this image while Corazon Aquino, a wealthy widow who seems to release funds in a niggardly way and who is criticized frequently in a free media, has not.

When choosing between candidates who are both Ilokano, ethnicity, of course, ceases to be a consideration. What becomes crucial is simply the degree to which either candidate approximates ideals of leadership. I am told that, after his victory, Fariñas's popularity has since declined vis-a-vis that of his vice-governor because he seems aloof, he bars slipper-shod visitors from his office, and he does not sit at table with just anyone. Unlike Rolando Abadilla, his vice-governor, he has the image of a baknang. Sometimes a contender may win, despite a frosty image, simply because the person campaigning on his or her behalf has exercised complex patronage. Thus Freddie, who as vice-mayor had bestowed favors on village friends, was able to swing votes in favor of Aquino during the constitutional referendum.

At this point in time, Marcos's legitimacy does not rest secure. Those most critical of him are below fifty, are college educated and are familiar with the world beyond the province. Some political and economic reforms by the Aquino administration have won respect from other young but not so educated members of the village.

According to Samuel Popkin, peasants make long-term as well as short-term investments, risky as well as secure investments in their relationships with their equals and their superiors.[12] The long-term commitment of Rangtayans is to their family's financial security. Loyalties to particular politicians, like Marcos, are probably short-term commitments that are subordinate to their aspirations for their family. Thus while Marcos's hold continues, it may not be that permanent or that tenacious. His supporters were not able to attract the expected multitudes to the birthday celebration in his honor at Laoag in 1988, despite the promise of a huge birthday cake. So small was the turnout that no similar attempts were repeated in 1989. Marcos symbolizes many things for the Rangtayans. However, he may become a mere symbol from the past if supporting him does not improve their present conditions.

Notes

Notes to Kerkvliet and Mojares, "Themes in the Transition," pages 1–12

1. For especially influential studies, see John A. Larkin, *The Pampangans: Colonial Society in a Philippine Province* (Berkeley: University of California Press, 1972); Reynaldo Clemeña Ileto, *Pasyon and Revolution: Popular Movements in the Philippines, 1840–1910* (Quezon City: Ateneo de Manila University Press, 1979); Alfred W. McCoy and Ed. C. de Jesus, eds., *Philippine Social History: Global Trade and Local Transformation* (Quezon City: Ateneo de Manila University Press, 1982); and Norman G. Owen, *Prosperity without Progress: Manila Hemp and Material Life in the Colonial Philippines* (Quezon City: Ateneo de Manila University Press, 1984).

2. These are the essential elements of such landmark studies of Philippine politics as Mary R. Hollnsteiner, *The Dynamics of Power in a Philippine Municipality* (Quezon City: Community Development Research Council, University of the Philippines, 1963); Carl H. Lande, *Leaders, Factions, and Parties: The Structure of Philippine Politics* (New Haven, Conn.: Southeast Asian Studies, Yale University, 1965); Remigio E. Agpalo, *The Political Elite and the People: A Study of Politics in Occidental Mindoro* (Manila: College of Public Administration, University of the Philippines, 1972); and Carl Lande, *Southern Tagalog Voting, 1946–1963* (DeKalb: Center for Southeast Asian Studies, Northern Illinois University, 1973). K. G. Machado made important modifications by analyzing the tendency away from family-centered factions toward political machines: "Changing Aspects of Factionalism in Philippine Local Politics," *Asian Survey* 11 (December 1971): 1182–99; "From Traditional Faction to Machine: Changing Patterns of Political Leadership and Organization in the Rural Philippines," *Journal of Asian Studies* 33 (August 1974): 523–47.

3. Many subnational studies have noticed this. For an analysis that is more national in scope, see Thomas C. Nowak, "The Philippines Before Martial Law: A Study in Politics and Administration," *American Political Science Review* 71 (June 1977): 522–39; and *idem* and Kay A. Snyder, "Economic Concentration and Political Change in the Philippines," in *Political Change in the Philippines: Studies of Local Politics Preceding Martial Law*, ed. Benedict J. Kerkvliet (Honolulu: Asian Studies at Hawaii, University Press of Hawaii, 1974), pp. 153–241.

Notes to Turner, "Politics in Zamboanga City," pages 13–35

1. Field research for this paper was undertaken in January 1987, October-November 1987, and February-March 1988. During these trips, the Comelec gave me access to electoral returns and other data in their files while City Hall and regional governmental offices furnished additional documentary information. Local newspapers were examined for the period under study. Numerous interviews and conversations were held with politicians, officials, journalists, and many other residents of Zamboanga City. I am most grateful for their cooperation.

2. National Economic and Development Authority (NEDA) Region IX, *Socio-economic Information on Western Mindanao* (Zamboanga City: NEDA, 1987), pp. 9–13.

3. NCSO (fn.2), p. 1.

4. NEDA (fn.3), p. 39.

5. NCSO (fn.2), p. 208.

6. NCSO (fn.6), p. 366, and Office of the City Planning and Development Coordinator (OCPDC), *Socio-economic Profile: City of Zamboanga.* (Zamboanga City: OCPDC, 1984), p. 6.

7. C.A. Carunungan, "He Left a Legacy of Courage and Honor," in A.M. Nieva, T.P. Torres and E. Sebastian, eds., *The Ballad of Nor Cesar: Selected Writings on a Legend of Far Zamboanga* (Manila: Dispatch Books, 1986), p. 71.

8. A.M. Nieva, "Coming Home, a Son of La Belle Finds Guns Outnumber Smiles," in Nieva et al., *Ballad of Nor Cesar*, p. 244.

9. J.M. Burns, *Leadership* (New York: Harper Colophon Books, 1978), p. 244.

10. Ibid., p. 246.

11. R. Fernandez, "Post Climaco Zamboanga," in Nieva et al., *Ballad of Nor Cesar*, p. 56.

12. *The Morning Times*, 28 January 1986.

13. *The Morning Times*, 11 January 1986.

14. *Zamboanga Times*, 27 January 1987.

15. *The Morning Times*, 5 February 1987.

16. *The Morning Times*, 3 February 1987.

17. *The Morning Times*, 11 February 1987.

18. *Philippine Daily Inquirer*, 24 February 1988.

19. *The Morning Times*, 20 June 1987.

20. Bureau of Agricultural Economics (BAE), *District III: Zamboanga City: A Municipal Data Base in Agriculture* (Quezon City: BAE, 1983).

21. *The Morning Times*, 14 November 1987.

22. *The Morning Times*, 10 January 1988.

23. See for example, W. Wolters, *Politics, Patronage and Class Conflict in Central Luzon* (The Hague: Institute of Social Studies, 1983) and O.D. van den Muijzenberg, "Political Violence in Ilocos Sur" (unpublished manuscript, n.d.).

24. *The Morning Times*, 1 and 2 October 1987.

25. Using OIC status to build political machines was noted at least in Central Luzon by B. Fegan, "The Rural Areas," in *The Philippines Under Aquino*, ed. P. Krinks (Canberra: Australian Development Studies Network, 1987), p. 68.

26. *The Morning Times*, 4 November 1987.

27. *The Morning Times*, 5 August 1987.

28. *The Morning Times*, 28 January 1988.

Notes to Bentley, "The Islamic City of Marawi," pages 36–58

1. The arrivals, departures, and intervening periods of research on which this paper is based were supported by Social Science Research Council Predoctoral and Postdoctoral Grants for Research in Southeast Asia. The research was facilitated through affiliations with the Institute of Philippine Culture (1977–79), the Dansalan Research Center (1977–79), and the University Research Center at the Mindanao State University (1977–79, 1987).

2. According to local clergy, who bore the sad duty of blessing the dead, over four hundred soldiers died in the battle, which was futile in any case since the rebels escaped.

3. I especially did not want to bring harm to Maranaos who answered my questions and who sometimes confided in me. People could choose to talk with me or not as their perceptions of their own interests dictated. It was, of course, not possible to completely avoid "choosing sides," and I felt there was little point in trying to hide my feelings about events as they transpired. At the same time, I tried to give all voices a fair hearing. I sometimes felt people overestimated the possible benefits of talking with me, but given their intimate awareness of local conditions and sensitivity to the political significance and possible consequences of virtually every action, I often let myself be guided by my informants' perceptions of risk.

4. *Bulletin Today*, 7 June 1987.

5. Local conditions precluded any but the most opportunistic selection of informants. Because of the limited time I was able to spend in Marawi (about four weeks in June–July and three weeks in August 1987) I tried to contact as many of my Maranao acquaintances as possible. By comparing recent reactions and assessments with those of an earlier time, I would better understand what changes had taken place and what they meant. In interpreting these comments, I have taken account of changes in my informants' lives (most are a decade older) and their changing expectations in life. I have also supplemented the interview material with information from several dozen new informants and substantial amounts of documentary materials concerning demographic and economic changes in Mindanao and Sulu.

6. For many years Marawi was the only chartered city whose tax receipts could not cover expenses, requiring that city operations be subsidized by the national government. I do not know if this situation still obtains.

7. These reverses include two earthquakes (in 1954 and 1976) that virtually destroyed the city's waterfront commercial district, and armed conflict, which for long periods disrupted local commerce.

8. For instance, the "Marawi pocket rebellion" in October 1972 provoked the Moro National Liberation Front into beginning its military drive to secede from the Philippine Republic and, thus, initiated open warfare between the AFP and BMA (Bangsa Moro Army). More recently, avid competition for local government appointments drew front-page coverage in Manila papers.

9. T. J. S. George, *Revolt in Mindanao: The Rise of Islam in Philippine Politics* (Kuala Lumpur: Oxford University Press, 1963), pp. 171ff; see also G. Carter Bentley, "Mohamad Ali Dimaporo: A Modern Maranao Datu," in *Politically Dominant Families in the Philippines*, ed. M. Cullinane, A. W. McCoy, and R. Paredes (Ann Arbor: Michigan Papers in South and Southeast Asian Studies, forthcoming).

10. Because he lacked a doctoral degree, Governor Dimaporo could not qualify for permanent appointment as president of the Mindanao State University (MSU). A budget officer of Region 12 pointed out to me that more money was spent on MSU than on all other government activities combined in Region 12 (Interview, 25 July 1987). Expendi-

tures per student at MSU consistently run about twice those at the University of the Philippines, Diliman, the flagship campus in the Philippine state university system.

11. As one MSU official said, "When he [Dimaporo] wanted something from Marcos, he just had to knock on his bedroom door" (Interview, 8 July 1987). Dimaporo was widely believed to have misappropriated millions of pesos from the MSU budget, though he repeatedly challenged his political opponents and the government's Commission on Audit to prove he had done so.

12. One faculty member half-jokingly called the dozen or so buildings comprising the MSU commercial center "the children of the gymnasium" since most of them were built from materials pilfered during the building of the athletic complex.

13. Steve Le Vine, "Filipino University Confronts a Legacy of Corruption and Violence," *Chronicle of Higher Education* 34 (7 October 1987):49–50.

14. *Veritas*, 27 April 1986.

15. In some ways Dimaporo's position in Marawi was analogous to that of Ilokano President Marcos and his Leyteña wife among the Tagalog blue-bloods of Manila. In Marawi, however, the elite are spoken of as "yellow-bloods" since yellow denotes royalty (Interview, 12 July 1987).

16. Melvin Mednick, *Encampment of the Lake: The Social Organization of a Moslem-Philippine (Moro) People*, Research Series No. 5 (Philippine Studies Program, University of Chicago, 1965).

17. Interview, 7 July 1987.

18. Interview, 8 July 1987.

19. G. Carter Bentley, "Comments on Maranao Kin Terms," *Dansalan Research Center Research Bulletin*, 3 (March 1978).

20. *Mr. & Ms.*, 15–21 March 1985.

21. *Veritas*, 29 January 1986, quoted in Lela Garner Noble, "Muslim Grievances and the Muslim Rebellion," in *Rebuilding a Nation: Philippine Challenges and American Policy*, ed. C. Lande (Washington, D.C.: Washington Institute Press, 1987), p. 426.

22. One possible factor in Dimakuta's decision to work against his son-in-law Dimaporo may have been lingering bitterness at the 1978 marriage of his grandson Abdullah to the daughter of Arsenio Quibransa, the Christian kingpin of Lanao del Norte and Ali's main opponent during the divisive election campaigns of 1970 and 1971. While this marriage had obvious political benefits for the Dimaporo family and for Abdullah's political career, his mother had opposed it, sentiments said to be shared by her father, ex-Governor Dimakuta (Interview, 4 July 1987).

23. Noble, "Muslim Grievances," p. 426.

24. Ibid.

25. Ibid.

26. Ibid., pp. 426–27.

27. According to Philippine Army records, Dimaporo signed a receipt for 1792 weapons, most of which were automatic and semiautomatic rifles (M–14 and M–16). See *Veritas*, 7–9 July 1987.

28. Communique of the IVth General Meeting of the MNLF Leadership (5 March 1985), p. 9.

29. A full-page campaign ad in the *Bulletin Today* (2 February 1986) bore the lurid headline "An Act of Betrayal" and showed a map of the Philippines with Mindanao, Sulu, and Palawan torn away. The text of the ad read in part,

It took the Filipino people centuries of search, at great sacrifice, to form a lasting unity, evolve a national polity and define their unique identity as a free and sovereign nation. Countless men and women have suffered and died for that cause. More will be summoned in the defense of our liberty.

And yet there are pretenders to leadership who have no qualms about subverting this priceless legacy. They seem to feel no remorse in diminishing it to serve an overwhelming ambition.

Such is the crime of the UNIDO which, through its representative Agapito "Butz" Aquino, compromised the national territory by agreeing to the formation of a separate Muslim state in Mindanao for the support of the MNLF warlord Nur Misuari.

Misuari himself has announced that Butz Aquino, brother-in-law and adviser to Presidential candidate Corazon Aquino, has entered into an agreement with him and the Moro National Liberation Front, giving away Muslim Mindanao to the secessionist group on behalf of a future Aquino-Laurel government.

This precipitate act borders on disloyalty to the nation. Political naivete may mitigate but cannot excuse the crime nor can it calm a nation's fears that such total recklessness can, at a future time, sunder a nation forged on the shared sacrifices of Muslim and Christian Filipinos alike.

30. They had good reason for their concern. For instance, in the 1978 referendum election on continuation of martial law, provincial vote totals were announced the day before the election and several ballot boxes were later found floating in Lake Lanao.

31. Noble, "Muslim Grievances," p. 427.

32. A *Bulletin Today* account (15 February 1986) of this interview continues

Dimaporo said that the overall margin of about 600,000 votes [sic] President Marcos [sic] over Corazon Aquino in the two autonomous regions (Region 9 and 12) were votes cast by grateful [sic] Muslims and Christians in recognition of the many developments that the President has given to the two regions.

He denied charges of alleged terrorism and rampant poll irregularities committed by the KBL. The charges were attributed to Member of Parliament Omar Dimaporo [sic] . . . He said there were instances in which MP Dianalan and his followers provoked KBL men during the election but they always avoided him (Dianalan) because a confrontation could trigger a bloody clash among his followers and Dianalan's armed men.

33. Muslim opposition figures met in Manila on 18 February and denounced the conduct of the elections in Regions 9 and 12. Among those attending were former Senator Mamintal Tamano, MP Omar Dianalan, Jamail Dianalan (Chairman of the Islamic Directorate of the Philippines), Saidamen Pangarungan (LABAN chair and president of the Muslim Association of the Philippines), and Haja Potri Zorayda Abbas Tamano (president of the Philippine Muslim Women's Association). Newspaper reports also list representatives from the Taraka Professional and Student Association, Young Muslim Association, Muslim Lawyers League, Basak Muslim Association, and Basak Youth Reformist Association, all of which were based in Lanao del Sur (*Bulletin Today*, 19 February 1986). Notably, this opposition meeting, which purported to represent all sectors of the Islamic Philippines, appears to have been dominated by Maranao from Governor Dimaporo's home province.

34. Leaders of Catholic religious organizations on the campus provided an organization focus for anti-Marcos and anti-Dimaporo protests at MSU, suggesting a structure of opposing forces similar in some ways to that arrayed at EDSA.

35. Noble, "Muslim Grievances," p. 427.

36 *Bulletin Today*, 4 March 1987.

37. He went on to say, "that his men will help identify those persons possessing loose firearms if the Constabulary is earnest in going after them. He, however, pleaded that the military should allow him and his men to keep their firearms because they have

killed many NPAs and MNLFs and they themselves will be easy targets if they'll lose their firearms, 'just like the late Gov. Federico Peralta of Tarlac after the military confiscated his guns.'" (*Veritas*, 27 April 1986.)

38. *Asiaweek*, 11 May 1986. With regard to possible autonomy, Dimaporo told a more recent interviewer, "I told this to Misuari, if he wants independence not only for the Muslim [sic] but for all the people of Mindanao, then maybe many people will join you" (*Mindanaw Week*, 10–16 August 1987, p. 9).

39. Noble, "Muslim Grievances," p. 431.

40. See, for instance, R. J. May, "A Perspective from Mindanao," *The Philippines under Aquino* (Canberra: The Australian Development Studies Network, 1987), p. 72, which says fourteen people were killed during the fighting. Other reports maintain that no lives were lost and only a few injuries were sustained in the transition (see, for instance, C. O. Arguillas, "The takeover," *Veritas*, (8 May 1987).

41. A series of meetings by opposition Muslim culminated in a 18 February rally of the Islamic Conference of the Philippines at the Makati Sports Complex which passed six resolutions (*Bulletin Today*, 5 March 1986; see also reports of 1 and 4 March) calling for

1. Immediate and full implementation of the Tripoli Agreement and renegotiation with the MNLF;
2. Appointment of qualified Muslims to government positions under a scheme of equitable representation;
3. Release of all Muslim political prisoners;
4. Appointment of MP Omar Dianalan to the Ministry of Agrarian Reform;
5. Repatriation of Muslim refugees; and
6. Muslim representation in the commissions on good government and re-organization.

42. Noble, "Muslim Grievances," p. 432.

43. Virtually any Manila newspaper from the first half of August may be consulted for details of the story. *Malaya* (12 August 1986), for instance, reported

Pangarungan, said to be the only PDP-LABAN governor in the region, has come under fire from political leaders in the area for his alleged "inability to contain the rash of kidnapings" in the province.

This developed as followers of Princes Tarhata Alonto Lucman belied Pangarungan's claim that the appointment of the princess—who was formerly Lanao del Sur governor before warlord Ali Dimaporo—would establish an Alonto dynasty in the province.

In a press statement furnished *Malaya*, they claimed instead that the 35-year-old governor-designate has tried to establish his own dynasty by appointing alleged relatives to posts in the local administration.

At a press conference, Pangarungan reportedly argued that the kidnapings had been solved, that peace and order were not deteriorating, and that kidnapings were nothing new in Lanao in any case. He further, "pointed to a probable 'troika conspiracy' among followers of Dimaporo, Princess Tarhata and ex-MP Omar Dianalan, to oust him from the governorship," while

Tarhata's followers, meanwhile, claim Pangarungan's support comes mainly from the military, and does not count the majority of the predominantly Muslim civilian populace. They charged that Pangarungan cannot even go out of Marawi proper without his usual band of 'heavily armed bodyguards.' 'So how can he claim there is peace in our province?' they asked. (*Malaya*, 12 August 1986).

44. I do not know official estimates of the crowd's size. Unofficial estimates given to me ranged as high as 15,000 people.

45. Noble, "Muslim Grievances," pp. 431–32.

46. The MNLF position was that President Aquino should implement the autonomy provisions of the 1976 Tripoli ceasefire agreement by decree. They maintained that the agreement represented a treaty obligation of the Philippine government which could not be altered by the new constitution which went into effect in February 1987. They also feared, realistically, that once the overwhelmingly Christian Congress became involved, prospects for meaningful autonomy would be greatly diminished.

47. Transcripts of the negotiations were published in installments by the *Mindanao Cross*, a weekly newspaper published in Cotabato City. While the newspaper took editorial positions supporting the government's hardening stand against Muslim autonomy, the transcripts themselves raise doubts about whether government negotiators, especially Philippine Ambassador the United States Emmanuel Pelaez, were disposed to regard any demand emanating from the MNLF as legitimate.

48. On the other hand, many Christian residents were relieved that the government had finally returned to its senses.

49. Lela Garner Noble, "Muslim Separatism in the Philippines: The Making of a Stalemate," *Asian Survey* 21 (1981): 1097–1114. See also Noble, "Muslim Grievances," pp. 428–29.

50. Despite the harassment and kidnapings to which Christian missionaries were occasionally subject in Lanao del Sur, none had ever been killed or even seriously harmed. Most kidnap victims commented on the care with which they were treated by their captors. The killing of missionaries was thus unprecedented in this area.

51. The crime remained unsolved during my stay in Marawi. Since most crimes in Lanao are solved quickly or not at all I expect it remains a mystery today.

52. See, for instance, *Manila Chronicle*, 3 July 1987; *Malaya*, 24 July 1987.

53. The only election to that point had been the referendum election on the New Constitution held in February 1987.

54. This odd alliance between members of the Marcos and Aquino parties in opposition to a Laurel partisan reflects the dominance of local and regional over national political alignments in Lanao.

55. Candidates in Lanao del Sur District 1 collectively spent between fifteen and twenty million pesos in the campaign. The largest spender was Normallah Pacasum, Gov. Lucman's daughter, who reportedly spent over six million pesos. Omar Dianalan spent the second largest amount, about five million pesos. Their opponents charged that each had siphoned off government funds during the campaign. Dianalan accused Governor Lucman of looting the provincial road maintenance fund. Dianalan's brother, Director of the Office of Muslim Affairs and Cultural Communities, was accused of paying for campaign travel and other expenses through his office. Accusations against the latter were sufficiently serious that the Commission on Audit suspended Dianalan's right to issue checks against the bank account of his office.

56. In Lanao del Sur, Congressional District 1 generally covers territory north and east of Lake Lanao while District 2 includes areas south and west of the lake. In Lanao del Norte, District 2 covers approximately the southwestern half of the province.

57. Interview, 2 September 1987.

58. This trend ran exactly counter to my expectations and caused me considerable disquiet during my stay in Marawi.

59. Alonto was elsewhere at the time. Security probably would have been tighter had he been present.

60. *Philippine Inquirer*, 12 August 1987.

61. *Malaya*, 14 August 1987. Informants on the MSU campus indicated that kidnapers also demanded the resignation of MSU Vice-President for Finance and Administration Tocod Macaraya and the university's Chief of Security (interview, 15 August 1987).

62. Interview, 15 August 1987.

63. In a wry comment on government development projects, the flurry of kidnaping prompted jokes (among Maranao) that "Kidnaping is now a cottage industry in Lanao."

64. "Islamic fundamentalism makes its mark in the Philippines," *Financial Times*, 8 March 1988.

65. The supposed plot, its discovery, and its aftermath, are described in the *Mindanao Cross*, 16 December 1989. None of the supposed plotters is named in the newspaper accounts, but several scholars from Mindanao with whom I spoke indicated that Congressman Dimaporo was supposed to have been one of its prime movers.

66. For a Maranao perspective on the autonomy issue, see the compilation of documents and commentaries in *Autonomy for Muslim Mindanao: The RCC Untold Story*, Taha M. Basman, Mama S. Lalanto, and Nagasura T. Madale (NP: B-lal Publishers, 1989).

67. May, "A Perspective from Mindanao," p. 73.

68. Interviews, 7 July, 12 July, 14 July 1987.

69. Interviews, 12 July 1987.

70. These issues are discussed in more detail in G. Carter Bentley, "Law, Disputing and Ethnicity in Lanao, Philippines" (Ph.D. diss., University of Washington, Seattle, 1982), pp. 150–206.

71. See, for instance, B. R. O'G. Anderson, "The Idea of Power in Javanese Culture," in *Culture and Politics in Indonesia*, ed. Claire Holt (Ithaca, N.Y.: Cornell University Press, 1972), pp. 1–70; G. Carter Bentley, "Indigenous States of Southeast Asia," *Annual Review of Anthropology* 15 (1986): 275–305; A. C. Milner, *Kerajaan* (Tucson: University of Arizona Press, 1983); Shelly Errington, *Meaning and Power in the Southeast Asian Realm* (Princeton: Princeton University Press, 1989).

72. G. Carter Bentley, "Hermeneutics and the World Construction in Maranao Disputing," *American Ethnologist* 11 (1984): 649.

73. Although all power ultimately comes from God, it suffuses the world and objects in it in differing concentrations. Hence one may seek amulets, special Qur'anic verses, special stones, and other objects by which to enhance one's own effectiveness in the world while natural repositories of spiritual power (e.g., balete trees) or its material manifestations (e.g., waterspouts) are treated with considerable respect (see Bentley, "Law, Disputing, and Ethnicity" pp. 189–90).

74. Anderson, "The Idea of Power."

75. The following observations are drawn from my notes of interviews conducted between 26 June and 4 July 1987. Surface levels in Lake Lanao actually have become less stable as a result of hydroelectric power projects along the Agus River. According to National Power Corporation records, however, in recent years flooding along the Agus River has been more of a problem than has lowering the lake surface and the surrounding water table. Nevertheless, the impression that the lake is receding continues to hold sway. Since Lake Lanao stands as a focal symbol of Maranao life and society, I take such statements to signify a sense of waning vitality, a sapping of life-force evident in references to a decreasing supply of food and the new difficulties in praying. The symbolic and economic centrality of Lake Lanao in Maranao life is discussed in G. Zaide and M. Saber, "How the Angels Built Lake Lanao," in *The Maranao*, ed. M. Saber and A. T. Madale (Manila: Solidaridad, 1975), pp. 1–3; D. K. Villaluz, "The Lake's Scientific and Socio-Economic Importance," in *The Maranao*, pp. 4–7; D. S. Rabor and L. Florendo-

Rabor, "Ecological Source of Life and Progress," in *The Maranao*, pp. 12–20; L. Washburn, "Our Lake for Others: The Maranao and the Agus River Hydroelectric Project," *Dansalan Research Center Research Bulletin* 3 (November–December 1977).

76. My companion at the time commented cynically that after local elections (then expected in November), the machinery would disappear and the garbage piles would continue their monumental growth.

77. Dimaporo made this statement during a radio interview on 16 July 1987. It struck me at the time that Dimaporo was making both an observation about the state of affairs and declaring his own capacity to bring that state of affairs about. After all, the capacity to act effectively and to bring order into the world is simultaneously the capacity to render one's opponent's actions, and words, ineffective. For this reason, I predicted (in my journal) that some dramatic act of lawlessness would soon occur to confirm Dimaporo's statement. Twenty-four days later the mass kidnaping of students, faculty, and staff from MSU took place.

78. See, for instance, M. Saber, M. M. Tamano, and C. K. Warriner, "The Maratabat of the Maranao," *Philippine Sociological Review* 8 (1960): 10–15; Carlton Reimer, "Maranao Maratabat and Concepts of Pride, Honor, and Self Esteem," *Dansalan Research Center Occasional Papers*, no. 4, 1976.

79. Bentley, "Law, Disputing, and Ethnicity," pp. 186–88.

80. *Philippine Inquirer*, 20 June 1987.

81. Melvin Mednick, "Sultans and Mayors: The Relation of a National to an Indigenous Political System," *Il Politico* (1961): 142–47; M. Saber, "The Transition from a Traditional to a Legal Authority System" (Ph.D. diss., University of Kansas, 1967).

82. The means by which the National Power Corporation obtained land in Saguiaran, Lanao del Sur, for its Agus II hydroelectric plant provides a dramatic illustration of this process. See L. Washburn, "Our Land for Others? Maranao Muslim vs. the Philippine National Power Corporation" (Paper presented to the Association of Asian Studies, Washington, D.C., 21–23 March 1980).

83. Programs aimed at enhancing agricultural production have been widely (and I believe accurately) interpreted by Maranao farmers as increasing Muslim farmers' dependency on external (esp. state) sources of credit, fertilizer, pesticides, and other production inputs.

84. Mednick, "Encampment of the Lake"; Bentley, "Law, Disputing, and Ethnicity."

85. For clarification of this point, see J. Black-Michaud, *Cohesive Force* (New York: St. Martin's, 1975); P. Bourdieu, *Outline of a Theory of Practice* (Cambridge: Cambridge University Press, 1977), pp. 183ff. In this regard, Kiefer characterized Tausug ideology as "rank conscious egalitarianism" (see T. M. Kiefer, *Tausug Armed Conflict: The Social Organization of Military Activity in a Philippine Moslem Society*, Research Series No. 7 [Philippine Studies Program, University of Chicago, 1969]).

86. Bourdieu, *Outline of a Theory*, p. 196.

87. G. Carter Bentley, "Ethnicity and Practice," *Comparative Studies in Society and History* 29 (1987): 24–55.

88. Interviews (12–14 July 1987); see also G. Carter Bentley, "Rebirth of the Moro: Philippine Muslim Responses to Christian Domination" (paper presented at the Social Science Research Council Conference on "Muslims under non-Muslim Rule," Delhi, India, 14–16 December 1987).

89. Bentley, "Mohamad Ali Dimaporo: A Modern Maranao Datu."

Notes to Mojares, "Rural District in Cebu Province," pages 59–81

This is a revised version of a paper presented at the "Local Perspectives on the Transition from Marcos to Aquino" Conference, University of Hawaii, Honolulu, Hawaii, USA, 16–18 May 1988. I wish to thank all the conference participants, particularly Ben Kerkvliet and Brian Fegan. I also thank Harold Olofson, my colleague at the University of San Carlos, for his comments.

1. My knowledge of Valladolid and Carcar is based on field and archival work done in rather discontinuous fashion over the years 1976–81, 1983–85, and 1987–88. My initial research was focused on local history and theater. I have since collected data on contemporary developments in the area and the theoretical issue of how "communities" are constituted. Recent data include interviews with 220 respondents in Carcar and Valladolid—conducted from April 1987 to January 1988—on a wide range of topics, including life histories and politics (see Resil B. Mojares, *Theater in Society, Society in Theater: Social History of a Cebuano Village, 1840–1940* [Quezon City: Ateneo de Manila University Press, 1985]; *Idem.*, "Constituting Communities: Ideological Formation in Rural Philippines" [paper prepared for the Rockefeller Foundation's "Reflections on Development" Program, Bellagio, Italy, August 1988]).

2. Paul Rabinow, *Symbolic Domination: Cultural Form and Historical Change in Morocco* (Chicago: University of Chicago Press, 1975), p. 4.

3. In 1907, the Philippine electorate was 1 percent of the population. It was 3 percent in 1916 and then rose to 10 percent in the 1930s, 20 percent in the 1940s, 30 percent by the 1960s, and 40 percent by the 1980s.

4. This is based on the examination of the national censuses of 1903, 1918, 1939, 1970, 1975, and 1980. The pre–1940 census figures indicate the following percentages for the agricultural sector: 44 percent in 1903, 49 percent in 1918 and 1939 for Cebu province, and 37 percent in 1903 for Carcar. For reasons that cannot be detailed here, the reliability of the 1903 census is questionable. Moreover, all three prewar censuses underreport workers in agriculture by classifying women engaged in housekeeping (who may be engaged in farm work at the same time) in the "Domestic & Personal Services" category. I estimate that the actual pre–1940 percentages must be closer to 50 percent or 51 percent. A further limitation in the census data is that, in most cases, no information is available on secondary occupations.

5. Canute Vandermeer, "Corn on the Island of Cebu" (Ph.D. diss., University of Michigan, 1962), p. 104. Vandermeer says that, as of 1960, farm families comprised 65.1 percent of the population of Cebu province but that well over half of these families obtained income from nonagricultural pursuits.

6. Sources for landholding data are (1) Lot Data Computation Records and Numerical List of Claimants, Carcar Cadastre, Case No. 3, 1914 (Bureau of Lands, Region VII, Cebu City), and (2) Tax Declaration Records, 1987 (Municipal Assessor's Office, Carcar, Cebu). These sources occasion the use of the cadastral lot (rather than 'farm') as the unit of analysis. No precise data on farm size exist for Valladolid although local estimates (official and unofficial) of an average farm size of a hectare for Carcar municipality and less-than-a-hectare for Valladolid support the general argument of increasing parcellization in this paper.

On fishponds, data are from the Bureau of Fisheries and Aquatic Resources (BFAR), Southern Cebu Field Office, Carcar, Cebu.

7. See Mary R. Hollnsteiner, *The Dynamics of Power in a Philippine Municipality* (Quezon City: Community Development Research Council, University of the Philippines, 1963); Willem Wolters, *Politics, Patronage and Class Conflict in Central Luzon* (Quezon City: New Day Publishers, 1984), p. 180.

8. *Excerpts from the Minutes of the Municipal Council, Carcar, Cebu* (a series of volumes from 1952 to 1987 at the Carcar Municipal Hall, Carcar, Cebu).

9. See Resolution Nos. 133 (3 October 1972), 21 (6 February 1973), and 90 (17 July 1973) (in *Excerpts*, 1972 and 1973).

10. The Valladolid chapter of the Federation of Free Farmers (FFF), with around forty members, was organized in 1972. Valladolid was the site of the regional seminar because it is partly within the limits of the Hacienda Osmeña, the major land reform site in Cebu, and also because of the presence of a religious house of the Sacred Heart Mission Seminary in the barrio. (The FFF, it is to be remembered, is closely associated with sectors of the Catholic Church.) On the raid: Interviews with Teofilo Navasquez and Homobono Apura, 22 April and 26 May 1987, Valladolid, Carcar; *The Freeman*, 26 November 1973.

11. In the 1978 elections, the Kilusang Bagong Lipunan fielded Eduardo Gullas, Emilio Osmeña, Antonio Cuenco, Rene Espina, Ramon Durano II, Pablo Garcia, Emerito Calderon, Lino Chatto, Tomas Toledo, Andres Bustamante, Gonzalo Catan, Romulo Senining, and Victor de la Serna. The Pusyon Bisaya candidates were Filemon Fernandez, Hilario Davide, Jorge Kintanar, Bartolome Cabangbang, Valentino Legaspi, Julian Yballe, Alfonso Corominas Jr., Mariano Logarta, Natalio Bacalso, Enrique Medina Jr., Eutiquio Cimafranca, Dominador Pernes, and Jesus Villegas.

12. See *The Freeman*, 12 June 1980; 5 July 1980; and 22 September 1980.

13. Voting statistics for Valladolid in the 1978 and 1984 elections are not available (though local sources say the results replicated the provincial outcome) due to the disorganized state of election records both in the municipal and provincial offices of the Commission on Elections (Comelec).

14. There is another link of the village to the firm. San Miguel Corporation owns 13.7 hectares in Valladolid, acquired for development as a dairy farm. This project, however, has been indefinitely shelved.

15. Bonifacio Kabahar of Cebu City, referred to as "Kumander Mike," was killed midmorning, 11 May 1987, near the schoolhouse of Balungag, San Fernando. Although he was prominently mentioned in anticommunist radio broadcasts as a leader of the New People's Army in Cebu, the military has no evidence that he was indeed one. His assailants (widely believed to be anticommunist vigilantes) remain unknown (see *Sun Star Daily*, 12 May 1987).

16. Even a cursory survey of occupational patterns in Valladolid shows this diversity: farm workers, fishermen, workers in shoe and handicraft factories, tuba gatherers and middlemen, civil servants, fishpond workers, tricycle operators and drivers, storeowners, bangus fry traders, artisans, and others. One is impressed by the multiplicity of linkages, whether it is the household or the individual which is the unit of analysis: e.g., a farmer who is a tenant to three different landowners, a bangus fry collector who trades independently or through a middleman who also works part time as groundskeeper for a city-based fishpond owner, a casual farm worker who also raises fighting cocks and is on the lookout for job opportunities in the city, or a tenant's wife who does piecework both for a handicraft capitalist and a local shoe factory.

17. Clifford Geertz, *Agricultural Involution: The Processes of Ecological Change in Indonesia* (Berkeley: University of California Press, 1963).

18. Hollnsteiner, *Dynamics of Power*; Carl H. Lande, *Leaders, Factions, and Parties: The Structure of Philippine Politics* (New Haven: Southeast Asia Studies, Yale University, 1965).

19. Nicos Mouzelis, "Ideology and class politics: a critique of Ernesto Laclau," *New Left Review* 112 (November–December 1978): 47.

Notes to Szanton, "A Western Visayan Municipality," pages 82–104

1. Cristina Blanc-Szanton, *A Right to Survive: Subsistence Marketing in a Lowland Philippine Town* (Quezon City: Institute of Philippine Culture, 1976); "The Uses of Compadrinazgo: Views from a Philippine Town," *Philippine Sociological Review* 27 (3) (1979): 161–80; "Personalized Exchange: The Suki Relationship," in *Society, Culture and the Filipino,* ed. Mary R. Hollnsteiner (Quezon City: Institute of Philippine Culture, 1979); "The New Filipino Transnationalism" in *The Transnationalization of Migration,* ed. Linda Basch, Cristina Blanc-Szanton, Nina Schiller (New York: CUNY New Series on Ethnicity) (forthcoming).

2. David Szanton, "Estancia, Iloilo: Town in Transition," in *Modernization: Its Impact in the Philippines,* IPC Papers No. 4, ed. Walden Bello and Maria C. Roldan (Quezon City: Institute of Philippine Culture, 1967); "The Fishing Industry of Estancia, Iloilo," in *Modernization: Its Impact in the Philippines,* II, IPC Papers No. 5, ed. George H. Guthrie, Frank Lynch and Walden F. Bello (Quezon City: Institute of Philippine Culture, 1967), pp. 64–86; "Entrepreneurship in a Rural Philippine Community," (Ph.D. diss., Department of Anthropology, University of Chicago, 1970); *Estancia in Transition: Economic Growth in a Rural Philippine Community,* IPC Paper No. 9 (Quezon City: Institute of Philippine Culture, 1971; reprinted by Ateneo de Manila with updated last chapter, 1979).

3. Cristina Blanc-Szanton, "People in Movement: Social Mobility and Leadership in a Central Thailand Municipality" (Ph.D. diss., Department of Anthropology, Columbia University, 1982); "Thai and Sino-Thai in Small Town Thailand: Changing Patterns of Interethnic Relations," *The Chinese in Southeast Asia,* ed. Linda Y.C. Lim and L.A. Peter Gosling (Center for South and Southeast Asian Studies, University of Michigan, 1983); "Big Women and Politics in a Philippine Fishing Town," in *Women and Politics in Twentieth Century Africa and Asia, Studies in Third World Societies,* n. 16 (Williamsburg: College of William and Mary, 1981); "Women and Men in Iloilo, Philippines, 1902–1970," in *Women of Southeast Asia,* ed. Penny Van Esterik (DeKalb: Northern Illinois University, 1982); "Collision of Cultures: Historical Reformulations of Gender Under Colonialism in the Lowland Visayas, Philippines," in *Power and Difference: Essays on the Paradox of Gender in Island Southeast Asia,* ed. Jane Atkinson and Shelley Errington (Stanford: Stanford University Press, 1990).

4. I would like to thank Willie Arce, Scott Guggenheim, John Girling, Jean Illo, Romana Pahilanga, Lourdes Franco, and Pablo, Adela and Stella Tamesis for sharing their thoughts about the Philippines and Estancia with me. A special note of thanks is also due David Szanton, with whom I worked side by side in Estancia up to the early 1980s and with whom I have compared and discussed data many times. The people of Estancia were hospitable and very gracious with their time, always interested in our effort. I am grateful to them. This article could not have been written without their help.

5. Three months after the election, the great excitement about People Power was still there, but there was also an increasing rift and much bitterness between Marcos and Aquino supporters because of bureaucratic appointments and the loss of able people in key government positions. Bureaucrats who had voted for Marcos to protect their jobs but secretly campaigned for Aquino felt inappropriately discriminated against. Not enough efforts were made to heal the wounds, was the recurring comment of Marcos's supporters.

6. The town of Estancia gave Marcos a slight majority (45 votes according to the official count). Aside from captive Bayas (a block of 658 votes) which opted overwhelm-

ingly for Marcos following the wishes of its owner, Mina Reyes, the barrios showed mixed voting. Fishing barrios, however, had often a strong showing, if not a majority, for Aquino, while rural interior barrios more often favored Marcos.

7. Aquino visited Estancia once, during her Iloilo campaign tour. But Butz Aquino visited it one week or so before the election and some assemblymen also came (Caram, Salcedo, Defensor). On the Marcos side, Jose Aldeguer, former Iloilo Representative and Speaker Pro-Tempore of the House, visited Mina Reyes three times before the elections, asking her to set up a campaign meeting in town. Since no action was taken, the KBL went from house to house to give money before the elections. It was said that the KBL spent between 10,000 and 700,000 pesos in "newly pressed" 20–peso bills in Estancia. Barrio captains were to get some thousands. Close to election time, hired KBL people went around town, according to informants, throwing money bundles into house balconies, then asking people if they had received them. People's affirmative answers at that moment, however, did not assure the KBL their vote, as they had hoped.

8. Blanc-Szanton, *A Right to Survive*, pp. 3–15; Szanton, *Estancia in Transition*, pp. 6–9, 15–17.

9. Blanc-Szanton, *A Right to Survive*, pp. 7, 40, 77; Szanton, "The Fishing Industry of Estancia," p. 8.

10. Because of a recent increase in the municipal income designating second-class municipalities (from 100,000 pesos to 300,000 pesos a year), Estancia had, in fact, slipped to a third-class municipality status in 1988. The overall population of the municipality had at the same time increased to well over 20,000 people.

11. The main successes were in the wholesale of fresh and dried fish. At night, one could hear the trucks, loaded with the boxes of fish on ice that had piled up during the day on the market landing- or in *bodegas*, leave for Iloilo City or Capiz. A few former policemen, teachers, shopkeepers, even fish retailers, had grown to own two to three fishing boats and even to open stores in Divisoria, Manila. (But there were comparable cases already in 1967.) A few of the larger fishing outfit operators and entrepreneurs were also doing well. Others who sold *ilada* (iced fish boxes) were said to be Tagalog transients from Manila. They came to make business, stayed in the town, bought fish and sent it to Manila. Most successful shopkeepers were now also "transients," who came from elsewhere to start a business and make money in Estancia.

12. At first, young men left for the Middle East as industrial workers, while nurses went to the U.S. Today, educated young women are following them as service workers in the Middle East, but are also going as domestics to Europe, Hong Kong, Singapore, as well as the U.S. Overseas remittances have become in the 1980s the major source of foreign exchange for the country, and overseas workers have been called by Mrs. Aquino as the "new Filipino heroes and heroines."

13. "Illegal Gambling in Estancia," *Panay News*, 23 June 1988.

14. Because of government shortage of funds, there are only fourteen regular Estancia policemen for a population of well over 20,000 people, far fewer than the Napolcom rule of one policeman for 1,000 people. Police operations were severely limited by the lack of a vehicle at the time. (They were particularly concerned about that handicap because of NPA sightings in the fishing barrios in May, June, July 1988.) Furthermore, a limited budget did not allow them to pay their informants properly. And they were concerned about the likelihood of being placed again under the mayor's control, a possibility currently envisioned by Mrs. Aquino. "When that happens, we acquire two new bosses," they would say, "the Mayor and the Congressman." The law and order situation seemed a little better by June 1989, but problems of illegal gambling and drug pushing had not yet been eradicated.

15. They would spend time discussing the state of people's present alliances and their potential strategies of factional association in the future. In other words, the political scientist's model was also definitely one of their conscious models as well. See Carl Lande, *Leaders, Factions and Parties: The Structure of Philippine Politics*, Monograph Series 6, Southeast Asia Studies (Yale University, 1965); James Scott, "The Erosion of Patron Client Bonds and Social Change in Rural Southeast Asia," *Journal of Asian Studies* 32 (1972): 5–37; B. Kerkvliet, "Understanding Politics in a Nueva Ecija Rural Community" (this volume).

16. Scott, "Erosion," pp. 5–37; *The Moral Economy of the Peasantry* (New Haven: Yale University Press, 1978), chapter 7; Szanton, *Estancia in Transition*, pp. 46–53.

17. Blanc-Szanton, "The Uses of Compadrinazgo: Views from a Philippine Town"; Szanton, "Entrepreneurship in a Rural Philippine Community"; Scott, "Erosion"; Scott, *Moral Economy*; Blanc-Szanton, *A Right to Survive*.

18. The road from Iloilo to Estancia was a good example of a checkered port barrel electoral road. It was a mosaic of cemented and noncemented sections, according to the level of commitment of the local political families to major politicians. The carrot-and-stick approach to the Estancia politics of the 1960s and early 1970s is particularly evident if one focuses on elite family politics and gender roles (see Blanc-Szanton, "Big Women and Politics in a Philippine Fishing Town").

The Estancia municipal council or the Reyeses generally took pragmatic decisions to support one candidate or another on the basis of keeping options open and satisfying all potential winners by promising but not necessarily delivering votes. Thus a Nacionalista candidate for governor, despite assurances, unexpectedly lost the Estancia votes to an Estancia-born Liberal incumbent in 1967. And unwanted runningmates were literally cut from voting lists to increase votes of other candidates who were close relatives. Pragmatic considerations about how to obtain barrio improvements in exchange for votes were also emphasized during mayoral campaigning in the barrios.

19. Szanton, *Estancia in Transition*, pp. 26–33, 118–21.

20. By July 1988, in Estancia, there were also about seventeen *likum-likum* —a new fishing technique with outriggers, introduced by Samareños, that used 22 people and cost about 500,000 pesos—and there were purse seine costing over a million pesos.

21. Those with more difficult landlords were already angry:

Just imagine if you owe the landowner 10 sacks, during harvest time, you pay another 10 sacks. If you cannot pay now the 20, by next harvest time, you pay 40 sacks. My! That was the situation before the land reform. But we managed to pay it all. Just imagine you have to sacrifice and sacrifice. While I was still an only child, my father had been making those kinds of payments for years. Now, with many more of us, brothers and sisters, it's still the same. Father was not able to send us to school because of the payments he can barely meet.

But in case land reform is discontinued and the owner takes back the land, we hope that he will allow us who farm the land to continue doing so, and not turn it over to other persons. It would be better if the farmers themselves will petition the President that their land will not be taken from them. That is the problem now, because the owners are taking advantage of the situation. They got back the land and put others to farm it. If the landowner takes the land back, he should make the one working it continue doing so. I think it's really unreasonable and painful that the land be worked by others. Yes, that's the fear, that the land taken back is given to another. If that happens, according to farmers, they will be forced to join the NPA rebels. That's really mean. What will happen once the people are deprived of their livelihood? How many years have we been farming? Almost twenty years, and just think if within an hour the farm is taken away from us! I think I will be forced to kill. Anyway, we will also die—of hunger, since we shall have no more livelihood. (English translations of other long quotes in Hiligaynon which were collected from farmers, men and women).

22. See in this volume, J. Eder, "Political Transition in a Palawan Farming Community"; also Ross Marlay, "The Political Legacy of Marcos; The Political Inheritance of Aquino" in *Rebuilding a Nation: Philippine Challenge and American Policy*, ed. C. Lande (Washington, D.C.: Washington Institute Press, 1987), pp. 327–28.

23. The Charismatics belong to Pentecostal movements (which originated in Ann Arbor, Michigan). They had grown strong among Catholic and Protestant groups in the Philippines, and actively campaigned for Aquino during the elections. Nationally, the National Council of Protestant Churches aligned itself with Aquino but looked with concern at the growing links between the Catholic Church and the Aquino government. The churches of Aglipay and Iglesia ni Kristo supported Marcos. Though represented in Estancia, none of these churches were particularly active during the 1986 elections.

24. The new land reform program finally received a definite initial commitment by the Aquino cabinet in June 1987 and was initiated in July 1987. The so-called category *A* (Tenanted Rice and Corn Lands), were to be transferred to the tenants by 1989. The other three categories of *B* (Foreclosed, Public and Sequestered Lands), *C* (Fishponds and Plantations), and *D* (Private Agricultural Lands in the hands of Corporations) were to be land-reformed in succession, every fourth year (*Salient features of the Comprehensive Agrarian Reform Program, CARP,* Department of Agrarian Reform, 1988, p. 25; interviews with officials of the CARP office in Batasan, July 1988). Final surveys were in process and titles were starting to reach farmers in Estancia in July 1988. However, the final Land Reform Law (Republic Act 6657), which was passed by both Houses on 7 June 1988, had undergone major revisions with respect to the initial CARP plan. It contained serious loopholes in favor of the landlords. This was to come to the farmers' attention, however, through direct experience, only by late 1988 and early 1989. They did not yet seem aware of the implications of Republic Act 6657 when I interviewed them.

25. Payment in kind (i.e., through rice sacks at harvest), favored by some landlords, was actually very costly to the farmers, because it was based on particularly low prices for rice at that time of the year (down to 35 pesos a sack at harvest). Even with controlled prices, a sack of rice could be sold in 1988 for 110–120 pesos during the year and for up to 140–150 pesos at planting time (i.e., three to four times as much).

Notes to McCoy, "Planter Power in La Carlota City," pages 105–42

This essay has benefited from critical comments by Daniel Doeppers, John Roosa and David Streckfuss of the University of Wisconsin-Madison; Ruby Paredes of the University of Michigan; Rosanne Rutten of the University of Amsterdam; and Brian Fegan of Macquarie University. I am also indebted to Ben Kerkvliet of University of Hawaii and Resil Mojares of the University of San Carlos for their thoughtful editorial remarks. Finally, I am grateful to Don Emmerson of the University of Wisconsin for his suggestions for the conclusion.

1. *Philippine Daily Inquirer,* 17 October 1986.

2. Frank Lynch, SJ, "Big and Little People: Social Class in the Philippines," in *Philippine Society and the Individual: Selected Essays of Frank Lynch, 1949–1976,* ed. Aram A.

Yengoyan and Perla Q. Makil (Ann Arbor: Center for South and Southeast Asian Studies, 1984), pp. 96–98; Frank Lynch, SJ, *Social Class in a Bicol Town* (Chicago: Philippine Studies Program, University of Chicago, 1959); Carl Lande, *Leaders, Factions, and Parties: The Structure of Philippine Politics* (New Haven: Southeast Asian Studies, Yale University, 1965), pp. 24–83; Kit G. Machado, "From Traditional Faction to Machine: Changing Patterns of Political Leadership and Organization in the Rural Philippines," *Journal of Asian Studies* 33 (1974): 523–47; Kit G. Machado, "Changing Patterns of Leadership Recruitment and the Emergence of the Professional Politician in Philippine Local Politics," in *Political Change in the Philippines: Studies of Local Politics Preceding Martial Law*, ed. Benedict J. Kerkvliet (Honolulu: University Press of Hawaii, 1974), pp. 77–129; Mary R. Hollnsteiner, *The Dynamics of Power in a Philippine Municipality* (Quezon City: Community Development Research Council, University of the Philippines, 1963), pp. 28–85.

3. Benedict J. Kerkvliet, *The Huk Rebellion: A Study of Peasant Revolt in the Philippines* (Berkeley: University of California Press, 1977), chap. 1.

4. Ibid., p. 251.

5. For Negros Occidental province as a whole, 70 percent of the arable land was planted to sugarcane in 1971. See National Census and Statistics Authority, Republic of the Philippines, *Negros Occidental: 1971 Census of Agriculture* (Manila: National Economic and Development Authority, 1974), pp. 3, 14.

6. See, Alfred W. McCoy, "A Queen Dies Slowly: The Rise and Decline of Iloilo City," in *Philippine Social History: Global Trade and Local Transformations*, ed. A.W. McCoy and Ed C. de Jesus (Quezon City: Ateneo de Manila University Press, 1982), pp. 311–26.

7. Central Azucarera de La Carlota, "District Final Estimate CY 1985–86" (La Carlota, 29 August 1986); Fr. Hector Mauri, "Eduardo Cojuangco" (memo, n.d.)

8. Asociacion de Agricultores de La Carlota y Pontevedra, *Memoria Anual 1924–1925* (Iloilo City: La Editorial, 1925), pp. 33–36; *Memoria Anual 1949–1950*, pp. 8–12; *Annual Report Crop 1974–75*, pp. 12–48.

9. Philippine Islands, Department of Commerce and Police, Bureau of Labor, *Third Annual Report of the Bureau of Labor* (Manila: Bureau of Printing, 1912), pp. 57–79; Philippine Sugar Association, *Summary of Information about the Philippine Sugar Industry* (Manila, 17 November 1933), pp. 25–26; Asociacion de Agricultores de La Carlota y Pontevedra, *Memorial Anual Ejercicio 1924–1925*, pp. 1–2 2.

10 . Asociacion de Agricultores de La Carlota, *Memoria Anual 1924–1925*, pp. 33–36; Asociacion de Agricultores de La Carlota, *Memoria Anual 1933–1934*, pp. 37–43.

11. Fritz von Kauffman to Ynchausti, Manila, 9 June 1931 (File Kauffman—April to June 1931, Elizalde Iloilo).

12. Interview with Carlos Hilado, 3 August 1975.

13. Fritz von Kauffman to Ynchausti, Manila, 9 June 1931 (File Kauffman—April to June 1931, Elizalde, Iloilo)

14. Ibid.

15. Interview with Jaime Marino, La Carlota City, 26 October 1981.

16. During my periodic visits to La Carlota City Hall in 1975–76, I observed Mayor Jalandoni's radio administration and his reliance upon Roberto Cuenca.

17. Ramon G. Alvanez, "A Brief History" (La Carlota City: Buas Damlag, 3 August 1985).

18. Central La Carlota, "District Final Estimate CY 1985–86" (n.d.)

19. *Asian Wall Street Journal*, 4 March 1985.

20. Interview with Jauncho Aguirre, mayor of La Carlota and Roberto Cuenca ally, La Carlota City, 17 January 1988.

21. Philippine Supreme Court, *Marino vs. Commission on Elections* (No. L–52479, 28 March 1985).

22. Ibid.

23. *Sugar News,* February 1974, p. 95.

24. Operations Evaluation Department, International Bank for Reconstruction and Development, "Project Performance Audit Report: Philippines Third Rural Credit Project (Loan 1010–PH)," 27 December 1979, pp. i–v.

25. Ibid., p. 9: National Economic and Development Authority, *1982 Philippine Statistical Yearbook* (Manila: NEDA, 1982), pp. 602– 3.

26. *Sugarland* (Bacolod) 17 (no. 5), pp. 14–16.

27. Hermilo S. Villanueva, Ernesto D. Buenafe, Reuben Geolingo and Florencio Alonso, "Preliminary Observations on Mechanical Cane Harvesting Using Massey Ferguson 105" (Philippine Sugar Commission, La Carlota, n.d.)

28. Scorpion Marketing Corporation, "Summary of Areas Planted to Hodge" (Bacolod, October 1981) and "Customer Files, Hodge Sales" (sales reports from August 1980 to October 1981; Makati, Metro Manila).

29. Hacienda Najalin, Elizalde & Company, "Field by Field Comparative production Cost (Hodge System vs. Conventional) Crop Year 1981–82" (La Carlota, 17 September 1981); interview with Antonio Corro, manager of Hda. Esperanza-Najalin, La Carlota City, 20 October 1981; interview with Fred Aplaon, manager of Hda. Najalin, La Carlota City, 27 October 1981.

30. Interview with Juan Gregorio, technical consultant of the Philippine Sugar Commission, Bacolod City, 17 February 1983.

31. Central Azucarera de La Carlota, "Final Estimate for CY 1980–81 (Tons Cane)," 18 August 1980; Victorias Milling Company, "1981–82 Crop Estimate Including Left Over Cane of 1980–81 Crop," n.d.; Hawaiian-Philippines Company, Crop Survey Department, "District Production Report No. 14 (Final) CY 1980–81," 13 May 1981.

32. Interview with Fred Aplaon, manager of Hda. Najalin, La Carlota City, 11 July 1982.

33. Interview with Florencio Alonso, manager of Hda. Carmenchica, Pontevedra, 12 January 1982.

34. Interview with Ms. Noemi Soccoro L. Damian, administrative assistant of the Buas Damlag Foundation, Asociacion de Agricultores de La Carlota y Pontevedra, Bo. Consuelo, La Carlota City, 15 July 1986.

35. *Visayan Times,* 2 December 1981, 26 February 1982.

36. NFSW, "A Brief Case-History of the NFSW's Legal Struggle to Become the Sole and Exclusive Bargaining Representative . . ." (n.d.)

37. Interview with Elizalde employee, La Carlota City, 8 February 1983.

38. Task Force Detainees, "Central Azucarera de La Carlota Strike Diary" (Bacolod City, n.d.).

39 . Task Force Detainees, "Let the Cane Trucks and Scabs Enter" (Strike Documents File, Bacolod City, n.d.)

40. Task Force Detainees, "Strike Diary"; Education Committee, NFSW-CAC Chapter, "A Day Long To Be Forgotten" (La Carlota City, 15 March 1982.)

41. Yoshiko Nagano, "Collapse of the Sugar Industry in Negros Occidental and Its Social and Economic Consequences," *Kasarinlan* 3 , no. 3 (1988): 60.

42. Simon A. Suarez, Jr. (asst. vice-president), "Comparative Milling Data" (Central Azucarera de La Carlota Laboratory, 1986).

43. Interview with Alfredo Balcells, planter and editor of *Sugarland* magazine, Bacolod City, 14 January 1985.

44. Nagano, "The Collapse of the Sugar Industry in Negros Occidental," p. 63.

45. *Philippine Daily Inquirer,* 7 September 1986.

46. *Asiaweek,* 31 May 1985, pp. 10–12.

47. Interview with Ben Aplaon (transportation manager at Central Azucarera de La Carlota), La Carlota City, 14 July 1986.

48. Interview with Fr. Irineo Gordoncillo (social action director of the Diocese of Bacolod), 13 January 1985.

49. Interview with Serge Cherniguin, NFSW secretary-general, Bacolod City, 13 January 1985; interview with Roy Mahinay, NFSW chairperson, National Organizing Committee , Bacolod City, 20 January 1988.

50. Alvanez, "A Brief History," p. 1–2.

51. *Visayan Times,* 29 November 1980; Philippine Supreme Court, "Petitioners' Reply," *Corazon Zayco et al. vs. Philippine Sugar Commission et al.* (Gr. No. 55798.)

52. *Visayan Times,* 2 January 1981, 3 January 1981.

53. *Visayan Times,* 4 June 1981; *Bulletin Today,*13 February 1984.

54. Emmanuel S. De Dios, et al., *An Analysis of the Philippine Economic Crisis: A Workshop Report* (Quezon City: University of the Philippines, June 1984), pp. 44–45.

55. *Business Day,* 7 February 1985; *Asian Wall Street Journal,* 12 February 1987.

56. *Business Day* (Manila), 15 February 1984, 17 February 1984.

57. *Malaya,* 8 June 1984.

58. Interview with Danilo Gamboa, opposition candidate for the Philsucom Board in May 1985, Bacolod City, 16 July 1986.

59. *Bulletin Today,* 5 May 1985.

60. Violeta Lopez-Gonzaga, *Crisis in Sugarlandia* (Bacolod City: La Salle Social Research Center, 1986), p. 27.

61. Interview with Serge Cherniguin, Bacolod City, 13 January 1985.

62. Interview with Edgardo Estacio (secretary-general of Bayan Negros Occidental), La Carlota City, 16 January 1988.

63. Escalante Fact-Finding Committee, "Report," p. 11, recommends that "Ex Congressman Armando Gustilo be charged as co-principa l or accomplice in Multiple Murder . . ."; anonymous, "Factsheet on the Escalante Massacre" (n.d.)

64. Interview with Edgardo Estacio, La Carlota City, 16 January 1988.

65. *Philippine Daily Inquirer,* 7 September 1986.

66. Interview with Evelyn Hinolan, OIC Mayor of Escalante, Escalante, 10 July 1986.

67. National Movement for Free Elections, *The Namfrel Report on the February 7, 1986 Philippine Presidential Elections* (Manila: Namfrel, 1986), pp. 89–91, 150.

68. Interview with Edgardo Canlas, then vice-chairman of the Cory Aquino for President Movement in La Carlota, 17 January 1988.

69. Interview with Edgardo Canlas, former OIC Mayor, La Carlota City, 15 January 1988.

70. Interview with Edgardo Canlas and Edgardo Estacio, former La Carlota mayor and councilor, La Carlota City, 15 January 1988. Councilor Estacio witnessed this meeting and recalled it in this joint interview with Mayor Canlas.

71. Ibid.

72. Interview with Fr. Gregorio Patino, La Carlota City, 16 January 1988.

73. Interview with Fr. Terence Nueva, assistant parish priest, La Carlota City, 5 February 1989; interview with Fr. Gregorio Patino, 16 January 1988; anonymous, "History of KK La Carlota Upod Kay Fr. Greg" (ms., La Carlota City, 29 September 1988.)

74. Interview with Fr. Gregorio Patino, La Carlota City, 16 January 1989.

75. Vicarate of St. John the Baptist, "Pentecost Primer" (La Carlota, n.d.)

76. *Worker's Voice,* 28 December 1986; interview with Fr. Terence Nueva, La Carlota City, 5 February 1989.

77. Agrarian Reform Alliance of Democratic Organizations—Negros, "Prawn Industry in Perspective" (Bacolod City, 23 November 1988).

78. Interview with OIC Governor Daniel Lacson, Bacolod City, 17 July 1986.

79. Peter Laurie, "Aid to a Feudal Order," *National Midweek*, 11 January 1989.

80. Interview with Greg Forbes (research coordinator of Gamboa Hermanos), Makati, Metro Manila, 24 February 1983.

81. Interview with Jim C. Carruthers, counselor (Development), Canadian Embassy, Manila, 22 January 1988; "The Negros Rehabilitation and Development Fund: Spreading the Hallmark of Progress," *Negros Development Digest* 1 (2nd Quarter, 1987): 8–9.

82. Ibid.

83. Peter Laurie, "Aid to a Feudal Order."

84 . Ramon G. Alvanez, "Buas Damlag—A Brief History" (Asociacion de Agricultores de La Carlota y Pontevedra, 3 August 1985).

85. Interviews with La Carlota political observers, January 1988.

86. Negros Independence Movement, "What is Happening to Us Negrenses" (n.d.)

87. Concerned Catholics of Negros Occidental, "Questions We Want to Ask Our Bishop," *Visayan Daily Star*, 10 April 1987; anonymous, "Vote for the Dismissal of the Following Priests from the Catholic Church Hierarchy" (leaflet, circulated in Bacolod City, n.d.); *The Manila Times*, 14 March 1987.

88. Interview with Modesto Saonoy, secretary to the president of the National Federation of Sugarcane Planters, Bacolod City, 14 July 1987; interview with Attorney Luz Dato Lacson, spokesman for the Negros Independence Movement, Bacolod City, 19 July 1987.

89. Interview with Edgardo Canlas, OIC mayor of La Carlota City, 15 January 1988.

90. Interview with Edgardo Canlas and Edgardo Estacio, 15 January 1988 and 18 January 1988. Both were confident about their estimates for these payments since Canlas had handled Araneta's money personally, his good friend Luis Jalandoni had controlled Oppen's funds, and Jalandoni knew the details of his nephew Cuenca's dealings on behalf of Matti.

91. Commission on Elections, "Province of Negros Occidental and Bacolod City" (Bacolod City, n.d.); Commission on Elections, "Statement of Votes by City/Municipality/Precinct" (Negros Occidental, 11 May 1987.)

92. *Workers' Voice*, 18 September 1987.

93. Interview with Edgardo Estacio, former secretary-general of Bayan Negros, 16 January 1988.

94. Interview with Lt. Col. Miguel Coronel, Bacolod, 14 January 1988.

95. Task Force Detainees, "Militarization and Human Rights Violations in Negros (1987)" (Bacolod City, n.d.); Negros Subregion, Task Force Detainees, "Negros: Human Rights Violations Report, January–June 1987" (Bacolod City, 15 July 1987).

96. National Federation of Sugar Workers, *Trade Union Repression and Human Rights Violations* (Bacolod City: NFSW, October 1988), pp. 23–44.

97. Task Force Detainees, "Victims of Military Operations" (Bacolod City, n.d.); interview with Edgardo Estacio, Bacolod City, 1 6 January 1986.

98. NFSW, "What's Behind the Forced Surrender of NFSW-FGT Members?" (n.d.)

99. NFSW, "Victims of Military Operations" (n.d.); *Workers' Voice*, 10 July 1987.

100. Ibid.; interview with Edgardo Estacio, NFSW vice-president, 16 January 1988.

101. Interview with Elma Alcala, La Carlota City, 19 January 1988.

102. *Philippine Daily Inquirer*, 28 August 1987.

103. Interview with Jack Teves, Manager, Central Azucarera de La Carlota, Central La Carlota, 18 January 1988.

104. Interview with Roy Mahinay, Bacolod City, 20 January 1988.

105. *Ang Kristianong Katilingban* (Bacolod City, October 1987), pp. 2–3.

106. Interview with Fr. Gregorio Patino, La Carlota City, 16 January 1988.

107. Basic Christian Community-Community Organizing (BCC-CO), "Ten Guidelines for Voters in the Coming Elections" (April 1987, reissued January 1988).

108. Interview with employee of Elizalde y Cia. who witnessed these events, La Carlota City, 19 January 1988.

109. Interview with Miss Jamora, La Carlota South Elementary School, 18 January 1989.

110. Commission on Elections, "Statement of Voters by Precinct Elections for City/Municipal Mayor . . . January 18, 1988 Elections" (La Carlota City).

111. Interview with Errol Gatumbatu, Task Force Detainees, Bacolod City, 2 February 1989; *Visayan Daily Star*, 3 February 1988.

112. Interview with Napoleon Dojillo, one of the dissident NPA, Bacolod City, 16 January 1988.

113. *Panay News*, 2 February 1989; interview with Serge Cherniguin, vice-president of NFSW, Bacolod City, 4 February 1989.

114 . Interview with Serge Cherniguin, vice-president of NFSW, Bacolod City, 4 February 1989.

115. Bishop's House, "A Chronology of Events Leading to the Suspension of Rev. Fr. Antonio P. Atillaga" (Bacolod City, n.d.); anonymous, "Fact Sheet: Background of the Anti-Church/Bishop Rally" (Bacolod City, 21 July 1988); Bishop Antonio Y. Fortich, "A Pastoral Letter on the Rally Against the Transfer of Priests" (Bacolod City, 22 July 1988); interview with Bishop Antonio Y. Fortich, 3 February 1989; interview with Fr. Felix Pasquin, medical director of the Diocese of Bacolod, 4 February 1989; interview with Fr. Irineo Gordoncillo, social action director, Diocese of Bacolod, 4 February 1989.

116. Concerned Catholics of Negros, Letter to Bruno Torpigliani, 22 July 1988; anonymous, "Pact with the Devil-II" (n.d.).

117. *Manila Chronicle*, 3 February 1989; interview with Fr. Niall O'Brien, Bacolod City, 4 February 1989; interview with Fr. Vic Rivas, vicar-general, Diocese of Bacolod, Bacolod City, 4 February 1989.

118. Interview with Fr. Gregorio Patino, La Carlota City, 5 February 1989.

119. *Philippine Daily Inquirer*, 8 June 1989; *Malaya*, 22 May 1989; Human Rights Alliance-Negros, "Update on Southern Negros Evacuation" (Bacolod City, 11 May 1989).

120. NFSW-FGT, "Mga Butang Nga Dapat Mahibalu-an Bahin sa SDF" (Bacolod City, 11 January 1989.)

Notes to Eder, "A Palawan Farming Community," pages 143–165

A National Institutes of Mental Health Pre-Doctoral Research Grant supported my fieldwork in San Jose during 1970–72; a sabbatical leave from Arizona State University and a grant from the Social Science Research Council supported my fieldwork there during January to July, 1988. I would like to thank Julieta Buaya and Evelyn Martinez for their assistance in gathering field data during this latter period.

1. James F. Eder, *Who Shall Succeed? Agricultural Development and Social Change on a Philippine Frontier* (Cambridge: Cambridge University Press, 1982).

2. The data on the rural Philippines is taken from the ILO's *Poverty and Landlessness in Rural Asia* (Geneva: International Labor Office, 1977).

3. Benedict J. Kerkvliet, "Martial Law in a Nueva Ecija Village, the Philippines," *Bulletin of Concerned Asian Scholars* 14 (1982): 17–18.

4. B. M. Koppel, "Agrarian Problems and Agrarian Reform: Opportunity or Irony?"

in *Rebuilding a Nation: Philippine Challenges and American Policy*, ed. C. Lande (Washington, D.C.: Washington Institute Press, 1986), 157–87.

5. Mary R. Hollnsteiner, *The Dynamics of Power in a Philippine Municipality* (Quezon City: Community Development Research Council, University of the Philippines, 1963); Carl H. Lande, *Leaders, Factions and Parties: The Structure of Philippine Politics* (New Haven, Conn.: Southeast Asian Studies, Yale University, 1965).

6. Ibid.

7. Benedict J. Kerkvliet, "Understanding Politics in a Nueva Ecija Rural Community" (see essay in this volume).

8. Willem van Schendel, *Peasant Mobility: The Odds of Life in Rural Bangladesh* (Assen, Netherlands: van Gorcum, 1981), p. 293, 37n.

9. Ibid., 295–96.

Notes to Pinches, "Tatalon, Manila," pages 166–86

1. For some of the voluminous literature dealing with the "February Revolution," see P. Krinks, ed., *The Philippines Under Aquino* (Canberra: The Australian Development Studies Network, Australian National University, 1987); J. Lyons and K. Wilson, *Marcos and Beyond: The Philippine Revolution* (Kenthurst: Kangaroo Press, 1987); M.A. Mercado, *An Eyewitness History: People Power—The Philippine Revolution of 1986* (Manila: James G. Reuter Foundation, 1986); M. Ordoñez, *People Power: A Demonstration of the Emerging Filipino Ideology* (Quezon City: Sampaguita, 1986); L.Q. Santiago, ed., *Synthesis: Before and Beyond February 1986* (Manila: Edgar M. Jopson Memorial Foundation, 1986); M. Turner, ed., *Regime Change in the Philippines: The Legitimation of the Aquino Government* (Canberra: Department of Political and Social Change, Monograph No. 7, Australian National University, 1987); A. Javate-de Dios, P.B. Daroy and L. Kalaw-Tirol, eds., *Dictatorship and Revolution: Roots of People's Power* (Metro Manila: Conspectus, 1988).

2. Fieldwork in Tatalon covers more than two years and was conducted over six visits: 1978–1980, 1982–83, 1985–86, 1986–87, 1988 and 1989. During most of this time, I lived in one of the settlement's communities known as the Visayan area. The 1985–86 fieldwork period covered most of the presidential election campaign, the election itself, and part of the election aftermath. It stopped a week short of Marcos's overthrow. Details on activities over the final days are drawn from interviews in Tatalon at the end of 1986, early 1987, and 1988. I wish to thank the Departments of Anthropology and Sociology at Monash University, General Studies at the University of New South Wales and Anthropology at the University of Western Australia for enabling me to conduct this research. In addition, I benefited from an Australian Research Council Grant and a special research grant from the University of Western Australia. I also thank the Institute of Philippine Culture at Ateneo de Manila University where I was a Visiting Research Associate in 1978–80. I owe special thanks to the people of the Visayan Area, Tatalon, who have always made my fieldwork both rewarding and enjoyable. Most of all I am indebted to my wife Lenny Campos, whose contribution to this essay has been considerable. For comments on an earlier draft, I wish to thank the participants at the Local Perspectives Conference out of which this book came.

3. S. Ossowski, *Class Structure in the Social Consciousness* (London: Routledge and Kegan Paul, 1963).

4. M. Pinches, "'All that we have is our Muscle and Sweat': The Rise of Wage Labour in a Manila Squatter Community," in *Wage Labour and Social Change: The Proletariat in Asia and the Pacific*, ed. M. Pinches and S. Lakha (Clayton: Centre of Southeast Asian Studies, Monash University, 1987).

5. Translation of the term *hiya* and its derivations into English is open to variable interpretation: see V.G. Enriquez, "Kapwa: A core concept in Filipino Social Psychology" in *Philippine World View*, ed. V.G. Enriquez (Singapore: Institute of Southeast Asian Studies, 1986) and Z. Salazar, "Hiya: Panlapi at Salita," in *New Directions in Indigenous Psychology: Sikolohiyang Pilipino, Isyu, Pananaw at Kaalaman* (Quezon City: National Book Store, 1985).

6. See, for example, J.C. Bulatao, "Hiya," *Philippine Studies* 12 (1964): 424–38 and F. Lynch, "Social Acceptance Reconsidered," in *Four Readings on Philippine Values*, ed. F. Lynch and A. de Guzman II (Quezon City: Ateneo de Manila University Press, 1973); T. Church, *Filipino Personality: A Review of Research and Writings* (Manila: De La Salle University Press, 1986). The wider literature includes, among others, J.G. Peristiany, ed., *Honour and Shame: The Values of Mediterranean Society* (Chicago: University of Chicago Press, 1966); A. Heller, *The Power of Shame* (London: Routledge and Kegan Paul, 1985).

7. Some come from the town but most come from neighboring inland and coastal villages. The economy of the municipality centers on copra production and a small-holding peasantry. As cash crop production has increased, and as Palompon's economy, polity, and cultural life have been further integrated into the national and international arena, more and more people have migrated to various parts of the Philippines. Many have settled in other parts of Manila but the Visayan Area in Tatalon is well-known as a place of Palomponganons.

8. Pinches, "Muscle and Sweat".

9. Cf. *Ibon Facts and Figures* 65 (1981): 7; E. Tan and V. Holazo, "Measuring Poverty Incidence in a Segmented Market: The Philippine Case," *The Philippine Economic Journal* 17(1979):484; J. Andrews, "The Philippines: A Question of Faith," *The Economist*, 7 May 1988, p. 4.

10. M. Pinches, "A Rocky Road to the Promised Land: Squatters, Oligarchs and the State in the Philippines" (unpublished paper, 1986).

11. "Sites and services" schemes have their origin in Latin America and were introduced as a relatively cheap solution to low-income housing. They essentially involve the sale of small plots of land—serviced with water, electricity and drainage—to low-income families who are expected to build their own houses as and when their resources permit.

12. For the first perspective, see, F. Lynch, "Social Acceptance"; for the second see A. Guerrero, *Philippine Society and Revolution* (Hong Kong: Ta Kung Pao, 1971).

13. This is especially the case in regard to the working class. For important exceptions on the study of peasant rebellion, see B. Kerkvliet, *The Huk Rebellion: A Study of Peasant Revolt in the Philippines* (Quezon City: New Day, 1979); R. Ileto, *Pasyon and Revolution: Popular Movements in the Philippines, 1840–1910* (Quezon City: Ateneo de Manila University Press, 1979).

14. See, for example, M. Hollnsteiner, "Reciprocity."

15. For the classic reference on this, see C. Lande, *Leaders, Factions and Parties: The Structure of Philippine Politics* (New Haven: Yale University Press, 1964).

16. While *amor propio* (sense of personal dignity) is widely referred to in the literature, this is not a term commonly used in the Visayan area of Tatalon. The high value placed on human dignity is evident, however, in a range of expressions and actions.

17. For a most revealing account of the condescending attitudes and behavior of Manila's rich toward their domestic staff see R. Ranby, *A Greedy Institution: Domestic Service in Manila* (M.A. thesis, University of Sydney, 1987).

18. Compare Kerkvliet's and Fegan's work on the "everyday forms of resistance" found among the peasants of Central Luzon: B. Kerkvliet, "Everyday Resistance to

Injustice in a Philippine Village," *Journal of Peasant Studies* 13 (1986): 107–23; B. Fegan, "Tenants' Non-violent Resistance to Landowner Claims in Central Luzon," *Journal of Peasant Studies* 13 (1986): 87–106.

19. See M. Pinches, "Muscle and Sweat."

20. This important distinction is explored first in C. Jayawardena, "Ideology and Conflict in Lower Class Communities," *Comparative Studies in Society and History* 10 (1968): 413–46.

21. Compare with J. Scott, *The Moral Economy of the Peasantry* (New Haven: Yale University Press, 1977). This issue is also explored in relation to the squatters' struggle for land rights in Tatalon, in M. Pinches, "A Rocky Road."

22. While the Philippine literature generally conceives *hiya* in unproblematic functionalist terms, this is not the case with Ileto and Rafael who offer brief but insightful interpretations that provide for elements of both accommodation and resistance: R. Ileto, *Pasyon*, pp. 12–13, 192–93; V. Rafael, "Confession, Conversion and Reciprocity in Early Tagalog Colonial Society," *Comparative Studies in Society and History* 29 (1987): 320–39.

23. M. Pinches, "People Power and the Urban Poor: The Politics of Unity and Division in Manila" in *The Philippines Under Aquino*, ed. P. Krinks.

24. V. Turner, *The Ritual Process* (Harmondsworth: Penguin, 1969).

Notes to Brillantes, "Smokey Mountain," pages 187–205

1. There were some of those I talked to who resented the label "Smokey Mountain," feeling it was an insult to their dignity as a people. However, there were also those who have accepted the label, feeling that it is an advantage since it is recognized both nationally and internationally. In fact, there is a "Welcome to Smokey Mountain" arch by the concrete all-purpose pavement in the area. There is a local basketball team that has "Smokey Mountain" emblazoned across the uniform. Regardless of negative references, "Smokey Mountain" has become an accepted name of the area by the residents. It is within this context that I will be referring to the area as "Smokey Mountain."

Unlike many other communities, Smokey Mountain is quite unique in that it is largely organized, and came to exist, around a single and highly visible issue: human beings living on garbage and their basic human rights. In this sense, Smokey Mountain's uniqueness arises from the dramatic visibility of poverty in the area where poverty can actually be seen and smelled. This has attracted the attention of local and international media and nongovernmental (mostly civic and religious) organizations.

2. *Anawim*, Manila: Share and Care Apostolate for Poor Settlers, August 1986.

3. National Housing Authority Proposal for Development of Smokey Mountain, attached to letter of NHA General Manager Raymundo Dizon to Metro Manila Governor Elfren Cruz, 23 June 1988.

4. Based on a fact sheet (no date c.1987) prepared by Eduardo de Jesus, Smokey Mountain Health Committee Leader, Pagkakaisa ng Mamamayan ng Navotas (PAMANA) office.

5. The essentials in Dollente's narrative were confirmed during interviews with other people, and also findings by other research groups that studied the area such as the Maryknoll Foundation Women's Resource Center. In July 1988, Dollente moved out of Smokey Mountain to the Bulihan relocation site in Cavite. Dollente's five children live in Bulihan. One works for a transnational corporation, one as a janitor in Quezon City, one as an employee of a furniture shop, and two as carpenters. The Dollente

children each have a house in Bulihan, where they claim, "Napakaganda ang klima, ang daming halaman" (the weather is so nice and there are so many plants.) In other words, Dollente's children are happy there, considering the clean environment and fresh air, as compared to the life in Smokey Mountain. Interestingly, Dollente is also the president of the homeowners' association in Bulihan.

6. Quoted by Manny Martinez and Cynthia Sycip, "The Economics of Smokey Mountain," *Manila Times*, 9 June 1987.

7. Although the efforts to unseat Dollente prior to the 1988 barangay elections did not succeed, he became a largely unrecognized (and ineffective) barangay captain because of the community's negative perceptions of him. Additionally, parallel organizations (such as those organized by the Catholic priest) were organized effectively, replacing the barangay as the prime community organization of the area.

8. The various community leaders I talked to during my regular visits to the area over a 20–month period (from October 1987 to June 1989) included the barrio captain, Isaias Dollente; the barangay executive officer; the acting barangay head, Ben Ignacio, who later was elected barangay captain; the parish priest, Benigno Beltran; the executive secretary of the Welcome Friends Organization, Manuel Manarang; the head of the Sambayanang Kristiyano, Manuel Borja, who later was elected as a barangay councilman; and the head of the leftist group in the area, the People's Committee on Smokey Mountain (PCSM), Alex Caballero. I also had casual conversations with many residents of varying backgrounds including scavengers, buyers, employees, and unemployed, to obtain their perspectives of national events.

9. "Smokey Mountain Development Project: A Comprehensive Plan for Smokey Mountain," National Housing Authority, 29 April 1988.

10. After he came from his studies abroad, Father Benigno Beltran, SVD, began to look for a more meaningful ministry in the Philippines, specifically one that involved dealing with the poor. He eventually got involved with the people in Barrio Magdaragat, and has worked with them ever since. He has lived in the area since the early part of 1989.

11. There are two other Catholic church infrastructure projects in the area. The first is the original chapel (*kapilya*) built in the 1960s. The second one was built on orders of Manila Mayor Mel Lopez right after the local elections. The original chapel has deteriorated and is not in use anymore. The other (which some residents cynically refer to as "basilika ni Lopez" (basilica of Lopez) has likewise not been used primarily because of its location. It is an imposing structure located on one of the highest points of Smokey Mountain literally surrounded by garbage that is freshly dumped daily. Aside from the physical distance from the residents, the smell of immediate surroundings has discouraged its use by the residents. It has been used by the Metro Manila Commission personnel doing work in Smokey Mountain.

12. There are a number of other nongovernmental organizations (NGOs)—mostly religious—operating in the area. However, unlike the Catholic Church, their involvement does not include community organizing. They are limited to providing social services. For instance, a Protestant group, the Youth with a Mission (YWAM) conducts informal religious services and sponsors a feeding program every Sunday morning. The YWAM's presence is very much felt considering that they actually have a building close to the Catholic church. A second Protestant group, the Christian Growth Ministry, offers free education for preschoolers. Another NGO that provides free education from the elementary level up to the collegiate level, including foster parenting to indigent children, is a Norwegian organization called the NORMA. Finally, the CANOSSA Health and Social Center also renders free medical and dental services.

Direct government presence in the area is through the Department of Social Services and Development (DSSD). It conducts a feeding program specially for malnourished children. Such a program is implemented through the community-based organization, the Samahang Magkakapitbahay (roughly translated, Organization of Neighbors) which is also affiliated with the Catholic organization, Caritas. Children one to six years old are the target of the feeding program. Flor Cabili of the Samahang Magkakapitbahay told me that she personally cooks the children's meals from Monday to Friday. She has a quota of some 68 underweight children who qualified for the feeding program. She said, "Pinapasobrahan ko ang pagluluto para kahit hindi nakalista nabibigyan" (I cook more than enough so that children not in the original list will be given food, too). On weekends, the DSSD has no feeding program. The Catholic church, though, serves meals on Sundays. Cabili told me that the supply provided by the DSSD is oftentimes incomplete: "Minsan, walang niyog, walang asukal, tubig o kahoy" (Sometimes, there is no coconut, sugar, water or wood). Water costs 20 pesos per container, firewood costs five pesos. As a result of the shortages in supply, and in order to cover rising costs, each child gives a fifty-centavo donation per meal.

13. The appendix is a comparative presentation of the voting turnout in Barangay 128 during three national political exercises, i.e., the February 1986 Presidential Elections, the February 1987 Plebiscite, and the May 1987 Congressional Elections. Since figures on the number of registered voters during the 1986 Presidential elections were unavailable, I used the figures of the Commission on Elections on the number of registered (and qualified) voters in 1987. I assumed that these same voters were living in the area even during the 1986 presidential elections. This is not an unreasonable assumption, considering that there were no major population movements during the period under study.

For purposes of this study, and in order to obtain a more accurate feel of the voter turnout during these events, I focussed on the election results in the major barangay of Smokey Mountain, specifically Barangay 128 composed of five precincts, all voters of which live in Smokey Mountain. Only a portion of Barangay 129 is covered by Smokey Mountain, thus 128 would be a sufficient sample for the area.

14. Alex Caballero had lived in Smokey Mountain since 1978. He initially rented a small space, but when many of the residents were relocated to Bulihan in Cavite, he built his own shack, where I talked to him. On the walls were banners and posters pertaining to significant national issues that concerned the Kongreso ng Pagkakaisa ng Maralita ng Lunsod (KPML), to which the PCSM is affiliated. There were banners all lettered in blood red—protesting the murder of former Bagong Alyansa (Bayan) Chairman Lean Alejandro and former Kilusang Mayo Uno (KMU) Chairman Rolando Olalia, decrying the increase in oil prices, and protesting demolition and relocation of the people in Smokey Mountain.

15. This question is being investigated further by a project at the University of the Philippines College of Public Administration.

Notes to Wolters, "Nueva Ecija Politics," pages 206–25

I have done field research in Cabanatuan City and other parts of Nueva Ecija in 1971–72, July–August 1979, June–August 1985, June–July 1986, and June–August 1987. Additional research for this paper was undertaken in July–August 1988. I gratefully acknowledge the support from the Netherlands Organization for Pure Scientific Research as well as from the Faculty of Social Sciences of the Catholic University Nijmegen.

This paper was written while I was a Fellow in Residence at the Netherlands Institute of Advanced Studies (NIAS), Wassenaar, the Netherlands, September 1988–January 1989. I want to thank my wife Ingrid Diaz for her collaboration in my research and in the writing of this paper.

1. Editorial, *The People's Examiner*, volume 1, no. 14, 9–15 December 1985, p. 4.

2. "Elections '86: Peaceful but Chaotic," *Examiner*, volume 1, no. 22, 3–9 Feb. 1986, p. 1.

3. Ibid.

4. Editorial, "Proclaim Revolutionary Government Now " *Examiner*, volume 1, no.28, 17–23 March, 1986, p. 2.

5. Interview with Atty. Antonio Paguia (OIC vice-governor of Nueva Ecija, 1986–1987), 21 August 1988.

6. Interview with Jay Vergara, assistant to Sedfrey Ordoñez, 1986-1988, 24 August 1988.

7. "Ordoñez Rapped," *Examiner*, volume 1, no. 35, 5–11 May 1986, p. 1.

8. Interview with Noli Santos (OIC governor of Nueva Ecija, 1986–1987), 18 August 1988.

9. Ibid.

10. Ibid.

11. Paulynn P. Sicam, "An Eerie Silence Blankets Scene of 10 February Massacre," *Manila Chronicle*, 16 Feb. 1987.

12. Editorial, "Transparency in Government," *Examiner*, volume 2, no. 50, 17–23 August 1987, p. 2. SOP means "Standard Operational Procedure."

13. J.C.Nuñez, "Media Range," *Examiner*, volume 2, no. 18, 5–11 Jan. 1987, p. 2.

14. "Concepcion Predicts Slim Yes Win," *Examiner*, vol. 2, no. 16, 22–28 Dec. 1986, p. 1.

15. "Bayan, PnB Lead 'No' Vote Demo," *Examiner*, vol. 2, no. 20, 19–25 Jan. 1987, p.4.

16. "NPA Rebels Meet with Barangay,"*Examiner*, vol. 2, no. 20, 19–25 Jan. 1987, p. 4.

17. Election results for Nueva Ecija have been provided by the Comelec Office in Cabanatuan City. National figures are taken from Mark Turner, "The Quest for Political Legitimacy in the Philippines: the Constitutional Plebiscite of 1987," in *Regime Change in the Philippines: The Legitimation of the Aquino Government*, ed. Mark Turner (Canberra: Department of Political and Social Change, Australian National University, 1987), pp. 58–101.

18. "PDP-Laban Councils Organized," *Examiner*, vol. 2, no. 16, 22–28 Dec. 1986, p. 1.

19. Interview with Jay Vergara (assistant to Sedfrey Ordoñez, 1986–1988), 24 August 1988.

20. Ibid.

21. Ibid.

22. "Lakas' Official Bet: Concepcion or Vergara," *Examiner*, vol. 2, no. 32, 13–19 April 1987, p. 1.

23. "BALANE Girds for Election," *Examiner*, vol. 2, no. 25, 23 February–1 March 1987, p. 4.

24. "Volunteers Root for Veneracion," *Examiner*, vol. 2, no. 34, 27 April–3 May 1987.

25. "A Quixotic Venture that May Down the Windmills," *Examiner*, vol. 2, no. 35, 4–10 May 1987, p. 4.

26. Editorial, "The Fragmented Majority," *Examiner*, vol. 2, no. 30, 30 March–5 April 1987, p. 2.

27. Official election results were provided by the Nueva Ecija provincial Comelec registrar.

28. Official election results, Nueva Ecija.

29. Interview with Jay Vergara, 24 August 1988; also *Examiner*, vol. 3, no. 5, 5–11 October 1987; *Business World*, 6 January 1988.

30. "Comelec Stops Poll Count in Nueva Ecija," *Manila Times*, 23 January 1988, p. 2.

31. Johnny Nuñez, "Were Nueva Ecija Polls Peaceful?," *Manila Standard*, 25 January 1988.

32. Official election results in Nueva Ecija were provided by Comelec.

33. Adrian Mayer, "The Significance of Quasi-Groups in the Study of Complex Societies," in *The Social Anthropology of Complex Societies*, ed. Michael Banton (London: Tavistock Publications, 1966), pp. 97–122.

34. Interview with Marcelo Diaz, former mayor of Talavera, 31 July 1988.

35. Interview with Noli Santos, 18 August 1988.

36. Ibid.

37. Benedict J. Kerkvliet, *The Huk Rebellion: A Study of Peasant Revolt in the Philippines* (Berkeley: University of California Press, 1977).

Notes to Kerkvliet, "Nueva Ecija Rural Community," pages 226–46

1. My wife and I returned to San Ricardo in July–August 1987 to conduct this inquiry. (I thank the University of Hawaii for a Fujio Matsuda scholarship awarded for this purpose and Melinda Tria Kerkvliet for her terrific assistance.) The visit was my fourth to this rural area. The first was in 1970 for four months. I returned in 1978–79 for a year to study its political economy and society. Melinda and I were again there for four months in 1985. These previous stays meant that in 1987, I was able to learn a great deal from a wide spectrum of people inside and outside the village about what had happened in 1986–87 and put that new information into local historical context.

Nearly all my information comes from conversations and observations; documents and other printed materials are rarely available. Names for village residents are fictitious.

I thank Dan Doeppers, Masahide Kato, Jack Larkin, Resil Mojares, Steven Rood, and Mark Thompson for their comments on initial drafts of this essay.

2. The election was apparently clean. Fraud reported elsewhere did not occur in San Ricardo and vicinity, according to voters, supporters of each candidate, poll watchers, and a NAMFREL representative in the municipality. NAMFREL agrees with the Marcos government's count that Marcos won in Nueva Ecija, though not with 63 but instead 59 percent of the votes (*The NAMFREL Report on the February 7, 1986 Philippine Presidential Elections* [Manila?: NAMFREL, 1986?], pp. 25, 86, 147).

3. See the introduction to this book.

4. I have elaborated this and related themes about San Ricardo life in *Everyday Politics in the Philippines: Class and Status Relations in a Central Luzon Village* (Berkeley: University of California Press, 1990).

5. A. Kintanar, Jr., "The Philippine Economy: An Analysis of the Economic Crisis," *Southeast Asian Affairs* (1985): 279–93.

6. The other reason for the drop in harvest payment is the small mechanical thresher. In 1979, no one in the San Ricardo area used this machine; by 1985, nearly every landholder was renting one of the half-dozen in the village to thresh their grain. This eliminated the hand threshing that harvesters had previously done and thus, became one justification landholders cited when reducing harvesters' pay.

7. Between 1978 and 1982, the National Irrigation Administration was unable to

collect half the fees that users owed (Republic of the Philippines, National Irrigation Administration, Upper Pampanga River Irrigation System, *Annual Reports*).

8. My information comes from discussions with several participants and newspaper accounts. See, for instance, Al Mendoza, "Farmers Bring Grievances to the Minister's Door," *Philippine Panorama*, 24 February 1985, pp. 4ff. AMGL began in 1981 in Bulacan province. Its most well-known leader is Jaime Tadeo.

9. The Marcos government's agrarian reform was barely noticeable or nonexistent in many other regions. However, because of Central Luzon's proximity to Manila and its history of unrest, and also because of the need for some show cases, the government expended considerable effort in that region to stop landlords from evicting tenants and to buy large estates for resale to tenants (see my *Everyday Politics*, pp. 29–42 and table B1).

10. After Manolo Tinio, owner of over 200 hectares, died in 1977, his heirs quarreled about who would manage the land. As a result, virtually no farming was done until 1981. Owners of the other hacienda, Vivencio Tinio and two sisters, had switched from rice to sugarcane in 1975. But poor management and little investment resulted in spotty use of the 120 hectares.

11. The 1986 "boycott" effort in parts of the country was not active in central Nueva Ecija and does not account for the proportion of nonvoting. The 35-percent figure is based on the assumption that the number of registered voters in 1986, which I was unable to locate, was nearly the same as the 788 registered voters in May 1987. The voter turnout in the May 1987 congressional elections was somewhat higher, 70 percent (figures come from the Commission on Elections office, Talavera, Nueva Ecija).

12. Final count, 1982 Barrio Elections, Commission on Elections office, Talavera, Nueva Ecija.

13. In early August 1987, a large organization of landowners did file a class suit before the Supreme Court saying that the agrarian reform decrees by President Marcos and executive orders by President Aquino are illegal. The case is pending (*Manila Chronicle*, 6 August 1987).

14. Previously, government authorities had portrayed the Hukbalahap as a subversive, illegitimate organization. Consequently, unlike veterans of anti-Japanese guerrilla units that were "recognized," Hukbalahap veterans had not been entitled to certain benefits.

15. The crime was never solved. There were rumors that the NPA had killed him in order to create a vacancy on the MT hacienda and deter anyone other than the local landless from trying to get those fields. Although the NPA has admitted to some killings in central Nueva Ecija, it denies this one. That fact and other information makes more credible the possibilities that the subtenant was killed by someone who wanted the land and/or someone who was angry because the tenant, although married, had tried to have sex with another woman.

16. I was unable to reach Mario Tinio for his views. Perhaps he did not want to talk to me. Although I had interviewed him at length in 1979, he would not agree to another interview in 1985 because he thought my book *Huk Rebellion* is unfair to the Tinio side of San Ricardo's history during the 1930s–1940s.

17. *Manila Chronicle*, 24 July 1987, p.7.

18. Executive Order 229, section 22, 22 July 1987.

19. For accounts of events prior to and after the Mendiola confrontation, see Jo-Ann Q. Maglipon, "The Mendiola Tragedy," in *A Smouldering Land* (Quezon City: National Council of Churches in the Philippines and the Forum for Rural Concerns, 1987), pp. i–xlii.

20. The rate is based on figures from the National Census and Statistics Office.

21. The drop is probably not the result of those peasant demonstrations in 1985 but the sharp decline in crude oil prices in 1985–86.

22. The top 24 senate candidates in village voting included sixteen from the Aquino slate, six from the Grand Alliance for Democracy (including former members of the Marcos government), and two from other parties. For the House of Representatives, 60 percent of San Ricardo voters favored Eduardo Joson, Jr., who ran on a ticket formed by his father, the former Nueva Ecija governor, that was neither pro-Aquino nor pro-Marcos (see Willem Wolter's essay in this volume). Joson's nearest rival was Leopoldo Diaz (36 percent). While factionalism and vote-buying helps to explain this outcome, as important if not more so is that many voters criticized Diaz for being extremely arrogant and, despite having been in the national legislature for many years, he had done little for the area.

23. The five included two notorious men (including a rapist), two alleged military spies, and one NPA member who had stolen money from the movement.

24. See, for instance, Remigio E. Agpalo, *The Political Elite and the People: A Study of Politics in Occidental Mindoro* (Manila: College of Public Administration, University of the Philippines, 1972), p. 374; and Carl Lande, *Southern Tagalog Voting, 1946–1963* (DeKalb: Center for Southeast Asian Studies, Northern Illinois University, 1973), pp. 6, 97–98.

Notes to Pertierra, "Ilokano Municipality," pages 247–65

1. B.A. Mistal and F. Mistal, "The State's Capacity to Change—The Case of Poland and the Philippines," SAANZ Conference Paper, 1986.

2. C. Geertz, *The Interpretation of Cultures* (New York: Basic Books, 1973).

3. R. Pertierra, *Religion, Politics and Rationality in a Philippine Community* (Quezon City: Ateneo de Manila University Press, 1988).

4. For a comparable example, see R. Agpalo, *The Political Elite and the People* (Quezon City: University of the Philippines Press, 1972).

5. E. Leach, *Political Systems of Highland Burma* (London: Bell and Son, 1964), p. 281.

6. B. Anderson, *Imagined Communities* (London: Verso, 1983).

7. J. Habermas, *The Theory of Communicative Action 1: Reasons and the Rationalization of Society*, trans. T. McCarthy (Boston: Beacon Press, 1984); idem., *The Theory of Communicative Action 2: The Critique of Functionalist Reason*, trans. T. McCarthy (Cambridge: Polity Press, 1987).

8. R. Pertierra, "An Anthropological Perspective on Philippine Politics," in *The Philippines Under Aquino*, ed. P. Krinks (Canberra: Australian Development Studies Network, Australian National University, 1987), pp. 115–34.

Notes to Zialcita, "Legitimacy in Ilocos Norte," pages 266–85

This paper was made possible through a research grant by the Center for Social Policy of the Ateneo de Manila University and the assistance of two Rangtay residents in the gathering of data. I would like to thank Mr. Joselito R. Jimenez and Mr. Andres M. Palmero Jr. for their invaluable help in typing and editing the manuscript.

1. Ronald Cohen, "The Political System" in *A Handbook of Method in Cultural Anthropology*, ed. Raoul Naroll and Ronald Cohen (New York: Columbia University Press, 1973), pp. 488–89. His categories allow a distinction between forced and voluntary consent. This is not the case with Seymour Lipset, *Political Man: The Social Bases of*

Politics (New York: Feffer and Simons, 1960, p. 29), and Barrington Moore, Jr., *Reflections on the Causes of Human Misery and upon Certain Proposals to Eliminate Them* (Boston: Beacon Press, 1972), pp. 54–55.

2. Cohen, "Political System," p. 490. He defines power as the ability to influence the behavior of others or gain influence over the control of valued action. Authority, on the other hand, is really an implicit constitution where superior and subordinate agree on their mutual roles. However, this relationship may change as both seek to expand their capacity to influence the other.

3. A definition of *class* that I lean towards is that of Weber which includes market potential (Max Weber, *Economy and Society*, vol. 2 [New York: Bedminster Press, 1968], pp. 926–28). See also Mark Turner, "Interpretations of Class and Status in the Philippines: A Critical Evaluation," *Culture et développement* 10 (1978): 293. However, for purposes of this essay, it suffices to define "class" in terms of assets while showing how those in nonmanual occupations fit in.

4. Turner,"Interpretations," p. 295.

5. Mark Turner, "Status Evaluation in a Philippine Town: Some Preliminary Observations," *Southeast Asian Journal of Social Science* 6 (1978): 79–89.

6. Willem Wolters (*Politics, Patronage and Class Conflict in Central Luzon* [Quezon City: New Day Publishers, 1984], pp. 198–99), distinguishes "patronage" and "patron-client ties."

7. Because of my interest in phenomenology, I tend to accept people's interpretation of the world, strange as the interpretation may seem, and figure out the underlying logic. For me, my informants' version of EDSA is on the same level as their perennial advice to be careful of such-and-such a village that is notorious for its sorcery. I have therefore tried to disclose the experiential context that has made their version possible. A question: Since radio and television programs detailing the dictator's abuses have reached the villagers, is there any defensiveness on their part, when relating the past? The answer is no, given the sum of their experiences.

8. Wanting to find out if these patterns were duplicated elsewhere in the region, I asked Ponciano Bennagen, an anthropologist who hails from Ilocos Sur, why Marcos was popular in his area. He repeated his friends' comments,"Marcos did not forget his origins. He came home regularly to the Ilocos; despite his high position, he still loved *dinengdeng* (an Ilokano dish of boiled vegetables and fermented fishpaste); once, while dining with Imelda, she happened to drop her fried chicken to the floor. He picked it up for her." Note the motifs: he acknowledged his origins; though he was in Tagalog country amid the wealthy, he remained attached to modest Ilokano food; despite his wife's carelessness—dropping a rich man's food to the floor—he bent over to pick it up. The image is that of a humble man.

9. The irony of it all was that the man allegedly responsible for the smuggling operation, Roque Ablan, Jr., was a Marcos ally.

10. Under Marcos, his sister, Elizabeth, became the governor of the province. After she died, the governorship passed over to Marcos's son, Ferdinand, Jr. (Bong-Bong). In the meantime Rodolfo Fariñas had become the mayor of the capital, Laoag. Bong-Bong and Rudy became good friends.

11. On the other hand, one might also argue that the election of Rolando Abadilla as vice-governor strengthens Marcos's hand. He has long been accused of being Marcos's henchman in violations of human rights. Although he was implicated for his alleged participation in a failed coup against the Aquino government, he was subsequently released by the court for lack of evidence. The Aquino government did not object.

12. Samuel Popkin, *The Rational Peasant* (Berkeley: University of California Press, 1979), pp. 20–21.

Index